SORCERY IN ITS SOCIAL SETTING

A Study of the Northern Rhodesian Cewa

Frontispiece

Plate I. A CEŴA DIVINER

SORCERY IN ITS SOCIAL SETTING

A STUDY OF THE NORTHERN RHODESIAN CEWA

BY

M. G. MARWICK

Professor of Sociology,
University of Stirling

MANCHESTER UNIVERSITY PRESS

© 1965, M. G. Marwick
Published by the University of Manchester
at THE UNIVERSITY PRESS
316–324 Oxford Road, Manchester M13 9NR

First published, 1965
Reprinted, 1970

ISBN 0 7190 0257 5

Distributed in the U.S.A. by
The Humanities Press, Inc.
303 Park Avenue South, New York, N.Y. 10010

Printed in Great Britain by Butler & Tanner Ltd., Frome and London

FOREWORD

I FIRST met Max Marwick in 1946, when I was Director of the Rhodes-Livingstone Institute of Social Studies in British Central Africa. He had been strongly recommended to me by colleagues and friends at the Natal University College where he had studied social psychology. I was immediately impressed by the quality and strength of his mind; and I put his name forward to the Colonial Social Science Research Council for a fellowship on which he could study social conflict in relation to secular and ritual action among the Cewa of Northern Rhodesia. His essays on this and related problems have won for him the high reputation which has been recognized in his appointment to two professorships; and they have greatly influenced the development of research into the sociology of sorcery and of social conflict. We are now given a book which develops and expands those early essays: it will enhance Marwick's reputation and rank as a most significant contribution to social science, for it establishes new techniques, sets new standards, and raises crucial theoretical issues. Marwick brings to bear on these issues both his initial training in social psychology and his later acquired expertise in social anthropology and sociology. The result is so rich that I can only sketch his general approach and touch on a few of the many points he raises.

I think all readers will be impressed by the manner in which Marwick places his own analysis in relation to previous studies both of sorcery and of conflict in general. His punctiliousness here contrasts sharply with the practice of some anthropologists who, in a contest of 'one-upmanship', score points either by ignoring earlier work or even by baldly asserting that it was all wrong. Marwick's scholarly use of others' work benefits both himself and the subject as a whole; for clearly by conning the others positively he is able to strengthen his own study; and by indicating the value as well as the limitations and shortcomings of their analyses, he enhances the worth of those analyses. This book is therefore more than a monograph on one tribe: it is an admirable summing up and development of existing theory in the field.

Following on the lead of E. J. and J. D. Krige, M. Wilson, and others, Marwick checks with quantitative studies the extent to which Cewa beliefs about sorcery as the cause of misfortunes are consistent with accusations actually made. And he finds, for example, that though

v

informants say that most sorcerers are female, in fact women are less often than men accused of being sorcerers, those who kill because of specific malice against the victim or an associate of the victim. On the other hand, 'witches' (real *nfiti*), those who kill from addiction rather than malice, are '. . . typically, though by no means exclusively, female'. Again, Cewa believe that polygyny produces, through the jealousy it provokes, much sorcery between co-wives; but Marwick found very few cases of misfortune explained in terms of these relationships. He suggests that this is partly because a weak marriage-tie and a high divorce-rate allow spouses just to separate, and they do not need sorcery as a catalytic agent for separation, in the way that members of the same matrilineage may. He suggests that, more deeply, in this matrilineal society sisters and sisters' daughters are the budding points of segmentation, rather than wives, who among, for example, the patrilineal South African Nguni are liable to be accused of witchcraft.

The quantitative analysis is based on 194 cases of misfortune which Marwick observed, or collected from informants, and had interpreted to him. (One weakness of the book is that the circumstances in which the data of specific cases were collected are not always made clear.) The 194 cases are reduced in number for calculation on certain problems. In discussing these cases, and how they can be used, and what they show, if they are examined in several ways, Marwick makes an important technical and theoretical contribution. Some calculations show that 'the frequency of inter-segmental [between segments of a matrilineage] believed attacks or accusations was about twice that of intra-segmental ones'. The conclusion that therefore 'inter-segmental relationships seem to be more tense than intra-segmental ones' may, however, be a 'reckless interpretation'. There might be an intervening variable, such as the fact that relatives are more often neighbours than are unrelated people. The greatest difficulty arises from the nature of the universe: a collection of cases of misfortune. It would seem that the incidence of accusations in varied types of particular relationships should be referred to the extent of interaction in each type of relationship. Marwick tackles these difficulties in various ways. I found most interesting of all his essays at working out the relative degrees to which persons in particular relationships with others were either accusers in their defence against sorcerers (i.e. were protectors), or were accused of sorcery. The discussion of these problems is intricate: and though Marwick emphasizes deficiencies and says he has not solved the difficulties, clearly he has posed an important problem of theory and technique for the study of social conflict and tension, and not merely of sorcery. And he sketches some possible solutions.

These beliefs crystallize through divination. Developing one of Mitchell's insights, Marwick writes that: 'The divining situation is important sociologically, since it is during divination that vague feelings of tension are organized and formulated into a belief that a particular person is responsible for a particular misfortune.' Working from this starting point, Marwick covers many problems, of which I can only list a few. Sorcery is only one of the mystical causes of misfortune in which Ceŵa believe. Misfortunes may be attributed to lineage spirits who punish certain derelictions, or to the wrath of elders, or to breaches of taboos, particularly those believed to keep the unborn, the newly born and the symbolically reborn safe from the heat of adult sexual life; for the innocent may suffer from the faults of those connected with them, notably from the last set of forces. And strikingly these beliefs, rooted in persisting forms of domestic life, survive more than beliefs in the lineage spirits. Marwick examines how these varied beliefs are invoked by sufferers and their associates, or put forward by the diviner, to explain various misfortunes according to the specific present situation of all the parties. These parties include accuser, as much as victim and alleged sorcerer. He calculates the distribution of these three categories of persons, according to sex and relative age, with results that lead him into an analysis of the inter-relationships between all categories of persons and groups in Ceŵa society. Accusations of sorcery are but one among many forms of reaction to man's lot in a society where comparatively poor technology leads to constant illness, death, and disaster. We learn how Ceŵa readjust after such crises; and when and how accusations of sorcery lead to (and are used to justify) ruptures of relations, and when and how they are not. Thus we learn that, while there is a chance that a group may remain united, struggle continues between contenders for leadership to control it; but when break-up of the group becomes apparent, an accusation of sorcery is a catalytic agent in the ensuring separation.

The problems are many-sided: for both the incidence of beliefs and that of accusations, which do not always coincide, have to be explained. The links are largely those between social relations, beliefs, and moral judgments. In the examination of these links, Marwick's quantitative and statistical analyses are particularly illuminating. It is striking that not only is the sorcerer or witch clearly an evil-doer, but also that in sixty per cent of cases the victim of sorcery, or a close associate of the victim, has also been guilty of a moral fault. And Marwick stresses that only a thin line divides approval from disapproval in moral judgment. Marwick relates that judgment to social action in a more or less stationary society, with limited property and a limited number of positions of prestige. Pursuing this analysis, he considers when judicial action and rational arbitration of behaviour can be used, as against situations when behaviour is believed to provoke mystical reactions. Here he constantly stresses that sorcery seems to be potential between fellow-members of a matrilineage because they cannot take one another to law, an argument linking with one stressed by V. W. Turner in *Schism and Continuity in an African Society* (1957).

I have been selecting a few points from a fascinating analysis of both social system and belief. One-to-one relationships are meticulously discussed, and then examined in their setting within wider fields of social action, and ultimately within the processes of development of marriages, matrilineages, villages and chiefdoms. Changes due to modern conditions are fully considered, with the effects of new forms of property, new standards of living, new activities, new values, and new authorities. The study of the Ceŵa concludes with an illuminating chapter on the misfortunes which befell one man between 1890 and 1950, and how allegations of sorcery, or of other mystical disturbance, were set within his changing relationships, which in turn were set in the absorption of Ceŵaland under British protection. The theoretical study culminates in the concluding general and comparative chapter.

I stress one further point, which may escape attention. Until Marwick reported on the Ceŵa, it was believed that patrilineally organized tribes were better able to sustain the effects of labour migration than matrilineally organized tribes. In the course of this book (and in an article on 'The Kinship Basis of Ceŵa Social Structure', 1952) Marwick shows that the Ceŵa matrilineage supported the women while their husbands were away. This implies that we must reconsider this whole problem; and I feel we would be led deep into the heart of the differences and similarities between consanguineal and conjugal relations in various situations. Marwick raises, and solves, problems of wide import.

                                                    MAX GLUCKMAN

Department of Social Anthropology and Sociology,
The Victoria University of Manchester,
June 1964

CONTENTS

LIST OF MAPS

LIST OF PLATES

xi

LIST OF TABLES

LIST OF CASES

LIST OF FIGURES

PREFACE

THE preface of my first book is an appropriate place for acknowledging the inspiration of the teachers who gave me my academic bearings, a psychologist, a geologist and a geographer, Dr Ella Pratt Yule, Dr L. C. King and Mr R. M. Jehu, all senior lecturers when I was a student at the Natal University College from 1936 to 1939, and subsequently all professors of their subjects in its successor, the University of Natal.

I should like to thank those of my colleagues who guided me when I took the formidable step of undertaking research for which my initial training (in psychology and geography) was not entirely appropriate. Dr Max Gluckman, then Director of the Rhodes-Livingstone Institute, awakened my interest in my native Africa and was my first mentor in the field. More recently, as Professor of Social Anthropology in the University of Manchester, he has given me invaluable inspiration and help in the preparation of this book—both directly, by finding time to read, comment on and discuss my draft, and indirectly, by being the creator of as lively and stimulating a department as any scholar could wish to work in anywhere. Professor I. Schapera, then of the University of Cape Town, with his colleague, the late Professor G. P. Lestrade, gave me a useful grounding in the principles and the practical aspects of anthropological field-work, as well as many stimulating approaches to problems. Professor Monica Wilson, who supervised the later part of my field-work and the protracted preparation of the Ph.D. thesis[1] on which this book is partly based, was generous of her time and constructive in her guidance. The late Professor J. D. Krige and his wife, now Professor E. J. Krige, both took a keen interest in my work from the time I joined the staff of the Department of Sociology in the University of Natal in 1950, as did the head of my department, Professor Leo Kuper and his wife, Dr Hilda Kuper. I record with gratitude the fact that my thoughts on the sociology of sorcery and witchcraft have been stimulated and clarified by many enjoyable discussions I have had during the last fifteen years with Professor J. Clyde Mitchell, now Head of the Department of African Studies in the University College of Rhodesia and Nyasaland.

---

[1] *Sorcery and Witchcraft in Their Social Setting: with Special Reference to the Northern Rhodesian Ceŵa*, University of Cape Town, 1961.

The encouragement that the late Dr A. Winifred Hoernlé has given South African anthropologists is legendary; and, though I was not one of her students in a formal sense, her helpfulness and kindness to me made me appreciate why she had become known as 'the mother of social anthropology in South Africa', though I always felt that, owing to her knack of treating even her most junior colleagues as her intellectual equals, 'grandmother' would, in terms of Radcliffe-Brown's principle of the combination of alternate generations, have been more appropriate.

Those of my colleagues in the United Kingdom who, during this year, have encouraged and helped me include: Professor Gluckman, Professor Meyer Fortes of Cambridge, Professor I. Schapera of the University of London (London School of Economics and Political Science), Drs John Middleton and Mary Douglas of University College, London, and Dr A. L. Epstein, Dr R. Frankenberg, Dr R. W. Mackenzie, Mr E. Marx, Dr E. L. Peters, Dr V. Pons, Dr V. W. Turner and Mr R. Werbner, all of Professor Gluckman's department at the University of Manchester.

At various times some of my colleagues have been kind enough to read and comment on parts of the draft of this book or of the thesis that preceded it. These include: Professor Monica Wilson, Professors J. D. and E. J. Krige, Professor J. Clyde Mitchell, Professor Gordon W. Allport of Harvard University (at the time Carnegie Visiting Professor at the University of Natal), Mr Julius Lewin and Dr M. D. W. Jeffreys of the University of the Witwatersrand, Dr Raymond Apthorpe then of the Rhodes-Livingstone Institute, Dr Mary Douglas, Professor Max Gluckman, Dr V. W. Turner and Mr R. Werbner. I have had advice on statistical aspects of my material from Professor Mitchell, Professor J. E. Kerrich of the University of the Witwatersrand, Mr A. O. H. Roberts of the National Institute for Personnel Research in Johannesburg, and Dr R. W. Mackenzie of the University of Manchester. In recording my gratitude to all these colleagues, I should add that I—and not they—must be held responsible for the accuracy of all facts and tables included and for the wisdom of all computations and interpretations.

I should like to thank my wife, who shared the excitements and alleviated the discomforts of my field-work, who took many texts from women who were too shy to dictate them to me (though they had no objection to my reading and using them), whose expert stenography often relieved me of the burden of recording my observations myself, and who, in general, has supported me in my resolve to use my limited free time to get my record of the Ceŵa into proper shape. I am also indebted to Miss F. M. O'Leary, Miss B. J. Le Maistre, Reverend E. M. Sholund and Mrs S. C. Wasem who helped prepare the final figures.

My thanks and those of my wife are due to the many people, African and non-African, in Rhodesia and Nyasaland whose encouragement, hospitality and friendship made my work possible and our stay enjoyable. These include: Mr and Mrs D. B. Hall (now Sir Douglas and Lady Hall) and Lt-Commander E. C. Cooper of the Provincial Administration, and Mr J. Hindson of the Department of Agriculture, in Northern Rhodesia; Mr and Mrs M. Gandy and Mr P. K. O'Riordan of the Provincial Administration in Nyasaland; Mr and Mrs J. H. du Plooy and Mr and Mrs M. Visagie of Katete, Senhor Lames-Franco of the Portuguese Administration in Moçambique and Reverend and the late Mrs A. S. Labuschagne of the Dutch Reformed Church Mission in Nyasaland. Among our Ceŵa friends we are especially grateful to Chief Kaŵaza Soŋgani and his successor, Chief Kaŵaza Maniŋu, Chiefs Mkanda Mateyo and Cimwala Catham'thumba, Headman Jeremiah Mvula, A Develiase Mvula[1] and the two young men who played the combined rôles of interpreter, language teacher and clerk, Messrs Raphael Almakio Mvula and David Misecky Mwanza. Among those of our Ceŵa friends who were always generous of their time and tolerant of inquisitive and eccentric Whites, we remember especially A Cuzu Phili, Headman Mceleka Luŋgu, Headman Jabesi Phili, A Yeleko Banda, A Thomo Daka, A Sindikani Phili, A Tuŋgase Mvula, A Ŋguzi Phili, A Mfukula Banda, Headman Kamphodza Phili and Mr Penias Thomo Phili, Court Clerk to the elder Kaŵaza.

My field-work was financed most generously by the Colonial Social Science Research Council, London, both during my tenure of a Colonial Research Fellowship in 1946–7 and on two subsequent trips to the Northern Rhodesian Ceŵa in 1948–9 and 1952–3. The Research Committee of the Council of the University of the Witwatersrand provided a grant for the typing of earlier drafts of the manuscript and the preparation of the maps and figures. The Simon Fund Committee of the University of Manchester awarded me a Simon Senior Research Fellowship which has given me the time and a near-perfect setting for work on the preparation of this book. The Committee of the Radcliffe-Brown Memorial Fund of the Association of Social Anthropologists of

[1] For an explanation of the title 'A', see footnote on p. 45.

the British Commonwealth awarded a grant which made possible the inclusion of the Genealogies in Fig. 3 and Appendix A. To all these bodies I am deeply grateful, as I am to Messrs Map Studio Productions (Pty) Ltd of Johannesburg for their public-spirited policy of assisting impecunious academics by providing their expert services at greatly reduced rates.

While engaged in research in Northern Rhodesia and Nyasaland, I invariably enjoyed the generous help and the confidence of the officers of the two Governments concerned. So much so, that I have been careful to seek formal permission for the use in this book of the unpublished material placed at my disposal. In all instances official permission has been granted.

M. G. M.

R.M.S. *Transvaal Castle*
North Atlantic Ocean
27 December 1962

NOTE ON NAMES

There is a possibility, however slight, that the use of the real names of persons involved in the cases described in this book might have identified them to their acquaintances and thus damaged their reputations. For this reason, in presenting these cases with the sole intention of advancing scientific understanding of the phenomena that they illustrate, I have, wherever necessary, disguised the identities of the persons concerned by giving them pseudonyms. These I have tried to make resemble as closely as possible the varied assortment of traditional and introduced personal names now to be found among the Ceŵa.

NOTE ON ORTHOGRAPHY

The Ceŵa speak a dialect—as it happens the majority dialect—of a language known to the world as Nyanja (*ciNyanja*). This is the official African language of the Nyasaland Protectorate, one of the four official African languages of Northern Rhodesia, and the alternative to Shona in the African townships of Salisbury, where many Nyanja-speakers have come froṃ Nyasaland and Northern Rhodesia to work. When Ceŵa is written, the official Nyanja orthography is usually employed.

I have found this orthography unsatisfactory in many respects, and have used one based on Atkins's suggested reforms,[1] though not conforming to them entirely. Thus I represent the velar nasal, a sound which sometimes occurs singly before vowels in Nyanja, by *ŋ* rather than the clumsy *ng'* of the official orthography; and, to be consistent, I use this symbol to represent it where it more often occurs—before *k* and *g*. This practice has led to some inconsistencies, especially in the spelling of ethnic or tribal names such as Nguni and Ŋgoni and of geographical names such as Kasungu and Luaŋgwa. Sẹcondly, I write nouns of Classes 9 and 10 always with an initial *n* or *ŋ* and not with the homorganic nasal permitted in the official orthography. In this way, two words of cardinal importance.in this study, 'sorcerer' and '(female) dependant', are written *nfiti* and *nbumba*—not *mfiti* and *mbumba*.

Thirdly, I distinguish between the radical and the aspirated *tʃ*-sound (which, roughly, the English *ch*, as in 'church', with less and with more aspiration respectively would represent) by using *c* and *ch*; and I do this consistently, with the result that the name of the people I describe is written 'Ceŵa', even though the rendering in the official orthography, 'Chewa', which violates a phonetic principle, is possibly an easier guide to a speaker of English.

Fourthly, although Atkins does not at this stage recommend for standard Nyanja separate symbols for the ordinary labiovelar *w* and the closely lip-rounded *ŵ*, he notes the important distinction between them in what he calls Northern and Western Cewa;[2] and the latter includes the speech of the people with whom I am concerned. Because in Northern Rhodesian Ceŵa (a form of Western Ceŵa) the distinction

---

[1] 'Amended Spelling and Word Division of Nyanja'.　　　[2] *Ibid.*, pp. 205–6.

between these two sounds is often of semantic significance, I have tried
to record it by using the two symbols mentioned. I may not have
consistently succeeded because one of the inadequacies of the official
orthography, especially for Western Ceŵa, is its failure to make the
distinction and thus to alert the beginner to its existence. In connection
with the closely lip-rounded $ŵ$, it may be worth noting that the Ceŵa
I knew used it in the prefixes of the more common Class 2 nouns, e.g.
ŵanthu ('people') and *ŵakaʒi* ('wife', honorific plural); but omitted it
from those of less common ones, e.g. *akadʒidʒi* ('owls') and *A Cite*
('So-and-so', hon. plur.). In standard Nyanja they are all written
without an initial consonant or semi-vowel, whereas, since it was
important for me to speak the dialect of the people I was studying
rather than what these people sometimes derisively called *ciZuŋgu*
('European [language]') or *ciBlantyre*, I developed the habit of recording words as I heard them; and I have retained this practice in what
follows.

PART I

Introductory

CHAPTER 1

THE SOCIOLOGY OF SORCERY

The Approach

ONE of the first things that impressed me about Cewa beliefs in sorcery was the fact that they had a social reference. 'Sorcerers never attack strangers,' my informants told me, 'they always attack their relatives.' As the Cewa trace descent through women, a statement such as this usually implied that sorcerers confine their attacks to their matrilineal relatives. When I asked why this should be, the analogy my informants gave me in reply was, 'If you want to slaughter livestock, you don't go and kill that of other people: you kill your own.' While this statement was consistent with their belief that sorcerers exhume and eat the corpses of their victims, it was nevertheless not very enlightening. There were, however, some less direct indications that this central item of dogma was based on an understanding of the link between sorcery (as they saw it) and the social process. They contended that matrilineal relatives 'practise sorcery against one another' because, belonging to a close-knit group, they are unable to settle their disputes by the judicial procedures available to unrelated persons who quarrel; and they pointed to the matrilineage as the natural arena for disputes about succession to office and the disposal of property.

Cewa allow certain exceptions to this general rule. They recognize that, when strong motives are involved, sorcerers may attack people who are not matrilineally related to them, and, as instances, they cite competing fellow-workers and the competing co-wives of a polygynist.

Thus the Cewa have some insight into the link that anthropologists and historians[1] have noted between sorcery and witchcraft and the social structure. This is one of the reasons why I have chosen to discuss the sociology of sorcery in the light of my research among them. Another is that I discovered at an early stage of my field work that virtually all Cewa believed in sorcery, and that many of them, especially those more advanced economically and educationally, were preoccupied to a considerable degree by fears of being attacked by

[1] In Appendix C I have indicated how my approach to the sociology of sorcery and witchcraft has been influenced by the writings of my colleagues.

sorcerers. It seems possible, therefore, that a study of sorcery in its social setting may help to advance the general theory of conflict and tension as well as to throw light on some of the changes taking place in present-day Africa.

The order in which this book has been written has been determined by the demands of intelligibility rather than those of strict scientific methodology.[1] Though I had developed certain hypotheses from reading the literature on witchcraft, sorcery and social tension, and though I had these hypotheses in mind when I collected and analysed my data, I have decided that I can present my results with greater clarity by making a unified advance through the material than by following the order implied in the methodologists' dictum that hypotheses should be formulated and then checked empirically. Although the order I have adopted may erroneously suggest that I have arrived at my generalizations by induction from particular instances,[2] I have avoided the alternative procedure because it involves a separation of theory, ethnography and the analysis of case material.

Instead of separating them, I have presented relevant items of sociological theory and specific cases of believed sorcery at appropriate points in my description of Cewa life. Thus, after this brief note on my approach, I try to illustrate my conception of the sociology of sorcery in three cases of a type that will be comprehensible to the reader without involving him in the minutiae of Cewa social organization. I follow this with an account of my field-work methods with special reference to the collection and classification of the cases I use for illustration and whose summarized attributes I include in my statistical tables, after which, in the two remaining chapters of Part I, I give an introductory account of Cewa life and beliefs. The first seven chapters of Part II describe the various contexts in which Cewa beliefs in sorcery are of social relevance; and the last one reviews the elements common to these contexts in an attempt to vindicate certain hypotheses which may be applicable, not only to the Cewa, but also to other societies.

Preliminary Illustration of Approach

The following two cases tend to be a little unreal; for they were ones in which I was personally involved. In an attempt to penetrate the secrecy surrounding the divination process, I decided to play the

[1] Cf. Wisdom, *Foundations of Inference in Natural Science*, Chapter 5.
[2] *Ibid.*, Part II; and Fisher, *The Design of Experiments*, pp. 6 ff.

rôle of diviner's client. I waited for parallels in my own experience of situations that would have prompted a Cewa to consult a diviner. These cropped up on two occasions; and I took what, in Cewa idiom, would have been appropriate steps. I played the client's rôle more skilfully on the second occasion than on the first. In both instances, the diviners' diagnoses had close parallels in the reported experience of many of my informants; though the first diviner, whose *Fanakalo*-laden[1] speech confirmed his reputation of having lived amongst, and learned about, Whites in the labour centres in the south, ingeniously transposed the Cewa doctrine regarding the typical kinship of sorcerer and victim from a matrilineal to a patrilineal mode.

Case No. 1—The Dancing Owls

In July 1947, my wife and I were losing a good deal of sleep because each night birds used to come and make a noise (as if they were dancing, *ngati kubvina gule*) on the reed-mat ceiling of the house we were using. We asked several Cewa what they thought these birds could be, and the consensus of opinion was that they were owls. Our servant, Jerusalem, felt sure that they were owls 'sent by people', i.e. that they were sorcerers' familiars, although he was puzzled about who could be sending them, since, from the cardinal Cewa belief that sorcerers do not attack people unrelated to them, it follows that African sorcerers do not attack Whites.

I decided to consult a diviner, and, as Dayton, one of my research assistants, told me that there was one at his home village, I went there with him early one morning. (At the time I did not know that it was necessary to 'put the divining apparatus to sleep' first.)[2] As this was my first meeting with the diviner, he was suspicious, and hesitant about taking on my case. He finally got rid of me by discovering that there was no suitable oil for working his speaking gourd.

Two days later he came to see me, and arranged that the séance should be held early the following morning. During the evening of the same day, however, he came to tell me that he had to leave the local village earlier than he had anticipated, and asked whether we could have the séance immediately. I assented, and, as my research assistants had gone home for the night, asked our servant, Jerusalem, to support me. We went with the diviner into a disused hut, using a petrol-tin brazier and a paraffin lantern for light. The diviner took a little black gourd out of a basket he was carrying, and, having

---

[1] *Fanakalo* (= 'like this' or 'like that') has become the scientific designation of 'Kitchen-Kaffir', a pidgin-Zulu used as a lingua franca in European settlements from Cape Town to the Copperbelt. The Cewa give it the expressive name of *ciLapha-lapha* because *lapha* ('here' or 'there', 'in' or 'on'—from the Zulu, *lapha*, 'here') is one of its commonest words.

[2] See below, Chapter 3.

put some powdered 'medicines' into it and having rubbed it on the outside
with an oily substance, he shook it hard and passed it round his head. He
then set it up on the floor and told us to clap hands (*kuomba m'manja*)—a
token of respect. Next, he asked me to turn down the lantern. When I had
done this, he started addressing the gourd in polite terms, calling it *A Mai*
('Mother', the term of address one would use towards any woman commanding respect). The gourd responded in a wheezing whistle. As the light
was poor, I was unable to tell whether this sound was the result of ventrilo-
quism or caused by the diviner's squeezing something in his hands. I could
not understand what the gourd was saying, though Jerusalem obviously
could. I concluded that what it said was intelligible only to someone
thoroughly acquainted with the tones of Ceŵa.

After some preliminary courtesies, the diviner asked me what the trouble
was. I said, '*Akadzidzi* (owls).' The gourd cackled, and the diviner said, 'So,
you knew all along, did you, Mother?', to which it replied in the affirmative.
The diviner and the gourd then had an argument. After respectfully disagreeing with his 'mother', the diviner turned to me, saying that she had
asserted that a younger brother of my father was using sorcery against me,
but that he had assured her that such a person must have died long ago. If
he had been mistaken in his assertion, he added, I should contradict (*-tsutsa*)
him. In this way I was drawn into the argument. When I told him that there
were two of my father's younger brothers still alive, a further argument
ensued about which of the two was responsible for sending the owls. It was
decided eventually that the one who had sought to do me harm was 'the one
who does not write regularly'. Unfairly perhaps, I did not reveal that, quite
deservedly, I seldom had a letter from either of my uncles. Instead, I asked
how it was that my wicked uncle could send owls over such a long distance.
The gourd found this question very amusing, and replied, 'Why, people can
send things across the sea, across Southern Rhodesia and even across the
Zambezi into Northern Rhodesia—don't be astonished!'

The diviner then passed on a warning from the gourd that my uncle would
kill me if I failed to take some steps in the matter. Not relishing the idea of
having 'medicines' rubbed into incisions in my skin, I told him that I would
write to my uncle telling him to desist from his sorcery. If that proved
ineffective, I said, I would call in his [the diviner's] assistance again. I paid
him five shillings and he left.

Case No. 2—The Broken Windscreen

At the end of 1948, on our way to Ceŵa country (during a university
vacation), we had a slight accident which provided a useful excuse for consulting a diviner. As we were driving through Southern Rhodesia, a car
going southward threw up a stone which struck the windscreen of ours,
which happened to be new, making a small round patch of splintered glass

in one corner. In January 1949, while talking to an old Cewa friend, who happened to be the local diviner, I mentioned this accident, saying that I was puzzled about its cause, and would probably consult him professionally about it. He showed no objection, and a few days later I went at sundown to his hut, accompanied by another friend, the headman of the village in which we were camped. In order to 'put the divining apparatus to sleep (*kugoneka ula*)', I handed him a fragment of the broken windscreen together with three shillings, reminding him of our earlier conversation. He told us to come back the following morning.

Before sunrise the next day, the headman and I went to the diviner's hut, into which he took us and seated us. He sat opposite us across the fire next to a forked stake which had been driven into the floor of the hut. From the top of the stake was suspended a fine string which was threaded through a hole in the middle of a tortoise shell about three inches long. Below the tortoise shell the string was fastened to a small disc (probably of wood). The diviner started to tell us the story that explained how the stone had jumped up and struck the windscreen. As he proceeded, he confirmed details by putting questions to his apparatus which he addressed in a familiar way as *Fulu* ('Tortoise'). Holding the disc in one hand so that the string was taut, he used the other to slide the tortoise shell up it as he asked a question. If the shell slid straight down, the answer was negative; if it came down slowly, positive. He probably controlled the movements of the shell by keeping the string still or by vibrating it slightly—as required—but, however he managed it, he did it skilfully enough not to be detected in the semi-darkness of a fire-lit hut before sunrise.[1]

The story he told me was as follows: Before I had bought my car, three other Europeans had seen it in the window. They had 'counted their pennies' with a view to buying it, but had found that they hadn't enough money. Soon after that, I went in and bought it, and this angered them very much. They decided to kill me by making a 'medicine line' (*mkhwekhwe*) across the road so that I would have a serious accident in the car. Fortunately for me, however, the spirit of one of my ancestors had taken pity on me because he felt that, having paid for the car, I was entitled to have it. He had therefore intervened, though by mistake he had not removed all the medicine from the road, with the result that the stone that broke our windscreen was thrown up by what remained. When I told the diviner that I was anxious about the journey back to South Africa, he asked his apparatus whether we would have any mishap. The shell came straight down, indicating a negative reply. He told me that, to be on the safe side, he would prepare a charm for me to keep in my car when travelling. I paid him ten shillings for the séance and the charm. He told me afterwards that the activating agent (*ci̧imba*) he had used in it had been a piece of human caul (*cibalilo*), which is of general use

[1] Essentially the same technique, except for the use of a gourd or small horn instead of a tortoise shell, is described by Stannus for the Nyanja ('Notes on Some Tribes', p. 304).

because of its protective function (anatomically) and of special value for improving social relationships because it makes one 'like a child' and therefore 'pleasing to people'.

These cases illustrate some of the principles that will become apparent when, suitably prepared, the reader is offered more authentically Cewa cases in their social setting.

In the first place, in both cases, the victim's misfortune was attributed to the malice of a mystical evil-doer. It was not made clear why my uncle should have wished to harm me with sorcery, but the diviner probably assumed that there was as much tension in a European surname group as he would encounter in a Cewa matrilineage.[1] In the second case the origin of the malice was clearer. Even by Western standards I had, from the point of view of my mystical assailants, 'jumped the queue', this having been at a time of post-war shortages; though, as the spirit of my (unidentified) ancestor had reasoned, I had had some right on my side, having paid for the car and having been unaware that others wanted to buy it.

Secondly, in the case of the Broken Windscreen, the issue between the sorcerers and their victim was assumed to have arisen in a situation in which they competed for a strongly desired object and in which there was a conflict of rights and claims.

Thirdly, in both cases there was some assumed impediment to the resolution of the conflict of rights and interests between victim and attacker. There is insufficient information about my uncle's reasons for using sorcery in preference to some other kind of expression; but Cewa would have reasoned that, belonging to the same descent-group as myself, he was unable to submit his (unspecified) grievance to an outside arbitrator corresponding in function to a Cewa chief, and had to adopt the direct, if illegitimate, course of using sorcery against me. In the second case, my co-consumers had to take the law into their own hands because they had no legal claim against me, even though I had violated a social convention that is emphasized in times of shortages. (It is debatable, of course, whether the second diviner was aware of such issues; though it so happens that he, like the first one, had been a labour migrant.)

Fourthly, the second case illustrates the fact that sorcery may have moral implications. The victim, in that he had 'jumped the queue', had failed to observe a social norm; and sorcery came as a punitive sanction.

---

[1] For my usage of 'matrilineage', see the beginning of Chapter 4.

Apart from the fact that both cases were ones of attempted sorcery, which by definition is anti-social, neither of them happens to illustrate clearly an allied principle, which is illustrated by other cases, viz. that the sorcerer is, through the very illegitimacy of his attack, at least a moral transgressor, and may be much worse; for, while the victim, as a wrong-doer, sometimes gets his deserts, the sorcerer is often portrayed as the personification of evil, who commits the gravest crimes, such as murder and incest.

The following case is taken from a text written for me by a literate Cewa. Although it refers to a few of the distinctive aspects of Cewa social organization, such as the vesting of the group's responsibility in the maternal uncle, its elements are otherwise sufficiently universal for it to serve as a further introductory illustration. As in the case of the Broken Windscreen, it involves believed sorcery between unrelated persons. In an attempt to convey the style of Cewa narrative, I have kept my translation of what my informant wrote as close to the original as possible, except that the persons involved have, as in all subsequent cases, been given pseudonyms.

Case No. 3—The Cow's Four Limbs

This is how I explain the deaths of my [classificatory] mothers, Zaŋgose and Yelezeti. These people died very astonishing deaths; and their deaths came about because Yelezeti's brother, Lekani, went and committed adultery with Ndalose, the wife of another man; and the man's father and mother were sorcerers. It happened that, when Lekani was committing adultery with that woman, he was caught and the one who caught him was the woman's mother. The scandal of Lekani's adultery with Ndalose became widely known. Ndalose's husband was [at work] in Southern Rhodesia. The case went to the Chief's court, and there Lekani's maternal uncle paid a beast of pregnancy [damages to Ndalose's husband's matrilineage]. The beast [a cow] stayed two weeks only and in the third week it had a heifer calf. After a while the calf died; and the cow itself also died. And the mother of the cuckolded husband, seeing that she was a sorcerer,[1] said words to this effect: 'This beast has died; you'll see indeed! I want this beast's death to be balanced by other things. Each front leg is the equivalent of one [junior] person; one hind leg, of an adult; and the other, of another adult. Altogether four people will die.'

[1] My reasons for translating *nfiti* as 'sorcerer' are given in Chapter 3. While in everyday speech 'sorcerer' is masculine and 'witch' feminine, in anthropological usage, which in this respect happens to correspond with Bantu usage, both terms are applied to men or women and are thus of common gender.

It was really true. Before a long time had passed, our maternal uncle fetched Ndalose and took her to Southern Rhodesia [to her husband]. This was in August 1942. In December my mother [mother's sister, classificatory mother], Zaŋgose, began to sicken. Some said it was a disease; but we, her guardians,[1] because of those words, 'This beast of mine has died; you'll see!', knew that it was those troubles [that caused her illness]. She became very ill

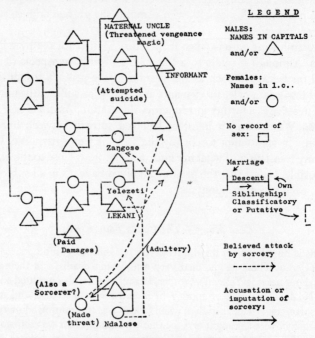

Fig. 1. The Case of 'The Cow's Four Limbs'

Note: Subsequent genealogies will follow the same conventions, but marriages will be shown only if material to the point being illustrated. In large genealogies, such as that in Fig. 3, the demands of space have made it necessary to show sex by only one or other of the two methods used here.

indeed and developed frightening symptoms; and we were unable to do anything for her. In the month of April 1943, Mother Zaŋgose died on a Monday; and that other one, Yelezeti, began to be ill. We buried Zaŋgose on the Tuesday; and on the Wednesday that other one died, too. We were sorely distressed. At this time my own mother tried to commit suicide because of these troubles. We buried Yelezeti on the Thursday. (I was at

[1] The word used, *eni* (sing., *mwini*), could also be translated as 'proprietors' or possibly 'owners'; but the context suggests 'guardians'. For an account of the Cewa system of guardianship, see Chapter 4.

[boarding] school at this time but I heard about all this from my mother who explained the manner in which things had gone on.) Those two people died, the two elders representing the hind legs of the beast, just as the sorcerer had said.

Of the two mothers, one left a boy who was old enough to be walking; and the other, a boy who was crawling. They [my relatives] tried to care for these children, but within a short time they began to be ill. One of them became very ill and died; then the other one was ill and after but a few days also died. These deaths caused great distress in our family. We wrote to our maternal uncle to tell him of them; and he, too, was greatly distressed and he begged those of us remaining at home, saying, 'How now? Why don't you let me send wild beasts to eat up those people who threatened us with death?' But we, on seeing a letter of this kind, said, 'No, these things [he suggests] are worthless nonsense not to be followed.' Then his heart softened and he returned to the village and heard about all that had happened there. The hatred between those people [the sorcerers] and us exists even until the present.

This case provides further illustration of the pattern of elements emerging from the first two. Firstly, a serious misfortune is attributed, even by a relatively sophisticated informant, not to the vectors of disease aided by tropical climate, ignorance of hygiene and inadequate medical services, but to the machinations of sorcerers (or of a single sorcerer, there being only one reference to the cuckold's father).

Secondly, there is an assumption that sorcery, especially when it occurs between persons who are not related matrilineally, springs from intense competition over highly desired objects. 'All's fair in love and war', we might say; and this would explain why the believed sorcerer in the struggle for her son's conjugal rights, was prepared to use extreme and illegitimate methods. Thirdly, methods of such extremity were resorted to after the socially approved machinery of reconciliation had failed to work because the cow awarded by the Court in settlement of the action for adultery, and later its calf, had died.

Finally, the case has moral overtones. The victims were close relatives (by Cewa standards) of the adulterer whose conduct was assumed to have precipitated the sorcerer's attack. And the sorcerer herself, though she could have petitioned the Court for a replacement of the cow, chose instead to take the law into her own hands—because, the informant says, 'she was a sorcerer', i.e. a person of evil disposition.

c

Field Work Methods

This book is based on research which I started during my tenure of
a Colonial Research Fellowship in 1946–7 and have since continued
in my spare time while lecturing at the South African Native College,
now the University College of Fort Hare (1948–9), the University
of Natal (1950–6) and the University of the Witwatersrand (1957
–1963). Since my original field-trip, which was divided between the
Northern Rhodesian Ceŵa and the Nyasaland Ŋgoni, I have been back
to the Northern Rhodesian Ceŵa twice during South African university
long vacations (1948–9 and 1952–3). Both these trips, like the original
one, were sponsored by the Colonial Social Science Research Council,
London. I have spent an aggregate of about fourteen months among
the Northern Rhodesian Ceŵa; but this has been spread over a considerably longer period, thus consolidating my grasp of Ceŵa language
and culture more effectively than would have been the case had my
period in the field been uninterrupted. Unless otherwise indicated,
when the present tense is used in the text, it refers to 1953.

I started research in Northern Rhodesia and Nyasaland with the
intention of making a comparative social-psychological study of the
Ceŵa and Ŋgoni, a scheme which had been conceived on the assumption that the Ŋgoni had retained the patrilineal institutions of their
forebears, the Swazi and Natal Nguni. The discovery that they had
not, more particularly that they had virtually abandoned the cardinal
institution of *lobolo*—together with my finding that 'projective' techniques were unsuited to the type of psychological study I had in mind
—led me to concentrate on the matrilineal Ceŵa and to shift my general
orientation from social psychology to comparative sociology. The
latter step involved no fundamental practical change; for my social-
psychological investigations had had to be preceded by ethnographic
study and sociological analysis.

The methods I used in acquiring my background knowledge of
the Ceŵa were those generally adopted by social anthropologists. I
learned the language. I collected texts, either written by literate informants or dictated to me or to my African assistants by illiterate
ones, and I asked semi-literate people who were strategically placed to
record in diaries anything that they considered worth the great effort
of writing it down. I observed everyday life in villages, gardens, the
Chief's court, trading stores and places of work; I questioned people
on what I had been told or what I had seen; I attended ceremonies, such

as funerals and subsequent mourning rites, with their attendant feast-
ing and dancing. I drew up genealogies of villages and made censuses
of population, marriage, religious affiliation and labour experience;[1] I
carried out a public opinion survey on a quasi-random sample of 268
people;[2] and I recorded fairly detailed life histories of nine selected
informants, five men and four women. I read—mainly after I had
completed my field work—what had been written on the Ceŵa in
travellers' records, in official documents, in scientific and popular
journals, and in books.[3]

In all these activities my aim could have been described as the empathetic exploration of Ceŵa life; for, though the social anthropologist
should and does rely on objective reporting, he relies, too, on attuning
his personality to the conditions of life of the people whom he describes
and then reporting on the resulting experience. In this attempt to feel
my way into Ceŵa life, I acquired habits that became almost uncon-
scious and were difficult to break when I left the field and they became
redundant. Some were simple matters of etiquette, such as, when
joining company, sitting down as low as possible and as quickly as
possible, lest I should give the impression that I considered myself
important enough to be fetched a chair; or clapping my hands in
greeting and simultaneously ducking my head (to avoid bumping it)
on entering someone's hut. Others were more fundamental, and one of
them at least has a bearing on the subject-matter of this book. I was
able to make some estimate of the effects on one's habits of thought
of a life-long association with a system of beliefs by reformulating
some of the questions I asked myself and others about what I had
observed. As I was an investigator rather than a teacher, I was in the
fortunate position of not having to refute my informants' beliefs but
rather of having to project myself into their situations as fully as
possible in order to gain a sympathetic understanding of their problems.
The ease with which I was able to do this, and to develop habits appropriate to the system, impressed upon me how firmly rooted beliefs in
sorcery must become in the course of time, especially when they are
held by one's peers. Whenever someone died—and the death-rate was
high—I found it relatively easy, if only as a means of detecting social

[1] Owing to my shorter period in the field, my statistical records are not as full as those
of some of my colleagues who have worked in Central Africa, e.g. Mitchell, *The Yao
Village*, and Turner, *Schism and Continuity*.
[2] Cf. Marwick, 'An Experiment in Public Opinion Polling' and 'The Rôle of the Social
Anthropologist in Assessing Development Programmes'.
[3] A select annotated bibliography is given at the end of the book.

tensions, to change from the Western thought, 'What disease or accident caused his death?', to the more typically Ceŵa one, 'What wrong has he committed; with whom has he quarrelled; who was jealous of him; in short, who has killed him?' So ingrained did this cultivated habit become that I sometimes had to remind myself that notorious 'sorcerers' in the local community were not in fact responsible for others' misfortunes, but were unfortunate people whose social positions or eccentric personalities had made them unpopular.

Collection and Primary Analysis of Sorcery Case Material

The reason why this last instance of empathetic exploration assumed such importance has to do with a special category of data I recorded, viz. cases of believed sorcery. Since I shall be referring to these data at various points throughout the book, it is as well to dispose now of the conditions under which they were collected and the qualifications that must therefore be made about their interpretation.

I collected this material during the course of field work, especially during my second (1948–9) and third (1952–3) field-trips. By the time of these two trips (both of short duration during South African university summer vacations), I had a clearer idea of the problem about which I intended orientating my study of the Ceŵa, and I was freer from the task of acquiring a knowledge of the language and culture than I had been on my longer, first trip (1946–7). I made a practice of recording all cases of serious misfortunes (mostly deaths) that I heard of. In some instances, these came my way with hardly any effort on my part, as when they occurred in the neighbourhood in which I was working. In others, I deliberately sought them out, either by asking informants from this neighbourhood to describe any misfortunes that had escaped my notice, e.g. those that had occurred during periods when I was not in the field, or by asking informants from other neighbourhoods to tell me about misfortunes occurring at any time in their areas.

I recorded the account of each case verbatim, and, then, by entering certain of its details under headings in a specially prepared note-book, checked that I had enough information on it to make it comparable with others, and to meet the requirements of the analysis I had in mind.[1] To facilitate tabulation, I transferred the main characteristics of cases on to cards which could be sorted and counted easily.

[1] I am grateful to Professor Monica Wilson for suggesting this procedure.

It is clear that the manner in which the cases came to be recorded precludes their being regarded as a random sample from the universe of Ceŵa misfortune; and the ratios between any of the categories into which they fall must be regarded as but crude estimates of the corresponding parameters of this universe. Without the complete listing of all misfortunes in a given area over a given period and the use of a randomizing technique for drawing a sample of these, the possibility cannot be excluded that selective biases were operating. For instance, it is possible that, in the earlier stages of recording cases, I was too often attracted by the exotic nature of explanations in terms of beliefs in sorcery to give due attention to the more humdrum ones attributing misfortunes to acts of God, of persons other than sorcerers, and of spirits. Furthermore, since some informants gave me details of more than one case each, their personal interests and problems may have influenced the selection of those that they remembered and related. There was, however, a sufficiently large number of informants— between thirty and forty for 194 cases of misfortune—for their biases to have been subject to some degree of mutual dilution.

A few of the cases I recorded have been excluded from the analysis that follows because I failed to ascertain sufficiently detailed information about them. I have retained in Table I only those related to me by informants who showed by the way they answered my questions that they were fully acquainted with the persons involved in the incidents they described. It must be noted that this criterion, that the informant should have full knowledge of the characters in the drama, does not ensure that he is necessarily impartial; and, to avoid misunderstanding and to anticipate criticism, I must record that in most cases I had only one person's view of any particular believed instance of sorcery. The limitations of this fact are obvious. There are often different versions of the account of a believed instance of sorcery, each espoused by persons differently placed and of differing loyalties. While recognizing the weakness of my material in this respect, I can only hope that, over the whole series of cases, the errors attributable to the informants' positions and attitudes may in some measure cancel one another out.

Table I shows that:

(1) in twenty-five per cent of the 194 cases retained for analysis, the misfortune was attributed to '[acts] of God', such as the victim's succumbing to recognizable disease, to old age, or to certain accidents not believed to be associated with malign or sinister circumstances;

TABLE I

TYPES OF EXPLANATIONS, WITH MORAL IMPLICATIONS, OF 194 CASES OF MISFORTUNES (MOSTLY DEATHS) COLLECTED DURING THE COURSE OF FIELD WORK

Type of Explanation Offered	Moral Implication			Total	Percentage of All Cases
	Victim Had Been at Fault	Victim's Friend or Relative Had Been at Fault	No One Had Been at Fault		
(1) Natural causes, '[acts] of God'	12	8	29	49	25·3
(2) Acts of persons other than sorcerers:					
(*) Vengeance for sorcery (V)	11	—	—	11 }	17·0
Other acts, e.g. breach of taboo, use of property-protecting or anti-adultery magic, suicide	13	9	—	22 }	
(3) (*) Acts of sorcerers:					
(V) Sorcerers killed by own sorcery or by other sorcerers	6	—	—	6 }	55·1
Other acts of sorcerers	39	15	47	101 }	
(4) Acts of spirits	2	2	1	5	2·6
Total	83	34	77	194	100·0
Less cases involving beliefs in sorcery (marked (*) above)	56	15	47	118	60·8
Cases not involving beliefs in sorcery	27	19	30	76	39·2

Summary with Reference to Many Subsequent Tables

Total cases involving beliefs in sorcery (marked (*) above) — 118

Less cases in which sorcerers were victims of people's vengeance, their own sorcery or the sorcery of others (marked (V) above) — 17

Cases in which misfortunes were attributed to sorcerers' attacking non-sorcerers — 101

Summary with Reference to Table XXV

Cases with:	Involving Beliefs in Sorcery	Not Involving Beliefs in Sorcery	Total
Moral implications	56 + 15 = 71	27 + 19 = 46	117
No moral implications	47	30	77
Total	118	76	194

(2) in seventeen per cent, to the actions of persons other than sorcerers, such as their failure to perform a ritual, their breach of a taboo, their use of property-protecting (*cambo*), anti-adultery (*likaŋkho*) or vengeance magic, and their suicide;

(3) in fifty-five per cent, to acts of sorcerers; and

(4) in three per cent, to the intervention of lineage spirits.

Before I give closer attention to the 55 per cent of cases in Table I in which misfortunes were attributed to attacks by sorcerers, their number, viz. 107 (101 + 6) should be adjusted if it is to reflect either (*a*) the total number of cases involving beliefs in sorcery or (*b*) the number of those in which sorcerers were believed to have attacked non-sorcerers. Reference to the foot of Table I will make these adjustments clear. (*a*) Cases involving beliefs in sorcery include all the 107 in the third category, in which sorcerers were believed to be the agents of misfortune, plus eleven in the second category, in which they were regarded as the deserving victims of physical or magical vengeance. Of the total of 118 thus arrived at, there were seventeen cases (eleven in the second category and six in the third) in which sorcerers were believed to be victims—of physical or magical vengeance, of other's sorcery, or of their own sorcery. (*b*) Deducting these from the total, we are left with 101 cases in which non-sorcerers were regarded as the victims of sorcerers. It is these 101 cases that will be analysed at various points throughout this book; and seventy-nine of them, those in which an accuser as well as a sorcerer and a victim was identified, are of particular importance.

Before leaving Table I, I should note that cases of misfortune have been classified (in the first three columns) according to whether they had any moral implications. Of the total of 194 cases, there were eighty-three (or forty-three per cent) in which the victim of misfortune had been at fault; and thirty-four (or eighteen per cent) in which one of his kinsmen or friends had been. In the second summary at the foot of Table I, those cases involving beliefs in sorcery have been separated from those that have no reference to such beliefs, since this procedure will enable me to test, at the appropriate point in my argument, whether the two categories of beliefs tend to sanction distinct categories of moral behaviour.

It will be immediately apparent that my sample of case material is small; and, as the analysis proceeds, the limitations imposed by this fact will become increasingly obvious. It is therefore fitting to refer to the reason why the sample is not larger. Adequate case material of this kind can be collected only after a high degree of rapport has been established. Most informants among the Ceŵa are aware of the fact that Whites disapprove of beliefs in sorcery. They tend, therefore, not to relate incidents implying such beliefs unless they are sure that their listener will take them seriously, will not try to eradicate them, and will be generally sympathetic. It was only by living in the community for an extended period, learning the language and participating in everyday and ceremonial life, that I was able to gain my informants' confidence. The collection of case material therefore had to come late in my field work. I might add that, even with ideal rapport, informants usually become reticent when they remember, not only that it is a criminal offence to impute witchcraft (including sorcery) to others,[1] but also that, by doing so, they may arouse the hostility and precipitate the vengeance of those to whom they impute it.

[1] Northern Rhodesia, *Laws*, Witchcraft Ordinance, No. 5 of 1914 as amended by No. 47 of 1948, Section 3, which also makes it an offence to assert 'that any person has by committing adultery caused in some non-natural way death, injury, damage or calamity' (a reference to *mdulo*, discussed in Chapter 3).

CHAPTER 2

INTRODUCING THE CEŴA

In the main this book will be a search for common elements in the various contexts in which Ceŵa beliefs in sorcery are expressed. Some of the significance of these contexts will escape the reader unless I provide him, in this and the next chapter, with accounts of the general conditions of Ceŵa life and the idiom of Ceŵa beliefs.

In this chapter I shall try to place the Ceŵa in preliminary focus by presenting such details of their history, environment and subsistence as will give an understanding of their present-day life and attitudes.

Origin of the Northern Rhodesian Ceŵa

The material I present on the Ceŵa is based mainly on observations made in the Cimbuna neighbourhood of Chief Kaŵaza's country in the south-west part of Fort Jameson district. For convenience, I refer to the people I studied as 'the Northern Rhodesian Ceŵa', especially since my few visits to areas outside Kaŵaza's chiefdom left me with the impression that the differences between his people and other Northern Rhodesian Ceŵa are not fundamental.

Chief Kaŵaza's people belong to a branch of the Ceŵa usually referred to as the 'Southern Ceŵa' of Fort Jameson district. There are two other branches of the tribe (using the term in the cultural rather than in the political sense) in Northern Rhodesia, the 'Northern Ceŵa' of the same district and the Ceŵa of Lundazi district, which lies north of Fort Jameson district. These three branches, though now under a common administration, that of the Eastern Province of Northern Rhodesia, differ in origin, and consequently in present political disposition. In particular, they vary in the degree of loyalty they show to Paramount Chief Undi; for those to the south, and nearer his traditional capital at Mano on the Kapoche river in Portuguese territory (see Map 1), are more closely affiliated to him than those to the north.

The three groups comprising the Northern Rhodesian Ceŵa form a part—and only a small part—of a larger group. 'Nyanja-speaking'

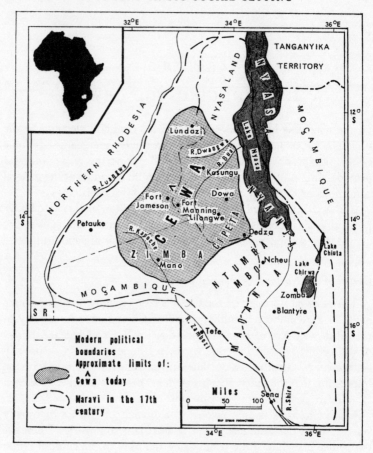

MAP I

Approximate positions of the Maravi in the seventeenth century and of
the 'Nyanja-speaking peoples' in the twentieth

peoples calling themselves Ceŵa (aCeŵa) are found, not only in the
Eastern Province of Northern Rhodesia, but also in the Central
Province of Nyasaland and in the northern part of the *intendência* of
Tete in the district of Manica and Sofala of Moçambique (see Map 1).
In Nyasaland and Moçambique, some of them use the designation
'Cipeta'; and in Moçambique alone, 'Zimba'.[1] The Cipeta are widely

---

[1] I am indebted to Mr A. Rita-Ferreira of the Portuguese Administration in Moçambique for providing me with information on the Zimba, and for helping me to increase
the accuracy of Map 1.

recognized as a division of the Ceŵa.[1] In 1951-2, the *de jure* Ceŵa-Cipeta-Zimba population of the three territories was probably between 900,000 and a million, with about seventy-seven per cent in Nyasaland, fourteen per cent in Northern Rhodesia and nine per cent in Moçambique. The Ceŵa, in turn, make up about two-thirds of the total 'Nyanja-speaking' population, the remainder of whom, comprising Nyasa, Nyanja, Maŋanja, Ntumba and Mbo, live in Nyasaland, in Moçambique and in the part of Tanganyika Territory along the eastern shore of Lake Nyasa.[2]

All these peoples, including the Ceŵa, Cipeta and Zimba, speak dialects of the same language, the standard, written form of which has become known as Nyanja (*ciNyanja*). This designation, whose more specific reference is to the dialect spoken on the south-western shores of Lake Nyasa, has arisen fortuitously. Either 'Ceŵa' or 'Malaŵi' would have been more appropriate—'Ceŵa', because of the numerical preponderance of this division; or 'Malaŵi', because the so-called Nyanja-speakers are descendants of a tribe or federation of related tribes referred to in seventeenth-century and later Portuguese records as the Maravi (Maraves, etc.).[3] The Nseŋga of Petauke district,

[1] Cf. S. S. Murray, *A Handbook of Nyasaland*, p. 68; A. G. O. Hodgson, 'Notes on the Achewa and Angoni', p. 127; and R. S. Rattray, *Some Folklore Stories and Songs in Chinyanja*, p. viii.

[2] These estimates are based on the following sources: Nyasaland Protectorate, *Report on the Census of 1945*, Tables 1, 3 and 4; Central African Statistical Office, *Monthly Digest of Statistics for the Federation of Rhodesia and Nyasaland*, 1, 3, June 1954, Table 1; letters from the Chief Secretary of the Nyasaland Government, dated 20 February 1955, and the Director of the East African Statistical Department, dated 1 March 1954, both cited by permission; Northern Rhodesia, *Eastern Province*, Annual Report on Native Affairs, 1951, appended tables—on file at Fort Jameson—cited by permission; Dos Santos Júnior, *Algumas Tribos do Distrito de Tete*, 1945, p. 21 and maps on p. 104 and between pp. 18 and 19; Rita-Ferreira, *Agrupamento e Caracterização Étnica dos Indígenas de Moçambique*, 1958, pp. 63 and 123; private communications from Mr A. Rita-Ferreira; and *Annuário da Província de Moçambique*, 1952-3, pp. 28-9. I have had to make various calculations from the figures given in these sources to make my estimates refer to the same date (1951-2) and to the *de jure* (domiciled) rather than the *de facto* (actually present) population. My estimate of the total 'Nyanja-speaking' population at 1½ millions is comparable with the one made by Guy Atkins in his paper, 'The Nyanja-Speaking Population of Nyasaland and Northern Rhodesia (a Statistical Estimate)', 1950, when allowance is made for the facts that he refers to a slightly earlier date, that he does not include Moçambique or Tanganyika Territory, that he counts Fort Jameson Ŋgoni as Nyanja-speaking (in fact they speak Nseŋga) and that he includes (where I have excluded) the Nyanja-speaking subjects of non-Nyanja (non-Ceŵa) chiefs, e.g. 10,000 Ceŵa in Petauke district, Northern Rhodesia.

[3] The reason why 'Maravi' was written with a *v* is probably because the ŵ in the modern rendering, 'Malaŵi', is a sound closely resembling a *v* and not unlike a *b*. *L* and *r*, both representing the same, flapped consonant, are used interchangeably in the present official orthography, and have been so used at least since the Monteiro expedition in 1831-2 (see A. C. P. Gamitto, *O Muata Cazembe, passim*). For convenience I shall use the form 'Maravi' for the people from whom the Nyanja-speakers are descended; and the form 'Malaŵi' for the dispersal area (see next paragraph of text).

Northern Rhodesia, and of the adjoining *circunscrição* of Zumbo in Moçambique are related to the Maravi, but, as a result of amalgamation with Lala-Lenje peoples west of the Luaŋgwa river,[1] they speak a language generally regarded as distinct from Nyanja. The modern descendants of the Maravi have not only a common language, but also a common basic culture.

The Ceŵa affirm that their ancestors came from the north—from the Luba country (*uLuŵa*) of the southern Congo basin. This statement conflicts, however, with an equally prevalent tradition that they were created in the hot lowlands immediately south-west of Lake Nyasa,[2] an area they call Malaŵi, where, on a hill called Kaphilintiwa,[3] the first men and animals are said to have left their footprints on the rocks. Hamilton, who has recently studied the history and tribal traditions of this region, resolves the conflict between these two accounts of the advent of the Ceŵa by suggesting that, though the story of the migration from the north is presented as if it were a movement of the whole people, it is more likely to have been the coming of chiefly invaders who gained control over long-established autochthones.[4] My own observations support this conclusion. For instance, Hamilton's hypothesis accords with the traditional division of function between the two main Ceŵa matriclans. The Phili, to whom the traditional chiefs belonged, have political power; and the Banda, who may be descended from the autochthones, have a close relationship with the land and are credited with the power of making rain.

Ceŵa history, as opposed to conjecture based on tradition, begins with the records of the Portuguese,[5] who established settlements on the Zambezi during the first half of the sixteenth century, and en-

---

[1] Cf. Poole, *Native Tribes*, 3rd ed., 1949, pp. 39–40; Winterbottom, 'Outline Histories', p. 24; and Bruwer, 'Note on Maravi Origin and Migration', p. 33. Dr Raymond Apthorpe (private communication) does not agree with the view, originating in Poole and expressed in the works just cited, that the Nseŋga are descended from the Maravi. *Note:* In the sections of this chapter dealing with traditional history, I rely, though not entirely, on secondary sources such as the ones cited—for two main reasons. Firstly, authors on whom I depend all preceded me in the field and most of them had contacts with the Ceŵa extending over many years. Secondly, with the spread of literacy and the popularity of Nthara's vernacular history, *Mbiri ya Acewa*, it is becoming increasingly difficult to obtain accounts of traditional history that are independent of what has been recorded.

[2] This location, described to me by Chief Mkanda Mateyo, corresponds roughly with the one given by Nthara, *Mbiri ya Acewa*, p. 4, and Rangeley, 'Mbona—the Rain Maker', p. 9.

[3] Referred to as Kaphiri-Ntiwa by Rangeley, 'Two Nyasaland Rain Shrines', p. 50; as Kaphirinthiwa by Stegmann, 'Die Godsbegrip van die Acawa [*sic*]', p. 256; and as Kapirimbuja by A. C. Murray, *Ons Nyasa-Akker*, p. 49.

[4] 'Oral Tradition: Central Africa', p. 21.

[5] For a more detailed résumé of these records, see my paper, 'History and Tradition'.

countered the Maravi about a century later. It was not until the end of the eighteenth century, as a result of expeditions into the interior, that they were able to record that the north-western limit of Maravi territory was the upper Luangwa river. For our purposes the most notable expedition was that led by Major Monteiro in 1831–2. Its deputy commander and chronicler, Captain (later Major) Gamitto, who was a systematic, competent and painstaking ethnographer, made detailed notes of the tribes through whose territories the expedition passed, including Undi's people, whom he called Maravi (*Maraves*), and Mkanda's and Mwase's, whom he called Ceŵa (*Chévas*).[1] Although these three chiefs were at this time politically independent of one another, their subjects showed few cultural differences.[2]

How and when the Ceŵa separated from the other Maravi is uncertain. It is possible that they broke away and moved northwards under a chief called Kalonga[3] (though Kalonga is a title rather than a personal name);[4] or it may be that Undi, the predecessor of the paramount chief (of the same name)[5] of the Ceŵa now living on either side of the Northern Rhodesia–Moçambique boundary, may have been leader of all the Maravi.[6]

According to the more orthodox tradition, a chief called Kalonga led the Ceŵa to the Malaŵi country south-west of Lake Nyasa. He then sent his 'younger brother' (which may mean any junior matrilineal kinsman—see below, Chapter 4), Undi, to colonize the headwaters of the Kapoche (see Map 3), the area in which Kaŵaza's chiefdom now falls. Undi was assisted by his 'younger brother', Cimwala, who is said to have cleared this part of the country of the 'little people without villages or gardens', known locally as *aKafula*.[7] Cimwala achieved a

---

[1] *O Muata Cazembe*, especially Chapters 2 and 4.

[2] *Ibid.*, especially p. 148. The opening sentence of footnote 3 on p. 21 applies *mutatis mutandis* to 'Chévas'.

[3] For details, see Hodgson, 'Notes on the Achewa and Angoni', p. 127; Nthara, *Mbiri ya Acewa*, p. 4; Winterbottom, 'Outline Histories', p. 21; and Bruwer, 'Note on Maravi Origin and Migration', p. 33.

[4] The title of 'Caronga' is bestowed even on Mkanda by the *Pombeiros* who travelled from Angola to Tete in 1811 ('Journey of the Pombeiros, P. J. Baptista and Amaro José', p. 195).

[5] Since, among the Ceŵa, succession to headmanship and chieftainship involves name-inheritance as well (see below, Chapter 4).

[6] Cf. Duly, 'The Lower Shire District', p. 17. de Lacerda e Almeida refers to 'Unde' as the 'Morave Emperor' ('Lacerda's Journey to Cazembe in 1798', p. 66).

[7] For this information I am indebted to Chief Cimwala Catham'thumba, the present-day descendant of Undi's lieutenant, who, disliking Portuguese rule, relinquished his sub-paramountcy in Moçambique, and, in 1953 when I visited him, was living as an ordinary village headman in the country of his traditional subordinate, Kathumba (Maps 4 and 5). For a discussion of the Kafula, see J. D. Clark, 'A Note on the Pre-Bantu Inhabitants of Northern Rhodesia and Nyasaland'.

position second only to that of Undi, being sub-paramount in the area west of the Kapoche, while Undi's area of direct control lay east of it. As we shall see later, both the Cimwala and the Undi of a later period managed to resist the attacks of the Ŋgoni.

Subsequent to his dispatching Undi to the Kapoche, Kaloŋga divided the country[1] stretching westward from Lake Nyasa over the Nyasa–Luaŋgwa divide among a large number of territorial chiefs, including Lukwa (and/or Culu in some accounts), who received territory now forming part of Kasungu district, Nyasaland; and possibly Mkanda,[2] who received the watershed country immediately north of where the town of Fort Jameson is now situated.

The traditions I have been considering provide the best available explanation of the existence today of three distinct groups among the Northern Rhodesian Ceŵa (see Map 2). The Ceŵa of Lundazi district are under chiefs whose predecessors derived the title to their land ultimately from one of Kaloŋga's designates in the Kasungu area of Nyasaland. In Fort Jameson district, the 'Northern' Ceŵa owe allegiance to Mkanda; and the 'Southern' Ceŵa, to Undi—either direct or through the sub-paramount, Cimwala. As our concern is mainly with the Southern Ceŵa, more detailed notes on the origin of the Northern Fort Jameson and the Lundazi Ceŵa have been relegated to a separate paper,[3] which contains some of the data on which Map 2 is based.

The country of the Southern Ceŵa was cut in two by the Northern Rhodesia–Moçambique boundary. Both Undi and Cimwala remained in Portuguese territory, and their subordinate chiefs were about equally divided between Portuguese and British territory.

Of the six Southern Ceŵa territorial chiefs whose authority has been entrenched under Indirect Rule in Fort Jameson district, the most important in respect of size and population of territory and of influence among his peers is Kaŵaza. The incumbent who succeeded in 1922 and died in 1950 (Kaŵaza Soŋgani) was a man of outstanding personality, who, before his succession, was a Divisional Messenger of the early Administration. He proved to be a wise and efficient ruler, and in effect became, and was recognized by Government as, 'Paramount Chief of the Southern Chewa of Fort Jameson district'.[4] Mkanda

---

[1] Nthara, *Mbiri ya Acewa*, pp. 4–10.
[2] This is disputed—see my 'History and Tradition'.
[3] 'History and Tradition'.
[4] Recommendation from the District Commissioner, Fort Jameson, to the Provincial Commissioner, Eastern Province, dated 4 July 1934, recording Kaŵaza's service in the named capacity from 1914 [*sic*] to 1934—on file at Fort Jameson.

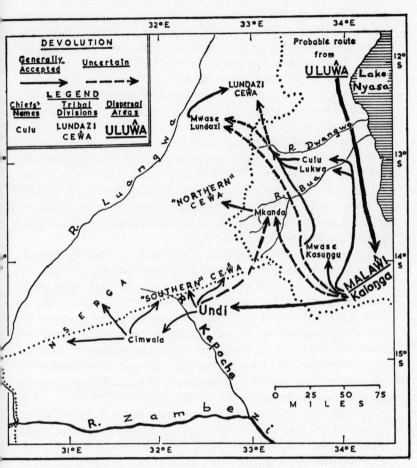

MAP 2

Devolution of Northern Rhodesian Ceŵa chieftainships

Mateyo came to occupy a similar position among the Northern Ceŵa and was granted similar recognition by Government.

The paramountcies of both Kaŵaza and Mkanda Mateyo turned out to be temporary. Their positions depended on the fact that the traditional paramount, Undi, being in Portuguese territory, could not be given a niche in the Northern Rhodesian hierarchy of Indirect Rule. As early as 1913, if not earlier, the British South Africa Company, which then administered the country under a Royal Charter, was aware of the fact that the Southern Cewa acknowledged Undi as their paramount;[1] and, when he paid a visit to Northern Rhodesia in 1921, his local subjects received him enthusiastically.[2] In the 1930's the Undi of the day (Cibvuŋga) got into trouble with the Portuguese Administration. The most plausible story is that he was imprisoned for two years for having wrongfully arrested a kinsman; but in 1952, when there was a movement 'to kill (*kupha*)' his paramountcy (see next paragraph), much more lurid tales of his misdemeanour and the length of his sentence were told. On his release from prison, he crossed the border, and from 1935 lived in Chief Kaŵaza's country. When the British Administration discovered him in their territory, they tried to unify all three groups of Northern Rhodesian Cewa under him. This was achieved in 1937,[3] though by then Undi Cibvuŋga had died and Undi Cinphuŋgu had succeeded him.

For various reasons, personal and historical, Undi Cinphuŋgu failed to gain the support of the Lundazi Cewa, and in 1947 the Administration's attempt to unite all three branches of the tribe under him was abandoned.[4] He remained paramount chief of the Cewa of Fort Jameson district. Even here, owing largely to the power of his two senior subordinates, Mkanda Mateyo of the Northern Cewa and Kaŵaza of the Southern, he did not succeed in welding the two elements together. This became especially apparent after his death in 1952, when there was a strong movement aimed at 'killing' his paramountcy and reverting to the position prior to 1937. At first this movement received the support of the new Kaŵaza (Maniŋu) whose succession had been blocked for two years by Undi, and who would probably not have succeeded at all if Undi had not died in 1952. Mkanda's traditional independence and his claim to a status co-ordinate with, rather than subordinate to, that of Undi lent strength to the movement to abolish the Undi paramountcy. It did not succeed, however. The Administration suggested that the opinions of Cewa labour migrants should be canvassed; and, as the majority of these were opposed to abolishing the paramountcy, Undi's matrilineal heir,

---

[1] Northern Rhodesia, *East Luangwa District*, District Note Book, Vol. 1 (kept at Fort Jameson): Notes of a meeting between the Magistrate and Chiefs on 28 June 1913.

[2] Northern Rhodesia, *East Luangwa Province*, Annual Report for Fort Jameson District, 1921–2, on file at Fort Jameson.

[3] Northern Rhodesia, *Department of Native Affairs*, Annual Report on African Affairs, 1937, p. 73.

[4] Northern Rhodesia, *Department of Native Affairs*, Annual Report on African Affairs, 1947, p. 42.

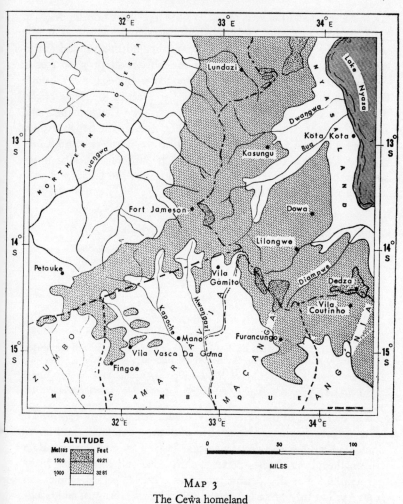

MAP 3
The Ceŵa homeland

Obster Cibvuŋga, was installed as Paramount Chief of the Fort
Jameson Ceŵa on 3 March 1953.[1]

The Ceŵa Homeland in General

The country in which the Ceŵa, Cipeta and Zimba live consists
of a roughly triangular plateau lying between about 12° and 15½°

[1] I am grateful to Mr A. St J. Sugg, District Commissioner of Fort Jameson district
at the time of my third field trip, for letting me know the outcome of this movement.

D

South Latitude and between about 31° and 34½° East Longitude (Map 3). This plateau forms the watershed between the Zambezi in the south and the Luaŋgwa and Lake Nyasa in the north-west and north-east respectively. Its general altitude varies from about 3,000 feet in Petauke district in the west to about 3,600 feet in Lundazi and Kasungu districts in the north-east and to about 3,300 feet in the *circunscricões* of Macanga and Angónia in the south-east. The Ceŵa, Cipeta and Zimba share this country with other tribes, notably the Seŋga, Kunda and Nseŋga in the west; the Ŋgoni in the centre, north-east and south-east; the Tumbuka in the north-east; and the Ntumba and Mbo in the south-east. Of these, only the last two are, like the Ceŵa and their associates, descendants of the Maravi.

TABLE II
MODIFICATION OF TEMPERATURE BY ALTITUDE

	Mean Annual Temperature
Valley Stations:	
Feira	89·5° F
Tete	80·2° F
Plateau Stations:	
Petauke*	76·3° F
Vila Coutinho	67·5° F

* This refers to the old site of Petauke some twenty miles north of the present one and very much lower than the rest of the plateau.

Sources: Trapnell, *North-Eastern Rhodesia*, pp. 1–2; and Dos Santos Júnior, *Algumas Tribos do Distrito de Tete*, p. 29.

The climate is of the savannah type with a single rainy season. The rains usually begin in November and may continue until April. Sometimes mid-season droughts occur in January or February. Rainfall on the plateau varies between thirty-one and thirty-nine inches per annum.[1] The dry season comprises a cooler period, which lasts from April to July, and a hotter one, which starts in August and reaches the time of highest temperatures in late October just before the rains begin. Temperatures are not as high as might be expected from the tropical latitude because they are modified by altitude (as Table II shows); because winds blow from the south-east during the hot season; and because clouds obscure the sun during the rainy season.

The predominant vegetation of the plateau consists of *Brachystegia-Isoberlinia* woodlands. These vary in density and type according to

[1] C. G. Trapnell, *North-Eastern Rhodesia*, p. 2; and Northern Rhodesia, *Eastern Province*, Annual Report: Department of Agriculture, 1951, on file at Fort Jameson.

(a) the nature of the soil, which, owing to the variability of the rocks of the basement complex forming the plateau, is far from uniform; (b) altitude and topography, flat watershed and drier lower-altitude areas being less wooded than those elsewhere;[1] and (c) the extent to which human cultivation has proceeded without intervals long enough to allow the regeneration of the original type of woodland, deforestation of this kind being especially marked in the older Native Reserves of Fort Jameson district.

The woodlands are cut up into blocks by wide, shallow valleys known in Northern Rhodesia and Nyasaland by the Nyanja term *dambo* (Nyanja plur., *malambo*; English plur., *dambos*). These *dambos* are grass-covered, and in the wet season are waterlogged. Except in the larger ones, the courses of the streams draining them are usually indeterminate. In some parts of the Ceŵa–Cipeta–Zimba homeland, the *dambos* are numerous and large enough to provide excellent grazing for cattle, which usually abound in localities free from tsetse fly.[2] *Dambo* cultivation is confined to occasional enclosed vegetable gardens and patches of rice.

Kaŵaza's Country in Particular

Kaŵaza's country (*dziko*) is in the south-west of Fort Jameson district in the No. III (Ceŵa)[3] Native Reserve (Map 4). His traditional capital is on the Katete river a few miles above its confluence with the Kapoche near the Portuguese border. In recent times he has administered his country from Kagolo, about seven miles west-north-west of his old capital, a village which, through being only sixteen miles south of the Great East Road, on a road that follows the divide between the Mzime and Katete rivers, is more accessible, especially in the rainy season (Map 5).

Kagolo is about seventy miles from Fort Jameson, to which town and its district I shall pay brief attention before turning to the residents of the Ceŵa Reserve, whose lives are influenced by the conditions and opportunities existing there. Fort Jameson, pleasantly situated in the hilly country where Northern Rhodesia, Moçambique and Nyasaland meet, is 380 miles by road (the Great East Road) from the Rhodesia Railway at Lusaka, and 180 from the Nyasaland Railway at Salima near Lake Nyasa. Twice a week an aircraft of the Central African Airways

---

[1] Trapnell, *ibid.*, pp. 12–13.
[2] See below, this chapter.
[3] Spelt 'Chewa' in official documents.

comes[1] to Fort Jameson from Lusaka and returns the same day; and once a week there is a similar link with Salisbury via Nyasaland. There is considerable lorry traffic between Lusaka and Fort Jameson.

In the town itself live 500 non-Africans, of whom 304 are Europeans; 191, Indians; and five, coloured. In servants' quarters and in the adjacent African compound, there live 5,239 gainfully employed Africans, some of whom have their dependants with them. Most of the gainfully employed Europeans are in Government service and commerce, Fort Jameson being the administrative and commercial capital of the Eastern Province, which, comprising the districts of Fort Jameson, Petauke and Lundazi, has a *de facto* population of about 310,000 (including about 2,000 non-Africans). Most of the gainfully employed Indians in the town are shopkeepers; and most of the Africans in employment are unskilled labourers; though here more than in the rural area is emerging a 'middle class' of African clerks, messengers, policemen, lorry-drivers, businessmen, etc.

In the rural part of the district there are about 200 tobacco farms. In recent years the number of these that are operated has varied considerably with fluctuations in the price of tobacco. The farms are in a series of irregularly shaped blocks, the largest of which, with a radius of from ten to fifteen miles, is centred on Fort Jameson. A smaller one, of about thirty farms, lies south of the Great East Road about thirty miles west of the town, and another fifteen miles west of this block is a third cluster, surrounding the Mpaŋgwe Hills and comprising about twenty farms. The surnames on farm sign-boards along the Great East Road reveal that a large proportion of tobacco farmers are of Afrikaans-speaking, South African origin. Most of the other names are British, including those of a few Coloured descendants of some of the earlier settlers; and one or two are Indian.

Most of the 570 Europeans and 302 Coloureds in the rural part of Fort Jameson district are supported by the tobacco industry, though a considerable number of Europeans are to be found on small Government stations concerned with administration, agriculture, public works, development, and game and tsetse control, and on mission stations. The rural Indian population, numbering 220, is dependent

---

[1] The present tense in this and in subsequent paragraphs refers to 1951. The statistics that follow are based on the 1951 Census of non-Africans and Africans in employment (Northern Rhodesia, *Census, 1951*, Lusaka: Government Printer, 1951) and on the Administration's 1951 estimates of the African population (Northern Rhodesia, *Eastern Province*, Annual Report on Native Affairs, 1951, on file at Fort Jameson). Statistics in this part of the text refer to the population actually present (*de facto*) and not to those locally domiciled (*de jure*).

mainly on shopkeeping and is distributed on trading posts of varying sizes adjacent to European farm blocks and Native Reserves. The rural African population of the district, estimated at about 154,000, is concentrated in Native Reserves and a few new settlement areas established on Native Trust Land.[1]

Although the position of Fort Jameson district makes contact with the outside world difficult, its flat relief and sandy soil make local communication easy. Roadmaking is largely a matter of removing treestumps. Consequently most rural villages are situated near roads or bush tracks on which motor transport may be used. Furthermore, Africans have taken readily to the bicycle, and nowadays are usually able to count the owner of one among those of their kinsmen on whose services they have a call. The distribution of farms, Government stations, trading centres and mission stations, together with the ease of communication just mentioned, makes them readily accessible to reservedwellers, who often make their first contacts with non-Africans on them during periods of work—usually of short duration. These rural centres of non-African enterprise employ about 12,000 Africans.

As I have said, Kaŵaza's people occupy part of the No. III (Ceŵa) Reserve. Recently some of them have been resettled on certain areas of Native Trust Land to the north of it. The Reserve, varying in width from six to twenty miles, runs along the Portuguese border eastwards from the Petauke district boundary for about sixty miles. It is 928 square miles in area, has an estimated population[2] of 43,722, and is divided unequally into six territorial chiefdoms and an uninhabited area of about 100 square miles, the Mwaŋgazi valley, which was evacuated in the 1920's because of sleeping sickness (Map 4 and Table III). Kaŵaza's chiefdom is the largest and most populous in the Reserve. It is separated from the most westerly chiefdom, that of Kathumba, by the Kapoche river which in the wet season is a formidable barrier. From many points in Kaŵaza's country, the salient features

---

[1] The Native Reserves have been established and defined by: United Kingdom, *Statutory Rules and Orders*, The Northern Rhodesia (Crown Lands and Native Reserves) Order in Council, 1928, amended by The Northern Rhodesia (Native Reserves) Amendment Order in Council, 1936. Native Trust Land has been established and defined by: United Kingdom, *Statutory Rules and Orders*, The Northern Rhodesia (Native Trust Land) Order in Council, 1947. For a brief history of land in the Eastern Province, see below, this chapter.

[2] The figures given in this and the next paragraph refer to *de facto* population estimates derived from tables appended to: Northern Rhodesia, *Eastern Province*, Annual Report on Native Affairs, 1951, on file at Fort Jameson. Areas given in the text or used in calculating densities are estimates included in a Memorandum dated 8 January 1953 filed at Chadiza.

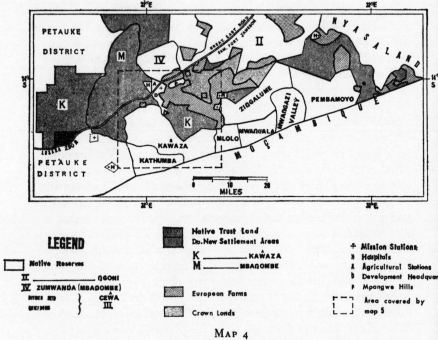

MAP 4

The (Southern) Ceŵa Reserve (No. III): its divisions and adjoining areas

TABLE III

DE FACTO POPULATION AND POPULATION DENSITY OF THE DIVISIONS OF THE CEŴA RESERVE, FORT JAMESON DISTRICT, 1951

Division	Area (square miles)	Population (de facto)	Density (per square mile)
Chiefdoms:			
Kaŵaza's	120	13,320	111·0
Kathumba's	100	8,339	83·4
Mlolo's	60	6,077	101·3
Ziŋgalume's	184	5,626	30·6
Mwaŋgala's	112	6,634	59·2
Pembamoyo's	252	3,726	14·8
Mwaŋgazi Valley	100	(Uninhabited: sleeping sickness)	
	928	43,722	47·1

Sources: Those given in footnote 2 on page 31.

of Kathumba's are visible, notably Nchiŋgalizya hill where, during the
Ŋgoni invasion, the Kathumba of the day and neighbouring chiefs
took refuge with their following.

Kaŵaza's and Kathumba's chiefdoms have population densities of
111 and eighty-three persons to the square mile respectively, compared
with the Reserve's average of forty-seven. In part at least this is a
reflection of their higher soil fertility. The chiefdoms to the east of
them, especially those of Mwaŋgala, Ziŋgalume and Pembamoyo have,
generally speaking, light, sandy soils which quickly lose their fertility
and require long periods of fallow. It is partly because of the degeneration of these areas that an administrative station, Chadiza, was established recently in their vicinity and is now the point from which the
whole of the Ceŵa Reserve is controlled.

In addition to the rehabilitative programme administered from
Chadiza, there is a resettlement scheme, of earlier date, aimed at relieving the pressure on the more fertile parts of the Reserve. To the north
of the Great East Road are two adjacent areas of Native Trust Land
which have been allotted to Kaŵaza[1] and to Mbaŋombe, a 'Northern'
Ceŵa chief most of whose country is in the No. IV (Zumwanda)
Reserve. As the resettlement scheme had been preceded by an ecological survey, it was possible to divide the new areas into village
blocks, their sizes being determined by the carrying capacity of the
land under indigenous methods of cultivation and by the sizes of the
village communities shifted from Kaŵaza's and Mbaŋombe's 'old'
areas.

The resettlement scheme had been put into operation before increased expenditure under the Colonial Development and Welfare Act
was approved in 1944. A conspicuous local effect of the increased funds
available for development is the Eastern Province's development team
with headquarters at Katete, near the junction of the Great East Road
and the road leading south to Kaŵaza's new capital at Kagolo. The
team, whose activities started in 1947, includes administrative and
technical officers from the whole Province, but those stationed at
Katete include two district officers, and technical officers in the fields
of agriculture, public health, water development and education. The
development programme, though directed to the Province as a whole,
touches more closely the people relatively near Katete. It includes the
setting up of peasant farms, the encouragement of 'improved farmers'

[1] When in the text I refer to 'Kaŵaza's chiefdom' I mean his area in the Reserve and
do not include his new settlement area.

under traditional tenure, the training of artisans, the improvement of health and of agricultural practices, and the development of fruit growing and vegetable gardening. The co-operative marketing of surplus crops, especially maize and ground-nuts, has made great strides in the last few years.

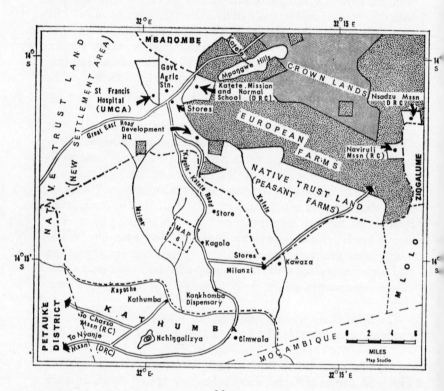

MAP 5

Kaŵaza's chiefdom and its environs

When the new settlement scheme started in the early 1940's, the Department of Agriculture built the road linking the Great East Road with Kaŵaza's new capital at Kagolo. The care with which it was made to follow the Katete–Mzime divide masks the fact that the Reserve is well watered. It is only at the end of the dry season that villagers sometimes have to walk far to water-holes dug in the larger *dambos* and stream beds. In respect of water supply the Reserve is better off than some of the new settlement areas to the north of the Great East Road where human habitation has been made possible only by the provision of wells and dams by the Department of Water Development and Irrigation. As many of the water resources of the Reserve consist of wide, shallow *dambos*, they are coupled with excellent grazing with the result that the Reserve, Kaŵaza's part of it especially, contains some of the best cattle country in the Province.

Kagolo is the centre of a very densely populated locality. Within a radius of about two miles there are no fewer than fifteen villages, most of them having upwards of sixty huts each. The concentration may be accounted for by the fact that many of the low ridges in this area have the main features that the Ceŵa look for when choosing a village site, viz. effective drainage and proximity to water and good soil.

The general impression given by a Ceŵa village is one of restfulness and prosperity. Except when the demands of garden work lead to neglect, the site is free from grass, weeds and smaller shrubs. Larger trees have generally been left, and provide shade in which women can sing and gossip while they pound maize and perform other household tasks. Goats, pigs and fowls abound, and are a constant menace to the maize the women are shelling or the maize-flour they are drying in the sun. Small, informal but influential groups of men gather under a favourite tree, some idly whittling as they converse; others busy at a productive hobby such as making baskets or reed-mats, or twisting bark rope against their thighs. Children play games, dance, tease one another, quarrel and scream. Little girls, and occasionally boys, look after their not-much-smaller siblings. Cattle low from their byres where an idle herd-boy has forgotten to let them out to graze on the *dambo*.

Except in villages where the Western obsession for straight lines has had influence, huts are dotted at irregular intervals all over the site. Maize stores, which are built of woven split bamboo on wooden stilts and roofed in thatch, are usually found on the edges of the village site, though they may sometimes be placed more centrally. The smaller size of the mud-plastered containers for ground-nuts and beans accentuates the sharpness of their conical thatched roofs. Hut designs vary with the energy and initiative of their owners. They vary, too, with their genealogical positions and the beer-making ability of their wives; for in this society labour resources are a function of kinship ties and of the ability to participate in the exchange of gifts, entertainment and services. The better type of hut consists of two concentric rings of posts, the inner one closely spaced and plastered with mud, the outer one lower and widely spaced, serving as verandah supports, the whole area being sheltered by a conical or a hemispherical thatched roof. The door is usually made of woven maize stalks and is kept in place by two posts immediately behind the door frame; when the owner is out, it is held closed by a loop of bark rope through which a pole is suspended across the outside of the doorway. The floor is raised about a foot above the ground, and it and the walls are finished in hard, black clay. Outer walls are often decorated in lighter-coloured clay. The designs include simple lines, birds and human beings, including pink, be-spectacled Europeans. The smaller type of hut, such as that built by a group of young unmarried men, lacks the outer ring of posts and has eaves only long enough to protect the mud walls from storms and roof run-off. An old hut stands out because of the brownish-yellow smoke-stain on its roof and the untidy finish of its thatch, innumerable hand-fuls of which have been pulled out for lighting fires. A few huts are rectangular instead of circular in plan.

On the outskirts of the village are found the ash-heaps and places where rubbish is thrown. Sometimes holes that were dug in the middle of the village to provide plaster for hut walls are gradually filled with refuse. An occasional pit latrine may be found—more a monument to some enthusiastic district officer than an object of daily use; for to most villagers 'to go to the bush (*kupita kutheŋgo*)' is still both the literal and the polite equivalent of 'to defecate'. Cattle byres, made of high poles in order to keep out hyenas and leopards, are usually built at the edge of the village. Pole-protected enclosures for pigs, goats and fowls and elevated crofts for pigeons are usually nearer the huts of their owners.

The generally favourable impression one gets of a Ceŵa village makes one overlook some of its health hazards. As Steytler has pointed out in reference to the Ceŵa of Central Nyasaland, huts are difficult to keep clean, badly ventilated and infested with rats and vermin; villages have no sanitary pits, and flies and mosquitoes are a constant threat to health; drinking water is never boiled and usually drawn from con-taminated sources; and clothes are infrequently washed.[1]

The limited knowledge of hygiene that these conditions reflect, when it occurs in an environment favourable to the vectors of serious diseases, can result only in poor standards of health. On the basis of a sample count of the African population of Northern Rhodesia carried

[1] *Educational Adaptations with Reference to African Village Schools*, pp. 123–4.

out in 1950,[1] the Central African Statistical Office estimated the crude
death-rate of the *de jure* Ceŵa and Ŋgoni population at 32·3 per 1,000
(cf. United Kingdom, 1950: 11·7 per 1,000); and the infant mortality
rate of the *de facto* Ceŵa and Ŋgoni population at 266 per 1,000 live
births (cf. United Kingdom, 1950: 31·4 per 1,000 live births).[2] Both
local rates are near the respective averages for rural Northern Rhodesia
as a whole. Statistics of admission to the Fort Jameson African Hospital
(about seventy miles from Kaŵaza's capital but the only one in the
district for which satisfactory statistics are available) reveal that
malaria, intestinal disorders, venereal diseases, bilharzia, hookworm and
malnutrition are the chief causes of ill-health in the district.[3]

Ceŵa diet[4] is undoubtedly a contributory cause of this ill-health.
Judging by the prevalence of running noses, infected eyes and tropical
ulcers, malnutrition is widespread. The staple food is a thick porridge
(*nsima*) made from maize-flour (*ufa*) which is over-refined by pounding, soaking, pounding again, sifting and drying in the sun. *Nsima* is
so stodgy that people would rather go hungry than eat it without a
'relish' (*ndiwo*). 'Relishes' are savoury dishes made from a great variety
of substances, for instance, pumpkin leaves, pumpkin flowers, shrubs
from the bush, flying-ants, beans, tomatoes, ground-nuts, edible fungi,
caterpillars, and, most favoured though rather rare, meat. By modern
nutritional standards most relishes are over-cooked. The commonest
beverage is beer (*moŵa*) usually made from sprouted maize. From it in
great secrecy a potent decoction called *kacaso*[5] is distilled.

The adverse health conditions described in this section constitute
one of the factors conducive to the development of an elaborate system
of beliefs in sorcery. The high incidence of disease and death provides
many instances of misfortunes requiring explanations.

Ceŵa Subsistence

In spite of its contribution to ill-health, the environment is, when
considered in relation to Ceŵa technology, a bountiful one. The soil,
when chosen wisely and not used too long, produces food crops. The

---

[1] Central African Statistical Office, *Report on the 1950 Demographic Sample Survey of
the African Population of Northern Rhodesia*, Salisbury, 1952, Revised Table XI (supplied
separately in typescript).

[2] The United Kingdom rates are taken from United Nations, *Statistical Handbook*,
1951, pp. 49 and 55.

[3] Northern Rhodesia, *Eastern Province*, Annual Report of the Medical Department,
1951; *ibid.*, 1952, on file at Fort Jameson.

[4] For an interesting, detailed account of the diet of the Nyasaland Ceŵa, see Steenkamp,
'Die Voedsel van die Acewa'.

[5] From the Portuguese *cachaca*, 'rum; a spirit drawn from the sugar cane': Michaelis,
A New Dictionary of the Portuguese and English Languages.

bush provides: building timber and firewood; bark for tying things together and for making rope and string; bamboo for making baskets; herbs and fungi used as 'relishes'; and the roots and leaves that people use in the treatment of illness and for the magical protection of themselves, their houses and their property. The *dambos* provide grass for thatching; reeds for making mats; clay for making pots; and grazing for cattle. Traditionally the bush was the home of game, though hunters now have to roam far—often into Portuguese territory—to find any. Fishing is likewise a part of the 'know-how[1] of the ancestors', though most of the local streams are too small to give adequate returns. In the past the earth used to provide the iron ore from which Ceŵa hoes, axes, arrow-heads and knives were smelted and forged. Nowadays smelting is no longer practised, and smiths confine their activity very largely to forging axes and knives from broken lorry springs.

As to negative aspects of the environment, Kaŵaza's people are not plagued by wild pigs and baboons which destroy crops elsewhere in the district. Nor do lions and leopards trouble them often, though hyenas take a considerable toll of their small stock. Droughts and other causes of crop failures are common enough for them to be taken up in the crude chronology of recent tribal 'history'.

By tradition the Ceŵa are shifting hoe-cultivators. It is only recently that they have owned cattle in large numbers.[2] Their methods of cultivation are by no means 'primitive'. Livingstone records Bishop Mackenzie's remark about those of the Maŋanja (to whom, as I have mentioned, the Ceŵa are closely related culturally):

> When telling the people in England what were my objects in going out to Africa, I stated that among other things I meant to teach these people agriculture; but I now see that they know far more about it than I do.[3]

The Ceŵa practise a form of mound cultivation which involves effective drainage, weed control and green manuring. Furthermore, scientific agriculturists commend their skilful soil selection, their practice of planting ground-nuts and other legumes simultaneously with maize, and their traditional methods of establishing an optimum plant population. At present many agricultural reforms are being carried out among the Ceŵa, but most of these relate to soil conservation; and the need for them springs from overpopulation rather than from any fundamental defect in the native system of cultivation.

[1] *Nẓelu*, which has the connotations of 'knowledge', 'plan' and 'technique'.
[2] See below, this chapter.
[3] David and Charles Livingstone, *The Zambesi and Its Tributaries*, 1866, p. 524.

The staple crop is maize. Other cereals, such as rice, millet and sorghum, are grown, but are of minor significance. Next in importance to maize are ground-nuts; other subsidiary crops include beans of various kinds, sweet potatoes, cucumbers, pumpkins, ground-beans and sweet stem.

The Ceŵa have a sound understanding of soil selection. The average villager knows, not only the potentialities of various soils and the respective forms of treatment they require, but also the types of trees that grow on them. Thus, while some Ceŵa have a detailed knowledge of the relationship between plant-life and soil-potentiality, the majority know at least that *msuku*, *kasokoloŵe* and *mfendaluẕi* trees (*Uapaca kirkiana*, *U. nitida* and *Brachystegia stipulata*) indicate a sandy soil which, though capable of producing a heavy crop, can seldom be cultivated for more than three seasons running; and that the presence of the shiny-leaved *mtondo* (*Isoberlinia paniculata*) marks the transition from sand to loam, where a longer period of cultivation is possible; and that *mkuti* (*Brachystegia spiciformis*), *mmaŋga* (*Afromosia ango-lensis*) and *mtsanya* (probably an *Acacia*) are pointers to the more fertile loams (*katondo*) and black soils (*ŋkhanda*).[1] In 1953 I was shown a garden on dark brown loam which the holder assured me had been continuously cultivated since 1930, drawing my attention to the fact that all the stumps (from the original clearing) had rotted away.

If the Ceŵa want to cultivate virgin land, they first clear it of trees and undergrowth. They stack and burn the brushwood, but, unlike the Bemba,[2] do not limit cultivation to the ash-beds. On them they grow special crops such as pumpkins, but they usually grow maize and other crops anywhere on the cleared ground. Gardens are slowly extended—or their sites gradually changed—by small lateral move-ments. The newly acquired parts of the gardens are usually broken in with a crop of ground-nuts on especially large mounds.

In Kaŵaza's overcrowded part of the Reserve the opening up of virgin land is exceptional. Thus at the end of the hot season—when the *ntyeŋgo* bird wakens people by singing '*Gwila mpini; kwaca!* (Grasp a [hoe] handle; it's daybreak!)'—it is usually on previously cultivated land that one finds Ceŵa working. By the time of the first rains in November, gardens have usually been cleared of grass and weeds, which are burnt to provide small patches of ash here and there. In a

---

[1] I am grateful to the Provincial Forestry Officer at Fort Jameson for lending me his Department's *Check List* for the purpose of identifying trees and shrubs.

[2] Richards, *Land, Labour and Diet*, Chapter 15; and Trapnell, *North-Eastern Rhodesia*, p. 33.

recultivated garden, mounds remain from the previous season, and on the edges of these Ceŵa plant three or four maize seeds in a single hole—'one for the wild pig, one for the guinea fowl and one for ourselves'.[1] Some Ceŵa argue that the first rains should 'find the maize in the ground', since this will enable it to germinate before the field-mice, smelling the wet grain, have time to dig it up. Others consider they are doing well if their gardens are planted by the time the rains really set in. In 1952 the Agricultural Supervisor of the area in which Kaŵaza's part of the Reserve falls estimated that about two acres of maize are planted per head of population and that the plant population for maize is about 7,000 to the acre.[2]

Planting is by no means a major hurdle in the cultivator's race. More formidable is weeding. This starts in early December; and, if the weeds and grass are not beaten by the first or second week of January, the unweeded patches of garden will have to 'sleep'; for, by then, as the sickly yellow of the maize plants indicates, permanent damage has been done them, and their root systems are too extensively developed to permit of effective weeding.

Part of the burden of cultivation springs from a thoroughness that belies the notion that these Africans are improvident. Cleaning a garden would not be the difficult task it is if Ceŵa were less conscientious mound-cultivators. As they hoe the weeds, they bury them with soil from the existing mounds which thus change their positions slightly from one season to the next. This ensures good drainage of the maize, effective disposal of the weeds and a supply of plant food for the coming season.

January and February are months when, either satisfied with work done or philosophically resigned to the loss of part of the crop, Ceŵa are in a position to relax a little. These, however, are the hunger months. Food from the previous season is running low in grain stores, and only pumpkin leaves, cucumbers and green maize are available from the current one's crops. It is at this time of the year that livestock and other possessions may be bartered for grain.

If Ceŵa wish to extend their gardens, and virgin or long-unused land is available for clearing, this will occupy much of their time in February. Otherwise there is not much work to be done until May, when crops such as beans, pumpkins and ground-nuts are ready to be

[1] Poole, *Human Geography of the Fort Jameson District*, unpublished MS., 1932 deposited at the Rhodes-Livingstone Institute, p. 28, quoted by kind permission of the author.

[2] Information placed at my disposal by the Agricultural Supervisor, Katete.

harvested, and the time for bringing in the maize is near enough to call for repairs to grain stores. During this time, however, people have to keep a constant watch on their gardens lest their neighbours' cattle eat up their crops. The irresponsibility of herd boys and the inadequacy of the crop-damage compensation awarded by the courts become common topics of conversation.

Human marauders are kept away from the crops by the fear of property-protecting 'medicines'. Although these are of different kinds, Ceŵa believe them to be of uniform function and place them in a single category (cambo). Cambo magic is believed to bring a wasting disease and ultimately death to anyone taking property of any kind (not only crops) that has been treated with it. It has the advantage, in Ceŵa eyes, of being able to discriminate between the thief, on the one hand, and the owner and his family, on the other, and of being able to operate even if applied after the theft has occurred—according to the principle that 'cambo follows up (cambo cilondola)'.

After harvesting, which usually continues into July, huts are repaired and other odd jobs about the village are done. In the slack time that is characteristic of the cool season and the early part of the hot season, people go on journeys; and, if considerations of hygiene, convenience to gardens, or social tension should indicate it to be necessary, they may move their villages to new sites.

There is not much seasonal variation in the tending of livestock, though the wet season usually focuses attention on the need for new, well-drained cattle byres and, as we have seen, on the danger of crop damage. At the end of the dry season the need for new waterholes becomes apparent.

In the last thirty years considerable progress has been made in confining the tsetse fly to hot lowlands such as the Luaŋgwa valley. Kaŵaza's country has now been free of it for many years, and cattle thrive on the rich pastures of the dambos. Many an owner of a large herd has told me that ten, twenty or thirty years ago he acquired his first beast from an Ŋgoni or a European with money earned on a labour journey to the south or, if an older man, when he was a porter in the East African campaign of the first World War.

Official records confirm these statements. Table IV gives statistics for the two cattle-owning tribes of Fort Jameson district.[1] (Since details for each chiefdom are not available for the earlier years, the

---

[1] A fuller account of the increase in the number of cattle in Fort Jameson district will be found in my paper 'Cattle Ownership and Labour Migration' (in preparation).

comparison has to be a tribal one.) These show an increase in Ceŵa
cattle-ownership from twenty-one per 1,000 population in 1914–15 to
398 per 1,000 in 1951. During the same period the increase in Ŋgoni

TABLE IV

CATTLE OWNERSHIP AMONG THE CEŴA AND ŊGONI OF FORT JAMESON
DISTRICT, 1914–15 AND 1951

	1914–15			*1951*		
		Cattle			*Cattle*	
Tribe	*Population (de jure)*	*No.*	*Per 1,000 Popln*	*Population (de jure)*	*No.*	*Per 1,000 Popln*
Ceŵa	48,101	987	21	84,524	33,607	398
Ŋgoni	40,321	6,891	171	66,589	25,623	385

Sources: Northern Rhodesia, *East Luangwa District,* Annual Reports, Fort
Jameson Division, 1914–15 and 1915–16; Northern Rhodesia, *Eastern Province,* Annual Report on Native Affairs, 1951 (all three on file at Fort Jameson);
and information supplied by the Provincial Veterinary Officer, Fort Jameson
(in a letter dated 4 April 1955).

cattle ownership was less marked, from 171 to 385 per 1,000 population. The special advantages of Kaŵaza's country are reflected in a
cattle ownership rate (565 per 1,000 in 1946) twice that of the Ceŵa as
a whole and more than twice that of the Ŋgoni (Table V). Most of the
cattle are of the humped variety (Zebu), though some show signs of
admixture with European strains.

TABLE V

OWNERSHIP OF CATTLE AND SMALL STOCK: KAŴAZA'S PEOPLE (EX-
CLUDING NEW SETTLEMENT AREA) COMPARED WITH OTHER POPU-
LATIONS OF FORT JAMESON DISTRICT, 1946

		Cattle		*Goats*		*Pigs*	
Tribal Division	*Population (de jure)*	*No.*	*Per 1,000 Popln*	*No.*	*Per 1,000 Popln*	*No.*	*Per 1,000 Popln*
Kaŵaza's Ceŵa Fort Jameson	15,920	8,989	565	3,232	203	6,352	399
Ceŵa Fort Jameson	81,795	23,255	284	8,204	100	13,211	162
Ŋgoni	72,960	18,727	257	4,155	57	6,529	89

Source: Northern Rhodesia, *Eastern Province,* Annual Report on Fort Jameson
District, 1946—on file at Fort Jameson.

The novelty of cattle among the Ceŵa is reflected in an absence of traditional usages for herding them, for distributing their meat and milk, and, especially important, for owning and inheriting them. Like other Ceŵa possessions, they are inherited matrilineally, but whether they belong to the individuals whose earnings bought them or to their matrilineages is an ever-present, tension-producing problem. As I shall show later, many accusations of sorcery originate in quarrels over cattle—quarrels that would probably not occur in a society with more definite usages regarding their disposal.

Ceŵa regard cattle mainly as a 'bank (*benki*)', a means of investing money earned at work or accruing from the sale of surplus maize or ground-nuts. Cattle play no specific part in ritual observances or in marriage transactions. Admittedly they are useful means of providing mourners with funeral fare, but goats, fowls or pigs are equally appropriate. Little use is made of milk. Only herd boys drink it with any regularity or cook their porridge in it. The fact that Ceŵa regard cattle as reproducing rather than productive capital is shown by the poor support of the Native Authority ghee factory near Kagolo.

Small stock rather than cattle are used as ceremonial gifts and means of atonement. Bruwer has written entertainingly of the part that the fowl plays in Ceŵa ceremonial.[1] Goats are used for important presents and payments, as when a man takes his wife away from her home village to live at a place of his own choosing. In a judicial system geared to the righting of wrongs rather than the punishment of offenders,[2] the judgment of the presiding headman, chief or court assessor is very often 'Catch a fowl! (*Gwila ŋkhuku!*)' or 'Tie up a goat! (*Maŋga nbuẓi!*)', which may generally be taken to mean 'Pay the person you have wronged a shilling' or '. . . five shillings', though neither amount is now equal to the market value of a fowl or a goat. Kaŵaza's people, again, as Table V shows, have higher rates of ownership of small stock than have other African populations in Fort Jameson district.

In general, the Ceŵa have a remarkably full knowledge of their bountiful environment and a technology that is adequate for tapping its resources. Though occasional droughts threaten their subsistence, their main source of insecurity lies in the fact that, in common with other non-Western peoples living in the tropics, they do not have the technological resources for countering the diseases that are rife in their country.

---

[1] 'By Ons Is 'n Haantjie', and 'Huweliksgewoontes onder die Acewa'.
[2] The Ceŵa have much in common with the Lovedu in this respect. Cf. Krige and J. D. Krige, *The Realm of a Rain Queen*, Chapter 11.

Labour: at Home and Abroad

In describing the annual cycle of activity, I have not referred to the way in which work is divided among sex and age categories. This subject, to which I now turn, leads naturally to the modern phenomenon of migration from the Reserve to work for wages; for this, affecting men almost exclusively, is an aspect of the division of labour between the sexes.

The social basis of day-to-day living is a group consisting typically of a woman, her husband, her daughters, both single and married, her unmarried sons, and the husbands and children of her married daughters.[1] For convenience I shall refer to this group as a 'household', though this is not the equivalent of any Cewa term. The matrilineage segment forming the core of the household is referred to as the 'breast' (*bele*) of its senior ancestress; and the whole group, i.e. including her daughters' husbands, as her 'family' (*banja*), a term which, however, shares the ambiguity of its English translation, ranging from a group as small as an elementary family to one as large as a village section. In the course of time, owing to the segmentation of its matrilineal core (the 'breast'), the household splits into derivative households of the same structural form, the focus of each of which is one of the married daughters of the parent household.

It is the household that jointly cultivates a garden and lives on its produce which is stored in a common set of receptacles (*ŋkhokwe*, sing., the same) in the village. The functional unity of the household has some influence on the grouping of huts in the village; but, as there are no compound walls or similar divisions, it is often difficult to distinguish a household's huts on physical cues alone.

Within the household, there is division of labour by both sex and age. As in other human societies, daily chores devolve mainly upon the women. We should not forget that the Cewa have no grinding mills, circular saws, piped water or delivery vans; and that the tasks of preparing food, fetching wood and drawing water are burdensome and time-consuming. In garden work there is but little division of labour between the sexes. The only task not done by both sexes is tree-cutting, which is men's work. In the village, men are responsible for building huts, grain stores and livestock pens; but some of the operations

[1] This definition is based on Richards's one of the corresponding group among the Bemba. It has, however, been modified to accommodate what appears to be a slightly greater matrilineal emphasis among the Cewa. Cf. Richards, *Land, Labour and Diet*, p. 124, and *Bemba Marriage and Present Economic Conditions*, p. 30.

involved, such as plastering hut walls and floors, are performed by women.

Children are inducted into economic life at an early age. Some tasks have an instant appeal to them; for instance, little girls may be found in most villages pounding maize—sometimes with their own miniature pestles and mortars—to the accompaniment of their breathless singing. Other tasks children find less attractive; for instance, herd boys seldom perform their duties properly without being constantly reprimanded; and, in the hoeing season, both boys and girls are sometimes starved into going to work in the gardens by being given their main meal there, and little or no food in the village. The garden work that is regarded as the children's special duty is catching field-mice. This they do willingly because they enjoy roasting and eating them.

Some tasks may be beyond the labour resources of the household, e.g. hoeing a garden before weeds choke the maize, or building a new hut or a new cattle byre. There are two ways in which the household may augment its labour supply. Firstly, it may persuade kinsmen to help. For instance, it is the duty of a man to help his sisters if they are in need. In 1949 I came across A Develiase,[1] the younger brother of Headman Jeremiah, building a hut for his widowed sister, A Mlela-manja. A man may call upon the young sons of his sister or of his sister's daughter to herd his cattle. He is more likely to succeed in inducing them to do this work than he is his own sons because, since inheritance is matrilineal, the former are potential heirs to the cattle and may therefore show more interest in them.

Secondly, the household may organize a working party. Whether it will attract labour depends on whether its members have enough maize and its women-folk the requisite skill for making good beer; for beer is the traditional entertainment given to helpers. This is reflected in the terms used to designate various types of working party, such as 'beer of hoeing (moŵa wolima)' or 'beer of hut-building (moŵa womaŋgila nyumba)'. Working parties attract, not only kinsmen, but also unrelated neighbours from other sections in the same village and from other villages in the neighbourhood.

In the sense that every Ceŵa works in a garden to produce his own food, and generally builds his own house, there is no specialization of labour from man to man or from family to family. There are, however,

[1] I am following Atkins's suggestion that the honorific plural prefix of names should be shown by a separated capital 'A' (cf. Guy Atkins, 'Amended Spelling and Word Division of Nyanja', p. 216n). This 'A' may be translated as 'Mr', 'Mrs', 'Miss' or 'Master', though it need not necessarily be appended to a clan-name (surname) rather than a personal name.

certain crafts practised by individuals in the time when they are not occupied with subsistence activities; and in some cases these may be lucrative enough to enable them to employ others (for beer, salt, soap or money) to carry out some of their garden work. But the difficulty one experiences in getting a 'specialist' of this kind to work for one in the hoeing season shows that he is still fundamentally involved in subsistence farming.

Some Ceŵa crafts have developed as a result of the advent of Europeans; and even those that are indigenous now show many European influences. Iron-smelting was practised by the Ceŵa before the Europeans came,[1] and smiths used to forge native iron into hoes, axe-blades, adze-blades, arrowheads, etc. Nowadays they use European scrap-iron, especially spring-steel which is plentiful in a country of rough roads and bush tracks. Some of the smith's products have been displaced by factory-made articles (including native-style tanged hoes and flat axe-blades). On the other hand, the advent of bicycles, guns and sewing machines has encouraged the smith to extend his craft to embrace the repair and production of intricate mechanisms, for which he forges small parts with great skill. He has become adept in the use of European tools such as hammers, hacksaws and files. A Mfukula Banda, who lives in Chief Mlolo's country, is a traditional smith whose modern speciality is making muzzle-loaders. The only part he is unable to make himself is the barrel, for which he uses water-piping or, if he can get it, boiler-tubing. Every other metal part, including levers, small screws (threaded with a file), springs and clamps, he forges from scrap iron.

Other indigenous crafts, such as pottery and basket-making, have not changed greatly in technique, though improved communications and the interest of local Europeans have increased the market for them. The ritual 'specialist', the diviner (*ŋaŋga* or *waula*, '[he] of the divining apparatus'), has widened his techniques through contact with other tribes at labour centres; and his clientèle has probably increased with the almost successful suppression of the poison ordeal (formerly used for detecting sorcerers) and the increase in social tensions characteristic of modern life.

Most of the indigenous crafts are inherited; but the line of their descent is irregular. A craftsman may teach his skill and magical trade-secrets to his son, younger brother, uterine nephew or some other

[1] Gamitto, *O Muata Cazembe*, pp. 38–9 and Est. II, gives a description and coloured sketch of a Maravi smelter which he saw or (more likely) had described to him in 1831.

relative, the choice depending mainly upon the aptitude and enthusiasm of the pupil. In the vernacular, 'skill' (*nʒelu*, also implying 'wisdom', 'knowledge' or 'plan') is virtually a material noun; and attitudes towards it are essentially proprietary. In 1946, by curing his septic big toe, I demonstrated to Headman Mceleka the healing powers of un-medicated hot water. I therefore suggested that he might tell other people about this simple remedy. 'Oh, no!' he replied, 'it's my life (*Ndimoyo waŋga*),' implying that, since I had given him this new technique, it was now his personal property.

Of the specialists whose emergence is the result of the advent of the Europeans, those found in the Reserve include brick-makers, brick-layers, sawyers, carpenters, Native Authority clerks and messengers and teacher-evangelists. On European farms, on Government stations and camps, at Indian trading posts, on mission stations and in the more remote labour centres, this list may be extended to include clerks, messengers, policemen, shop-assistants, tailors, lorry-drivers and veterinary and agricultural assistants. Even in introduced specialist occupations, the old and the new are effectively combined. For in-stance, A Jim Phili, the deputy headman of Bezaliele village, is a carpenter who uses a Ceŵa adze and axe as skilfully as he does a European saw, plane and chisel.

From this new specialization and from the general differentiation resulting from the introduction of a money economy, a Ceŵa middle class is emerging. It consists of the specialists mentioned in the last paragraph together with younger headmen, village shopkeepers and farmers producing surplus crops. Middle-class Ceŵa may be recognized by their European-style dress and their more substantial houses furnished with chairs, tables and beds and decorated inside with magazine pictures and calendars. They are usually literate and sub-scribe to vernacular newspapers. They have some European items in their diet, especially tea. They have a dawning political consciousness and a consequent sense of frustration and insecurity which probably contribute—along with universal middle-class 'conspicuous consump-tion'—to the greater addiction to *kacaso*-drinking and *dagga*-smoking[1] of which their unsophisticated compatriots accuse them and which they readily admit.

No account of labour among the Ceŵa would be complete without

[1] Pronounced *daxa* (I.A.I. script), this term—probably of Hottentot origin—is current in Southern Africa for *Cannabis Sativa*, a kind of narcotic hemp. (I am grateful to Professor D. T. Cole for this information.) To the Ceŵa it is known as *camba*.

a reference to their migration from their villages to work for wages. As one drives towards the Ceŵa Reserve along the Great East Road, the sight of human cargo perched precariously on lorries loaded with goods, or packed tightly into an occasional passenger bus, reminds one of the two-way stream of migration between the Eastern Province and the distant labour centres—on the Northern Rhodesian line of rail, on the Copperbelt, in Southern Rhodesia and in the Republic of South Africa. Not all migrants follow this modern route in and out of the Province. Many still walk or cycle across the Zambezi valley direct to and from Southern Rhodesia. Most of the migrants are men, though an increasing proportion of women among them shows that the rural conservatism which nick-named the Great East Road the 'conveyor of prostitutes (Mteŋgamahule)'[1] is breaking down. Its strength is still shown, however, by the fact that, to comply with a Native Authority order, women passengers unaccompanied by their husbands have to produce marriage certificates before passing westward out of the Province.

Labour migration dates from the first contacts with whites, who have always regarded African labour as one of the important resources of the country.[2] Increasing gradually during the first decade of this century, labour migration reached its first peak in 1917, when the combined demands of the local tobacco industry, Southern Rhodesian mining and agriculture and East African military transport induced about two-thirds of the taxable men of what is now the Fort Jameson district to leave their homes and work for wages.

Except for a decline during the depression of the early 1930's, the absolute number of labour migrants has steadily increased. Population growth has, however, kept pace with it, with the result that the proportion of Fort Jameson district's taxable males at work for wages was much the same in 1951 as it had been in 1917 (Table VI).

Table VI shows that, of every twenty taxpayers (i.e. able-bodied men over the age of eighteen) leaving Kaŵaza's country to enter paid employment, about eight work within the Eastern Province and the remaining twelve go to the distant labour centres; of these, five go to other parts of Northern Rhodesia, e.g. Lusaka and the Copperbelt;

---

[1] *Hule* (plur. *mahule*), 'prostitute', is the only word I have encountered in Ceŵa having an *h* as an independent consonant (rather than a sign of aspiration). The fact that this *h* is voiced makes it virtually certain that the word is derived from the Afrikaans *hoer*, in which the *h* is also voiced.
[2] For a résumé of the development of labour migration in what is now the Eastern Province of Northern Rhodesia, see my paper, 'Cattle Ownership and Labour Migration'.

about five, to Southern Rhodesia; and about two, elsewhere, usually the Republic of South Africa.

TABLE VI

ADMINISTRATION'S ESTIMATES FOR CERTAIN FORT JAMESON
AFRICAN POPULATIONS OF THE PERCENTAGE OF TAXABLE MALES AT
WORK FOR WAGES, AND THEIR DISTRIBUTION BY PLACE OF
WORK, 1951

	Percentage of Taxable Males at Work for Wages	Percentage Distribution by Place of Work				
		Northern Rhodesia				
Population		Eastern Province	Elsewhere	Southern Rhodesia	Else-where	Total
Fort Jameson Ŋgoni, Ceŵa and Kunda*	62·5	39·1	29·4	25·1	6·4	100
Ŋgoni	65·2	42·2	29·9	24·4	3·4	100
Kunda	69·3	30·0	43·9	22·3	3·7	100
Ceŵa:						
Total for district	58·5	38·4	25·1	26·5	10·0	100
S. Ceŵa Reserve	55·4	37·4	19·8	28·9	13·9	100
Kaŵaza's in Reserve	54·6	37·4	24·5	29·8	8·3	100
Kaŵaza's in new settlement area	46·8	41·5	30·0	22·8	5·7	100

* The Kunda live in the Luaŋgwa valley north-west of Fort Jameson.

Source: Northern Rhodesia, Eastern Province, Annual Report on Native Affairs, 1951, on file at Fort Jameson.

The Administration's estimates of the proportion of taxable males at work for wages usually falls between a half and two-thirds. My estimates based on limited genealogical information do not differ reliably from this range. Boys under taxable age and women, neither of whom are included in Table VI, are involved to a considerable extent in short-term work on tobacco farms adjoining the Reserve.

Elsewhere[1] I have suggested that Ceŵa society, on account of its extreme consanguineal organization, is well adapted to a high labour migration rate. The consanguine matrilineage, consisting typically of a man, his sisters and his sisters' uterine descendants, is the basic social group among the Ceŵa; and it is a group which remains functional under a disturbed sex ratio. This does not mean that labour migration

[1] M. G. Marwick, 'The Kinship Basis of Cewa Social Structure', pp. 261–2.

is not socially disruptive. The abnormally low masculinity of the adult
Reserve population (Fig. 2), which is mainly the result of labour
migration, is conducive to social problems such as adultery, prostitution and the excessive dependence of married women on their matrilineal male relatives as a result of their husbands' being away at work.

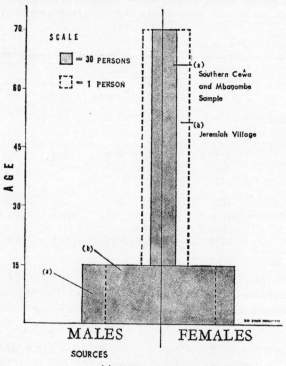

Fig. 2. Simple Age–Sex Structure of (*a*) a Population Sample Drawn from
Southern Cewa and Mbaɲombe Chiefdoms, 1950, superimposed on that of (*b*)
the Population of Jeremiah Village, 1953

It may have led, too, to an increase in polygyny, which, though rooted
in tradition, is in serious conflict with Christian norms which, as I
show at the beginning of Chapter 3, are respected by a wider circle
than those who have been formally converted.

    These ill-effects of labour migration are in some measure balanced
by its enriching Reserve life both economically and culturally. It is

the main source of the money needed for paying tax, for buying new essentials such as cloth, salt and soap and for making traditional payments that now have cash equivalents, e.g. a man's payment (*nthakula*) for the right to take his wife from uxorilocal to virilocal residence, formerly a goat, now five shillings. Among the invisible assets accruing to labour migration are its cultural effects. Undertaking a journey to a distant labour centre is a test of manhood which fills in one of the gaps left by the decay of tribal initiation. The experience that the migrant gains does much to adjust him to the money-conscious, faster-moving, modern world with its higher standard of living for those who progress. The stories told by migrants on their return give some idea of the trials, the excitements and the rewards of a 'journey to work'.

It is precisely because labour migration accelerates the adaptation of the African to the culture of the modern world that it becomes relevant to the theme of this book; for, by making it possible for young adults to raise their own standard of living instead of ploughing back their income into established relationships and, in general, by being the chief cause of economic differentiation, it imposes strains that sometimes find expression in beliefs in, and accusations of, sorcery.

Ceŵa Attitudes and Their Determinants

The account I have given of tribal origin, environment, subsistence and labour may have created too serene a picture of Ceŵa life. The past has had its storms as well as its calms, and the peace of the present is not without its tensions. I shall therefore try to sharpen the relief of the picture by shading in some of the details. The most convenient procedure will be to examine Ceŵa attitudes; for in these are precipitated both the main themes of the past and the outstanding conflicts of the present. Among these, the attitude towards the European occupies a cardinal position.

'If it were possible,' I asked in my public-opinion survey among the Ceŵa in 1947, 'would you chase the Europeans from this country or allow them to remain in it?' Informants were asked this question three times, once for each of the three local types of Europeans, the administrator, the farmer and the missionary. Of the combined responses of the 268 persons interviewed, twenty-six per cent were in the 'hostile', affirmative category; and seventy-two per cent in the 'favourable', negative category. (Two per cent failed to respond.) Many of those who were in favour of allowing the Europeans to remain in the country added spontaneously the reasons for their choice. Of administrators they said, 'They keep peace amongst us'; and 'There was nothing but mutual killing (*kuphana*) before they came'; of farmers, 'They give us work and we get clothes [with the wages]'; and 'Where would we work?' And of missionaries, 'They help people to know things'; and 'They made us see'.

Responses such as these indicate that the Cewa attitude towards the European cannot without distortion and oversimplification be scored on a simple 'favourable-hostile' scale. Though hostility may be present, it is often tempered by a sense of dependence and by some appreciation of the advantages accruing from the introduction of the European way of life with its cultural equipment. In short the attitude is complex and ambivalent.[1]

The attitude may become more comprehensible if I try to isolate some of its historical determinants—if, that is, I review the events that made the Cewa regard the coming of the European as a mixed blessing. The European has sometimes been the hero, sometimes the villain, in the drama of the last hundred years during which Cewa prestige and self-respect have been assailed and, on balance, diminished.

The prestige of the Cewa devolved from their relationship to the land; and their self-respect, from their ability to live the good life as defined by tribal morality. Both these foundations of their security have been shaken, and informants' statements reflect feelings of inadequacy, helplessness and hostility.

Although the Ŋgoni conquest of a century ago and more has blotted out many links with the past, the Cewa recall with nostalgic pride the days when they were the owners and dividers of the country and when their way of life, especially in its moral aspects, was uncontaminated by the evils of the present. The first aspect of this golden age, the relationship to the land, Cewa preserve by affectionately referring to the country they inhabit as 'this country of ours (*dʒiko lathu lino*)' and by bestowing on Paramount Chief Undi the praise-name of Gawa (loosely, 'the Divider'), since he is the successor to Kaloŋga and the first Undi who parcelled out the country among a vast array of petty chiefs, and whose lieutenants, such as Cimwala and Mkanda, cleared it of its only inhabitants, the Kafula. The second aspect, traditional morality, they memorialize by depicting the 'good old days' when harsh punishments kept sorcery, theft, adultery and disobedience at a minimum.

---

[1] I am grateful to Professor Max Gluckman for drawing my attention some years ago to the complexity of African attitudes towards the European.

Their golden age, no doubt as idealized as any other, serves as a reference point for their present degradation. And it is when they are assessing their decline and accounting for it that their attitudes are forcibly expressed. For the loss of their land they apportion the blame about equally between the Ŋgoni and the Europeans. This is not unreasonable in the light of what happened. But, for the decline in their morality, they hold the Europeans mainly responsible. Was it not the Europeans, they ask, who forbade the poison ordeal, their only effective means of detecting sorcerers? Was it not they, too, who prevented them from executing sorcerers and adulterers, or selling them into slavery, and from cutting off the hands of thieves and the ears of the disobedient? And have not the Europeans frowned on their 'great drum' society, the *nyau*, which prepared youths for decent, effective manhood?

When they ask some of these questions, the Ceŵa betray what appears to be a contradiction in values; for the brutality of the punishments they hark back to is in sharp contrast to their veneration of the 'meek in heart (*ofatsa mtima*)', those who never lose their tempers nor let their 'hearts burn [with anger] (*-pya mtima*).'

This apparent inconsistency has its parallel in tribal history. Tradition asserts that the Ceŵa have always been peace-loving and unaggressive. There is almost a touch of pride in their admission that 'when it comes to war, we are as if women'; and this characteristic is confirmed by the impressions made by the Nyanja-speaking peoples on the Europeans who came into contact with them at the end of the nineteenth century.[1] Yet the Portuguese writers of the seventeenth and eighteenth centuries regarded their ancestors, the Maravi, as formidably warlike[2] an impression that is consonant with another tradition, viz. that they were inveterate wanderers.

There are various possible explanations for this contradiction. Firstly, it may spring from the fact that the impressions gained by the two groups of Europeans were relative to their own military strength. The militarily weak eighteenth-century Portuguese expeditions had greater reason to fear the Maravi than the late nineteenth-century British had to fear their descendants, whom, in any case, they inevitably contrasted with the powerful Ŋgoni.

Secondly, it is possible that there always has been a contradiction in

[1] See, for instance, Johnston, *British Central Africa*, 1897, p. 62; L. T. Moggeridge, 'The Nyasaland Tribes: Their Customs and Their Ordeal Poison', 1902, p. 467; and Hugo Genthe, 'A Trip to Mpezeni's', 1897.
[2] The relevant literature is reviewed in my paper, 'History and Tradition'.

Ceŵa values between those of war and peace. Perhaps the toning down of aggression in everyday life, which is a conspicuous Ceŵa characteristic, can be achieved only by releasing it on certain occasions. This hypothesis is supported by the fact that an orgy of violence traditionally accompanied the production of the *nyau* mimes (Chapter 8 below).

Finally, perhaps the eighteenth-century Maravi were actually more aggressive than their descendants. Even before the Ŋgoni invasion, Gamitto contrasted Mkanda's and Mwase's Ceŵa with their neighbours, Undi's Maravi, suggesting that the former had greater moderation, sobriety and industry.[1] This difference, if it actually existed, must have been accentuated, by the time the British arrived, by more than a generation of Ŋgoni raiding if not actual bondage. Ceŵa may have found that their very existence depended on their being meek and compliant.

Whatever the explanation happens to be, the following description by a European hunter and trader of the effects of an Ŋgoni raid on a Ceŵa village in 1897 recaptures some of the hopelessness and despondency of a conquered people:

On my arrival I found the male population all under arms, and the women crying. A raiding party of Mpezeni's [Ŋgoni] people had attacked them suddenly that morning. Ten women were killed in the gardens and twenty-two were taken away as prisoners. An old man and one of the headman's children had been severely wounded. Their entrails hung out of frightfully torn wounds, inflicted most likely by barbed spears. It was a pitiful sight—the groans of the wounded, the women crying over their dead, whose bodies were brought from the gardens, the men standing about helpless and depressed. As the raiding party could not have been far off, I proposed to the men to follow them up at once, and try to release the prisoners, but they were disheartened by the misfortune that so suddenly had overtaken them.[2]

This account was written about sixty years after the Ŋgoni first went through Ceŵa country. Led by Zwangendaba, this offshoot of the Natal Nguni (or, loosely, the Zulu) crossed the Zambezi in November 1835.[3] After sojourning a few years among the Nseŋga, to the west of the Ceŵa, the Ŋgoni passed through Ceŵa country about

[1] *O Muata Cazembe*, p. 148.
[2] Genthe, 'A Trip to Mpezeni's' (1897).
[3] On the basis of Ŋgoni traditions, notably that they waded across and that there was an eclipse of the sun on the day of the crossing, Poole established that this occurred in November 1835, giving the date as 19th. Barnes corrected it to 20th. Cf. Poole, 'The Date of the Crossing of the Zambezi by the Ngoni', and Barnes, *Politics in a Changing Society*, p. 3.

1840 on the start of their invasion of East Central Africa, the effects of which are well summarized by Lane Poole as follows:

Geographically, this migration extended as far north as the Victoria Nyanza; ethnologically it introduced into that part of Central Africa which they finally occupied a tribe of patrilineal descent and pastoral customs among peoples matrilineal and agricultural by occupation; historically it led to the extermination or reduction to servitude of a population computed to be a million in number.[1]

Many Ceŵa were among those exterminated or reduced to serfdom. Some succeeded in defending themselves by climbing natural fortresses such as Nchiŋgalizya hill, in Kathumba's country near the present boundary between Northern Rhodesia and Moçambique, and Mount Mbazi, at Undi's capital, or by constructing mud forts, the ruins of which are still to be found in parts of Central Nyasaland.[2]

They had useful weapons of defence in bows and arrows, some of them tipped with a 'virulent poison decocted from the strophanthus plant';[3] in poisoned spikes which were left in paths; and in muzzle-loaders obtained from the Portuguese to the south and the Arabs to the north-east. Mwase Kasuŋgu is famous for the resistance he put up;[4] and Codrington records that Maseŋgela's people of Mkhoma mountain were not subject to the Ŋgoni, having successfully beaten off three separate groups of them.[5] Other Ceŵa lay too far from the paths of the various groups into which the Ŋgoni split to be greatly affected. Thus among Kaŵaza's people today there are many immigrants from the south, where their ancestors, apart from occasional raids, were free from the depredations of the Ŋgoni; and where Undi and Cimwala, though repeatedly raided,[6] were never defeated.[7]

The ancestors of the rest of Kaŵaza's people, including the Kaŵaza

[1] Poole, ibid., p. 290, quoted by kind permission of the Editor of the Journal of the Royal African Society.
[2] See Foà, Du Cap au Lac Nyassa, 2nd ed., 1901, pp. 277 ff.; Rangeley, 'Some Old Cewa Fortresses in the Kotakota District', 1951; 'W.H.M.', 'The Achewa', 1896; 'W.D.L.', 'Machemba—Primitive Citadels', 1950, and Codrington, 'The Central Angoniland District', 1898, p. 518.
[3] Codrington, ibid., p. 518.
[4] Cf. Stigand, 'Notes on the Tribes in the Neighbourhood of Fort Manning, Nyasaland', 1909, pp. 35–7; and T. D. Thomson, Preliminary Notes on the Constitution of Mwase's Chewa (unpublished MS. cited by kind permission of the author).
[5] Codrington, 'Central Angoniland District (Extracts from a Report)', 1896.
[6] See Foà, Du Cap au Lac Nyassa, pp. 277 ff., who arrived at Undi's while an Ŋgoni raid on Mount Mbazi was in progress.
[7] George Russell Deare ('A Durban Man'), 'Eighteen Months with the Last of the Slave Raiders', 1929, describes how he visited Undi and Cimwala in 1897, finding them independent of the Ŋgoni, which is in accordance with Ceŵa tradition.

of the day himself, did not escape. In the 1860's, a section of the Ŋgoni under one of Zwangendaba's sons, Mpezeni, returned to the western part of the plateau between the Luaŋgwa and Lake Nyasa; and, some ten years later, settled not far from where the town of Fort Jameson now stands.[1] A large proportion of the Ceŵa in what are now the districts of Fort Jameson, Northern Rhodesia, and Fort Manning, Nyasaland—including the Northern Ceŵa of Mkanda after their chief had been killed—became members of a subordinate class in Mpezeni's chiefdom, and remained in this position until the Ŋgoni power was broken by the British forces in 1898.

Ever since the Ceŵa were conquered by the Ŋgoni, the whole basis of their claim to 'their' country has been threatened. Under the Ŋgoni, political power became dissociated from the reciprocal rights and duties of persons involved in a system of land tenure, and was more dependent upon size of human following and disposition of tribal cattle.[2] And, under the Europeans, though the political power of the Ceŵa has greatly advanced, there have been times when they have had to assert their claims strenuously. During the period when the country was administered by the British South Africa Company, the Ŋgoni objected strongly to the assignment of land to the Ceŵa, and asked that the Southern Ceŵa be made definitely subject to them under a proposed native reserve scheme. The Administration refused to recognize the subjection of the Ceŵa to the Ŋgoni, but took no active steps to separate those Ceŵa whom they found living among the Ŋgoni.[3] It would appear, however, that, during the first two decades of this century, many Ceŵa took advantage of the eclipse of Ŋgoni power, and moved off to the areas where they are now found living on their own, where they were subsequently joined by fellow tribesmen who had come from Portuguese territory.[4]

Though the advent of the Whites freed the Ceŵa from the Ŋgoni, it brought threats of a new kind to their claim to the land. A grant of land and mineral rights over an area of nearly 10,000 square miles (the greater part of what are now the districts of Fort Jameson and Petauke) was made to a company in lieu of certain concessions it had bought from an early White trader who claimed he had obtained them from

[1] Poole, *Native Tribes*, Chapter 1 and Appendix I.
[2] Cf. Barnes, *Politics in a Changing Society*, p. 30.
[3] Northern Rhodesia, *East Luangwa District*, District Note Book, Vol. 1 (kept at Fort Jameson): Notes of a meeting between the Magistrate and Chiefs on 28 June 1913.
[4] Northern Rhodesia, *East Luangwa District*, Annual Report, 1912–13, on file at Fort Jameson.

Mpezeni. This became known as the North Charterland Concession.[1]
A rider to the Concession, that it was subject to the possessory
rights of the native inhabitants, was incorporated in the revision of the
British South African Company's Royal Charter in 1900,[2] and retained
when North-Eastern and North-Western Rhodesia were amalga-
mated in 1911[3] and when the Northern Rhodesia so formed was transferred to the Crown in 1924.[4] This rider has provided the legal authority
for creating the present Native Reserves which came into being in
1928.[5] Subsequently, Government bought the unalienated portion of
the Concession, amounting to nearly sixty per cent of its original area,
and had almost all of it scheduled as Native Trust Land in 1947.[6] It
was on parts of this Native Trust Land that, after an ecological survey,
people were settled in an attempt to relieve pressure on the overcrowded reserves (p. 31 above).

The Ceŵa regard this land history as an incomprehensible series of
arbitrary European actions. Having found themselves land south-west
of their Ŋgoni captors, they were displaced into what is now the Ceŵa
Reserve by the advent of European farmers. Having lived there for
two or three decades, many of them were then sent forty or fifty miles
to the new settlement areas. My public-opinion survey of 1947 included the question, 'Why are the Europeans sending African people
to the new settlement areas?' Only thirty per cent of informants[7] gave
answers that reflected the intentions of the Government, e.g. 'There
was hunger in the Reserve; in the new areas there is plenty.' Eight per

---

[1] For a detailed account of the origin of the North Charterland Concession, see Barnes,
Politics in a Changing Society, pp. 73–8, and Fraser, 'Land Settlement in the Eastern
Province of Northern Rhodesia'.
[2] United Kingdom, *Statutory Rules and Orders*, The North-Eastern Rhodesia Order in
Council, 1900.
[3] United Kingdom, *Statutory Rules and Orders*, The Northern Rhodesia Order in
Council, 1911.
[4] United Kingdom, *Statutory Rules and Orders*, The Northern Rhodesia (Crown
Lands and Native Reserves) Order in Council, 1928, preamble.
[5] *Ibid.*
[6] United Kingdom, *Statutory Rules and Orders*, The Northern Rhodesia (Native Trust
Land) Order in Council, 1947.
[7] The effective sample for this item of the schedule was 156, since the responses recorded
by one of my three African assistants had to be eliminated because they showed statistically
significant differences from those of other interviewers (he probably used supplementary
questions that had the effect of suggesting answers to his informants); and those of
another assistant have been excluded because he interviewed only nine informants in only
one area. The remaining 156 is made up of responses to me (sixty) and to my third
assistant (ninety-six) between whose records there were no differences falling outside the
range of normal sampling fluctuations. For a discussion of the technical aspects of this
survey, see Marwick, 'An Experiment in Public Opinion Polling among Preliterate
People', and, for its results, 'The Rôle of the Social Anthropologist in Assessing Development Programmes'.

cent gave answers not seriously in conflict with official intention, considering especially that the resettlement policy was coupled with a rigorous programme of soil conservation; they said that people were being sent to the new areas to learn agricultural methods. A large proportion (forty-two per cent) gave vague or accommodating answers, indicating either that they really didn't know or that they felt their function was 'not to reason why'. Examples from this category were: 'I am unable to tell what lies in the chests [minds] of the Europeans'; 'They gave us no reasons when they ordered us to move'; 'The Europeans are the owners of this country and do as they please'. The majority of the remainder (eighteen per cent) were openly suspicious or hostile, expressing, for instance, the belief that Africans were being sent to clear the country of lions and tsetse flies for European settlement, or that they were being sent there to enable Europeans to settle in the old Reserve.

I can best sum up Ceŵa feelings of insecurity in relation to their land in the words of an old woman who was living in the new settlement area in 1947 and who had experienced many moves. She said: 'In this country the Europeans are the people; we are the birds!' Had the public-relations programmes of the various land policies been as efficacious as the application of the ecological survey to the recent resettlement scheme, it is probable that Ceŵa attitudes might not have been at such variance with the constitutional security of their land rights.

The historical events that have led to pressure on the land are relevant to the theme of this book; for, by intensifying the conflict of rights to a basic natural resource, they have increased one of the ingredients in tensions sometimes expressed in the idiom of beliefs in sorcery.

Although land history has been the most outstanding cause of Ceŵa hostility towards Whites, it is not the only one. There are other friction-points in the application of European administration. Some of these arise from misunderstanding on the part of the governed of the process of government; others spring from more substantial causes, past or present.

Taxation is one of these friction-points. It was introduced at the turn of the century, when the rate was three shillings per annum per hut. It was later changed to a head tax, and by 1952 amounted to ten shillings per annum, being payable by males over the age of eighteen who had not been exempted on grounds of old age or infirmity. This amount included a Native Treasury local levy of half a crown. While there are grounds for believing that the main function of taxation in the early years of European administration was to force Africans to work for wages, there is less cause for attributing this motive to the Administration nowadays, since as much as ninety per cent of the money paid in tax and levy returns directly or indirectly to the Native Treasury. In spite of this, the Ceŵa man-in-the-village still believes that most of the tax money is 'eaten' by successive categories of Europeans, ranging from the District Officer to the British Sovereign.

Cross-examining a witness in 1949, one of Chief Kaŵaza's court assessors asked: 'Would you be able to recognize the beast [involved in the case], or are cattle just like Europeans, their faces all alike?' It is not only on this simple, physical level that Ceŵa tend to regard the Whites as a uniform, undifferentiated group. They fail, also, to distinguish between European groups of different function and consequently of different political alignment in relation to them. This fact, coupled with ineffective communication, leads to misunderstandings about the origin and rationale of instructions, both real and imaginary. It is not surprising that, in a society where communication is almost entirely by word of mouth and where the exchange of news is an important form of entertainment and a means of expressing goodwill, rumours—both endemic and epidemic—come into being. These rumours, furthermore, concern the activities and intentions of 'the Europeans' in general—not the Administration, or the missionaries or the farmers. Examples of outstanding epidemic rumours are the 'sugar story' of 1952-3, according to which the Europeans had 'doctored' supplies of sugar for African consumption in such a way that Africans would become impotent and sterile, and the complex of rumours, rife in 1947-8, about Bwanali and Mpulumutsi who were to save the country from the ravages of sorcerers.[1]

The endemic rumours consist of myths whose function is to rationalize firmly rooted, but not necessarily true, beliefs regarding the intentions or characteristics of Europeans. An instance is the belief that the *cinamwali* dance, the one performed at girls' initiation, is illegal. This misconception springs from two causes. Firstly, until very recently the *nyau*, the esoteric mime-production involving boys' initiation and associated with the mortuary rituals of important persons,

[1] Chapter 3 below, and Marwick, 'Another Anti-Witchcraft Movement in East Central Africa'.

F

was banned by the Europeans—at first by the direct action of the
Administration, and, after the introduction of Indirect Rule, by
persuading the Native Authorities to pass an order prohibiting it.
Secondly, the *cinamwali* dance, while not illegal, is strongly disapproved of by European missionaries. Thus to say that 'the Europeans
forbid it' is in a sense correct.

The reasons given by my informants for not favouring the hypothetical policy of chasing away European farmers point to some of the
positive components in the Cewa attitude towards the European. 'They
give us work and we get clothes [with the wages],' they said. Although
they dislike many aspects of European contact, they look upon
Europeans as a necessary evil. Before Europeans came to their country,
Cewa had had experience of trade goods such as cloth and guns which
came to them from the Arabs in return for ivory and slaves. The scale
of this trade was, however, very small by modern standards, and hardly
involved persons other than chiefs and headmen. The prestige value
that cloth acquired by this scarcity may account for the enormous
demand for it by the Cewa and for the fact that it still forms one of the
chief items in their trade with the outside world. In any event, there
have been remarkable changes since early European residents and
visitors commented on the scanty bark-cloth and goatskin covering of
the Cewa.[1] Nowadays Cewa look upon cloth as essential and by comparison with other African peoples, e.g. the Natal Nguni, are rather
prudish in the way they cover themselves with it.

Apart from cloth, other trade goods of strong appeal to Cewa are
salt, soap, enamel basins and hoes (factory-made, but still of the
traditional, tanged design). As I have mentioned, salt and soap are
sometimes used for rewarding people who have helped with hoeing or
hut-building.

All these goods cost money. Furthermore, services, ceremonial
presents and compensation-awards are to an increasing degree being
changed into money payments. For instance, I have noted that 'Tie up
a goat' means 'Pay five shillings', while 'Catch a fowl' means 'Pay a
shilling'. Ever since money was introduced to the Cewa, its chief source
has been the sale of labour. From the time that Europeans first came,
Cewa men have worked for them both locally and in more distant
areas such as Southern Rhodesia. The local labour market—on tobacco

[1] Codrington, 'The Central Angoniland District', 1898, p. 518; Byatt, 'Chewa-land',
1900; 'W.H.M.', 'The Achewa', 1896; A. C. Murray, *Nyasaland en Mijne Ondervindingen
Aldaar*, 1897, pp. 151 and 167; and du Plessis, *A Thousand Miles in the Heart of Africa*,
1905, p. 68.

farms, in Government departments, in Fort Jameson township and on smaller European and Indian settlements—is convenient but not lucrative. Southern Rhodesia (*Walale*) has a great attraction to Ceŵa; and going there has almost become a substitute for tribal initiation. Most men have been on a labour journey to one of the distant urban areas such as Salisbury, Gwelo, Bulawayo, Lusaka or the Copperbelt; and most women have had experience of work on nearby tobacco farms.[1]

As I have mentioned, my public-opinion survey differentiated between three types of Europeans: farmers, administrators and missionaries. When informants were thus forced to separate categories that they generally lump together, results showed more favourable attitudes towards missionaries than towards farmers and administrators, the attitude towards the last two being ambivalent. The farmer is regarded as the one who has displaced the Ceŵa from their land and who, by comparison with the Southern Rhodesian employer, pays a niggardly wage; and yet he is often a considerate employer and is conveniently situated. The administrator is, in Ceŵa eyes, in league with his fellow Europeans, and an arbitrary ruler; yet his presence preserves peace. The Ceŵa attitude towards the missionary, apart from being more favourable on balance, shows less ambivalence. Though his intolerance of native customs such as polygyny and, depending on denomination, beer-drinking and cousin-marriage, is resented, his cordiality (*cipfundo*) and his primary desire to help and enlighten are appreciated by Christian and pagan alike.

It should be remembered that the relative lack of ambivalence in the attitude towards the European missionary is exceptional. Marked ambivalence is characteristic of the Ceŵa attitude towards the European in general, and it is intensified when the Ŋgoni enters the picture. Traditionally, the Ŋgoni is the ruthless conqueror from whose tutelage the European set the Ceŵa free; and yet he is a fellow African subjected to the same deprivations and into whose arms the Ceŵa is driven by the new racially defined nationalism emerging from the structural oppositions of the modern social and administrative system.

African nationalism has not yet made the Ceŵa a prejudiced anti-White. Though he has mixed feelings about the European and thus about his general position in the modern world, this does not prevent him from sorting out the ingredients in the mixture with remarkable

---

[1] For a more detailed account of working for wages, see Chapter 2 above, and my paper, 'Cattle Ownership and Labour Migration'.

insight and objectivity. This is illustrated by an informant's statement, which will serve to conclude this chapter:

We used to be the owners of this country, but now we are as if cattle which the herdsman drives to wherever there is grass. When the grass is finished, he drives you elsewhere. Europeans are of some good; for without them we Africans would be left to our own ways. The Europeans came with seeds of various kinds and clothes of various kinds. Each type of European who has come to this country has come with something good.

CHAPTER 3

THE IDIOM OF CEŴA BELIEF

BEFORE I examine the contexts in which Ceŵa believe that sorcery operates, I shall present the main outlines of their mystical beliefs; for these constitute the medium through which sorcery or one of its alternatives is invoked as an explanatory principle.

I have already noted (see Chapter 1) that, in a sample of 194 cases of serious misfortune, a slight majority were attributed to the machinations of sorcerers; about a quarter, to natural causes; under a fifth, to the actions of persons other than sorcerers; and a very small proportion, to the intervention of lineage spirits. It is conceivable that, if less serious misfortunes, such as passing illnesses, had been included in the sample, these proportions would have been different. Spirits, for instance, are believed often to indulge in admonitory visitations of illness, but seldom to cause death.

References in the last chapter to Ceŵa subsistence show that their technology, though it is based on tradition rather than scientific enquiry, nevertheless has firm rational foundations. A poor crop, for instance, will usually be attributed to the cultivator's failure to weed his garden in time or to a more fundamental failure to adapt his methods to the type of soil he is working, e.g. not making mounds high enough, or planting on sandy soil beyond its normal period of fertility.

The Supreme Being

It is therefore not surprising to find that a considerable proportion of misfortunes are attributed to natural causes, to what we, with legal precision rather than religious piety, would call acts of God. This is what Ceŵa call them—or most of them—too: they refer to 'deaths of God (*imfa ʒaMuluŋgu*)', implying that they are the result, not of the negligence, malevolence or retribution of human beings, nor of similar attributes of quasi-human spirits, but of more inscrutable causes.

The God, Muluŋgu, to whom is assigned the control of the major forces of nature, probably represents a Christian elaboration of an indigenous Supreme Being. Muluŋgu is only one of his names. Some of the others refer to the rôles that Ceŵa traditionally ascribed to him.

63

Thus, Mleŋgi means creator; and Ciuta (sometimes Cauta), 'the big bow', the rainbow, the reference being to his function of providing rain. In his rôle of creator, he is distant in both time and space; and even in his rôle of rain-provider he is not approached direct but through the leader (cisumphi) of a rain-making cult (asumphi). Thus the Ceŵa Supreme Being resembles that of other Bantu-speaking peoples both in being remote and in having been the indigenous stock on to which the Christian God has been grafted. It is now difficult to separate the stock from the graft. Formal converts to Christianity probably make up no more than a fifth of the adult population and include considerable numbers of persons whom the missionaries call 'backsliders'—those who have reverted, or, because of enhanced social status, taken for the first time, to bigamy or concubinage, or, according to denomination, beer or cousin-marriage. In spite of this relatively low rate of formal and lasting conversion, and perhaps because of keen competition between the two main missions represented in Ceŵa country, the (Roman Catholic) White Fathers and the (Protestant) Dutch Reformed Church, the influence among the Ceŵa of Christianity is extensive. Thus, of the almost innumerable funerals I attended during the course of my field work, not one lacked some Christian element, such as a Bible-reading, a prayer or a sermon. The first one I went to promised to be a good example of a pagan funeral; but, soon after we were settled outside the hut of the deceased, a man appeared, carrying a Bible. I turned in disappointment to my interpreter, a Roman Catholic: 'So it's to be a Christian funeral after all!' 'No', he replied, 'Dutch.'

All Ceŵa nowadays, Christian and pagan alike, observe the Sabbath, and in speech and belief find it easy to assimilate the Christian God to the position of their indigenous Providence, Creator and Rain God. On leaving for Nyasaland in February 1947, I bade farewell to a pagan friend, saying that we would see each other the following June. 'Muluŋgu akatisuŋga (If God preserves us),' he corrected me. He may have been expressing a cautious pagan sentiment, but it certainly fitted the Christian mould.

Lineage Spirits

In general, if Ceŵa have any opposition to Christianity, they are very reticent about it; and, converted or not, they tend to be shameful and secretive about the cult of the spirits, who traditionally were much

(a)

(b)

PLATE II. IMPORTANT TREES

(a) Sacrificing a fowl to the lineage spirits at a shrine built at the base of an *msolo* tree; (b) an *mwabvi* tree, bushy because branches from it have been cut for use in hut-frames as protection against sorcerers.

more important than the Supreme Being. During my stay among them, I was able to attend only two purely indigenous rituals involving them. The first was the offering of a libation of *cale* (beer a day before it matures) and maize-flour to the spirit of a headman at the end of the mourning period following his death. The second was the sacrifice of a fowl to the lineage spirits of the woman leader of a rain-making cult on the occasion of a rain-making dance (*mgwetsa*), which, having long been neglected, was revived during a particularly serious drought in January 1949.

The spirits that were approached on these occasions were those of deceased members of the matrilineages of the persons approaching them. As Mitchell has pointed out,[1] the term 'ancestor', because of its connotation of lineal rather than collateral senior kin, is not an appropriate designation in a matrilineal society for these everyday domestic deities, since in many cases they are collaterals, such as the mother's brothers or mother's mother's brothers of those approaching them.

The lineage spirits usually manifest themselves negatively. Someone, very often a child, falls ill, and members of his lineage, such as his elder brother or mother's brother and possibly his mother or his mother's sister, consult a diviner. The diviner very often finds that the illness is merely the means by which one of the lineage spirits is expressing his or her anger at having been neglected. No offering may have been made to him or her; rituals may have been incorrectly carried out; or the spirit's name may not have been handed on to a successor.[2] As an emergency measure, a libation of maize-flour and water will be poured at the base of an *msolo* tree (*Pseudolachnostylis maprounaefolia*), a species which spirits are believed to frequent; and plans will be made for a full propitiation—or perhaps the omitted ritual—as soon as the persons concerned can be assembled and certainly no sooner than the end of the four- or five-day period required for making beer. Beer is usually offered when it is *cale*, a day off being mature (*wakupya*). The offering may be made at a specially built shrine (*kaimba, kacisi*), a miniature hut at the base of an *msolo* tree in the village.

Much of the ritual following someone's death, expecially that carried out at the shaving of the chief mourners from three to five weeks after the burial, is aimed at settling his spirit as a helpful domestic

[1] Professor J. Clyde Mitchell, private communication.
[2] For an account of the custom of nominal reincarnation, see below, Chapter 8.

deity (*mẓimu*, plur., *miẓimu*) rather than allowing him to remain a haunting and troublesome ghost (*ciwanda*, plur., *viwanda*).

Although the commonest manifestations of the lineage spirits are negative, in that their intervention usually indicates that they have been neglected, a more positive rôle—a protective and supporting one—is sometimes attributed to them. It will be remembered that, in the case of the Broken Windscreen, the diviner stated that I had been saved from a serious accident by the intervention of the spirit of one of my ancestors (Chapter 1 above). The same diviner relied on the spirit of his mother's brother for help in dreaming solutions to the problems his clients brought him.

The Mdulo Complex

Apart from the religious beliefs described in the last two sections, Ceŵa are preoccupied by another set of mystical notions—ones that cannot be classified as religious because they conceive, not of supernatural beings who have to be persuaded to soften their hearts when angry and to provide help when it is needed, but of supernatural, impersonal forces that determine automatic and invariable consequences of certain human actions. Most prominent among these are beliefs centring on the idea that an innocent, susceptible ('cold', *woẓiẓila*) person will 'get cut in the chest' (*-duka m'cifuwa*) and suffer the state of being cut (*mdulo*) if he comes in contact—mystically, physically (e.g. sexually) or through the medium of salted 'relish'— with someone who is ritually impure or dangerous ('hot', *wotentha*).[1]

The dangers of *mdulo* dog the Ceŵa from the womb to the grave. A man should refrain from committing adultery when his wife is pregnant because she and her unborn child are 'cold', and adultery will make him 'hot', with the result that he will kill the foetus as soon as he comes to the doorway of his wife's hut, or he will make her labour difficult. The child's 'coldness' can be removed only by performing a ritual known as 'taking the child' (*kuteŋga mwana*), which is performed by the parents when, at the age of four or five weeks, the child smiles for the first time. This consists of *coitus interruptus* while the mother holds the baby to her chest and after which the child is 'warmed' and strengthened by having mixed seminal and vaginal fluid rubbed on him and by being passed across the fire in which medicinal herbs may be burnt.

[1] A fuller account of the *mdulo* complex will be found in my paper, 'Notes on Some Ceŵa Rituals' (in preparation).

A strong mystical tie between father and child is assumed to exist; for if the father does not 'make firm [his] heart' (-limbika mtima) sufficiently to break off intercourse at the right moment, the child will not receive from him any strength of character. Once the child has been successfully 'taken', it is 'warm' (wofunda) or 'hot' (wotentha); for the ritual, including his being passed across the fire, has driven out the 'coldness' (nphepo) of the womb. 'Hotness' is believed to come from men; it is their 'hotness' that makes them desire coitus.

The only time a man can kill his wife with mdulo is when he commits adultery when she is pregnant. If, in this way, he 'cuts' her, he has to pay her matrilineage damages known as mpaŋgo or canthumbi; and, if any of his children die, he is seldom able to establish his innocence and almost invariably has to make the payment 'of the spirit' (camẓimu) for settling the child's ghost.

A woman, it is believed, can kill her husband by committing adultery when he has been on a journey and comes home and has intercourse with her. In this case adultery has made her 'hot', and, if he has been continent on his journey, he will be 'cold' and therefore susceptible to mdulo. Another way in which, according to belief, an adulterous woman may kill her 'cold' husband is by seasoning his 'relish' with salt. Should the husband be engaged in any dangerous or hazardous undertaking, such as hunting, distilling kacaso, smelting iron or, in modern times, mining, his wife must refrain from adultery lest she ruin the enterprise and also endanger him. A menstruating woman is 'hot', and avoids seasoning food with salt lest she should 'cut' those who will eat it. A pregnant woman can kill herself (-dẓipha yekha, the expression used for 'commit suicide') by committing adultery.

At all stages of life, neophytes and mourners are 'cold', and special taboos are imposed on all those close to them, e.g. their spouses, parents and the headmen of their matrilineage and village, lest they 'get cut in the chest'. This applies to boys' and girls' puberty ceremonies, entry into the nyau secret society, and installation in office, e.g. headmanship or chieftainship. The defloration that completes the Ceŵa female puberty ritual (cinamwali) is simply the means of formally re-introducing the girl, who has been in a 'cold' condition, to the dangerous, 'hot' forces prevalent in the village. Exactly parallel is the instruction given to a boy at the end of his induction into the nyau society to have intercourse with a woman 'lest he should die'.

Ceŵa believe that, should the taboos be broken, the 'cold' person will 'get cut in the chest', the symptoms in the post-natal period approximating those of what Western doctors would diagnose as pulmonary tuberculosis. The number of cases of pulmonary tuberculosis brought in to the Fort Jameson African Hospital is considered to be very small in proportion to the probable prevalence of the disease;[1] and this may well be the result of the fact that, because Ceŵa, and other tribes in the district, regard it as the condition of 'getting cut in the chest' and a natural consequence of human negligence, they think it unlikely that Western methods of treatment will help to cure it. The whole complex of beliefs concerning *mdulo* exerts a strong influence on every Ceŵa, and appears to have withstood the onslaught of modern changes far better, for instance, than the cult of lineage spirits.

An important aspect of the *mdulo* complex is the notion that the breach of a taboo will not affect the one who breaks it, but that some innocent person connected with him will suffer. Thus, although a supernatural sanction is apparently operating, the ultimate sanction preserving the taboo is a secular one. Usually people who break *mdulo* taboos at inauspicious times, such as when their wives are pregnant or mourning, are successfully sued for damages—in spite of the fact that the allegation made against them falls within the Witchcraft Ordinance's wide definition of 'imputing witchcraft' (end of Chapter 1 above).

The effect of these ritual prescriptions bolstered by secular authority is the preservation of the social relationships conducive to effective human reproduction. Their ultimate reference, through the obscurer channels of symbolism and mystical belief, is to the fertility of the soil and the fecundity of animals and men. An indication of this is to be found in the belief that a woman who has died in childbirth should be cut open to release the harmful tension (*nphamvu*, 'strength'), and her corpse either thrown into a deep pool or tied in the branches of a tree lest its 'heat' should destroy the fertility of the soil.

Magic

Following Evans-Pritchard's terminology,[2] I take magic to have a morally neutral connotation. It comprises ritual involving the mani-

---

[1] Discussion with the Provincial Medical Officer of the Eastern Province in Fort Jameson, early in 1953.
[2] E. E. Evans-Pritchard, *Witchcraft among the Aʒande*, p. 21.

pulation of material substances believed to have powerful specific properties (and sometimes inadequately referred to as 'medicines' [1]) and the use of verbal spells or addresses directed towards the influencing of forces, conceived of as impersonal, that are believed to govern the course of events. Many of the practices associated with the *mdulo* complex, described in the last section, would fall within this definition; and I have kept my account of them separate only because they have an internal consistency and lack the close association with material substances ('medicines') that characterizes the beliefs I am about to describe. Magic may be used for either (*a*) productive, protective or curative purposes or (*b*) destructive ones. Sometimes protective magic may be destructive and punitive in its implications, as when a 'medicine' for protecting one's property or ensuring the fidelity of one's wife is intended to bring death or illness to the thief or adulterer.

Magic is morally neutral in that it can be put to either legitimate or illegitimate purposes. Some writers, especially those dealing with Oceania,[2] use the term 'sorcery' to embrace all forms of destructive magic, including those applied with social approval; others restrict its meaning, as I shall in this book, to those applications of destructive magic (and sometimes more positive forms) that are socially disapproved or deemed illegitimate.[3] According to this narrower meaning, the sorcerer and the witch have a fundamental similarity: 'Both alike are enemies of men . . .';[4] and this fact makes sociological generalizations about either type largely applicable to the other. The implications of beliefs in their existence and activities can, therefore, be taken up in a single set of sociological propositions.

In other respects, according to Evans-Pritchard's widely accepted definitions, witches are clearly distinguishable from sorcerers. Witches are believed to harm others, not by the use of destructive magic, but by means of psychic emanations from an inherent physiological condition that is transmitted biologically. I shall, however, postpone a detailed discussion of the differences between sorcerers and witches until I raise the problem of finding a suitable translation of the Ceŵa word for mystical evil-doer (*nfiti*, plur., the same) (see end of this chapter).

---

[1] As a reminder of the inadequacy of this translation I shall write 'medicines' between inverted commas where appropriate, e.g. where it is the translation of the Ceŵa *maŋkhwala* (no sing.).

[2] See, for instance, Malinowski, *Crime and Custom*, pp. 85 ff.; and Hogbin, *Law and Order in Polynesia*, pp. 216–24.

[3] Evans-Pritchard, *Witchcraft among the Aʒande*, p. 10

[4] *Ibid.*, p. 387.

Ceŵa employ magic for a variety of purposes. There is magic for making children and crops grow, for curing barrenness and diseases of various kinds, for bringing success in enterprises such as employment, gambling, hunting and love-making; and there is magic for protecting oneself, one's hut, one's crops and one's conjugal rights from the evil designs of others. Protective measures may be punitive. Thus, Ceŵa believe that branches of the ordeal-poison tree,[1] if woven into a hut-frame before the walls are plastered or if buried near the doorway, will cause an approaching sorcerer to bleed from his rectum and even to die; that a 'medicine' called *likaŋkho* applied secretly to one's wife will cause her lover to die in a variety of ways according to the activating agent (*ciɀimba*) used; and that *cambo* magic will protect one's crops and other property from thieves by causing them to die from a wasting disease. As with other forms of magic, *cambo* can be made selective, e.g. to exclude members of the owner's family, by being suitably addressed when it is applied. A peculiar advantage possessed by *cambo* is that it can be applied after a theft has occurred—on the principle that '*Cambo* follows up' (Chapter 2 above).

Ceŵa 'medicines' are made from the roots, leaves and other parts of trees and shrubs; but, to be effective, they require the addition of activating agents (*viɀimba*, sing., *ciɀimba* (Chapter 1 above)) of human or animal origin; and especially potent forms require that the operator should commit incest with, or kill, a near relative. Such potent 'medicines' include those used in hunting and gambling and are often regarded with suspicion and disapproval because of these sinister associations, i.e. they are on the borderline between legitimate magic and illegitimate sorcery. Distinctly across it, in the realm of sorcery, is magical maize-stealing (*nfumba yacimaŋga*) by means of which the operator entices either other people's living maize plants into his garden or their harvested maize into his grain store.

Even in modern situations, magic is frequently employed, e.g. for keeping on good terms with one's employer and for protecting oneself against the sorcery of those jealous of one's economic or educational success. While for most purposes Ceŵa regard Western medicine as superior to their own, their acceptance of it does not necessitate a change in underlying rationale. Thus, they recognize that the Western method of introducing 'medicines' into the body by means of a syringe is more effective than their own method of rubbing them into incisions

---

[1] Probably *Crossopteryx febrifuga*. See below, this chapter, for a discussion of the botanical identification of this tree.

THE IDIOM OF CEŴA BELIEF

in the skin; and they are enthusiastic about injections, for this reason sometimes trying to be treated for venereal diseases even when one of these has not been diagnosed. To them the substances being introduced by this method into the system are of the same kind as the 'medicines' of their own tradition, but are much more potent. The successes of local doctors and hospitals are attributed, not to modern hygienic routines, nor to the destruction of disease-bearing germs and parasites, but to the power, i.e. magical power, of the drugs they administer. Ceŵa believe that these modern 'medicines', like their traditional ones, can be put to good or evil uses; and fear of going into hospital is rationalized by the assertion that Africans employed at hospitals are in the habit of killing patients with 'medicines' selected from the formidable armoury at their disposal.

Beliefs in Sorcery

Such actions would, of course, be deemed illegitimate and would be called 'sorcery' (ufiti), the characteristic activity of the 'sorcerer' (nfiti).[1] Since this book will be concerned mainly with the social contexts in which beliefs in sorcery are expressed, it will be necessary to consider them in greater detail.

(a) Prevalence and Preoccupation

Every year the Provincial Commissioner of the Eastern Province of Northern Rhodesia devotes a small section of his annual report to 'witchcraft', a term defined in the relevant Ordinance to include sorcery.[2] His remarks usually show that there have been very few cases of it in the three districts falling under his control.[3] Since this section is included in the chapter on 'Law and Order', the reference is, of course, to cases involving 'witchcraft' that have come before the courts—the subordinate courts of District Commissioner and Provincial Commissioner, and the High Court, since such cases are specifically excluded from the jurisdiction of the native courts.[4]

The number of court cases involving 'witchcraft' cannot, however,

---

[1] For a discussion of the translation of these terms, see below, this chapter.

[2] Northern Rhodesia, Laws, Witchcraft Ordinance, No. 5 of 1914, as amended by No. 47 of 1948, Section 2.

[3] See, for instance, Northern Rhodesia, Department of Native Affairs, African Affairs: Annual Reports, 1951, p. 63; 1952, p. 69; and 1953, p. 75.

[4] Northern Rhodesia, Laws, Native Courts Ordinance, No. 10 of 1936, Section 11.

be taken as an indication of the number of accusations of it that actually take place or of the prevalence of beliefs in it. Although it is an offence to name a person a 'witch' or to impute 'witchcraft',[1] there appear to be strong social pressures preventing a person accused of sorcery from bringing his accuser to court. The law may be on his side, but public opinion may not be. The chief effect of taking his accuser to court may be to bring greater publicity to his social condemnation; for the weight of popular prejudice is loaded heavily against him.

Even if there were records of the accusations that take place, these would still provide an incomplete picture of the prevalence of belief in sorcery. Suspicions may remain vague and unformulated; and accusations, especially in view of the provisions of the Witchcraft Ordinance, are cautiously expressed and seldom made in public. In these circumstances an estimate of the prevalence of belief in sorcery has to be based on impressions. From my contacts with Cewa of all types—Christian and pagan, educated and illiterate, old and young— I would say that the basic belief that certain persons are sorcerers is held by close on 100 per cent of the population. For instance, only one of the 268 persons interviewed for my public-opinion survey rejected as unanswerable the question, 'Are there more or fewer sorcerers nowadays than there were long ago?' Incidentally, sixty-two per cent of an abridged sample of 156 persons[2] said there were more nowadays; twenty-five per cent said there were more long ago; and most of the remaining thirteen per cent, who included the person who specifically rejected the question, said they didn't know.

If, as my impressions suggest, belief in sorcery is almost universal, it is necessary to consider, not so much its prevalence, as people's preoccupation with the fears that spring from it.[3] Pointers to this preoccupation are the relative frequency with which people attribute misfortunes to sorcery and their related tendency to take precautions against possible attacks by sorcerers.

My first impressions led me to believe that Cewa were intensely absorbed in beliefs in sorcery. This was probably because of the common discrepancy between people's general statements about a phenomenon and their specific references to it. In this case I encountered dogma first. After hearing a few accounts of the wonderful but wicked ways of sorcerers, and after being assured that people were

[1] See Chapter 1.
[2] The reason for abridging the sample on certain items has been given in Chapter 2.
[3] I owe this distinction to Schapera, 'Sorcery and Witchcraft in Bechuanaland'.

constantly troubled by their actual deeds and the dread of their possible deeds, I had one of my assistants interview ten men and nine women individually and ask them to estimate how many of twenty hypothetical deaths in a village they would expect to be caused by sorcerers. Their estimates ranged from sixteen to twenty, i.e. from eighty to 100 per cent; the residual category (if any) they described as 'deaths of God' (*imfa ʒaMuluŋgu*).

As I mentioned in the first chapter, during the course of field work, I collected information relating to deaths and other misfortunes (mainly the former) about which my informants had first-hand knowledge; and the summary of believed instances of misfortunes given in Table I assigns a lower proportion than dogma does to those resulting from acts of sorcerers, and, in addition to showing misfortunes resulting from natural causes, or acts of God, it introduces two other categories, those resulting from acts of people other than sorcerers and those attributed to lineage spirits.

Although the fifty-five per cent of misfortunes attributed to sorcery in this table is lower than that usually estimated by informants, it nevertheless indicates a considerable degree of preoccupation with fears of sorcery. This is borne out by the fact that virtually all Ceŵa take precautions against the possible attacks of sorcerers. A later section will deal with some of the details of these precautions. All I need to note here is that they regard the procuring of protective charms as an essential part of the normal pursuit of health; and that, though they recognize that the protection of a hut from sorcery is magical rather than technological, they look upon it as an essential part of normal building procedure.

(b) Content of the Beliefs

What is the content of the beliefs with which Ceŵa are thus preoccupied? In general, they may hold sorcerers responsible for most forms of misfortune that may befall them. They believe that sorcerers disturb one's relationships with useful persons such as chiefs or employers; that they impoverish one by sending 'their' hyenas and wild cats after one's livestock and poultry, or by using *nfumba* magic to entice living plants from one's garden into theirs; that they prevent some pregnancies and end others disastrously; that they send one insane; and that they kill one in a variety of ways. Two beliefs are of cardinal importance, viz. (*a*) that sorcerers are necrophagous and (*b*) that they usually attack their matrilineal relatives.

Informants are unanimous that sorcerers are dependent on material magic for their evil deeds. The idea of their killing anyone by using words alone or by using some means other than 'medicines' seems absurd, though they attribute this sinister power to some of the missionaries. When questioned, they say that it is possible for older people to curse their matrilineal juniors by using words alone. (The effects of this cursing may be removed by blowing water on to a live coal held near the victim's head.) In practice, however, younger informants seldom make the distinction between socially tolerated cursing and the use of threatening words, which is one of the characteristic practices of the sorcerer. A cross-tabulation of age category of informant and the relative generation of sorcerer and victim revealed a slight, but statistically insignificant, tendency for younger informants in my sample to cite a larger proportion of cases with sorcerers in a senior generation. Ceŵa say, too, that sorcerers often step in and kill a person who has been cursed or threatened by someone else, thus throwing their guilt on to someone who in a fit of anger may have said more than he intended.

Ceŵa believe that the tendency to use threatening and prophetic words is nevertheless the surest mark of the sorcerer; and it often serves to identify him without the bother of holding an ordeal or consulting a diviner. If A threatens B by saying, 'You'll see this year! (*Mudʒaona caka cino!*)' or 'You'll fall into a game pit! (*Mudʒagwa m'mbuna!*)', and B later dies, it is considered obvious who killed him. In addition to this fondness for threatening language there are other traits that set off sorcerers from people (Ceŵa sometimes use this dichotomy as a means of stressing the inhumanly anti-social nature of sorcerers). These traits include: red eyes, from staying up all night; fatness, from eating human flesh (cf. the gaunt European stereotype of the witch); and what may best be described as a kind of extra-sensory perception which enables its possessor to tell where a death has occurred in the neighbourhood.

Informants seem quite familiar with some of the more straightforward of sorcerers' techniques, but tend to stall when questioned about details of their more amazing feats. They refer to the latter as *matseŋga* ('tricks'), by which they mean that they are incomprehensible to ordinary people. I often noticed that informants would show agreement about the more mundane practices of sorcerers, but, when asked for details of their more astonishing accomplishments, would begin to discuss these heatedly, and then would stop with dramatic suddenness as each remembered that to pose as an authority on sorcery is to endanger one's reputation. Shrugging their shoulders, they would turn to me and say, 'Why ask us? Go and ask the sorcerers themselves!'

Starting with some of the items that are familiar to most Ceŵa, I may note the widespread belief that sorcerers injure and kill people by putting magical substances (*maŋkhwala*, into which category European poisons and medicines also fall) into their food or beer. It is doubtful whether Ceŵa originally distinguished between poisoning and sorcery. They have to now, however; for, though it is a public duty to report a case of murder-by-poisoning, it is an offence in terms of the Witchcraft Ordinance to accuse anyone of sorcery. In effect, Ceŵa have come to recognize that the Administration believes in one type of sorcery, viz. poisoning.[1] They therefore now distinguish between 'visible magical substances' (*maŋkhwala apoyela*, lit., 'magical substances of in-the-light'), which they hope will impress the Administration, and others that will probably not. Despite this emphasis on poisoning, enquiries I made of the Health Department revealed that very few cases of it are brought in to hospitals or dispensaries.

Another point on which there is fairly general agreement is that sorcerers attack people by making concoctions that incorporate various forms of 'dirt' obtained from their prospective victims, e.g. nail-parings, hair, bodily excretions and soil from a footprint. The Ceŵa objection to pit-latrines is in part probably due to the fear of this 'contagious' sorcery.

Most informants are prepared to describe how sorcerers use their magical concoctions for drawing lines (*mikhwekhwe*, sing., *mkhwekhwe*) across paths that their would-be victims frequent. They add that the magic is made selective by having 'dirt' from the intended victim included in it, and by the sorcerer's addressing the 'medicines' as he applies them in a manner similar to the following:

If now this person [naming him] and I agree, then he will pass over this line [without ill effect]; but, if we don't agree, then he is going to see [i.e. experience] something today [specifying the intended victim's injuries in detail].

Another item of common knowledge—if not of common reported experience—is the tendency for sorcerers to trouble one when one is asleep. The sorcerer evokes a feeling of oppression—of being paralysed

[1] I am grateful to Mr D. B. Hall, now Sir Douglas Hall, formerly of the Northern Rhodesia Provincial Administration, for pointing this out to me.

G

yet conscious—a condition which can be got rid of only by a strong effort to throw off the sorcerer. An informant states:

> Sorcerers cut off a person's head, he remaining alive, and go and play with it at the graveyard [their favourite meeting place]. When they realize that dawn is about to break, they go and put it back on that person. This is why, when he wakes up, he has a sore head and neck.

Sorcerers using a socially disapproved method of enticing other people's crops into their own gardens (*nfumba*) sometimes make doubly sure of a large, but illicit, crop by seizing people at night and setting them to work without their knowing it. In one story of wide currency a missionary was the victim of this kind of abuse.

Many informants believe that tropical ulcers (which are very common in Ceŵa country) are the result of sorcerers' eating people's flesh without following the more usual practice of killing them first. They allege that *nsima* (stiff maize-flour porridge) is often found on tropical ulcers, indicating that the victim's living flesh is being used as *ndiwo* ('relish') by the sorcerer concerned.

I have described how Ceŵa believe that sorcerers meanly take advantage of hot-headed people by killing those whom they have cursed or threatened. They also believe that sorcerers take advantage of other opportunities, too, and quote the instance of how, if a person has been weakened by the visitation of a spirit, a sorcerer may finish him off and thus escape blame for his death. Informants state that sorcerers always attack the weak and unprotected. That is why, they argue, there are many deaths among young children, and why many people die in January and February [the malaria season] 'when people's stomachs are weakened by eating the new crops'.

I come now to those practices attributed to sorcerers about which informants (perhaps for reasons of respectability) disclaim a detailed knowledge. Thus they say that sorcerers have familiars who work for them; that they belong to a necrophagous guild; that they teach their sorcery to their favourite children or grandchildren; and that they perform supernatural feats such as operating over great distances by flying around in winnowing baskets (*visese*, sing., *cisese*). But, apart from putting forward some general principles such as the one that a sorcerer lacking magical substances is helpless, they are unable (or unwilling) to speak authoritatively or consistently about any details relating to these beliefs. The descriptions that follow thus represent modal rather than standard opinions.

Sorcerers are believed to employ familiars. These include hyenas, owls, red ants, nightjars, lions, leopards, puff-adders and mythical, crested black mamba snakes (*nbobo*, sing., the same). Hyenas and owls are mentioned most frequently. This may be related to the facts that hyenas cause considerable losses in small stock and poultry, and that the owl's weird cries are heard in Ceŵa as '*Muphe! Muphe nimkukute!* (Kill him! Kill him that I may munch him!)'. Informants do not believe that a sorcerer has sexual relationships with his[1] familiars, but they describe a kind of mystical sympathy that exists between them. They quote instances of how, when a sorcerer has imbibed heavily, drunken hyenas are found in his hut; and of how, when a sorcerer dies, his hyenas die too. They reject the idea that there is any transformation of sorcerer into familiar. As one informant puts it:

When sorcerers send hyenas or other animals to catch pigs or fowls [for them], this does not mean that they are inside them, but rather that these animals are their soldiers or messengers who are sent by them. These [animals] all stay in their masters' huts, some being roots [i.e. magical constructions]; others, real animals. . . . Hyenas are like sorcerers' servants, or they are sometimes like their bicycles or donkeys.

Some of the information about the sorcerers' guild[2] comes from those who have taken part in grave-watching (see below, this chapter). Grave-watchers claim that, owing to the magical substances they use for making themselves invisible, they have been able to observe the sorcerers without being detected. Such informants say that sorcerers, after the burial of someone they have killed, send various of their familiars to the graveyard to test whether they will meet with any opposition from grave-watchers or from graveyard magic which may have been used for 'closing' entrances and circumscribing the grave.

When sorcerers want to go to the graveyard, they send birds, such as nightjars and owls, and then there comes a wind blowing from west to east which brings flying winnowing baskets on its return [from the east].

We were sitting down [reports a grave-watcher] and we saw a great many red ants. They were coming along the path, but where they came from was impossible to say. At this stage the elders [present] knew that this day we

---

[1] Masculine pronouns and possessives referring to sorcerers should be read as common gender, since they are so in Ceŵa statements. Informants usually assert that the majority of sorcerers are women, though this doctrine is contradicted by totals derived from actual allegations of sorcery. (See below, this chapter.)

[2] *Msoŋkhano*, which is the general term for 'gathering' or 'meeting'. 'Sabbat' might possibly be a better translation, except that it is too specific and has become associated with some of the special features of European witch beliefs, e.g. satanism.

would indeed be beating sorcerers. Secondly, we saw crows, fowls, snakes and also chairs. And all these things I saw with my own eyes.

After having sent their familiars ahead in this way, the sorcerers themselves are said to approach. They have a leader whom some informants call Nyamawila. He supervises the sharing of the flesh of the victim, who is cut up by one of his own matrilineal relatives, this person having been responsible earlier for reviving him so that the sorcerers may torment him before they slaughter and eat him. The grave-watcher continues:

When these things had happened, the sorcerers themselves arrived. We heard them speaking just as ordinary people would speak. They walked in single file along the path, and the woman who had killed the dead girl with sorcery was in front; I heard her saying, 'All the meat of the two legs is mine.' And Headman Kamteŋgo sat in the chair, and it was he who said 'Hurry up!' The others called for the dead girl's relative, the one who had killed her with sorcery, and told her to revive her. She came forward and again insisted that the meat from both legs was to be hers.

Informants say that, if sorcerers elude the grave-watchers, they disinter the corpse by striking the grave with a 'root' (i.e. magical object) and by calling out the name by which the deceased was known as a small child. By their 'tricks' (matseŋga), they cause him to come up to the surface where they revive him into a semi-conscious state. He can hear and feel but is paralysed and dumb. They torment him, perhaps saying, 'You stinted me beer; do you think you'll get any in this graveyard?' When they have finished this, they kill him again—just as they would any kind of livestock, i.e. they cut his throat. Then they share the 'meat'. It is not clear how they cook it, though informants do not think they eat it raw. If any is left over, they dry it. The victim's fat is rendered down for making magical substances, e.g. those for bringing success at gambling. When they have finished, again by using 'tricks', they close up the grave in such a way that it does not appear to have been disturbed. They are said to build a fire (as any other company of people probably would); and some informants claim to have seen this fire.

Like any other body of its kind, the sorcerers' guild protects the general interests of its members and regulates the relationships between them. The first of these functions is illustrated by informants' assertions that, if anyone in the neighbourhood acquires particularly strong anti-sorcery 'medicines', the guild chooses some of its most skilful and

experienced members to try their strength. A man I knew had just
returned from a visit to Portuguese territory, where he had obtained
some of Mpulumutsi's famous anti-sorcery magic,[1] and he was boasting
about his immunity from the attacks of sorcerers. People hearing him
thought his demeanour was very foolish, if not suicidal. The second
function is illustrated by beliefs that the guild ensures a fair distribution among members of flesh from corpses, and that it forces everyone
in turn to contribute a corpse. If a member shows a lack of reciprocity
by living too long on what is described as 'credit' (cikweleti), his guild-
fellows enjoin him to kill one of his matrilineal relatives or perhaps
even his own child in order that he may discharge his obligations
towards them. An informant says:

If a sorcerer simply eats the meat killed by his fellows, the latter will tell
him, 'You must kill some of your children so that we may partake of them.
Why do you just eat our meat?' And, overcome with shame, the sorcerer
proceeds to kill his own child so that he can give [meat] to his fellows.

Another illustration of how the guild is believed to regulate relationships between members is found in the rationalization of the belief
(to be discussed later) that a sorcerer attacks the members of his own
matrilineage. This is expressed by analogy: 'If you want to kill livestock, you don't go and kill that of other people: you kill your own.'
The implication here is that the member's matrilineage is his special
preserve, and that the guild will arbitrate in his favour if anyone
trespasses on it.

Although Ceŵa habitually speak of all mystical evil-doers (and
poisoners, too) as nfiti, they sometimes, if questioned about the
motives of sorcerers, distinguish between two types. Firstly, there is
the mphelanjilu ('killer-for-malice'), the person who, untrained and unskilled in the art of sorcery and motivated chiefly by hatred, begs or
buys destructive magic or poison and kills his enemy; and, secondly,
the nfiti yeni-yeni ('real nfiti') who has been one from childhood, and
who is driven by 'meat hunger' (ŋkhuli), and whose characteristic activity is 'digging up people' (kufukula ŵanthu). My informants were
unable to answer the crucial question whether the mphelanjilu subsequently eats the corpse of his victim. This distinction between 'real
nfiti' and 'killer-for-malice' is similar to that made by certain South
African tribes between terms that some writers[2] have translated as

[1] I shall refer towards the end of this chapter to the anti-sorcery movement of which
Mpulumutsi was one of the leaders.
[2] See, for instance, E. Jensen Krige and J. D. Krige, The Realm of a Rain Queen,
pp. 250 ff.

'night-witch' and 'day-witch' and, in a general way, to that made by the Azande[1] between terms that Evans-Pritchard translated as 'witch' and 'sorcerer'. I shall return presently to the translations I use.

How does a child become a 'real *nfiti*'? Cewa maintain that when a sorcerer gets old he takes his favourite child or grandchild and initiates him into eating human flesh. He gives him 'medicines' to prevent him from being nauseated by its smell, and he inoculates him against the skin-rash that is believed to be the normal consequence of eating it. People say that this training takes up a good deal of the child's time and interest, and that he is often scolded by his mentor for ingenuously letting the cat out of the bag. Says one informant:

At our village there is a woman called Maŋgose, who has a daughter, Lusia; and Lusia has a daughter, Velonika. Now Maŋgose is teaching her granddaughter, Velonika, to be a sorcerer; and she takes her with her wherever she goes at night riding on her hyena. In the daytime Velonika tells other people: 'Granny and I went to the graveyard, and to kill people with sorcery, and we rode on our hyena.' Her grandmother, Maŋgose, becomes very angry with her and tells her to stop saying these things.

Some informants assert that a sorcerer does not achieve any power until he has had sexual intercourse with his sister. Other references to power derived from contact with incestuous objects are to be found in descriptions of maize-sorcery (*nfumba yacimaŋga*), by means of which the sorcerer entices young plants from other people's gardens into his own. In preparing his 'medicines', the maize-sorcerer is said to make use of activating agents (*viʒimba*, sing., *ciʒimba*) such as the caul from his sister's child or his mother-in-law's loin cloth stolen from her while she sleeps. Similarly, some owners of muzzle-loaders are believed to increase the accuracy of their shooting by persuading their sisters to sleep with their bullets in contact with their private parts. These practices are referred to as *ufiti* (sorcery).

In general, Cewa describe sorcerers as 'very clever' (*ʒocenjela kwambili*). They believe that there is no limit to the means they can employ for attaining their sinister ends—provided they have the requisite magical substances and the knowledge of how to use them. I have mentioned that informants credit sorcerers with the power of using animal familiars, and of operating over long distances by flying in winnowing baskets. They tend, however, to be rather inconsistent in that they attribute omniscience to sorcerers and yet believe it possible

[1] *Witchcraft among the Aʒande*, p. 21.

to hoodwink them without much difficulty, e.g. the practice that returning labour migrants follow of entering their home villages under cover of darkness (see below, this chapter and Chapter 9), or that of bereaved people of postponing wailing for a few hours after someone has died. One gets the impression that Ceŵa conceive of sorcerers as both very clever and very stupid.

By now I have probably presented enough details about Ceŵa beliefs regarding the characteristics of their mystical evil-doers to make it possible to examine the appropriateness of my use of 'sorcerer' and 'sorcery' as translations of the Ceŵa terms *nfiti* and *ufiti* when used in a generic sense. Evans-Pritchard's recognition of the Zande distinction between two types of evil-doers has alerted his successors to the fact that both may coexist in the same society.

Starting with the distinction that Evans-Pritchard elucidated, anthropologists now apply the following interrelated criteria. Firstly, the sorcerer uses magic to perpetrate his evil deeds, whereas the witch carries out his crimes by having a special type of personality. From this it follows, secondly, that people who are sorcerers are conscious of their actions and deliberate in their intentions; whereas those who are witches may not know of the evil life they lead after normal waking hours, and, even if they do, may be driven by an uncontrollable urge, in some instances personified in the form of a familiar. Thirdly, the sorcerer may be driven by anger, envy or malice of a passing kind; whereas the witch has a permanent addiction to his anti-social actions, one that is rooted in heredity or in early conditioning. Fourthly, the actions of the sorcerer, depending as they do on material substances ('medicines') and/or on specific verbal magic, are not as baffling to ordinary minds as are the supernatural machinations of the witch. Finally, the anthropologist can usually believe that sorcery is attempted (even though he may not accept allegations regarding its prevalence or its effectiveness); whereas he can only dismiss as fantastic the idea that witchcraft is ever practised, let alone that it is effective.

Applying the first four criteria to the *ufiti* of the Ceŵa, I find that according to belief:

(1) With the exception of the curse (which is rare and not necessarily illegitimate—see above, this chapter, and Chapter 4), there is no means by which people can bring harm to others without the aid of material magical substances; thus, 'The *nfiti* does not kill-by-*ufiti* without anything—without magical substances (*Nfiti silodʒa cabe—popanda maŋkhwala*).'

(2) All *nfiti* are conscious of their actions, and most of them are motivated by hatred and envy; the only cases where this is not so are those in which they are driven by their lodge-mates to kill someone in order to pay their debts of flesh.

(3) The 'killer-for-malice' (*mphelanjilu*) is usually satisfying a short-term urge for vengeance, whereas the 'real *nfiti*' (*nfiti yeni-yeni*) is driven by a 'flesh hunger' (*ŋkhuli*) that is directed specifically towards human flesh, to which he was habituated in early childhood by his mentor.

(4) Some of the *nfiti*'s actions are comprehensible; whereas others are beyond ordinary understanding, being designated as 'tricks' (*matseŋga*, the term that is also used for conjuring tricks).

Applying the fifth criterion, I would say that, although I have no first-hand evidence of anyone's ever having practised *ufiti*, I have no reason to believe that some forms of it are never attempted.

This summary of the evidence shows that Cewa usage of the term *nfiti* is ambiguous. Sometimes it is a generic term to cover both the types of mystical evil-doer that they recognize; and sometimes, when they qualify it with *yeni-yeni* ('real', plur., *ʒeni-ʒeni*), it is a specific term for those mystical evil-doers who are driven by addiction rather than passing, and not necessarily characteristic, hatred or malice. As to general usage, there are sound reasons for translating *nfiti* as 'sorcerer' rather than as 'witch'. The *nfiti*'s techniques are based on the use of material magical substances ('medicines'); he is conscious of his aims and is deliberate in his purpose. Against these reasons there must, however, be weighed two facts that make Cewa *nfiti* closely resemble the witches rather than the sorcerers of other societies. Firstly, to them are attributed certain fantastic actions and characteristics, such as flying around at night, belonging to a necrophagous guild, and having familiars. Secondly, the Cewa designate as 'real *nfiti*' those who are driven by addiction rather than by passing malice.

On balance, I have decided for convenience to use 'sorcerer' and 'sorcery' as generic terms equivalent to *nfiti* and *ufiti* (unqualified). I have chosen this pair of terms rather than 'witch' and 'witchcraft' because there is no trace in Cewa doctrine of the idea that *ufiti* is anything but socially (as opposed to biologically) inherited; and because there is every indication in both doctrine and case material that the average *nfiti* is believed to be a deliberate evil-doer.[1]

As to specific usage, I translate *nfiti yeni-yeni* as 'witch' and *mphelanjilu* as 'killer-for-malice'. I realize that the *mphelanjilu* is clearly a

---

[1] I am grateful to Professor Max Gluckman and to Dr D. H. Reader for discussions that have helped to clarify this problem for me.

'sorcerer', but, having chosen 'sorcerer' for generic usage, I find the literal translation convenient for usage in those situations where a distinction is made between the two types of evildoers on the basis of their motives.

(c) Social Consequences

I turn now to the practices associated with the basic belief that sorcerers exist and harm people. These include: protective measures; the direct combating and punishing of sorcerers; and the methods of determining, in specific cases of misfortune, whether sorcery is the cause, and, if so, who the sorcerer is.

Fears of sorcerers are sufficiently general to make practically every Ceŵa take precautions against their possible attacks. It is customary for a person to protect magically both his body and his hut (*kutsitikila thupi* and *kutsitikila nyumba* respectively). The modern movements directed against sorcery[1] have had a strong appeal because they have capitalized the widespread insecurity basic to these practices by offering dual-purpose 'medicines' for destroying mystical evil-doers and for protecting their potential victims.

Ceŵa protect their bodies by wearing amulets (*vithumwa*, sing., *cithumwa*), consisting of 'medicines' sewn into small pieces of cloth, or by having 'medicines' rubbed into incisions in the skin (*kutemela maŋkhwala*). They believe that these measures have the effect of diverting sorcerers from the person using them. Some amulets have the specific purpose of warning their wearer of the approach of sorcerers. Thus, he believes, if he is walking along a road or path, the amulet may grip his arm tightly to tell him exactly where a sorcerer lies in wait for him. If he is sleeping in his hut, it will, so he believes, wake him up so that he can challenge the sorcerer as soon as the latter comes near; and, if the sorcerer fails to give a satisfactory account of his presence at a time when people are not normally in the habit of paying calls, the projected victim can deal with him. This he does by hitting the evil-doer (usually below the knee) with a hammer specially treated with destructive 'medicines' which cause the sorcerer to return to his hut and die at a later date. One sorcerer-alarm 'medicine' is kept in a small horn hung on the doorway of the hut. Informants say that, when a sorcerer approaches, the horn falls to the ground, and of its own accord jumps across the floor and wakes up its owner by tapping him

[1] See below, this chapter.

on the head. Ceŵa regard the protection of the body against sorcery as especially important if going on a journey.

Convenient though they may be, protective 'medicines' are considered dangerous. Firstly, they are always a challenge to the sorcerer-fraternity, who, if it hears that someone is protected by new kinds of 'medicines', may send one of its leading members to test their strength. Secondly, the more powerful the protective 'medicines' the greater the dangers attending their use. In 1952 I was told the story of a man who, when he was at work in Southern Rhodesia, had been treated by some Nyasalanders (who are believed by Northern Rhodesians to have strong 'medicines') in such a manner that he would wake up on the approach of sorcerers. The 'medicines' may have helped him during his lifetime; but, when he died, they caused his ghost to wake up, and he has haunted the bush every since, sometimes making himself known to his widow and daughter. The fact that some of these 'medicines', like the one described in the last paragraph, are kept in horns is significant. It is only powerful, sinister 'medicines' that are kept in horns. The leaders of the two modern anti-sorcery movements (see below, this chapter) urged people to throw away all their horns, which was a safer way, given the Witchcraft Ordinance and cognate legislation in the territories in which they operated, of telling them to give up sorcery.

I have not heard of any instances in which European medicines have been used specifically as prophylactics against sorcery, but it is possible that they are. Ceŵa show great faith in European medicines—especially ones that are injected—even in what they regard as sorcerer-sent ailments. As an informant puts it:

God created many trees [from the roots of which most Ceŵa 'medicines' are made]. There is no reason why the Europeans should not have acquired some of the good trees which can be effective against the bad ones.

The 'doctoring' of a hut starts while it is being built. Branches of the ordeal-poison (*mwabvi*) tree[1] are incorporated in the wooden frame before it is plastered, and various 'medicines' are buried under the threshold and in the part opposite the doorway known as 'at the heads' (*kumitu*). These measures are aimed at injuring any sorcerer who may come near. Ceŵa believe that he would bleed from the rectum, return to his hut and die. In addition, 'medicines' are placed in the roof. Some of these are believed to keep away bird-familiars, such as owls and

---

[1] See below, this chapter.

nightjars. Others, especially a concoction made from water-lily roots, are intended to cause the sorcerer to see, not a hut, but a pool of water or some other such misleading object.

Since Ceŵa regard 'digging up people' (*kufukula ŵanthu*) as the activity characteristic of sorcerers, the most active and organized steps that they take to destroy them are to be found in the institution of lying in wait for them at the graveyard (*kukhalisyila nfiti kumanda*).[1] The beliefs that sorcerers are necrophagous and that many deaths are the result of their actions inspire elaborate precautions immediately after someone dies. Since it is considered necessary for the graveyard to be 'closed' against sorcerers and for the site of the grave to be marked out with 'medicines', wailing is usually delayed for some hours lest sorcerers approach the grave before the relatives of the deceased have fetched a graveyard magician (*mabisalila*) to carry out these steps. Ceŵa consider it possible, however, that sorcerers may have preceded the graveyard magician and may have drawn lines with their own 'medicines' in an attempt either to influence him or to neutralize in advance any of the magic he uses. In order to be sure that sorcerers will not disinter and eat the corpse, Ceŵa believe it necessary, therefore, to keep a vigil at the graveside for two or three nights after the burial. Graveyard magicians have a variety of 'medicines' for facilitating this task: some for circumscribing the graveyard with a line which, if crossed by sorcerers, will make them visible; some for sprinkling on the grave in order to paralyse any sorcerers approaching it; and some to render the grave-watchers invisible and inaudible to the sorcerers. One informant describes how the magician must be naked when he applies the first of these; and how, as he does so, he addresses his medicines as follows: 'If it is God who has killed this one, no matter; but if he has died by death sent by a person, then I would like to see this person.' Some informants assert privately that graveyard magicians are people who were once sorcerers themselves but who have given up their evil ways. Graveyard magicians whom I knew did not admit this, but said they had acquired their skill from friends or relatives.

The grave-watchers go to the graveyard just after sundown on the day of the burial. When the graveyard magician has applied his 'medicines' appropriately, they lie in wait for the sorcerers. They report that the latter, after preliminary tests already described, arrive, and, by asking one another whether so-and-so and such-and-such are

[1] For an account of the graveyard vigil among the Nyanja, see H. S. Stannus, 'Notes on Some Tribes', p. 314.

expected, reveal the identity of many of the neighbourhood's sorcerers. When the graveyard magician is satisfied that all the sorcerers have arrived, he grips his 'medicine'-horn firmly 'lest the sorcerers run away', and he tells his fellow watchers to 'harden their hearts' and start punishing the sorcerers. Grave-watchers say that, aided by being invisible and inaudible to the sorcerers, they approach these, and, with calm deliberation, drive thorns (or, in modern times, nails) into various parts of their bodies. Finally they ram a sharpened stick (cisoŋga, plur., visoŋga) through the anus of each sorcerer and 'stir up his entrails' (-vundula matumbo). A sorcerer treated in this way does not die immediately, but returns to his village where he dies in due course. Before dying, they say, he inadvertently reveals what has happened to him by his tendency to sit on one buttock. It is probable that persons suspected of sorcery are actually subjected to treatment of this kind. During my third field trip, a woman from Fort Jameson district was convicted by the High Court of having murdered another woman by forcing a stick up her vagina. No suggestion of sorcery was, however, to be found in the evidence.[1]

A graveyard vigil I attended had a distinctly modern flavour about it. After the graveyard magician had anointed our foreheads with ' "medicines" to make us invisible', he said a prayer to Muluŋgu, as the Christian God. (Before his second—polygynous—marriage, he had been a mission teacher.) It ran:

We know, O Lord, that You disapprove of people's killing one another; but when people do it, as they have in the case of this one here [indicating the grave], we have to get even (kuliŋgana) with them. So, Lord, if they [the sorcerers] come tonight, please excuse us if we chop them with axes [-patsa ŋkhwaŋgwa, 'give axes'].

Had the sorcerers come (they didn't 'because of strong "medicines" used for closing the graveyard'), they would have been shot with muzzle-loaders and finished off with axes. The only exciting incident occurred when a second party of grave-watchers approached, and their electric torch was mistaken for the sorcerers' fire.

Fortunately for ordinary people, sorcerers are considered unlikely to disinter corpses after about 9 p.m., and grave-watchers seldom need keep an all-night vigil—especially if they 'doctor' the grave against any atypical sorcerers who may come in their absence, who will be caught by the 'medicines' as birds are caught in bird-lime. At the end of

[1] See Northern Rhodesia, *Department of Native Affairs*, African Affairs: Annual Report, 1952, p. 69.

(a)

(b)   (c)

PLATE III. DETECTING SORCERERS

(a) The poison ordeal among the Maravi in 1831 (after Gamitto); (b) 'medicines' on grave-mound aimed at ensnaring sorcerers who try to exhume and eat the corpse; (c) A Bwanali Mbewe, leader of anti-sorcery campaign in 1947-8.

the vigil mentioned, one of the graveyard magicians left some 'medicines' in a small horn and in a gourd on the grave-mound (see Plate III (b)).

Informants assert that, if sorcerers approach the grave during a vigil, it is not essential to establish their identity before punishing them. Anyone who goes to a graveyard, except as a mourner in a funeral procession or as a member of a grave-digging or grave-watching party, is assumed to be up to no good; and for practical purposes he or she is regarded as a sorcerer. So diligently do people avoid the graveyard that it is considered to be a safe place at which to leave the highly secret, life-sized representations of animals (nyau ʒolemba) inside which men dance during the evening performances of nyau mimes.[1]

Since Ceŵa feel that many sorcerers elude the grave-watchers, they often consider it necessary to establish the identity of the sorcerer who is responsible for a particular case of misfortune or for a series of such cases. This they do by means of ordeals and other kinds of divination.

Before the Europeans came, at the behest of chiefs and village headmen, an infusion of the bark of the mwabvi tree was regularly administered to whole village populations at a time. Sometimes an ordeal of this kind would be held when a series of deaths, or perhaps the death of a chief or headman, had led to the impression that sorcerers were active; but apparently it was also held as a routine measure of social hygiene. Ceŵa say that there are two types of mwabvi tree. The one found in Nyasaland, known to Northern Rhodesian Ceŵa as ciŋkhundu, is said to be so strong that the infusion made from its bark causes people guilty of sorcery to die outright from its effects. The one found in Kaŵaza's country is said to be weaker; if a sorcerer drinks an infusion prepared from it, he does not die but he purges; and this is taken as a sign of his guilt. Long ago it led to his enslavement or death. If enslaved, he would generally be sent as tribute to the territorial or paramount chief; otherwise he was either killed with an axe by a ritual friend of his matrilineage, who was given a red bead as a token of instruction and rewarded for his services with a goat; or he was bound hand and foot and thrown on to a fire.[2]

Both varieties of mwabvi are believed to make innocent people vomit. If the ordeal clears an accused person, there is great rejoicing,

---

[1] See Chapter 8 below and my paper, 'Notes on some Ceŵa Rituals' (in preparation).
[2] Stannus, 'Notes on Some Tribes', 1910, p. 291, records that, among the Nyanja, the 'mphiti' was burned on a pile of wood, which accords with the accounts of my Ceŵa informants and with the extended description of the burning of sorcerers and the poison ordeal given by Gamitto, O Muata Caʒembe, 1854, pp. 128–32; or, in Cunnison's translation, King Kaʒembe, Vol. 2, pp. 104–6.

and he is compensated by his accuser. One of my informants described an animated scene of rejoicing that occurred when a village headman in his home neighbourhood was cleared of suspicion. This was in the middle 1940's. A very similar incident, which happened at the foot of Mount Zomba in Southern Nyasaland in 1860, is recorded by Livingstone.[1]

In this part of Africa, the ordeal-poison tree has usually been identified as *Erythrophloeum africanum*; this is probably the one that the Northern Rhodesian Ceŵa refer to as the Nyasaland kind of *mwabvi (ciŋkhundu)*. I collected specimens from a shrub designated as the local variety, and the Northern Rhodesian Forestry Department tentatively identified it as *Crossopteryx febrifuga*.[2]

According to the *Nyasaland Handbook*, poison ordeals still occur 'over the border in Portuguese territory'.[3] According to an official of the Portuguese Administration whom I met, '*Mwabvi*-drinking no longer occurs in Moçambique, but across the border in British territory'. I am unable to judge whether both statements are true in the sense that people cross the border in both directions for the purpose of holding ordeals; but it is certain that, though *mwabvi*-drinking at large-scale ceremonies has been successfully suppressed, it still occurs —in great secrecy—as a family (i.e. matrilineage) affair, when an accusation of sorcery is countered by a challenge that all possible suspects, including very often the accuser, should submit to the ordeal. As I have noted, branches of the *mwabvi* tree are still used as defences against sorcery by being woven into hut-frames before these are plastered.

The poison oracle, in which *mwabvi* is administered to fowls and its effect taken as confirmation or refutation of some proposition formulated when the medicine is addressed, is known to some Ceŵa but unknown to many; and I doubt whether it is often resorted to. My enquiries about it produced this unexpected statement:

There are some people who know they are sorcerers, and when they realize that on the morrow they are going to drink *mwabvi*, they shut a cock in a basket, and when they have drunk the *mwabvi* it is the cock that purges in their stead.

In Ceŵa the term *mwabvi* is used to refer to any kind of ordeal. In addition to the poison ordeal, there are ordeals by fire and by boiling

---

[1] David and Charles Livingstone, *The Zambesi and Its Tributaries*, 1866, pp. 131–2.
[2] Letter dated 29.9.54 from the Conservator of Forests, Ndola, for whose co-operation and that of the Provincial Foresty Officer at Fort Jameson I am grateful. See my 'A Note on Ordeal Poison in East Central Africa'.
[3] S. S. Murray, *A Handbook of Nyasaland*, p. 90.

water. As these are used more often for discovering thieves and adulterers than for detecting sorcerers, they are not especially relevant here.

Although the use of the poison ordeal has been greatly reduced, this does not mean that sorcerer-finding has stopped. My impression is that the Ceŵa, on being forced to depend less upon the poison ordeal for detecting sorcerers, have turned to other methods of divination, those falling into the general category of *kuombeza ula*.[1] These appear formerly to have been used only for determining whether a case of misfortune, usually illness, was the result of a visitation of a lineage spirit and, if so, which spirit was responsible and should be appeased. I found that, whenever I asked for information about this kind of divining, informants gave me descriptions of steps taken to establish the identity of an angry spirit rather than of a sorcerer; yet, in most cases of actual divination that I investigated, I found that the client's trouble was traced to the activities of a sorcerer, who might or might not be named—depending sometimes on the fee paid.

Although divining does not follow every case of death or misfortune—even when sorcery is suspected—Ceŵa nevertheless consider it important in many cases to know who the sorcerer is. An informant states:

Among village people those with [divination] magic know who the sorcerers are; those who lack it are simply killed without knowing a thing.

Ceŵa are familiar with a variety of methods of divination. I make no attempt here to determine which of these are indigenous. Many are obviously not, since some diviners of high prestige are foreigners. In the neighbourhood I know best, of four well known diviners, one is a Yao from Nyasaland, and another, though professing to be a Ceŵa, has, judging from his own account and from his *Fanakalo*-laden speech,[2] been away from Ceŵa country for many years; the other two are local Ceŵa. The Yao, who is a Mohammedan, divines with the aid of the Koran. The much-travelled Ceŵa uses a speaking gourd, and one of the local diviners depends mainly on dreaming, but

---

[1] *Ula* (plur., *maula*) means 'divining apparatus or medium'. In Nyanja literature it is sometimes translated as 'lot'. I do not consider this appropriate because there is more in the meaning of *ula* than 'one of a set of objects used to secure a chance decision . . .' (*Concise Oxford Dictionary*, 3rd ed.). It may be a chance decision from the Western viewpoint, but it is not for the Ceŵa. *Ula* is impersonal. The diviner is referred to as *Waula*, i.e. '[The person] of *ula*'.

[2] See Chapter 1.

checks his results with a tortoise shell on a string. I have already described in Chapter 1 the techniques of the last two, since I had occasion to consult them personally.

A divining method known to the Ceŵa but one which I was unable to observe personally is that of the *mpondolo*, or lion-diviner. The *mpondolo* enjoys high prestige and is always addressed as *Mambo*, a title shared only with important chiefs (Chapter 4 below). The Ceŵa say that *mpondolo* divining came from the Cikunda people on the Zambezi; and it is interesting to note that Livingstone referred to a man at Kebrabasa on the Zambezi who called himself a '*Pondoro*' and claimed that he could change into a lion, and that the village gained from the hunting he did when in that form.[1] Chief Kaŵaza Maniŋu gave me the following account of the *mpondolo*:

Among the Cikunda there is a kind of diviner known as an *mpondolo*. If you want to know anything, you hand him some tobacco and a shilling. He grinds the tobacco and snuffs it, and in the middle of the night he turns into a lion and starts roaring. Next morning he is able to tell you the answer to your problem. He owes his gift to a spirit which he owns during his lifetime and which moves on to another person, not necessarily a related person, when he dies. The new possessor of the spirit receives all the knowledge of the person who had it before. The *mpondolo* diviner is always addressed as *Mambo*. Being a lion is useful for many purposes, e.g. wreaking vengeance (your victim dying by whatever way you lay down—accident, suicide or ordinary death); protecting people; and hunting.

The main function of any divining apparatus or medium is to say 'yea' or 'nay' to a proposition, though the range of response of a speaking gourd is naturally somewhat wider. Ceŵa say that some diviners place a horn in a gourd, and interpret the way in which it falls when the gourd is moved; that others speak when delirious (-*bwebweta*), or rely on dreaming (*kulota*); that others, again, gaze into a dish of water and see the sorcerer's face reflected on the surface (a technique modernized by vendors of Mcape medicine in the 1930's, who used mirrors (see below, this chapter).) Two interesting beliefs exist about the practices of Christians. The first is that they use the Bible as a means of divining; and the second, that the taking of the sacraments is the Christian form of the poison ordeal, a view that was held in medieval Europe.[2]

If the diviner is to manipulate his apparatus with success, or in

---

[1] *The Zambesi and Its Tributaries*, p. 177.
[2] Taft, *Criminology, a Cultural Interpretation*, p. 305.

some other way give satisfactory solutions to his clients' problems, he has to know a good deal about their present social relationships; and, if he is to attribute their misfortunes to the displeasure of their matrilineage spirits, he has to be acquainted with their genealogies. For these reasons, he is usually a keen student of local friendships, animosities and kinship ties. In addition, he usually insists that the client should be accompanied by a relative or a close acquaintance. Most diviners require a period during which they can give consideration to the client's problem; hence there are two distinct phases in the divining process, firstly, 'putting the divining apparatus to sleep' (*kugoneka ula*), i.e. handing over some token with a request that a problem (often only vaguely mentioned at the time) be investigated; and, secondly, returning later for the séance proper (*kuombeẓa ula*). Usually the divining apparatus is 'put to sleep' as the sun goes down, and the séance is held the next morning before sunrise. It is at the séance that the fee (referred to as the 'fowl' though nowadays commonly paid in money) is offered. The diviner will accept the 'fowl' only if he feels reasonably confident that he will satisfy his client; and, if he makes a false diagnosis or prognosis, he is expected to return his fee.

Material magic plays an important part in the smooth running of the apparatus, or in the effective response of the medium. Horns, gourds, tortoise-shells and other devices have to be treated with 'medicines' before being used. The diviner who relies on dreaming rubs a few drops of a concoction into incisions behind each ear, and sleeps with his head on the vessel containing the rest of it. The activating agents used in preparing this concoction are of great symbolic interest. They may include the brain of a hyena 'because a hyena dreams where people have left their livestock pens open'; or the heart of a vulture 'because the vulture keeps what it has dreamt in its heart, and knows where to go next day'. If a diviner has been treated with vulture-activated magic, he will be careful to remain standing (normally considered rude in Ceŵa society) if he goes to visit a sick person 'lest he kill him, since, if a vulture alights on a tree above an animal you have shot, it is a sure sign that the animal is going to die'.

The divining situation is important sociologically,[1] since it is during the divination that vague feelings of tension are organized and formulated into a belief that a particular person is responsible for a particular misfortune. Unless one joins Ceŵa in believing that diviners have actual occult power, one cannot escape the fact that the person who

---

[1] I am grateful to Professor J. Clyde Mitchell for impressing this on me.

H

goes to the diviner is the one who feels and afterwards expresses tension against the alleged sorcerer; for any diviner worth his 'fowl' gives
an answer acceptable to his client.[1] I shall return to this in a later
chapter.

A diviner's séance is usually conducted under conditions of great
secrecy, and the most effective way I could find of gaining first-hand
knowledge of it was to play the rôle of client. I have already given
accounts (Chapter 1 above) of the two occasions on which I consulted
diviners. Although these two cases are atypical because a White with
his special circumstances and social relationships was involved, they
nevertheless illustrate some of the basic principles at work. The client
comes to the diviner with a problem, about the solution of which he
has a number of unformulated ideas. By investigating his client's case
during the period between the initial consultation and the final séance,
and, during the séance, by skilfully drawing him into the conversation,
the diviner helps him to arrive at a satisfying conclusion (in terms of
Ceŵa belief), and may supply him with charms and other forms of
assistance that will help to relieve his anxiety. In the case of the Dancing Owls, the diviner, it will be remembered, ingeniously transposed
Ceŵa doctrine regarding the typical kinship of sorcerer and victim
from a matrilineal to a patrilineal mode. It is interesting to note, too,
that the second diviner, in the case of the Broken Windscreen, attributed our accident ultimately to a tense social relationship (that
between me and the people who wanted to buy the car).

To the Ceŵa the European ban on the poison ordeal or on any
other form of sorcerer-finding is quite incomprehensible. The majority
of informants believe that there are more sorcerers nowadays than
there used to be, and attribute this to the fact that the Europeans do not
allow them to make accusations of sorcery or to take any action
against sorcerers.

There is a popular myth about the sorcerer who was caught red-handed
and whose case eventually came before the District Commissioner. The D.C.
imprisoned the man whose sense of public duty had led him to report the
'crime'; and, turning to the sorcerer, he discharged him and presented him
with a bag of salt and a large knife, telling him to go back to the corpse he
had been eating. 'This is one of the reasons why the Europeans forbade the
poison ordeal; so that they could sell salt to people.' Another reason is that
'the Europeans are afraid of being detected themselves if the ordeal is used;
for they, too, are proprietors of sorcery just as they are of whisky'.

[1] Cf. Hunter (now Wilson), *Reaction to Conquest*, pp. 308–9.

An informant complains:

Long ago there were hardly any sorcerers, and you could not find the path
to the graveyard, but today it looks like a well-trodden road; and this is
because of the Europeans. If you catch a person killing his fellows with
'medicines', the Europeans ask, 'Did you see him killing?'; and, if you lack
words in reply, they set him free and arrest you. Or, if you find him eating
human flesh and take him to the Europeans, they say to you, 'If you find
dead game, do you not pick it up?'; and all they do is give the sorcerer a bag
of salt with which to eat his 'relish'.

The general attitude underlying these myths is probably of wide
currency in Northern Rhodesia. In 1947, a member of the African
Representative Council, speaking in English, disagreed with the
official doctrine that witchcraft does not exist, and reported that his
electors wanted him to tell the Council that African doctors, instead of
being tried by their District Commissioners, should be allowed to
detect witches and wizards.[1]

The 'African doctors' he referred to were probably followers of
Bwanali and Mpulumutsi whose anti-sorcery movement was then at its
height. The consequences of beliefs in sorcery that I have thus far
considered have been of a chronic nature. More acute forms occur
from time to time in movements directed against sorcery and witchcraft (the term depending on the tribe being considered) that sweep
across the country. As I shall argue in Chapter 9, the causes of tensions
expressed in these movements, and indeed in the beliefs in sorcery
underlying them, must be sought, not only in specific reactions to the
provisions of the Witchcraft Ordinance, but also in the general conditions of changed social life.

My present task is descriptive. Two of the movements have been
recorded,[2] that of the Mcape 'medicine' vendors, who were active in
the early 1930's, and that led by Bwanali and Mpulumutsi in 1947. Both
started in Nyasaland and spread to adjoining territories; and both
aimed at the complete removal of witchcraft and sorcery from the
country by the systematic destruction or reform of witches and sorcerers
and by the protection of their potential victims. Each had its dual-purpose 'medicine' for achieving these objectives. The Mcape 'medicine'
was a red solution of soapy appearance which was administered
orally. It was intended, firstly, to deter people from witchcraft

[1] Northern Rhodesia, *African Representative Council*, Debates, 18 July 1947.
[2] Richards, 'A Modern Movement of Witchfinders'; and Marwick, 'Another Anti-
Witchcraft Movement in East Central Africa'.

or sorcery by making them severely ill the moment they turned to it and by killing them if they persisted in it; and, secondly, to protect people from all possible attacks by witches and sorcerers. The 'medicine' of Bwanali and Mpulumutsi had similar aims but was administered through incisions in the skin. Both movements gave rise to widespread excitement and speculation regarding the disappearance of witchcraft and sorcery from the country; and both engendered a series of beliefs and rumours which *inter alia* attributed a Christ-like resurrection to the leaders, and predicted their 'second coming'.

Since 1947 other movements have occurred which are reminiscent of the two described. In October 1953, a Nyasaland Toŋga, known as Richard Bwanali (but apparently no relation of the other Bwanali, who was an Ŋgoni from the *circunscrição* of Angónia in the Tete *intendência* of Moçambique) was convicted in the High Court in Salisbury on four counts of culpable homicide and sentenced to four years' imprisonment. Evidence at his trial showed that he conducted ceremonies in a native reserve near Salisbury in which he administered 'medicines' orally to people standing in queues; that he encouraged confessions of witchcraft; and that he detected alleged witches by using a mirror (a practice of the Mcape vendors, some twenty years previously).[1]

During the first half of 1954, it was reported in the press that a number of instances had occurred in Sambawanga in south-east Tanganyika in which a person had suddenly appeared in a district, claiming that he had returned from the grave to become a 'Kamchape' who would smell out witches. This, with the aid of local 'unpopularity-scouts', he would proceed to do, and would be warmly accepted by a witch-ridden community. One of these witchfinders was found guilty on twelve counts of imputing witchcraft with intent to cause injury and misfortune, and was sentenced to three years' imprisonment and twelve cuts with a cane. In addition he was ordered to pay compensation to the witnesses for the prosecution.[2]

(d) Ceŵa Insight into Social Relationships Involved

Informants' statements show a clear recognition of the relationship between social tension and believed instances of sorcery. Such statements usually affirm that persons who have quarrelled 'practise sorcery

[1] *The Chronicle* (Bulawayo), 7 and 8 October 1953, and further information kindly placed at my disposal by the Secretary for Native Affairs, Southern Rhodesia.
[2] *The Central African Post* (Lusaka), 31 May 1954. I am grateful to Professor J. Clyde Mitchell for sending me information on this and the Richard Bwanali case.

against each other' (-lodʒana, lit. 'kill each other with sorcery'). Less often they assert that those who have quarrelled 'grasp [accuse] each other [of] sorcery' (-gwilana ufiti). Thus, the belief that sorcerers generally attack their matrikin is supported by a number of arguments that reveal considerable insight into the connection between believed instances of sorcery and strained social relationships. Similar insight is revealed by acknowledged exceptions to this central doctrine.

Ceŵa maintain that matrilineal relatives 'practise sorcery against each other' because they are unable to settle their quarrels by the ordinary judicial procedures available to unrelated persons who quarrel. Litigation is generally between one person supported by his matrikin and another supported by his.

If you try to take legal action against your 'sibling' [i.e. matrilineal relative], the court people [chief and assessors] just laugh at you, and you have to go home and settle your quarrel there.

This jural identification of matrilineage members appears to cause intra-matrilineage tensions to be relieved, not by catharsis and adjustment, but by suppression; and informants believe that the smouldering hatred resulting from suppression flares up in due course in the form of sorcery. They express this belief neatly when they assert that the hatred leading to sorcery is more common among matrikin because with them there is a tendency 'to leave [unspoken] words of speech with one another' (kusiana mau oyaŋkhula). The implication here is that, if there were some legitimate means of getting the angry words off their chests, there would be less danger that smouldering hatred would later lead to their 'practising sorcery against each other'. 'To keep words in the chest' (kusuŋga mau m'cifuwa) is regarded with an almost neo-Freudian disapproval.

Informants assert, however, that own siblings are tied by bonds of affection and loyalty and do not practise sorcery against each other. It is matrilateral parallel cousins (ortho-cousins, designated as 'siblings of different wombs'), they say, who are the ones who do. If 'sibling' is taken in its wider meaning of 'matrikinsman',[1] this is to say that persons belonging to different 'breasts', or matrilineage segments, are more prone to practise sorcery against each other than those who belong to the same segment.

The matrilineage is the natural arena for quarrels over succession to office and over the inheritance and disposal of property; and informants

[1] See below, Chapter 4.

link this with their assertion that sorcerers generally attack their matrikin. Referring to quarrels over office, one informant says:

Headmanship kills many people in this country of ours because, if you have succeeded to it, it isn't everybody that rejoices with you; others oppose you very much. . . . Sometimes the people of a family [*banja*, which in this context means 'matrilineage'] choose a junior child to be headman of it, if they see that his character is better than that of the senior 'brother' [which may include ortho-cousin]. Thus, when the junior brother succeeds to the headmanship, the senior one seeks 'medicines' that he may kill him and seize the headmanship.

Another informant makes a similar statement about quarrels over the inheritance of property:

If a person is rich, his younger relative or his elder relative kills him with sorcery so that he may take all his wealth (*cuma*) for himself.

A third informant makes a general statement which would apply to both office and property, and adds an interesting observation about the believed increase in the prevalence of sorcery since the Cewa acquired property. He says:

Of your brothers [i.e. matrikin] and your children, your brothers are the ones more likely to kill you with sorcery. Your children would not get any return (*phindu*) from doing so, but your brothers would get a return. Before people used to go to Southern Rhodesia and acquire property such as cattle, there was not much sorcery.

As I have hinted, Cewa recognize certain exceptions to their central doctrine that sorcerers attack only their own matrikin. The most important of these is the belief that the co-wives of a polygynist practise sorcery against each other or against their husband. An informant says:

Polygyny causes many deaths among women. If a man becomes a poly-gynist, he knows that, though he may survive for a long time, [one of his wives] will in the end kill him, or the wives will kill each other with sorcery. If the man loves one of his wives only—either the senior or the junior wife—the other one will procure 'medicines' and kill him or kill her co-wife and say, 'Now we are all even.' Sometimes she will kill her co-wife and say, 'Now my husband will have to love me only.'

This is a convenient point at which to record that Cewa assert that the majority of sorcerers are women. A sample of ten men and nine women (the same one referred to in ch. 3, p. 73) estimated on average that of twenty hypothetical sorcerers about fifteen, or seventy-five per cent, would be women (male informants' estimates averaged 14·9; and female informants' estimates, 14·7). As I shall show in the next subsection, this general statement is at variance with the sex ratio of my sample of alleged sorcerers.

Another exception to the belief that it is typically matrikin who practise sorcery against each other is the one that persons competing for the favours of a superior may do so. Ceŵa point out that, if a man has a quarrel with his employer or with his chief, he may attribute this to the sorcery of someone who is jealous of his relationship with this influential person. Those competing for the favours of a European or a chief are not necessarily related to one another.

Ceŵa believe sorcery to be on the increase. Although, as I have said, they attribute this to the European ban on ordeals and accusations of sorcery, they nevertheless seem to have considerable insight into the connection between accusations and some of the relationships that are typical of modern times. They believe that people who have become rich—and becoming rich is largely a modern phenomenon—are in constant danger of being attacked by sorcerers. As one of them put it:

Some people kill a fellow human being simply because of the jealousy [they feel] on seeing him possess good things. They do not feel well in their hearts, and they simply want to kill him, saying, 'He is very proud.'

I have already mentioned how, when a labour migrant returns from his place of work, he enters his home village under cover of darkness. This practice is attributed to his fearing the sorcery of his matrikin. According to African mores, he should be sharing his newly acquired wealth with them, and thus reinforcing matrilineage bonds; but his newly acquired attitudes impel him rather to the more universal norm of raising his own standard of living. The same applies to people who have become rich locally, e.g. from selling maize or vegetables or from running a village shop. Their preoccupation with fears of sorcery is, according to informants, reflected in their keen interest in acquiring strong protective medicines.

An important instance of how, in this manner, modern socioeconomic changes may have exacerbated social relationships that were probably already strained under indigenous conditions is to be found in conflicts arising from the ownership of cattle. Ceŵa assert that these conflicts are frequent causes of persons' practising sorcery against one another. The fact that Ceŵa have only recently acquired cattle seems to have accentuated the friction inherent in the relationship between men of the same matrilineage. What typically happens is that a labour migrant sends home some of his earnings to his mother's brother who invests them in cattle. When the migrant comes home—sometimes after many years' absence—quarrels often arise over the ownership of the cattle. Since both cattle and wage-earning are new elements in Ceŵa life, this situation has no indigenous precedents and no, or very few, customary solutions. In any case, cattle are a form of wealth, and, as I have just noted, Ceŵa consider the desire for wealth to be behind many misfortunes attributed to sorcery. It is not surprising that one informant summed up the causes of sorcery by saying, 'Cattle and polygyny finish people.'

(e) Theory and Practice

Thus far I have tried to give an inside view of Ceŵa beliefs in sorcery. My account has therefore been biased towards informants' general statements of opinion and has not yet included references to the characteristics of specific persons believed to be sorcerers. I shall now try to correct this bias by comparing theory with practice, or general statement with specific instance. For this purpose I shall turn to the case material introduced in Chapter 1, more particularly to the 101 cases shown at the foot of Table I in which sorcerers were believed to have attacked non-sorcerers.

Table VII shows for these cases the relationships, both social and spatial, between alleged sorcerer and believed victim. In some cases, more than one sorcerer or more than one victim were designated, with the result that the 101 cases provided 115 relationships. The figures in brackets take these 'multiple' cases fully into account; whereas those not in brackets include in respect of such cases only the first sorcerer or the first victim mentioned. As the percentage distributions vary only slightly with the two methods of counting, the figures in brackets will sometimes be disregarded in the tables and calculations that follow.

The material summarized in the table is consistent with the main Ceŵa doctrine that sorcerers tend to attack their matrikin; for nearly three-fifths of the cases are ones in which this is believed to have happened. Within the 'matrilineal' category, differences are generally too small for it to be possible to check some of the subsidiary beliefs, such as the one that it is commoner for classificatory than for own siblings to attack each other. However, if the broader categories into

TABLE VII

SOCIAL AND SPATIAL RELATIONSHIPS BETWEEN SORCERER AND VICTIM IN THE 101 CASES IN WHICH MISFORTUNES WERE ATTRIBUTED TO SORCERERS' ATTACKING NON-SORCERERS

Social Relationship	Spatial Relationship			Total	Percentage of 101 (115)* Cases
	Same Village	Different Villages or at Great Distance	Unknown		
Kinsmen:					
Matrilineal:					
Different segments	20 (22)*	7 (7)	5 (5)	32 (34)	31·7 (29·6)
Same segment	13 (17)	3 (3)	— (—)	16 (20)	15·8 (17·4)
Segment membership indeterminate	9 (9)	— (2)	2 (2)	11 (13)	10·9 (11·3)
Total matrilineal	42 (48)	10 (12)	7 (7)	59 (67)	58·4 (58·3)
Non-matrilineal:					
Involving a co-wife	— (1)	—	1 (1)	1 (2)	1·0 (1·7)
Spouses and father–child	7 (8)	—	—	7 (8)	6·9 (6·9)
Other affinal	11 (13)	—	—	11 (13)	10·9 (11·3)
Other non-matrilineal	9 (10)	3 (4)	—	12 (14)	11·9 (12·2)
Total non-matrilineal	27 (32)	3 (4)	1 (1)	31 (37)	30·7 (32·1)
Total kinsmen	69 (80)	13 (16)	8 (8)	90 (104)	89·1 (90·4)
Non-kinsmen	6 (6)	3 (3)	1 (1)	10 (10)	9·9 (8·7)
Victim not specified	1 (1)	—	—	1 (1)	1·0 (0·9)
Total	76 (87)	16 (19)	9 (9)	101 (115)	100·0 (100·0)

* In some cases more than one sorcerer or more than one victim were designated. The figures in brackets take these 'multiple' cases fully into account; whereas those not in brackets include in respect of such cases only the first sorcerer or the first victim mentioned.

which classificatory and own brothers fall are compared, the proportion of believed attacks between members of different matrilineage segments[1] is about twice the proportion of those between members of the same segment (thirty-two and sixteen per cent respectively). The magnitude of this difference must, of course, in part be attributed to the greater frequency with which Ceŵa villagers fall into the first relationship category rather than the second, i.e. to the larger universe of interaction that exists between persons belonging to different matrilineage segments and therefore the greater probability of their being associated in believed instances of sorcery. This reservation, incidentally, applies to all the conclusions based on tables, such as this one, which present unstandardized proportions rather than comparable rates; but a discussion of the problem that necessitates the reservation will be postponed to the next chapter where its effects are of greater consequence. Table VIII, though presented for another reason, to which I shall return presently, confirms the Ceŵa contention that the matrilineage is the natural arena for quarrels over succession to office and over the inheritance and disposal of property, especially cattle.

I noted above that Ceŵa recognize certain exceptions to their central doctrine that sorcerers confine their attacks to their own matrikin. The first of these is that the co-wives of a polygynist tend to practise sorcery against each other or against their husband. This subsidiary doctrine is not reflected prominently in Table VII, where cases related to polygyny amount to only one per cent of the total. However, a fuller analysis of this finding will be attempted in Chapter ·5, in the context of Ceŵa marriage.

The second exception, that unrelated persons competing with each other for the favour of a chief or an employer tend to practise sorcery against each other, is reflected in ten per cent of the cases, in which the sorcerer and victim were unrelated. The implication that, in such cases, sorcery breaks its usual bounds because of intense rivalry is largely sustained, and will be given further attention in Chapter 7. It is sufficient to note here that, of the ten cases we are considering, only one was not preceded by a quarrel, and the remaining nine were preceded by quarrels about love (five cases) or politics (two cases) or unspecified issues (two cases). The statistics derived from summarizing the case material showed no significant association between relationship of sorcerer to victim and whether a quarrel had preceded the believed attack. There was, however, as Table VIII shows, an associa-

---

[1] For a description of lineage-segmentation, see below, Chapter 4.

TABLE VIII

ASSOCIATION BETWEEN TYPE OF QUARREL (IF ANY) AND WHETHER OR NOT SORCERER AND VICTIM WERE MATRILINEALLY RELATED

| Attack Believed to be Linked with: | Relationship between Sorcerer and Victim | | |
	Matrilineal	Not Matrilineal	Total
Quarrel over:			
Social obligations, cattle and other property	24	8	32
Other issues, including sexual jealousy and politics	17	23	40
No quarrel	18	10	28
	59	41	100
Sorcerer not identified			1
			101

Significance of association	$\chi^2 = 8.211$; $.02 > p > .01$

tion, at between the one and two per cent levels of probability,[1] between type of quarrel and whether the sorcerer and his victim were related matrilineally or not. Quarrels preceding attacks between matrikinsmen tended to be connected with social obligations and the disposal of property, especially cattle, whereas those preceding attacks between persons not matrilineally related tended to arise from other issues, notably sexual jealousy and political rivalry.

Before leaving the question how the relationship of sorcerer to victim is associated with the type of quarrel, if any, that preceded the sorcerer's believed attack, I shall take advantage of the opportunity of checking certain Ceŵa beliefs about the distinction between the 'killer-for-malice' (*mphelanjilu*) and the 'witch' (*nfiti yeni-yeni*). In many of the 101 cases, the informant stated whether he considered the sorcerer fell into one or other of these categories. In most others, where the informant had not been explicit and I had not specifically asked his opinion, it was possible to judge into which category the sorcerer would have been placed. For instance, if his motive was given as 'flesh

[1] This means that the distribution shown in the table could result from chance between once and twice in a hundred times. A probability of one in twenty ($p = .05$) is widely accepted as the upper limit of safety in tests of significance (cf. Hagood, *Statistics for Sociologists*, pp. 449–50). In subsequent interpretations of statistical data I follow the widely observed convention (see, for instance, Hagood, *loc. cit.*) of using the expression 'moderately significant' when p lies between .05 and .01; 'highly significant' when p lies between .01 and .001; and 'extremely significant' when p is less than .001.

hunger' (ŋkhuli), or if it was stated that he had acted from addiction to sorcery rather than from hatred or a desire for revenge, it could be assumed that he would have been classified as a 'witch'. In eleven cases it was not possible to determine in which category he would have been placed.

This classification revealed two statistically significant associations. Firstly, as might be expected from the definition of the two categories, there was an extremely significant tendency, in the beliefs reflected in the data, for killers-for-malice to have been involved proportionately more often in quarrels than was the case with 'witches' (see the first part of Table IX). This finding supports the hypothesis that, where it is difficult to find persons with whom the victim may have quarrelled, there is a tendency for those with a long-standing addiction to sorcery, rather than with a strong specific motive, to be blamed for his misfortune.

Secondly, killers-for-malice have a higher masculinity ratio than witches, the difference being moderately significant (see the second part of Table IX). This finding has a bearing on the question of the

TABLE IX

TYPES OF SORCERERS DISTRIBUTED (1) BY WHETHER OR NOT A QUARREL PRECEDED THE BELIEVED ATTACK AND (2) BY SEX

Classification of Sorcerer	(1) Attack Preceded by			(2) Sex		
	A Quarrel	No Quarrel	Total	Male	Female	Total
Killer-for-malice (mphelanjilu)	64	1	65	43	21	64
Witch (nfiti yeni-yeni)	6	19	25	11	14	25
Uncertain	2	8	10	4	7	11
	72	28	100	58	42	100
Sorcerer not identified			1			1
			101			101

Significance of
association $\chi^2 = 6.343$; $.05 > p > .02$ $\chi^2 = 64.560$; $p < .001$

translation of nfiti, discussed above. Taken together with the fact that Cewa say that nfiti (unqualified) are more often women than men, it may mean that, when they say this, they may have the specific category of 'real nfiti', which I translate as 'witches', in mind; and in this case their witches resemble those of other societies in being typically, though by no means exclusively, female.

If, however, they do not have *nfiti ʒeni-ʒeni* specifically in mind, but are referring to *nfiti* generically, the case material is not consistent with the assertion that the majority of *nfiti*, which in this context I translate as 'sorcerers', are women. Table X shows the distribution by sex and age (the latter in four broad categories) of the 101 sorcerers we are considering. Nearly three-fifths are men; and slightly over two-fifths, women. Though these proportions do not differ significantly from the normal proportion, taken as ·50, they show a trend opposite to that postulated by informants, and might well differ significantly from the actual proportion (lower than ·50 because of labour migration), if a suitable estimate of it could be made.

TABLE X

SORCERERS BY AGE AND SEX

Age Category	Male	Female	Sex Unknown	Total
Child	—	—	—	—
Adolescent	1	—	—	1
Adult	43	22	—	65
Old	14	20	—	34
Unknown	—	—	1	1
Total	58	42	1	101
Sex proportion	·57	·42	·01	1·00

Significance of difference of sex proportions from ·50:
Males: CR = 1·06; p = ·29.
Females: CR = 1·20; p = ·23.

TABLE XI

VICTIMS BY AGE AND SEX

Age Category	Male	Female	Sex Unknown	Total
Child	4	7	5	16
Adolescent	6	5	—	11
Adult	36	24	1	61
Old	11	1	—	12
Unknown	—	—	1	1
Total	57	37	7	101
Sex proportion	·56	·37	·07	1·00

Significance of difference of sex proportion from ·50:
Males: CR = 0·91; p = ·36.
Females: CR = 1·91; p = ·06.

As to age, about two-thirds are mature people; and about one-third, old. Table XI gives similar details for the victims in the sample. Here, too, though the lower-age categories are better represented, the highest frequencies are for mature people and for males. Taken together, these two tables support the hypothesis that those believed to be involved in sorcery, either as sorcerers or as victims, tend to belong to the more socially active segments of the population, a finding which is important in a study that seeks the social functions of beliefs in sorcery. It must be noted, however, that, since it is difficult to set up norms with which to compare the observed age distributions, the statistical foundation for this proposition is not as firm as it should be.

This reservation applies also to the following two tables. Table XII indicates that, in a small minority of cases (nine in ninety-nine), the believed sorcerer was younger than his victim. In the others he was believed to be either in the same age category as his victim (forty-nine) or in a senior category (forty-one). Table XIII, which shows the relative generations of those sorcerers and victims related to one another, shows a similar belief that sorcery is more often directed towards juniors (forty-two cases out of eighty-nine) and equals (thirty-four) than towards seniors (thirteen).

Reference back to Table VII reveals one type of relationship between

TABLE XII

RELATIVE AGES OF SORCERERS AND THEIR VICTIMS

Age Category of Victim	Age Category of Sorcerer					Total
	Child	Adolescent	Adult	Old	Unknown	
Child	—	—	7	9	—	16
Adolescent	—	—	4	6	1	11
Adult	—	1	45	15	—	61
Old	—	—	8	4	—	12
Unknown	—	—	1	—	—	1
Total	—	1	65	34	1	101

Analysis

Sorcerer and victim in the same age category	49
Sorcerer older than his victim	41
Sorcerer younger than his victim	9
Age relationship unknown	2
	101

TABLE XIII

RELATIVE GENERATIONS OF RELATED SORCERERS AND THEIR
VICTIMS IN THREE KINSHIP CATEGORIES

Kinship Category	Sorcerer and Victim in Same Generation	Sorcerer in Senior Generation	Sorcerer in Junior Generation	Total
Belonging to different matrilineage-segments	9	20	2	31
Other matrilineal relatives	9	12	5	26
Non-matrilineal relatives	16	10	6	32
	34	42	13	89

Victim unknown	1
Sorcerer unknown	1
Sorcerer and victim unrelated	10
	101

sorcerer and victim which informants hardly mentioned at all, but which is represented by eleven per cent of the 101 cases. This is the relationship between affines (other than spouses). Prior to collecting my case material, I had heard of only one instance of a sorcerer's being believed to have attacked an affine; and this case, having been exposed by Mpulumutsi, one of the leaders of the 'anti-witchcraft' movement of 1947,[1] seemed to have been quoted as something so unusual as to be incredible—as a tribute to Mpulumutsi's great powers of detection.

The third character in any sorcery drama, the accuser, is of great sociological importance.[2] While from the investigator's point of view the relationship between sorcerer and victim is an imaginary one, that between accuser and sorcerer is a real, observable one, and so, for that matter, is the affiliative relationship between accuser and victim. Sorcerer–victim relationships may thus be regarded as representing peoples' estimates of interpersonal tensions; and accuser–sorcerer relationships, as actual expressions of them.

With this difference in mind, I now turn to some of the character-

[1] Cf. Marwick, 'Another Modern Anti-Witchcraft Movement in East Central Africa', p. 104.
[2] Again I have to thank Professor Mitchell for impressing this on me.

istics of accusers. As I mentioned in Chapter 1, in only seventy-nine of the 101 cases were accusers identified. The more obvious definition of an accuser as the person who accused someone else of sorcery is not wide enough for the purposes of sociological analysis, and I have included the person who carried out investigations, such as consulting a diviner or arranging a poison ordeal, that led to the identification of the sorcerer. This wider definition is based on the assumption that 'any diviner worth his fowl gives an answer that his client finds acceptable'. It makes possible the rather incongruous category of 'self-accusation' into which two cases fall. In this type of case, the diviner, perhaps through being unable to unravel a client's tangled social relationships and knowing him to have the reputation of being addicted to sorcery, accused the client himself of being the sorcerer. In twelve of the seventy-nine cases, the victim—sometimes on his death-bed—was himself the accuser.

Table XIV shows the distribution by age and sex of the seventy-nine accusers (the first named in those cases in which more than one were designated). Table XV indicates the steps, if any, that they took

TABLE XIV

ACCUSERS BY AGE AND SEX AND COMPARISON OF THEIR SEX
PROPORTION WITH THOSE OF SORCERERS AND OF VICTIMS

Age Category	Male	Female	Sex Unknown	Total
Child	—	—	—	—
Adolescent	1	—	—	1
Adult	48	16	—	64
Old	8	5	—	13
Unknown	—	—	1	1
	57	21	1	79
'Self-accusations' (as defined in text)				2
Accuser unknown, e.g. sorcerer designated by diffuse gossip				20
Total				101
Sex proportion	·72	·27	·01	1·00

Significance of difference of sex proportions from ·50:
   Males: $CR = 3·16$; $p = ·0016$.
   Females: $CR = 3·35$; $p = ·0008$.

Comparison of the sex proportions of:
(a) Accusers and Sorcerers (cf. Table X)

	Accusers		Sorcerers		Difference (%)	CR	p
	f	%	f	%			
Male	57	72·1	58	57·4	+14·7	2·04	·04
Female	21	26·6	42	41·6	−15·0	2·09	·04
Unknown	1	1·3	1	1·0	+ 0·3	—	—
	79	100·0	101	100·0	0·0	—	—

(b) Accusers and Victims (cf. Table XI)

	Accusers		Victims		Difference (%)	CR	p
	f	%	f	%			
Male	57	72·1	57	56·5	+15·6	2·16	·03
Female	21	26·6	37	36·6	−10·0	1·42	·16
Unknown	1	1·3	7	6·9	− 5·6	—	—
	79	100·0	101	100·0	0·0		

to establish the identity of the sorcerer. Accusers, like sorcerers and victims (Tables X and XI), tend to fall into the 'adult' age category and include a higher proportion of men than of women to a degree of significance at about the level of $p = ·001$. Again they tend to represent the socially active members of Ceŵa society. To a moderately significant degree in three out of four categories tested, accusers include a higher proportion of males than do either sorcerers or victims (see foot of Table XIV). Table XV shows the importance of diviners in the detection of sorcerers and the relative unimportance of other means. This is interesting when considered against the fact that, in all the texts on divining that I collected, the traditional function of the diviner was portrayed as that of ascertaining the wishes of the spirits. It would appear that, with the suppression of the poison ordeal, other

TABLE XV

INVESTIGATIONS MADE OR OTHER GROUNDS OF ALLEGATION IN THOSE CASES IN WHICH ACCUSERS WERE DESIGNATED

	f	%
Diviner consulted	33	41·77
No steps taken (no reason given for inaction)	16	20·25
No steps taken because identity of sorcerer was considered obvious	9	11·39
Poison ordeal	7	8·86
Questioning by village headman	5	6·33
Questioning by others	5	6·33
Sorcerer identified by grave-watcher	4	5·06
	79	100·0

I

types of divining have taken its place as the main means of detecting sorcerers.

Though Ceŵa more commonly assert that persons who have quarrelled 'practise sorcery against each other', they sometimes speak of their grasping, i.e. accusing, each other of sorcery; and to test such general statements against case-material it is necessary to turn to the relationships between accuser and alleged sorcerer. The percentage distribution of all such relationships, i.e. with full counting of 'multiple' cases, is given in the second column of Table XVII. About half of the recorded accusations (following the definition noted) were between persons matrilineally related; about two-fifths, between persons related but not matrilineally; and about nine per cent, between unrelated persons.

These results will be analysed in more detail in their appropriate social contexts, to the exploration of which I shall now turn. The aim of the present chapter has been to facilitate such an exploration by making the reader familiar with the nature of Ceŵa beliefs in the form of both general statements and the explanation of specific instances of misfortune.

PART II

The Contexts of Ceŵa Sorcery

CHAPTER 4

THE MATRILINEAGE FROM WITHIN

THE aim of the last two chapters has been to describe who the Cewa
are, where they live, how they subsist, how the events of the past have
conditioned their present attitudes, and what form their beliefs take
when they seek explanations of misfortunes. I shall now start a systematic exploration of Cewa social structure, and, as I proceed, illustrate
the functions of Cewa beliefs in sorcery by presenting cases of believed
instances in their appropriate contexts.

I have several times referred to the dogma that, in theory, limits the
operation of sorcery to the matrilineage. Because this proposition is an
important one, it will be appropriate to start by examining the Cewa
kinship system and the framework it provides for local organization.

Residence and Kinship

A fundamental social group among the Cewa is the matrilineage.[1]
I may demonstrate this fact by examining, firstly, the social composition of the Cewa residential group, and, secondly, the patterns of
prescribed behaviour among kinsmen. I propose therefore to enter one
of the villages of which in Chapter 2 I gave glimpses from the road,
and see who lives there.

For this purpose I have chosen Jeremiah village, not only because I
know it well, having many times enjoyed its hospitality, but also
because my investigations elsewhere have shown that its social composition is typical of villages in Kawaza's chiefdom. Its size, however,
is larger than average. In 1952 there were 203 people domiciled in it
(but only 183 present at the end of the year, when I made my census)
at a time when the average *de jure* population of the 132 villages in the
section of the chiefdom falling within the Reserve was 122.[2]

Jeremiah village is situated on a flat-topped ridge running roughly

---

[1] For convenience I use 'matrilineage' for what, strictly speaking, should be called a
'matrilineage remnant' (adapting the terminology of Wilson *et al.*, *Social Structure*, p. 47).
I use 'matrilineage fragment' for a group too small to be regarded as the portion remaining
behind when the others dispersed.
[2] Northern Rhodesia, *Eastern Province*, Chadiza Tour Report No. 2 of 1952, on file at
Fort Jameson. These figures refer to 'administrative villages' (see below, this chapter).

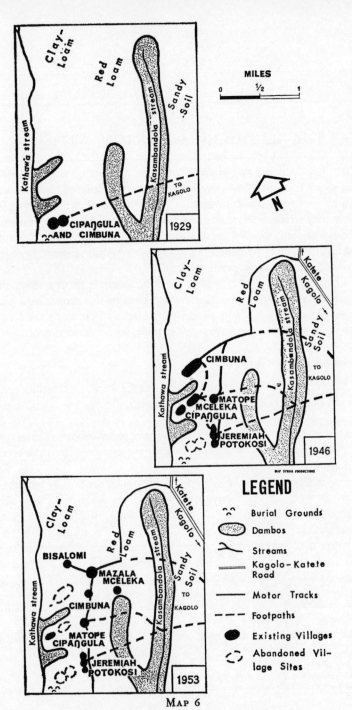

MILES

0 ½ 1

1929

Clay-Loam

Red Loam

Sandy-Soil

Kathawa stream

Kasambandola stream

TO KAGOLO

CIPAŊGULA AND CIMBUNA

N

1946

Clay-Loam

Red Loam

Sandy Soil

Kathawa stream

Kasambandola stream

Kagolo - Katete

CIMBUNA

TO KAGOLO

MATOPE
MCELEKA
CIPAŊGULA

JEREMIAH
POTOKOSI

MAP STUDIO PRODUCTIONS

1953

Clay-Loam

Red Loam

Sandy Soil

Kathawa stream

Kasambandola stream

Kagolo - Katete

BISALOMI

MAZALA
MCELEKA

TO KAGOLO

CIMBUNA

MATOPE
CIPAŊGULA

JEREMIAH
POTOKOSI

LEGEND

Burial Grounds

Dambos

Streams

Kagolo-Katete Road

Motor Tracks

Footpaths

Existing Villages

Abandoned Village Sites

MAP 6
Development of the Cimbuna neighbourhood, 1929–53

north and south between the Kathawa and Kasambandola streams, both of which are tributaries of the Mzime, which flows into the Kapoche (see Maps 5 and 6). It lies west of Chief Kaŵaza's capital at Kagolo, just over a mile by bush path, but longer by the motor track round the head of the Kasambandola stream. From the shade of its spreading trees, three land-marks are visible and help to stave off the feeling of oppressive isolation that sometimes descends on one in the flatter parts of the Rhodesian bush. The Mpaŋgwe hills to the north remind one of the proximity of the Great East Road, the link with the outside world. Nchiŋgalizya hill, to the south-west across the Mzime and the Kapoche, takes one back to the days of the Ŋgoni invasion when it was the refuge of the Chief Kathumba of the day. And the compact bulk of Milanzi to the south-east, beyond Kagolo, locates Kaŵaza's traditional capital on the lower Katete.

A *dambo* lying a quarter of a mile to the east provides the village with its water supply and much of its grazing. The gardens spread in all directions from the village, but especially to the north, along the Kagolo–Katete road, where there is a belt of rich red loam which changes westwards towards the Kathawa into an equally fertile black soil. Nearer the village, on the south-western slope of the ridge, is the old site of Cimbuna village from which Jeremiah village was derived; and, beyond it, the burial ground that has served this and the neighbouring villages of Matope, Cimbuna, Mceleka, Mazala and Bisalomi ever since 1929, when, having been displaced from land that is now a European tobacco estate, they came to this locality from near the Katuule stream about seventeen miles to the east.

They came as a single large village called Cimbuna, and joined Cipaŋgula village which, six years previously, had established itself on what is now referred to as 'the ruins' (*matoŋgwe*, *mainja*). Whereas Cipaŋgula has greatly decreased in size, Cimbuna has expanded and split into the six villages that have been mentioned. Increase in population is one of the factors in the emergence of the new villages. I have no information about the size of Cimbuna when it was established at 'the ruins' in 1929, but the Administration's estimates[1] show that, between then and 1951, the population of the Northern Rhodesian Ceŵa as a whole has increased by sixty-eight per cent. Judging by local soil fertility, higher stock-ownership rates (see Table V) and the

---

[1] Northern Rhodesia, *Report on Native Affairs for the Year 1929*, Livingstone: Government Printer; Northern Rhodesia, *Eastern Province*, Annual Report on Native Affairs, 1951, on file at Fort Jameson.

presence of many recent immigrants from Portuguese territory, there is reason to suppose that the local human population has increased by at least as much as that of the tribe as a whole.

Though population increase may be the ultimate cause of village fragmentation, the more immediate one—and the one of which people are more aware—is social tension. Barely two years after Cimbuna had been established in the neighbourhood, an accusation of sorcery led to the expulsion of one of its sections (the name of which I deliberately omit). This section was too small to satisfy the Administration's rule regarding the minimum size of a village,[1] and it was joined by five other sections, whose members, none of them tied to Headman Cimbuna by kinship, were glad of the opportunity of a change. The largest of these was that of Jeremiah, who, with the consent of Chief Kaŵaza Soŋgani, became headman of this assorted band.

I shall return in the next chapter to the relationships between village sections. It is sufficient to say here that what brought together the ones that founded Jeremiah village in the early 1930's was not kinship but expediency. Jeremiah's and Jombo's matrilineages were both of the Phili matriclan, and therefore referred to one another by sibling terms and their extensions. Jombo, in turn, was the cross-cousin of Kabvinde. But the other three section-leaders, Matope, Kaŋkhanoŋgo and Cimseleti, were related neither to one another nor to the first three.

Since it was founded, Jeremiah village has changed in composition by both losses and gains. The headman of one of its six sections was suspected of sorcery, and, when he died, people believed that their vengeance magic had at last found its mark. After his death, his matrilineage left for another village, though his widow stayed on because, having been captured by her husband far away in Portuguese territory, she had no nearby relatives to turn to, and her daughter had married into a neighbouring village section. Later, another matrilineage was disrupted by a quarrel involving mutual accusations of sorcery, and one faction moved elsewhere, leaving the other one in the charge of an old woman, Mniŋga. A third section rejoined Cimbuna village—for

[1] The Administration has at various times stipulated the minimum size of villages. In the days of the British South Africa Company, it was from twenty to thirty huts in 1908 and forty huts in 1912–13 (Northern Rhodesia, *East Luangwa District*, District Note Book, and Annual Report, 1912–13, both kept at Fort Jameson). By the time the Colonial Office took over in 1924, it had been fixed at fifteen taxpayers, and was later reduced to ten taxpayers, which is the minimum now applied by the Native Authority (information supplied verbally by the Native Courts Adviser, Lusaka, November 1952). It is not clear whether the fifteen- or the ten-taxpayer rule was operative at the time I am referring to.

reasons I failed to ascertain. Finally, in 1945, Matope hived off from Jeremiah after a quarrel arising from the fact that, in a detail of village administration, Jeremiah had dealt with members of Matope's section without due reference to him as their section headman. Matope succeeded in having his village registered as independent, and built on a lower part of the ridge about a quarter of a mile to the north (Map 6).

Of the gains, the numerically larger one was Potokosi's section, which came from Portuguese territory. Potokosi claimed to be Jeremiah's mother's brother; though my investigations showed this to be nothing more than a putative relationship. Not without foundation, Jeremiah suspected him of being after his village headmanship, and it was only the formality expected between mother's brother and sister's son that prevented an open breach between them. Potokosi retained a measure of independence by building what was virtually a separate village just to the south of Jeremiah's (see Map 6 and Fig. 3). He tried without success to 'have his own book', i.e. to be registered as a separate village. His case illustrates the distinction, which Mitchell makes for the Yao,[1] between an 'administrative' village and a discrete cluster of huts that people recognize as a village. From the viewpoint of Chief Kaŵaza, and more so from that of the District Commissioner, Potokosi's section comprises a part of Jeremiah village; whereas in fact it is functionally separate, though not entirely independent. The same applies to the now depleted Cipaŋgula village, which, though having a separate site and a virtually independent headman, is 'written with' Mceleka village, one of the derivatives of Cimbuna, because its size has fallen below the limit set by the ten-taxpayer rule.

The smaller of the gains was the matrilineage-fragment of Mwaiŋga, a woman related to Jeremiah, though not matrilineally. Having no male head, this group settled at the northern end of the village, close to Jeremiah's section (see Fig. 3).

While Jeremiah village was sustaining these losses and gains, the people remaining on the old site were regrouping (Map 6). In 1938, Cipaŋgula moved about half a mile to the north. The following year, when the Administration suggested in the interests of health that the old site should be abandoned altogether, Mceleka, the leader of a senior segment of the matrilineage to which Headman Cimbuna belonged, having been disappointed at the Chief's not recognizing him as headman of the village, led his followers away to form a new village just east of Cipaŋgula. It was soon after this that Cipaŋgula,

[1] Mitchell, *The Yao Village*, pp. 3 and 84 ff.

now containing only six taxpayers, was absorbed administratively by Mceleka. At the same time Cimbuna abandoned the old site, which, by the time of my arrival in 1946, had become a flourishing maize garden, and settled a stone's throw from Mceleka on a spur pointing towards the Kathawa. By the end of 1952, both Cimbuna and Mceleka had moved again. Mceleka found a new site north-east of Matope; and Cimbuna split into three groups all of which moved to new sites. Cimbuna built north of Matope; Mazala, the leader of a section unrelated to Cimbuna, moved about a quarter of a mile to the north; and Bisalomi, a cross-cousin of Cimbuna III and IV, settled north-west of Mazala. I shall return to some of these villages when I discuss lineage segmentation (see below, this chapter).

From what I have related about Jeremiah village, it is apparent that kinship does not necessarily play a part in linking sections together. For this reason, if the relationship between kinship and residence is to be examined, attention must be focused on a single village section rather than on a whole village or a neighbourhood of villages such as I have been exploring. I shall take the senior section of Jeremiah village, that of the headman, as it was at the time of my third field-trip (1952–3). Its genealogy (Fig. 3) shows that it comprises:

1. *A Matrilineal Core*, consisting of the following matrikinsfolk of the recently deceased headman, Jeremiah[1] (Generation C, No. 14):—

   (a) his mother's mother's sister's son (classificatory mother's brother), Kabuula (B.10);

   (b) his four living sisters, Loda (C.6), Tungase (C.8), Lowase (C.18) and Mlelamanja (C.21);

   (c) his younger own brother, Develiase (C.23), who is acting headman, and his two classificatory brothers (both mother's mother's sister's daughters' sons), Kenala (C.35) and Galantia (C.37), both of whom are away at work;

   (d) his sisters' children, including those of his late sister, Mailesi (C.32)—all of whom are in Generation D;

   (e) his sisters' daughters' children, only one of whom, Violeti (E.16), is married (all in Generation E); and

   (f) his sister's daughter's daughter's daughter, Ailesi (F.1).

2. *The Spouses of Matrilineage Members:* there are six wives and ten husbands of matrilineage members domiciled in the village, though some of them, e.g. Kenala's wife, Zelesi (C.34), and Violeti's husband, Makadani (E.15), are away at work.

[1] For convenience, in reference to genealogies, I drop the honorific plural indicated elsewhere by a separated capital 'A' (cf. p. 45).

3. *The Children of Male Matrilineage Members*, who belong to the respective matrilineages of their mothers, e.g. Jeremiah's daughter, Ezelia (E.26), and the two children of his sister's son, Yelesani (E.22) and Esita (E.23).

4. *Others*, such as Ezelia's husband, Simon (E.27), and the daughter's daughter, Besi (D.33), of Kabuula's wife, Msalota (B.9) (the issue of her first marriage).

This genealogy illustrates most of the outstanding features of the kinship structure of the Ceŵa residential group. Firstly, as to general composition, the matrilineage forming the core of the section group consists of the headman, who is married virilocally, and his sisters, who are married uxorilocally, together with the uterine descendants of the latter. Table XVI shows that this core makes up nearly sixty

TABLE XVI

SUMMARY OF THE SOCIAL COMPOSITION OF THE HEADMAN'S SECTION OF JEREMIAH VILLAGE, JANUARY 1953 (EXCLUDING MWAIŊGA'S SECTION)

Relationship to (Deceased) Headman and Sex		Domiciled and Present		Domiciled and Absent		Total Domi- ciled	Per- cent- age
		Un- mar- ried	Mar- ried	Un- mar- ried	Mar- ried		
Headman's Matrilineage:							
1st ascending generation	male	—	1	—	—	1	1·54
Contemporary gen.	male	—	1	—	2	3	4·62
Contemporary gen.	female	—	4*	—	—	4	6·15
1st descending gen.	male	4	—	4	1	9	13·85
1st descending gen.	female	3	5†	—	2	10	15·38
2nd descending gen.	male	4	—	—	—	4	6·15
2nd descending gen.	female	5	1	—	—	6	9·23
3rd descending gen.	female	1	—	—	—	1	1·54
Total		17	12	4	5	38	58·46
Others:							
Spouses of matrilineage members	male	—	7	—	3	10	15·38
	female	—	5*	—	1	6	9·23
Children of male matrilineage members	male	3	—	1	—	4	6·15
	female	1	1	—	—	2	3·08
	unknown	—	—	1	—	1	1·54
Others—see text for examples	male	1	1	—	—	2	3·08
	female	2	—	—	—	2	3·08
Total for Section		24	26	6	9	65	100·00

* This figure includes one widowed person.
† This figure includes one divorced person.
Source: Fig. 3.

per cent of the members of the section. This general pattern is repeated in Cimseleti's section and in Tenje's (from Matope village) (see Appendix A, Nos. 4 and 1 respectively). Sometimes it is modified by a larger-than-usual proportion of virilocal marriages. This occurs in Headman Matope's section, of which an abridged genealogy is given in Appendix A, No. 2, and in Potokosi's (Appendix A, No. 5); but the latter is further complicated by the intertwining of long-associated matrilineages and the effects of having recently migrated from Portuguese territory, where fragments of the section have been left behind.

Secondly, as to succession, it should be noted that the line of headmen of this matrilineage is: Kabuula I (A.3), Mgwinda (B.2), Ziyambe (B.4) and Jeremiah (C.14). After Jeremiah's death in 1952, Develiase (C.23) acted as headman, but Ciŋgaipe (D.26), then away at work, was regarded as the most likely permanent successor. This illustrates both the general form and the elasticity of Ceŵa succession. The general rules are that a man is succeeded by his younger own brothers and then by the eldest son of his eldest own sister; and that, as the matrilineage expands and differentiates, the headmanship should remain in the senior segment (*bele lalikulu*, 'big breast'), i.e. the group comprising the descendants of the eldest sister in every generation remembered. Thus Kabuula II (B.10) has been passed over because, as the son of a younger sister of Kabuula I, he belongs to a junior segment (*bele laliŋono*, 'little breast'). The elasticity with which Ceŵa apply these rules springs from their appreciation of the fact that headmanship demands personal qualities not found in every candidate. Thus Ciŋgaipe (D.26) on personal grounds is looked upon as a better candidate than either of Loda's sons (D.13 and D.14), and he may succeed in spite of his belonging to a junior segment of the matrilineage. There is an element of dramatic irony in the fact that the formula for rejoicing at the birth of a boy is 'A headman is born!' (*Kwabadwa nfumu!*); for every boy is a potential headman. As I shall show later, the uncertainty, in succession issues, created by the weight Ceŵa attach to 'character' (*makalidwe*) is an important source of accusations of sorcery; for, in a society with a well-developed system of beliefs in sorcery, calling a rival candidate a sorcerer is perhaps the most effective way of blackening his character and eliminating his competition.

This genealogy is atypical in regard to one aspect of succession. Each of the succeeding headmen has not inherited his predecessor's name; and one of the names, Kabuula, has been given to a man who, as I have shown, has been passed over. Usually the headman takes his predecessor's name, which thus becomes perpetual.

The third feature illustrated by this genealogy is the intertwining of matrilineages that have been associated in adjoining village sections over many years. The matrilineage fragment now presided over by Tasokalelo (C.19) has provided spouses for Kuliale I (B.7), Loda (C.6), Jeremiah (C.14), Lowase (C.18), Develiase (C.23), Mlelamanja (C.21) and Solopia II (D.17). Similar intertwining may be expected between Jeremiah's matrilineage and those in adjoining sections if they continue to live in the same village; for its beginnings are to be seen in the second marriage of Mlelamanja (C.21) to Obistala of Cimseleti's and of the sixth marriage of Develiase (C.23) to Sodonia of Mniŋga's. An advanced and complicated phase of this process is, as I have noted, illustrated by the genealogy of Potokosi's section (Appendix A, No. 5).

Although this intertwining is intricate, it is not, in one sense, inextricable. This is because of a fourth feature of the Cewa system of kinship and marriage, viz. a high divorce rate. In addition to Develiase's four divorces and one separation (C.23–8), there are other instances shown on the genealogy, e.g. those of Serenia (D.50) and Ezelia (E.26); and some have been omitted because, not being material to either the kinship links shown or the social composition of the section, they would have complicated it unnecessarily. Some of (though not all) these divorces may be attributed to modern conditions. For instance, Ezelia (E.26) divorced Vinileŋkoni when, by long absence in Southern Rhodesia, he became regarded as a 'lost one' (mcona).[1]

A fifth feature of Cewa kinship that is illustrated by this genealogy is a decline in the frequency of marriages between persons and their cross-cousins or their cross-cousins' children. In Generation C, both Loda (C.6) and Lowase (C.18) married their father's sisters' sons. Develiase (C.23) married his father's sister's daughter. Jeremiah (C.14) married his father's sister's daughter's daughter (patrilateral cross-cousin's daughter), Emelia (D.32); and Mlelamanja (C.21) married her father's sister's son. These five marriages make up a considerable proportion of those involving locally domiciled matrilineage members of Generation C. In the next generation, only one marriage, that of Solopia II (D.17), to her mother's father's sister's daughter's son (son of mother's patrilateral cross-cousin), belongs to the type I am

---

[1] Probably from the Zulu *ukushona*, 'to descend, to set (of the sun)', sometimes a euphemism for 'to die'. There are many Zulu words in the *Fanakalo* (Kitchen-Kaffir) that Cewa learn at the distant labour centres (see Chapter 1).

considering. It is worth noting that, of the six cross-cousin marriages mentioned, four were, from the bridegroom's point of view, matrilateral; and two, patrilateral. One cannot, of course, present this as evidence for, rather than in illustration of, either the slight predominance, from the viewpoint of the male Ego, of matrilateral over patrilateral cross-cousin marriage or the decline in the frequency of marriages between cross-cousins and relatives of similar type. There is, however, some other support, albeit slight, for the two trends illustrated. As I shall try to show, there is some evidence from kinship terminology to suggest that matrilateral cross-cousin marriage is the more common type; and informants' statements give the impression that the appeal of cross-cousin marriage in general is declining, one of them going so far as to state:

In these days, young people don't like marrying their cross-cousins because, they say, this is like marrying your sister, since she [your cross-cousin] is the child of your maternal uncle. Some refuse, saying, 'Marrying a cross-cousin creates confusion and is a bad omen (malodʒa).' There are others who favour marrying their cross-cousins, but, even if they do this, their marriage does not remain one of strength because they scorn each other, saying, 'You married me; did you see no unrelated people [to marry]?' and the woman doesn't work well. That's why they've given up marrying cross-cousins.

Roman Catholicism is one factor in the decline. As I said at the beginning of Chapter 3, Christianity, whether Catholic or Protestant, has influenced a wider circle than those who have been formally converted.

A feature that the Jeremiah genealogy does not exemplify, but which should be mentioned, is the tendency, noted by Mitchell among the Yao,[1] for groups to arise in the village section that are related patrilaterally to its matrilineal core. These groups originate in the virilocal marriages of male members of the matrilineage, typically those of the headman and his predecessors. The headman's children belong to his wife's matrilineage, which is domiciled elsewhere. They do not necessarily return to their mother's village of origin, and, in the course of time, may form a local fragment of their matrilineage led by the headman's son. As this group grows, it may form a separate section of the village or may move to another village. When the original section headman is succeeded by his sister's son, he and the headman of the patrilaterally linked group are cross-cousins. An example of a group of this kind is Bisalomi's following, which grew large enough to

[1] *The Yao Village*, Chapter 7.

separate from Cimbuna and form an independent village. As reference
to Fig. 6 will show, Bisalomi (E.4) is the son of a male member,
Catuluka (D.5), of the junior primary segment of the Mceleka-
Cimbuna matrilineage. His following consists of the matrilineage
fragment centring on his mother. He is a cross-cousin of Cimbuna III
and IV (E.9 and E.8). I shall refer to him when we discuss perpetual
relationships later in this chapter.

The Kinship[1] System

Perhaps my examination of the pattern of residential grouping has
not yet convinced the reader of the validity of the opening statement
of the last section, viz. that a fundamental social group among the
Ceŵa is the matrilineage. Residential customs need to be taken in
conjunction with the pattern of reciprocal rights and duties existing
among kin. I have, in fact, already introduced this second line of evidence by making the headman the focus of description. By referring
to him as headman, I have implicitly assumed that mutual obligations,
involving responsibility and dependence, authority and obedience,
exist between him and the members of his matrilineage and, to a lesser
degree, the other residents of his section. It will be necessary now to
make explicit these and other aspects of the system of reciprocal
rights and duties among kinsmen. As a preliminary to this, I shall
present the main reference points of the Ceŵa kinship system.

This system (summarized in Fig. 4) is a kind of phenomenon that
is highly satisfying to the scientific observer. In spite of its apparent
complexity and its wide range of terms, it may, with a little study, be
brought within the compass of but a few general principles; and to
these it conforms with symmetry and consistency. I shall consider six
principles altogether. The first three sketch the main outlines of the
system, and the others fill in some of the details. The first three are:

(a) what Radcliffe-Brown calls 'the unity of the sibling group',[2] which
  underlies the classificatory kinship system widespread among Bantu-
  speaking Africans;

(b) the assumption that the preferred form of marriage, that between cross-
  cousins, has taken place; and

(c) what Radcliffe-Brown calls 'the combination of alternate generations'.[3]

---

[1] Here I follow Radcliffe-Brown in including affinity in the concept of kinship (cf.
Structure and Function, p. 51).

[2] *Ibid.*, pp. 54 ff.   [3] *Ibid.*, pp. 69 ff.

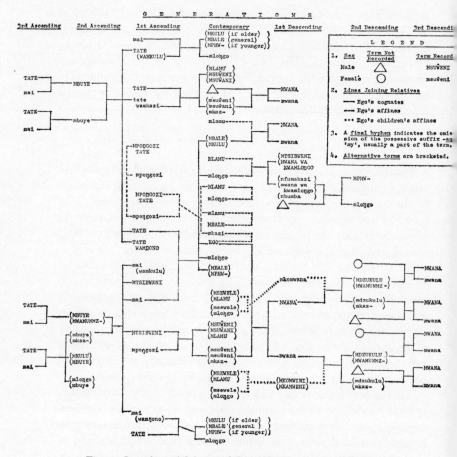

Fig. 4. Genealogical Scheme of Cewa Kinship Terms of Reference
used by a Male Ego

Note: Legend (4). Optional additions to terms are in parentheses.

In accordance with the first of these principles, Ego uses the same
term, *tate*,[1] for his father's brothers and his mother's sisters' husbands
as he does for his father; and he uses the same term, *mai*, for his

---

[1] At this stage, except where the context indicates otherwise, the vernacular terms given
are in the singular of the form in which they are used in reference, not address. Terms of
address will be dealt with under Principle (*d*) (see below, this chapter). In both reference
and address, the honorific plural is used where appropriate. Thus a child both refers to
and addresses his father (own or classificatory) as *A Tate*.

mother's sisters and his father's brothers' wives as he does for his mother. His father's sister is his 'female father' (*tate wamkaʒi*); and, though the term of reference applied to his mother's brother, *mtsibweni*, does not, as far as I know, mean 'male mother', the corresponding term of address is 'mother' (*mai*); and the term, *malume*, 'male mother', current among the South African Bantu, is known to the Ceŵa. Parallel cousins are referred to by sibling terms—'sibling-of-the-same-sex' (*mbale*) and 'sibling-of-the-opposite-sex' (*mloŋgo*).[1] In reference to both own and classificatory siblings, 'sibling-of-the-same-sex' is sometimes displaced by a pair of terms involving seniority—'senior sibling-of-the-same-sex' (*mkulu*) and '(my) junior sibling-of-the-same-sex' (*mphw(aŋga)*). All the terms so far considered are subject to wide extension. The terms for father, mother, mother's brother and father's sister are applied, not only to Ego's parents' own siblings, but also to their classificatory siblings. Similarly, sibling terms in their wider reference are not confined to first parallel cousins but include distant matrilateral and patrilateral ones as well. The logical extreme is reached in the application of sibling terms (or parental terms and their reciprocals, according to relative generation) to fellow matriclansmen who are regarded as uterine descendants of the same distant ancestress.

Although Ego's own parents and siblings are, in his own mind, clearly differentiated from classificatory ones to whom the same terms apply, the relationships that these terms define are fundamentally uniform. This is clearly illustrated by the fact that one pair of Ego's matrilateral classificatory parents, i.e. one of his mother's sisters and her husband, become his foster parents if his mother dies and his father goes back to his home village.

'Why do you call A Akiele your brother (*mbale*)?' I asked A Develiase in 1953. His reply was rhetorical, 'Did we not marry into the same family [matrilineage]?' The use of sibling terms between persons marrying into the same matrilineage applies whether they are of the same or of opposite sex and whether they marry into the same generation or into different generations. It is covered by a tradition of dual clan organization and the logically extreme application of the principle being considered, i.e. the use of sibling terms among fellow clansmen. Ceŵa say that originally there were only two matriclans (*mafuko*, sing., *pfuko*), Banda and Phili, and that between these there has always

---

[1] These translations, though clumsy, cover both possible instances, i.e. (a) when the speaker is male, *mbale* means 'brother' and *mloŋgo*, 'sister'; and (b) when the speaker is female, *mbale* means 'sister' and *mloŋgo* means 'brother'.

been a relationship of 'cross-cousinship' (*cisuŵeni, cisuŵani*), i.e. a potential marriage relationship. On the assumption that this dual organization still holds (in fact it does not; for other matriclans have emerged by differentiation), people who marry into the same matrilineage must belong to the clan (note singular) other than that of their spouses' matrilineage. They are therefore clan-siblings and refer to each other accordingly. This has an important social function; for typically they are representatives of the 'outsider' spouse group in the village community, and their classificatory siblingship establishes a bond between them.

Some interesting effects spring from Principle (*b*). Cross-cousin marriage is the enjoined, traditional form of union, and kinship terms and associated behaviour patterns are based on the assumption that it has occurred. There is slightly greater emphasis on a man's marrying his mother's brother's daughter than his father's sister's daughter, but both types of marriages are, traditionally at least, considered desirable. In addition to calling his mother's brother's or father's sister's child of either sex 'cross-cousin' (*msuŵeni, msuŵani*) a male Ego may call a female cross-cousin 'my wife' (*mkaʐaŋga*), she calling him 'my husband' (*mwamunaŋga*). A joking relationship exists between cross-cousins regardless of sex. Perhaps more interesting is the fact that not only this pair of terms but the whole system with its attendant behaviour patterns is adapted to expected cross-cousin marriage. Thus cross-cousins of the same sex, whether male or female, call each other 'sibling-in-law' (*mlamu*) as well as 'cross-cousin'; and a man, whether he has married his cross-cousin or not, refers to his mother's brother's wife as 'avoidance relative' (*mpoŋgoʐi*), and avoids her as he would his actual mother-in-law. Similarly, a man avoids his sister's daughter (*nfumakaʐi*) because she is his potential daughter-in-law These two facts, anticipating in particular the matrilateral cross-cousin marriage of a male Ego, constitute, with informants' statements, the slender evidence for a slightly greater emphasis on this type as against patrilateral cross-cousin marriage.

The secondary terms used for one another by the parents of a married couple would fit either the matrilateral or the patrilateral form of cross-cousin marriage. These terms are 'sibling-of-the-opposite-sex' (*mloŋgo*) between the father of one of the married couple and the mother of the other, and 'sibling-in-law' (*mlamu*) between a married couple's parents of the same sex. The primary term they use in both same-sex and opposite-sex relationships is *msewele*, for which there is no equivalent in English. This term is derived from *kusewela*, 'to play', and implies a free-and-easy relationship.

A final illustration of the ramifications of assumed cross-cousin marriage (as well as the logical consistency of the system of kinship terminology) is to be found in the fact that the children of cross-cousins, who are second cousins of a particular kind, call each other 'sibling', the Ceŵa term depending on whether they are of the same or of opposite sex. The case of Solopia II (D.17 in Fig. 3) indicates that marriage between them is not barred; and that of Jeremiah (C.14) to Emelia (D.32) shows that marriage between a person and his cross-cousin's child is possible. Marriages such as these, which depart from the normal preferred pattern, may, however, involve adjustments in patterns of enjoined behaviour. Thus Jeremiah, when he married Emelia, had to substitute an avoidance for a joking relationship with her mother, his cross-cousin, Cikweni (C.13) (see below, this chapter).

Principle (c), the combination of alternate generations, accounts, not only for joking relationships between children and the parents of both their father and their mother (the latter being more commonly encountered in a predominantly uxorilocal society), but also for a general equivalence of grandparents and grandchildren. There is, however, interaction between this principle and Principle (a), that of the unity of the sibling group. Ego may sometimes refer to his mother's mother's brother, who in English would be a great-uncle of a particular kind, as 'grandparent' (*mbuye*)—according to Principle (a). Very often, however, he refers to him as '(my) senior sibling-of-the-same-sex' (*mkulu (waŋga)*), which is a logical consequence of Ego's membership, according to Principle (c), of his mother's mother's generation. An interesting implication of the reciprocal of this relationship, but with a female Ego, is the fact that, though a man refers to his daughter's daughter as his 'grandchild' (*mdzukulu*) or 'my wife' (*mkazaŋga*), and, though his marriage to her is possible (though unlikely), he refers to his sister's daughter's daughter, in English a grand-niece of a particular kind, as 'sibling-of-the-opposite-sex' (*mloŋgo*). This usage is in conformity with the fact that she is a member of his matrilineage, and the matrilineage is a strictly exogamous group.

Because grandparents and grandchildren are identified, there are in effect only two generations at a given time. Ego, his grandchildren and his grandparents belong to one; and his children, parents and great-grandparents belong to the other. With characteristic consistency he refers to his great-grandparents as 'father' (*tate*) and 'mother' (*mai*);

and to his great-grandchild as 'child' (*mwana*).[1] The relationship between the two sets of combined generations is formal and restrained.
The three principles that I have presented, viz. (*a*) the unity of the
sibling group, (*b*) the assumption of cross-cousin marriage and (*c*) the
combination of alternate generations, are sufficient to determine the
general framework of the Ceŵa kinship system. I turn now to three
supplementary principles which will make kinship terminology clearer
to the reader and thus prepare him for an examination of patterns of
interaction and of reciprocal rights and duties among kinsmen. These
supplementary principles are:

(*d*) the distinction between terms of reference and terms of address;
(*e*) greater differentiation of the matrilineage with internal than with ex-
    ternal orientation;[2] and
(*f*) succession to genealogical position.

There is a distinction between terms of reference, the ones thus far
given, and terms of address.[3] For instance, Ego refers to his daughter's
husband as 'son-in-law (*mkamwini, mkomweni*) but addresses him as
'father' (*A Tate*).[4] He refers to his mother's brother as *A Tsibweni* but
addresses him as 'mother' (*A Mai*) or as *Ŵaŵa*.[5] He refers to his sister's
daughter as *nfumakazi* or *mwana wa kwamloŋgo* (lit., 'child of a sibling-
of-the-opposite-sex'); but, because she is potentially his daughter-in-
law, he respectfully addresses her as 'mother' (*A Mai*). Although this
is a term of address, I have heard its use given as the reason why a man
refers to his sister's daughter's daughter as 'sibling-of-the-opposite-sex'
(*mloŋgo*). 'Her mother is my mother,' said the informant. Furthermore,
it identifies the women of the first ascending generation of the matrilineage (mothers) with those of the first descending generation (sister's
daughters). The males of these two generations are similarly identified
because the term of reference for mother's brother (*mtsibweni*, hon.

[1] Bruwer, 'Kinship Terminology', pp. 185-6, and Pretorius, 'The Terms of Relationship', p. 48, record that a person calls his great-grandchild *cidzukulu cotukwanitsa* or
cidzukulu cacimbuye, a point on which I unfortunately have no information. Judging by
the meanings attributed to them by these writers, these terms would appear to refer
primarily to the great age of the person employing them.
[2] This seems to be a special case of Radcliffe-Brown's principle of the unity of the
lineage (*Structure and Function*, pp. 70 ff.).
[3] Pretorius, *ibid.*, p. 49, is explicit on this point, but not Bruwer, *ibid.*
[4] From this point onwards, I give terms in the forms in which they would actually
be used, i.e. in the honorific plural where appropriate.
[5] I suspected that *ŵaŵa* was of Ŋgoni origin (cf. Zulu: *ubaba*, 'father'; vocative, *baba*)
until I found that Gamitto recorded in 1831—before the Ŋgoni invasion—that *Bába* was
the title of the village headman (*Muéne muzi*, now written *mwini mudzi*)—cf. *O Muata
Cazembe*, 1854, p. 83.

plur., *A Tsibweni*), being a self-reciprocal, is used for sister's son as well.

The examples I have given of terms of address show that 'father' and 'mother' are widely used. In addition to their normal uses, for referring to and addressing Ego's own and classificatory parents, they serve as polite titles to bestow on any persons to whom respect is due, this being in conformity with the rather formal relationship existing between parents and children. They are applied to unrelated persons as well as to respected kinsmen and affinal avoidance partners. An alternative to *A Tate* is *Bambo*, which in my experience is commoner in Nyasaland than in Northern Rhodesia. Its honorific plural, *Mambo*, is reserved for important chiefs and certain types of diviners. *Bwana* ('master') is a term used for chiefs and for non-African men in authority. *Dona* (or more often its honorific plural, *A Dona*) is used for non-African women.

One reason why 'father' and 'mother' are ubiquitous in Ceŵa speech is that there is an equivalence of the males of a matrilineage which increases enormously the number of affinal avoidance relationships that are observed. Ego avoids his wife's mother and treats his wife's father with marked respect. Because he is identified with his own and his classificatory brothers, mother's brothers and mother's mother's brothers, all these join with him in avoiding his wife's parents, formally addressing them as 'father' and 'mother'.

This is actually an instance of Principle (*e*). The Ceŵa matrilineage, like any other social group, is more differentiated to its own members than it is to outsiders (including affines). If one remembers to distinguish between the internal and the external view of the matrilineage, then one will revise one's almost inevitable first impression that Ceŵa are slapdash in their use of terminology. From within, the generations of male matrilineage members are distinct, and terms acquire specific meanings. The younger brothers of the headman are referred to as 'his junior siblings-of-the-same-sex' (*aziphwaŵo*).[1] His sisters' sons are referred to as his *azitsibweni* or *ŵana ŵa kwamloŋgo*, the first term meaning specifically 'sisters' sons' (and, since it is self-reciprocal, 'mother's brothers'); and the second, 'sisters' children'. Because of the identification of his generation with the second descending one, his sisters' daughters' sons are referred to as 'his younger siblings-of-the-same-sex'

[1] The prefix *azi-* is often used for forming an ordinary plural when the more regular prefix *a-* or *ŵa-* is used for the honorific plural. *Aziphwaŵo* means literally '*their* junior siblings-of-the-same-sex', the possessive suffix *-ŵo* being in the honorific plural in deference to the headman.

(*aẕiphwaŵo*).[1] To an outsider, these distinctions between generations are of no concern, and all matrilineage males junior to the headman are lumped together in the category of 'his junior siblings-of-the-
same sex' (*aẕiphwaŵo*).

This lumping together is not surprising when one remembers that,
in regard to succession, a man stands in the same relationship to his
mother's brother as he does to his elder brother; and in the same relationship to his sister's son as he does to his younger brother.

There is a similar link between orientation and degree of precision
in regard to the term *mbale* ('sibling-of-the-same-sex'—without age
differentiation). If Ego is orientated within the matrilineage, *aẕibale*
(*ŵ*)*aŋga* means 'my siblings-of-the-same-sex', i.e. his own and his
classificatory siblings of the same sex. If, on the other hand, he is considering his matrilineage in relation to another matrilineage, or if an
outsider is referring to Ego's *aẕibale*, then the term may be translated as
'kin', or, more precisely, 'matrikin'.

Perhaps the most interesting and important application of this principle is to the female members of the matrilineage; for, to designate
them, the headman uses a term, *nbumba*, which, if he is orientated externally, may sometimes include the whole matrilineage except himself.
Within the matrilineage, any man, not necessarily the headman, refers
to his sisters as his 'siblings-of-the-opposite sex' (*aẕiloŋgo*); to his
sisters' daughters as his 'female dependants' (*nbumba*, sing., the same);
and, as a result of the combination of alternate generations, to his
sisters' daughters' daughters as his 'siblings-of-the-opposite-sex' (*aẕiloŋgo*). If this man is a headman, he will normally have inherited a name
and succeeded to its associated genealogical position, in which case these
two terms (*aẕiloŋgo* and *nbumba*) will be used to designate the sisters and
sisters' daughters of his predecessors. Now, an outsider, or the headman himself when orientated towards other matrilineages, will drop the
distinctions between generations and simply refer to all females of the
matrilineage as his (the headman's) 'female dependants' (*nbumba*). A
distinction that Mitchell discovered among the Yao[2] applies also to the
Ceŵa: whereas the headman refers to the women members of his matrilineage as 'my *nbumba*', his male juniors refer to them as 'our *nbumba*'.
Provided that orientation remains external, the term *nbumba* may be

[1] My investigations confirm neither Pretorius ('The Terms of Relationship', p. 47) nor
Bruwer ('Kinship Terminology', p. 186), who both give the term for 'sister's son' as
mupwa. This difference may, of course, be the result of our having made our investigations
among different groups of Ceŵa.
[2] Mitchell, 'The Yao of Southern Nyasaland', p. 320.

stretched on occasion to refer to all the headman's dependants, male and female. There are thus three meanings of *nbumba*. The most precise is the one understood when the speaker is orientated within his matrilineage, i.e. 'sister's daughter'. Then there is the one of wider reference when the speaker is orientated externally, i.e. 'female dependant'. Finally, there is the one of widest reference, again applying when the speaker is orientated externally, i.e. 'dependant' (male or female). The usage of key terms in varying orientations is summarized in Fig. 5.

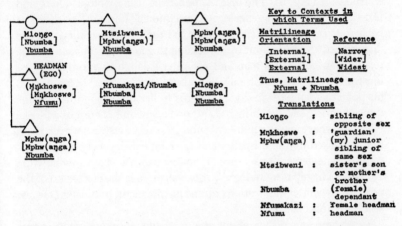

Fig. 5. The Unity of the Cewa Matrilineage reflected in Kinship Terminology

The fact that the headman has succeeded to the genealogical position of his predecessor is an instance of the final principle, (f), succession to genealogical position as a result of nominal reincarnation.[1] Before exploring other implications of this principle, it is necessary to repeat that, in accordance with it, a headman's *nbumba*, whether the term be used in the wider or the widest sense, includes not only matrilineage members of his own generation and descending ones, but also those of ascending generations who were the *nbumba* of one or other of his predecessors. This makes comprehensible an informant's statement that, if a sorcerer's lodge-fellows urge her to provide them with flesh by killing one of her relatives, she will if possible avoid killing her son because, when he has grown up, he will be 'as if a brother to her' (*ngati mloŋgo wace*).

I shall now follow up another instance of the final principle. When a male name, with its attendant genealogical position, is handed on, it

[1] As Stefaniszyn appropriately calls it ('African Reincarnation Re-examined').

follows (though not always closely) the usual matrilineal principle, i.e. it goes to younger brothers and then to the eldest son of the eldest sister. A female name, on the other hand, usually skips a generation, i.e. it goes from a woman to her daughter's daughter (usually own, but sometimes classificatory). These facts are amply illustrated in the genealogies. Take for instance the inheritance of the male name, Cimbuna (C.5, D.7, E.9, E.8 and F.3), and the female name, Citondola (C.7 and E.13), in the skeleton genealogy of the Mceleka-Cimbuna matrilineage (Fig. 6). The case of the female name, Solopia (A.10 and D.17), in the Jeremiah genealogy is exceptional (Fig. 3). This different behaviour of male and female names has the effect of minimizing the disturbance brought about by succession to genealogical position. The relationship between a man and his sister's daughter affords the best illustration of this. He normally addresses her as 'mother' because she is his potential daughter-in-law. Now it is to her that his mother's name typically goes, and this brings about no change in his term of address. Although she now calls him 'my child', the relationship between them is still marked by the formality and restraint existing between persons of proximate generations. Since my immediate task is to show how the system of kinship terminology works, I shall leave the discussion of the possible structural implications of this phenomenon until later (see last section of this chapter).

Ceŵa are punctilious about the etiquette springing from name inheritance. This was forcibly brought home to me by the case of A Kanyama and A Ŋguzi,

both of whom I met soon after I first arrived in the Ceŵa Reserve in 1946. I went to see some dancing at the village of which A Kanyama was headman, and happened to take his photograph, afterwards supplying him with a print of it. A Ŋguzi was an old woman living in Mceleka village. During the period before I had learnt the language well enough to dispense with an interpreter, I once sat on the verandah of her hut and had a friendly chat with her. An elder of the village came by, and, seeing me, asked me whether I was visiting the village. I said: 'Yes, I'm visiting my old friend here' (indicating A Ŋguzi). Since Ceŵa knows no Platonic friendship, my interpreter translated 'old friend' as 'mistress', much to the amusement of the elder, who asked whether they should go ahead with marriage negotiations. Henceforth, to put the joke on a decent basis, I became A Ŋguzi's putative grandchild.

Soon after my return to the Reserve in 1952, I was sorry to hear that A Ŋguzi was seriously ill. I decided to visit her the next day with a present of tinned soup. That evening I had a visit from Headman Kanyama, whom I had not seen since 1946 but whom I recognized because of the photograph. After a pleasant reunion with this jovial, middle-aged headman, now a peasant farmer, I heard him telling people in the village that he was on his way to visit a sick child. Next day when I went to see A Ŋguzi, I found that she had aged a great deal since I had last seen her (four years previously), and that her mind was wandering. Because of this, I was not surprised to hear her say that her father had come to see her the previous night. Then, on the point of dismissing this statement as a symptom of senile dementia, I suddenly remembered that, in 1946 when I had drawn up the genealogy of Mceleka village, I had recorded her father's name as Kanyama. I do not know how many holders of the name had intervened between A Ŋguzi's father and my middle-aged acquaintance. The casualness with which they both used the appropriate terms—in spite of a reversed age difference—was remarkable. So was the persistence of the 'father's' obligation to visit his sick 'child'.

The consequences of a headman's succeeding to the genealogical position of his predecessor are not confined to the readjustment of relationships within his matrilineage. They also have the effect of linking him, and thus the group he leads, with other similar groups. Most important among these external links are the 'perpetual relationships'[1] that grow out of patrilateral links. I have noted how the headman's son may become the leader of the local fragment of the matrilineage to which he belongs. Sometimes he is referred to as the 'child' of his father's successors. Thus Bisalomi, the headman of an offshoot of Cimbuna village, is referred to as the 'child' of Cimbuna although the present incumbent (Lazalo, Cimbuna V) is a generation junior to him (see Fig. 6). More often the perpetual relationship that emerges is one of 'cross-cousinship' (cisuẇeni)—presumably because the first leader of the new group is a contemporary of his father's first successor, i.e. his father's sister's son. Many of the links between Ceẇa chiefs are of this kind. It would appear that, though succession to Ceẇa chieftainship is invariably matrilineal, there are occasions when a chief, wanting to expand or reorganize his chiefdom, may, especially if he is caught by conflicting loyalties to son and sister's son, award his son a tract of land. The case of Chief Mkanda Mateyo of the Northern Ceẇa is recent enough to provide a clear illustration of the effects of this. The traditional territory of Mkanda, extending over the Nyasa-Luaŋgwa watershed, was bisected by the Nyasaland-Northern Rhodesia border. At this time the Mkanda chieftainship, owing to the Ŋgoni conquest, was virtually defunct. After about twenty years of British occupation, it began, like other Ceẇa chieftainships, e.g. Kaẇaza's, to show signs of

[1] To borrow Cunnison's term (Kinship and Local Organization on the Luapula, pp. 14–15).

recovery from the effects of bondage; and the problems arising from its
falling under two separate systems of European administration took on
a semblance of reality. In 1917 the incumbent of this chieftainship was
Mkanda Kamwendo whose capital was in Northern Rhodesia. On the
death of his perpetual sister's son, who had been in charge of the
Nyasaland section, Mkanda Kamwendo decided to take charge of it
himself. He assigned the section falling in Northern Rhodesia to his
son, Mkanda Mateyo. When he died in 1922, he was succeeded (in
Nyasaland) by his sister's son, Mkanda Gudu. The two Mkandas are
thus cross-cousins, and their successors will perpetually be 'in cross-
cousinship' (pacisuŵeni).

Dating from earlier times, and thus subject to varied explanations,
are the relationships between other Ceŵa chieftainships. The Mkanda
matriclan is Mbeŵe; whereas that of Undi is Phili. Mkanda (Gudu, not
Mateyo) is described as the cross-cousin of Undi. The links between
Mkanda and his subordinates include some perpetual 'cross-cousinships', e.g. that with Mbaŋombe whose matriclan is Sakala. Similarly,
among the Southern Ceŵa, there are some chiefs not belonging to
Undi's matriclan (Phili), who are his perpetual cross-cousins or those
of his perpetual younger brother, Cimwala. For instance, Undi's subordinate, Mŵaŋgala, is of the Mbeŵe matriclan; and Cimwala's subordinate, the Nseŋga Paramount Chief, Kalindawalo, is of the Mwanza
matriclan. When, in 1952, Chief Cimwala gave me a rather random
list of thirteen of his and Undi's subordinates among the Southern
Ceŵa of Fort Jameson and of neighbouring Portuguese territory, he
included only five who were of his and Undi's matriclan, Phili. He
stated that the 'cross-cousinships' with the eight non-Phili chiefs had
arisen from the habit chiefs have of giving chiefdoms to their children
when the expansion of their territory warrants a reorganization.

Prescribed Behaviour among Kin

Having presented the salient features of the system of kinship terminology, I shall now describe the patterns of enjoined behaviour between
kinsmen.

One criterion according to which relationships between kinsmen may
be classified is the degree of intimacy that is expected of them. According to this criterion, Ceŵa prescribed behaviour patterns range from
boisterous familiarity through friendly intimacy and reserved formality
to precipitate avoidance. I shall examine these four categories, which

represent the extremes and, roughly, the quartiles of the range under consideration.

The 'joking relationships' of anthropological literature are best represented among the Ceŵa by the licensed familiarity between persons calling each other 'cross-cousin' (*msuŵeni*) or 'sibling-in-law' (*mlamu*). Between Ego and his cross-cousins of the opposite sex there exists a relationship known as 'cross-cousinship' (*cisuŵeni*); and between him and his cross-cousins of the same sex, brothers' wives, sisters' husbands, wife's brothers and wife's sisters, there is a relationship known as 'sibling-in-law-ship' (*cilamu*). Cross-cousinship, a potential marriage relationship, is slightly freer than 'sibling-in-law-ship'. A man can fondle his female cross-cousin's breasts in public; for, as one informant put it, he is the 'proprietor of them' (*mwini wao*). He can have sexual intercourse with her, and this will not lead to serious trouble even if she is married, though it may cause quarrels between her and her husband because the latter will abuse her as an 'adulterous woman' (*mkaẓi wa vigololo*).

Ego's joking relationship with his wife's sister or his brother's wife does not go quite as far as this. Though he may fondle her breasts, he is deterred from having intercourse with her for fear of trouble with her husband or, if she is unmarried, her mother's brother. A man who kept a diary for me recorded with indignation the improper conduct of his sister-in-law, who sat on the verandah of his hut instead of entering it. 'I asked her, "Wherefore, since you are the proprietor of [privileged person in] this hut ... !" And I was greatly troubled. And I poured much scorn on her because she is a bad sister-in-law.'

Between cross-cousins and between these affines of the same generation, social relationships are characteristically tense. Cross-cousins belong to opposed patrilaterally linked matrilineages (see p. 120) and are involved at the receiving end, in a man's conflicting loyalties towards his children and his sister's children. Tensions between affines have been so well documented that it is unnecessary to say more than that in this respect the Ceŵa conform with the world-wide pattern. Joking relationships have, in addition to this tension-relieving function, another function of considerable moral importance. They provide a means of effectively censuring a miscreant's conduct. His joking partners may jeer at him in public with impunity; and, though their words are assumed to be in jest, there may be more than a grain of truth in some of the things they say. Their taunts, which may condemn bad temper or petty meanness, or expose clandestine affairs, are effective sanctions, since among the Ceŵa there is a highly developed sense of shame (*manyaẕi*).

It is not a far step from the almost aggressive familiarity I have been describing to the more affectionate, playful goodwill existing between members of alternate generations. The closeness of these two categories is indicated by the tendency Ceŵa have of using the terms 'cross-cousinship' (*cisuŵeni*) and 'grandchildship' (*cidẕukulu*) synonymously. More precisely, however, 'grandchildship' designates the relationship between Ego and the parents of both his father and his mother. The latter are more often near him in a predominantly uxorilocal society, and are of greater social significance since his mother's mother is one of the important elders of his matrilineage. The relationship is given full scope in Ceŵa society; for, from the time of weaning (at the age of two or three years), the child goes to live in the hut of his mother's parents (see, for instance, Fig. 3, p. 116, where Mwesanji and Salavia (E.19 and 20) are shown as living in the hut of their mother's mother, Tuŋgase (C.8)). He remains there until he is 'clever enough' to realize that his grandparents are in the habit of having sexual intercourse, at which stage he joins some of his age-mates (not all necessarily from his own village section) in a 'dormitory' (*nphala*). During the time he is with his grandparents, the child comes very much under their spell. It is they who tell him bedtime stories about Hare, Baboon, Lion and Hyena and who teach him proverbs and riddles. So conducive to learning is the atmosphere of 'Granny's nursery school' that a missionary friend of mine confessed that he regarded the grandmother as his chief rival. She is the repository of tradition, and has the advantage of being on very intimate terms with her 'pupils', both male and female. The joking relationship between grandparents and grandchildren is in keeping with the spirit of this period in the child's life. In addition to the terms 'grandparent' (*mbuye*) and its reciprocal, 'grandchild' (*mdẕukulu*), there are others used by persons of alternate generations; and these are constant reminders of their friendly, sometimes hilarious, relationship. Grandsons call grandmothers 'my wife' (*mkaẕaŋga*), and grandfathers 'my co-husband' (*mwamunmẕaŋga*). Granddaughters call grandfathers 'my husband' (*mwamunaŋga*), and grandmothers 'my co-wife' (*mkaẕi-mẕaŋga*). Typical of the friendly banter that goes on is Pretorius's example of the boy who, when his demands for food from 'his wife' (i.e. his mother's mother) are refused, turns to his 'co-husband' (i.e. his mother's father) and suggests that they divorce their wife.[1] This

---

[1] 'The Terms of Relationship', p. 47.

relationship has lasting effects; for later in life it is their grandparents rather than their parents to whom a young married couple turn if tribal initiation has left them incompletely equipped with 'the facts of life' or if they need arbitrators in their minor quarrels.

This leads to the next point along the scale from familiarity to formality. It is because of the socially prescribed behaviour between proximate generations that a young couple cannot consult their parents on the intimate details of marital adjustment. There are other situations, too, from which the members of the parental generations are excluded. If a person is undergoing the instruction associated with any *rite de passage*, such as that at puberty, marriage or name inheritance, he is supported by a joking partner. And in the physically intimate process of childbirth a woman is assisted by her grandmothers, sisters-in-law and cross-cousins—not by her mother. This slight formality colours Ego's relationships with all the members of the first ascending generation—with his fathers and mothers, both own and classificatory, and with his 'male mother' (mother's brother, *mtsibweni*) and his 'female father' (father's sister, *tate wamkaʒi*), though in their case the formality is even greater since they are potential parents-in-law.

This brings us to the fourth point on the scale, the formal extreme. Here we find the avoidance behaviour that exists between affines of proximate generations. This is most marked in cross-sex relationships, i.e. between a man and his son's wife or his sister's son's wife; and between a woman and her daughter's husband. Since among the Ceŵa the members of the last of these pairs encounter each other more often than do the others, discussions of the avoidance relationship (*cipoŋgoʒi*) implicitly refer to a woman and her daughter's husband. These two observe a very strict etiquette, the nature of which is revealed by the two verbs commonly used to describe it, 'to fear each other' (*kuopana*) and 'to flee [from] each other' (*kuthawana*). They may not mention each other's names (as I soon discovered in my early attempts to draw up genealogies); and, if they should meet on the path, they give each other a wide berth, leaving, as one informant expressed it, 'the path by itself in the middle' (*njila iyokha pakati*). It should be remembered (see above, this chapter) that, owing to the equivalence of the male members of the same matrilineage, these avoidance relationships are widely extended.

In the course of time, on the initiative of the mother-in-law, the avoidance taboos observed by her and her son-in-law may be removed by the exchange of gifts (usually a fowl and a shilling) and the ritual of eating together. Henceforth the partners treat each other in much the same way as mother and son. Some mothers-in-law delay this step for many years, and these cases illustrate the important function of the avoidance relationship. One woman I knew had still done nothing to remove the taboos after at least seven years. She explained that she knew her son-in-law to be hot-tempered and quarrelsome and believed that any closer contact with him would inevitably lead to an unpleasant clash of wills.

None of these behaviour patterns is rigidly immutable. Occasions arise when they have to be changed. I have described how generally the inheritance of a name, with its associated genealogical position, causes a minimum of disturbance to the system of kinship terminology. Sometimes, however, it necessitates changes in behaviour patterns. Thus, when Headman Matope III inherited the name associated with the headmanship (ultimately) from his mother's brother, Matope I, he had to drop his joking relationship with his cross-cousin, A Cawo, who became his 'child'.

Another type of change occurs when, for reasons of relative age, a person marries into a generation other than his own. When Headman Jeremiah (C.14 in Fig. 3) grew up, his father, Kaliza (B.15), sought a bride for him from his own matrilineage. Kaliza's sister's daughter's daughter, Emelia (D.32), was of a suitable age. On marrying her, Jeremiah changed from a joking to an avoidance relationship with her mother, Cikweni (C.13), who was his cross-cousin. Generally, if two kinship links determine conflicting relationships, such as those in the instance just cited, avoidance suppresses joking. Another example of this is the fact that, though Tasokalelo (C.19 on the same genealogy) is the 'sibling-in-law' of Develiase (C.23) because he married the latter's sister, Lowase (C.18), Develiase treats him with great respect because he is the mother's brother of Emelia (D.32), the widow of his brother, Jeremiah.

Behaviour patterns such as those I have been examining may form the basis of interaction between groups lacking actual kinship bonds. Thus the Banda and Phili matriclans are in a relationship of 'cross-cousinship' (cisuweni) with each other, with all that this implies regarding joking and preferential marriage. Another instance is a ritual alliance called 'grandchildship' (cidʒukulu) that exists between a particular matrilineage and individual members of other matrilineages in the same village or neighbourhood. Stefaniszyn has referred to this alliance as 'funeral friendship',[1] a term which, though possibly too specific, is satisfactory, since a funeral is the occasion *par excellence* on which it is operative. These ritual friends, who are not kinsmen at all,[2] are designated as 'grandchildren' (*adʐukulu*, sing., *mdʐukulu*), and have an asymmetrical joking relationship with the matrilineage they have served.

Stannus in his thorough study of the Nyanja[3] states that the relatives of the deceased 'ask some *friends* [my italics] to act as *adʐukulu*' and he adds:

For ever after having acted as a *Mdʐukulu* a man is expected to behave as a funny man. He may swear, use obscene language, insult people, commit adultery, make obscene overtures to women, pull off their clothes, etc., take chickens, take beer and drink it when he sees it being made in the village where he acted.[4]

This relationship, as applying to funerals rather than in its more general form, did not escape that acute observer, Gamitto, who in 1831 noted that, among the Maravi, those helping when another dies acquire in relation to his family a mutual term of address, *sabuhira* (a term I did not come across among the Ceŵa), and are henceforth entitled to say and do to them whatever they wish, even to take their possessions without fear of a court case.[5] Gamitto's describing the relationship as mutual conflicts with my finding (and, in a sense, with his own implication) that it is asymmetrical. It is clear from his statement that funeral friends do not belong to the family of the deceased.

[1] B. Stefaniszyn, 'Funeral Friendship in Central Africa', p. 290. See also Tew, 'A Further Note on Funeral Friendship'. Colson, 'Clans and the Joking-Relationship among the Plateau Tonga of Northern Rhodesia', has expressed dissatisfaction with the translation 'funeral friendship', and has reverted to the older term 'clan joking relationship'. This solution is not, however, satisfactory for the Ceŵa; for, though the joking relationship may have been one between clans in the past, it is nowadays essentially one between a particular matrilineage and individual members of other matrilineages in the vicinity. To meet Colson's objection to the specificity of 'funeral friendship', I use 'ritual friendship'.
[2] Neither Pretorius nor Bruwer distinguishes 'ritual friends' from grandchildren. Pretorius, 'The Terms of Relationship', p. 47, says: '*Mdʐukulu* means gravedigger: A man thus regards grandchildren as those who will dig his grave.' Bruwer, 'Korswelverhoudings en die Belangrikheid Daarvan by Begrafnisgebruike', p. 27, refers to the grandchildren as the actual *eni maliro* [proprietors of the funeral] whose functions he details as those of undertakers; and in 'Kinship Terminology', p. 186, he states that it is the grandchildren's sole responsibility to provide their grandparents with a proper burial. Similarly, Young (*Headman's Enterprise*, p. 191, footnote 2) writes: 'Mdzukulu: a relationship implying "one of those upon whom falls the duty of burying", and specially applicable to grandsons.' In contrast to these statements, my informants made a clear distinction between grandchildren who are related (*pacibale*) and ritual friends who are not; and at funerals I attended those who performed the functions of undertakers were not members of the deceased's matrilineage.
[3] Stannus, 'Notes on Some Tribes,' p. 315.
[4] *Loc. cit.*
[5] *O Muata Caʐembe*, p. 120 (my *précis* of a translation from the Portuguese by Mr José Cotta).

My informants among the Northern Rhodesian Ceŵa gave me descriptions of this institution very similar to those of Stannus and Gamitto. They added, however, that nowadays people were less tolerant of the depredations of ritual friends, and tried to attract their services more by entertaining them to good funeral fare than by permitting them extravagant liberties. During my stay among the Ceŵa, I certainly saw no incidents conforming with the traditional account of the behaviour of ritual friends.

I am translating *mdʒukulu* in this context as 'ritual friend' rather than 'funeral friend' because the service rendered is not confined to funerals. A headman who is being installed is supported by a ritual friend, just as a more junior person receiving a name is supported by an actual grandchild or cross-cousin. When offerings are made to the spirits, ritual friends of the matrilineage concerned are entitled to consume these the day after they have been offered. A ritual friend may even participate in a libation, saying to the spirits of the matrilineage to which he is linked: 'I am only a ritual friend (*mdʒukulu*), but remember me when I come looking in your village for a marriageable woman (*nbeta*).' When Ceŵa refer to someone as a 'hyena' (*fisi*) who comes in to complete some ritual for them, such as the defloration of a girl who has reached puberty, they generally mean a ritual friend.

Ceŵa show great ingenuity in exploiting situations provided by kinship links. A good example is the quarrel that occurred in 1947 between Msaŋkhulana of Matope village and Samba of Jeremiah village.

At a beer drink, Samba was given a gourdful of beer, and Msaŋkhulana drank some of it before Samba had tasted it. 'Hey, you,' said Samba, and slapped Msaŋkhulana on the knee. Msaŋkhulana took offence, and the quarrel eventually went before Headmen Matope and Jeremiah. Discussion of the case had gone on for some time when Cuzu, an elderly, highly respected 'son-in-law' of Cimseleti's matrilineage, pointed out that, since (*a*) Msaŋkhulana was his wife's sister and (*b*) Samba was a member of his own matriclan, a joking relationship must exist between these two women, and it had therefore been improper for Msaŋkhulana to take offence. Cuzu's argument was accepted, and Msaŋkhulana's complaint was dismissed as groundless.

Leadership and Segmentation

The familiarity-formality scale, along which I have found it convenient to place joking, avoidance and other, less spectacular patterns of enjoined behaviour, represents but one of the dimensions of human interaction. Another important dimension has to do with mutual

PLATE IV. BEHAVIOUR PATTERNS

(a) Avoidance between affines (posed but realistic); (b) old woman with
sick grandchild; (c) A Develiase Mvula building a hut for his *nbumba*
(widowed sister in this case); (d) ritual friend tying mourning band (*mlaẓa*)
on a bereaved person's head.

dependence. Kinsmen are enmeshed in a series of relationships involving reciprocal rights and duties. Most conspicuous are those between a leader and his following. The leader has the privilege, with its attendant prestige, of directing the affairs of his followers, who, enjoying a freedom from responsibility, are obliged to obey his orders. In return for the privilege and prestige that he enjoys, the leader is obliged to place his wordly wisdom, ritual power and economic strength at the disposal of his followers.

The relationship between leader and followers, better than any other aspect of its structure, throws light on the organization and the integration of the Ceŵa matrilineage. The group comprises, as I have shown, the headman (*nfumu*) and his dependants (*nbumba*, in the widest sense). Like other human leaders, the headman has lieutenants, both male and female. For convenience I shall consider the female lieutenants first. In every generation each woman is the source, and in a sense the president, of her own group of uterine descendants—her children, her daughters' children, her daughters' daughters' children, and so on. She is the 'ancestress' (*kholo*) of this group, which, since she has metaphorically suckled them, is referred to as her 'breast' (*bele*). The status that her 'breast' or segment occupies in the matrilineage as a whole has several determinants. Firstly, the generation to which she belongs determines the depth of her segment and consequently its span.[1] Thus, in Fig. 3 the segment of the late Kuliale I (B.7) has a depth of five generations and so wide a span that it includes all local matrilineage members except Kabuula II (B.10), Kenala (C. 35) and Galantia (C.37); whereas that of her daughter, Loŵase (C.18), has a depth of three generations and includes only her seven children and one daughter's child.

Secondly, an ancestress's order of birth makes her segment senior or junior to that of her own sister; and the order of birth of her mother, mother's mother, and so on, determines the status of her segment in relation to the segments of her female collaterals of the same generation. Thus the segment of Kuliale II (D.15 in Fig. 3) is senior (*a*) to that of her younger sister, Solopia II (D.17), and (*b*) to that of her mother's younger sister's daughter, Eledia (D.24). This type of seniority, dependent on the birth-order of the ancestress herself or of her lineal ancestresses, is designated by saying that a segment is a 'big breast' (*bele lalikulu*) or a 'little breast' (*bele laliɲono*) in relation to any other segment of same order with which it may be compared. As I have

---

[1] Cf. Fortes, *The Dynamics of Clanship*, p. 30.

L

mentioned, headmanship is supposed, in theory at least, to remain in the 'big breast' of the matrilineage as a whole ('biggest' would be more precise, but I am following the Cewa expression). In other words, a headman should be succeeded by his own (as opposed to his classificatory) brothers; then by his eldest own sister's sons, in their order of birth; then by his eldest own sister's eldest daughter's sons, in their order of birth—and so on.

Thirdly, the random distribution of fecundity and mortality, of opportunity and accident, makes some segments prosper and multiply; others, decline and die out. Similarly, the ordinary fluctuations in heredity and environment produce sub-strains that are intellectually bright or dull, emotionally serene or irascible. From the viewpoint of a scientific observer, these variations are random—due to chance. From the viewpoint of the Cewa, many, though not all, of them are due to personal intervention—the inscrutable works of Providence (Mulungu, Ciuta etc.), the essentially human reactions of the spirits, or the evil machinations of sorcerers. And the Cewa tend, as do certain classes in Western society, to over-emphasize the influence of sheer heredity. Such-and-such a woman's sons, they say, will never make good headmen because their father, the man who placed them in her womb, was a knave (*mambala*[1]) or a fool (*wopusa*).

These factors of random incidence must be taken into account; for, without them, there can be no explanation for the decline and disappearance of a segment which may have had great depth and potential span, and whose ancestress and her lineal ancestresses were the firstborn among sisters with issue. They may account also for the decline of whole segments and ultimately of whole villages. I have described at the beginning of this chapter how, when Cimbuna village expanded and proliferated, Cipangula village contracted until it lost its independence as an administrative unit.

Even in as prosperous a group as the matrilineage from which the kinship-nucleus of the headman's section of Cimbuna village derived, growth may be uneven. Fig. 6, to which I shall return shortly when I discuss matrilineage segmentation, presents its skeleton genealogy. This shows how the junior primary segment,[2] the 'breast' of Mnowa I (B.3), has proliferated far more than the senior one, the 'breast' of

---

[1] In South Africa, where this word is current in the form *mompara*, its meaning is nearer to 'fool' than it is to 'knave'. Dr N. J. van Warmelo has suggested (private communication) that it is derived from the Afrikaans adjective *baar*, meaning 'raw' or 'crude', converted into a noun by the use of the Bantu (Sotho) personal prefix *mo-*.

[2] Cf. Fortes, *The Dynamics of Clanship*, p. 35.

Makalila (B.2) from which the kinship-nucleus of the headman's section of Mceleka village has derived.

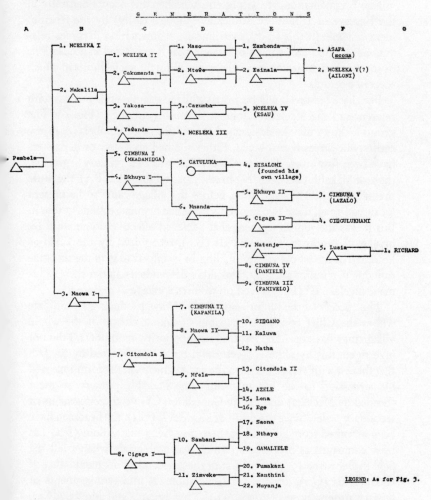

Fig. 6. Skeleton Genealogy of the Mceleka–Cimbuna Matrilineage

The process of matrilineage segmentation, which this diagram serves to illustrate, is basic to an understanding not only of Ceŵa social structure in general, but also of some of the specific problems with which this study is concerned. Segmentation is intimately related to the long-distance migrations of the past; for instance, Kaloŋga, Undi and

Cimwala were probably the leaders of their respective mothers' matri-lineage segments. And it plays an important part in the less memorable village fragmentation of the present, whether this occurs naturally in the Reserve or is induced artificially (though easily) by the resettle-ment scheme. In this study, matrilineage segmentation becomes rele-vant as an important source of tension that is expressed in accusations of sorcery and projected into beliefs regarding the social limits in which sorcery operates.

For these reasons it will be worth while to examine this process with reference to the Mceleka-Cimbuna skeleton genealogy (Fig. 6). The group it shows may be designated as the 'breast' of Pembela (A.1), the earliest ancestress remembered. Either she had no sisters or her sisters have been forgotten. This group divided into two primary segments, those of Makalila (B.2), the 'big breast', and of Mnowa I (B.3), the 'little breast'. At an early stage, long before the village came to its present locality in 1929, these two segments occupied distinct sections within it. But it was the junior segment that achieved effective domination by having its headman, Cimbuna III (E.9), recognized by the Chief as headman of the whole village. Failing in its efforts to gain the recogni-tion due to a senior segment, Makalila's descendants, under their head-man, Mceleka III (D.4), hived off to form a village of their own.

The success of the junior segment in always producing a candidate whom the Chief considered capable of taking charge of the whole village may have been the result of its superiority in numbers. I did not investigate this hypothesis specifically, but it is supported by the fact that there is a difference between the two segments in the form followed by succession to the headmanship. The Makalila primary segment (headed by Mceleka) divided (in Generation C) into three segments of secondary order. Since the death of Mceleka II (C.1), the headmen have been recruited from all three of these (assuming that Ailoni (F.2) has been confirmed as Mceleka V, which was not certain when I left the field in February 1953). The first of these secondary segments, that of Cakumanda (C.2), divided (in Generation D) into two segments of tertiary order, those of Maso (D.1), 'big breast', and Mtewe (D.2), 'little breast'. The male heir, Asafa (F.1), of the senior of these two tertiary segments did not succeed because he became a 'lost one' (mcona) in Southern Rhodesia.

In the junior primary segment, on the other hand, succession to the headmanship has been closer to the orthodox pattern. After the death of Cimbuna I (C.5), the headmanship passed only once to a junior segment, the 'breast' of Citondola I (C.7), returning and remaining in the senior secondary segment, that of Ŋkhuyu I (C.6), and, within it, going to the senior fourth-order segment, that of Ŋkhuyu II (E.5).

The difference between the two primary segments, which I have tentatively attributed to a difference of population with a corresponding difference in the field of candidates from whom to choose the headman, may, however, be fortuitous; for the almost perfect regularity of the succession to the Cimbuna headmanship (i.e. within the junior primary segment of Mnowa I (B.3)) has not occurred without opposition. Firstly, there were uncertainties regarding who would succeed Cimbuna IV (E.8). In 1946–7, when Cimbuna IV was headman, Ciŋgulukhani (F.4), the son of the second sister in his generation, Cigaga II (E.6), was his chief assistant and his most likely successor. At the end of 1948, after Ciŋgulukhani's death, Richard (G.1), the daughter's son of another junior sister of Cimbuna IV's generation, occupied this position and had similar prospects. In 1952, however, after the death of Cimbuna IV, Lazalo (F.3), of the segment senior among those of the fourth order, returned from work in the south and succeeded to the headmanship, becoming Cimbuna V. Incidentally, the reason why Cimbuna III (Faníwelo, E.9) preceded his elder brother, Cimbuna IV (Daniele, E.8), was that the latter was away at work when Cimbuna II died.

Secondly, just as the primary segmentation of the whole matrilineage ended in the emergence of two villages, Mceleka and Cimbuna, where formerly there had been one, so did secondary segmentation within Cimbuna itself nearly split it asunder. At the end of 1948, Gamaliele (E.19), an elder of the 'breast' of Cigaga I (C.8), one junior to the other secondary segments, succeeded in leaving what was then Cimbuna village and starting an independent settlement, to which he attracted, not only the tertiary segment of which he was a member, that of his mother, Sambani (D.10), but also the (secondary) segment of his mother's mother's sister, Citondolo I (C.7), and the (tertiary) segment of his mother's sister, Zimveke (D.11). This movement was foiled when the rest of the village abandoned the site from which he had moved with his following, and joined him at the new one, where he again became subject to Cimbuna IV, the leader of the senior secondary segment, that of Ŋkhuyu I (C.6).

My discussion of segmentation is only an apparent digression from the subject of the female sub-leaders of the matrilineage. To borrow a metaphor from Fortes, these women are the growing points[1] of the matrilineage and thus the origin of new segments. This is an appropriate moment to remark that the Cewa matrilineage is free from complications corresponding to those arising among patrilineal peoples from polygyny.[2] Though, as I shall show in the next chapter, the importance of a child's having an established physiological paternity is reflected in both doctrine and mystical belief, his having a particular paternity has no effect on his status in the segment of his mother or in the matrilineage at large.

I referred earlier to the ancestress as the president of her segment. She is a president in the pre-De Gaulle French, rather than the American, sense. Cewa matriliny is not matriarchy. Although she is an important figurehead and a person whose opinion has influence, she is not one of the executive officers of the matrilineage unless the absence of a suitable male heir necessitates her becoming the head (*nfumu*) of it. Gamitto records a few instances of women chiefs among the Maravi and Cewa.[3] During my first and second field trips, Kagolo village had a woman *nfumu*. But generally Cewa assert that women 'lack strength' (*alije nphamvu*), implying social as much as physical strength. It is the men of the matrilineage who normally perform executive functions.

This brings me to the headman's male lieutenants. They form a hierarchy with the headman at its apex. The form of the hierarchy is defined by the institution of 'guardianship' (*uŋkhoswe*).[4] In discussing the system of kinship terminology, I mentioned that any man, not necessarily the headman, has female matrilineal dependants known to outsiders as his *nbumba*. These are his sisters, sisters' daughters, sisters' daughters' daughters—and so on. He also has male matrilineal dependants known to outsiders as 'his younger brothers' (*aẓiphwawo*), though they include members of both his own and descending generations. The term *nbumba* may sometimes be stretched to include these male dependants.[5]

---

[1] *The Dynamics of Clanship*, p. 32.

[2] For instance, the segmentation of the Tale patrilineal units into matrilateral sub-units (*ibid.*, pp. 198 ff.).

[3] *O Muata Caẓembe*, pp. 416, 425 *et passim*.

[4] From *mŋkhoswe*, which, with some hesitation, I translate as 'guardian'. It also connotes 'representative', 'advocate' and 'surety'. As a reminder of my hesitation, I shall continue to write 'guardian' between quotation marks. Mitchell has translated the corresponding Yao term as 'warden' ('The Yao of Southern Nyasaland', p. 317). For an excellent account of 'guardianship' among the South Nyanja, which closely resembles that of the Cewa, see Malekebu, *Uŋkhoswe waa Nyanja*.

[5] In a neighbouring society, it has been stretched even further to include a large matrilineally extended family and the homestead it occupies. Cf. Lawson, 'An Outline of the Relationship System of the Nyanja and Yao Tribes in South Nyasaland', p. 181.

The relationship between any man and his dependants is expressed by saying that he is their 'guardian' (*myŋkhoswe*)[1] or, if they are of his own rather than of descending generations, their 'junior guardian' (*myŋkhoswe wamyono*). *Myŋkhoswe* is thus the reciprocal of *nbumba*. The relationship between a dependant and his or her 'junior guardian' becomes clearest in the context of marriage. The 'junior guardian' represents his matrilineage in the handing over of the marriage-token (see beginning of Chapter 5), and, having played this part, is charged with the future supervision of the marriage partners. He has to reconcile them when they quarrel, and, if he should fail in this, to arrange for their divorce. Typically the 'junior guardian' is responsible for the marriages of his own sisters and brothers. I have, however, recorded instances in which a man has acted as marriage 'guardian' of his classificatory siblings where these have lacked a brother of their own.

The 'junior guardian's' duties are not confined to acting as a marriage negotiator. He also sees to the general welfare of his dependants. If one of them should fall ill, it is his duty to take whatever steps appear to be necessary, e.g. arrange for members of the segment to consult a diviner and pay the diviner's fee, procure 'medicines' or arrange for the propitiation of a spirit or the prosecution of a sorcerer. And he must settle those of their quarrels that he can, and support them in those that he cannot, whether in the more intimate atmosphere of the matrilineage or village meeting (*kabuŋgwe*) or in the harsher glare of the Chief's court.

Among all the 'junior guardians' of a matrilineage, one stands out. He is the 'junior guardian' in the most senior segment (the 'big breast') a generation below the headman. Typically he is the headman's eldest own sister's eldest son, though this general rule may be upset by considerations of character (*makalidwe*) or by the absence at work or in uxorilocal marriage of the most likely candidate. Generally regarded as the headman's successor, this man is referred to as the 'junior headman' (*nfumu yaiŋono*) or the 'headman of the Administration' (*nfumu yaboma*), the latter designation arising from the fact that he is young enough to undertake journeys to Chadiza or Fort Jameson if the need should arise.

I now come back to the person whose female and male lieutenants I have been considering at some length, i.e. the matrilineage headman (*nfumu*). He is usually the 'senior guardian' (*myŋkhoswe wamkulu*) with whom 'junior guardians' are in continual consultation and to whom

---

[1] I am writing this term and the next few in the singular. In use they are more often in the honorific plural, e.g. *A ŋkhoswe, A ŋkhoswe waŋono.*

they defer, especially in matters in which their dependants are involved with members of other matrilineages. Sometimes, if the matrilineage is large and highly proliferated, the hierarchy may include 'guardians' of intermediate status. Thus, in Cimbuna village, Gamaliele (E.19 in Fig. 6) is referred to as the 'guardian' of the segments he succeeded in leading away to the new village site. He is senior to the 'junior guardians' of these segments, but junior to Headman Cimbuna, who is 'senior guardian' of the (primary) segment of Mnowa I, now domiciled in Cimbuna village.

The headman, or 'senior guardian', has a larger group of dependants than any of his male lieutenants either because he is actually of the same generation as the ancestresses of the primary segments or because he has succeeded to this, or an even more ascendant, genealogical position. Like his lieutenants, he takes an interest in the marriages, divorces and illnesses of his dependants; settles quarrels among them; supports them when they sue or are sued in the Chief's court; takes responsibility for their conduct, e.g. pays damages awarded against them in the Chief's court; and helps them when they are in need, e.g. clothes a female dependant neglected by a labour-migrant husband, and helps a male dependant to pay his tax. His range of contacts is wider than that of any of his lieutenants (except, possibly, his deputy, the junior headman) because, firstly, each segment within the group he leads looks ultimately to him; and, secondly, he interacts with the 'guardians' of other matrilineages, with chiefs and with administrators.

There are several reasons why the headman does not always attend in person to the affairs of the matrilineage, but delegates his authority to a 'junior guardian' or the junior headman. Firstly, he may be too old to undertake frequent journeys to the Chief's court or farther afield. Secondly, there are certain of his dependants, notably his sisters' daughters, about whom it would be improper for him to learn at first hand of intimate details of marital adjustment or of bodily condition. Thirdly, there is the general principle, which applies here, that a leader's best way of securing the loyalty of his lieutenants is to maintain their prestige by working through them.[1]

Sorcery and Segmentation

It is matrilineage segmentation that provides one of the most important contexts for beliefs in sorcery. As the matrilineage grows and

[1] Homans, *The Human Group*, pp. 429–31.

becomes unmanageable in terms of ecology and leadership, it divides, usually along its natural planes of cleavage, those between segments. Beliefs in sorcery express this inevitable but nevertheless disturbing process in that they provide a means of formulating tensions between the segments. In terms of the hypothesis I put forward in 1952,[1] Ceŵa beliefs in sorcery are, *inter alia*, catalytic to the normal process of matrilineage segmentation in that they are a means by which redundant, insupportable relationships, which through being close and personal cannot be quietly contracted out of, are dramatically blasted away.

Tensions between segments, which may be expressed in the form of rivalry between groups, or more specifically between their leaders, pass through two phases. So long as the matrilineage remains united, segment leaders compete for its overall control; and accusations of sorcery have the function of discrediting rivals. Once division has started, segment leaders may abandon hope of ever achieving overall control; and accusations of sorcery then have the function of accelerating and justifying the incipient separation.

As I have mentioned, when a headman dies, he is succeeded in turn by his surviving younger own brothers; and, when the last of these dies, by his eldest own sister's eldest son, i.e. by the genealogically senior male member of the first descending generation. The first phase, that of rivalry for overall leadership while the unity of the matrilineage persists, may start at any point in the succession sequence, but it is especially likely to begin on the death of the last surviving brother of the original headman. Since the succession rule may be disregarded on grounds of personal qualification or disqualification, this event may throw the men of the first descending generation into competition. Each of them stands a chance of succeeding if he can demonstrate his qualities of leadership and if he can discredit his more important rivals. The virtually irreconcilable conflict of rights and interests between rival candidates, together with the fact that headmanship is a highly valued goal, creates tension between them; and this tension cannot be contained or resolved for two reasons. Firstly, the judicial process cannot be applied to the settlement of the issue because the contestants belong to the same matrilineage. Secondly, a competitor, on the lookout for defects in his rival's character, may find evidence that enables him to believe, and to persuade others to believe, that his adversary is a sorcerer; and in this way he may secure a more effective method of

[1] 'The Social Context of Cewa Witch Beliefs', pp. 232–3 *et passim*.

discrediting a rival than any other available to him. In these circumstances, a high incidence of accusations may be expected between male
matrilateral parallel cousins, i.e. male ortho-cousins in this matrilineal
society.

Once the headmanship has left the headman's contemporary generation and passed to the first descending one, the second phase begins.
Hitherto one of the men of the senior generation, through not being
a member of any of the primary segments of the matrilineage (assuming
that its ancestress is his sister), has managed to keep the group together.
He has done this by being, to borrow a term from Fortes,[1] the keystone
of the arch. Once he falls away, the fragmentation of the matrilineage
may proceed. The successful candidate in the junior generation, even
if he is in its senior segment, may find it difficult to weld his followers
together; and tension may develop between the various segments, the
leader of each perhaps abandoning hope of ever being overall leader.
The resulting separation may be punctuated by accusations of sorcery.

Here are two cases that provide simple illustrations of what may
occur in this context. Both are in what I have described as the first
phase. In the first case, genealogical seniority wins; and, in the second,
personal qualification for leadership is on the way to winning, though
I have no record of the outcome.

Case No. 4—His Uncle's Bed

A Ceŵa chief, whom we shall call Kabambo, had no own sister's son, and
it was generally accepted that he would be succeeded by a classificatory
sister's son, Kasinda; so much so, that Kasinda had been given the pre-
succession name associated with the chieftainship. Kasinda was not, however,
universally liked, and a more distantly related classificatory sister's son of
Kabambo, whom we shall call Katete, who had gained an enviable reputation
as an arbitrator of disputes, was regarded as a possible alternative. When, at
an advanced age, Kabambo died, Katete, claiming that the old man had made
a death-bed statement to him, accused Kasinda of having killed him with
sorcery, adding that he had penetrated Kabambo's strong magical defences
by employing the unusual technique of committing adultery with one of
Kabambo's wives, an avoidance partner, thus rendering his bed dangerous
to its owner. Many people believed Katete's allegation, but, although it
blocked Kasinda's succession for a long period, Kasinda eventually succeeded
because of his closer genealogical relationship.

[1] *The Dynamics of Clanship*, p. 224.

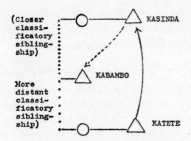

Fig. 7. The Case of 'His Uncle's Bed'

Note: This and subsequent genealogies follow the conventions used in Fig. 1, including the use of an unbroken arrow to represent an accusation; and a broken one, a believed attack.

Case No. 5—The Fertile Patch

Mtele, the headman of a matrilineage, had quarrelled, and come to blows, with his senior sister's son, Zabdiel, over a garden which Mtele had allotted to his own son, and the more fertile portion of which Zabdiel had claimed [an instance of the common conflict of loyalties a Ceŵa man experiences in

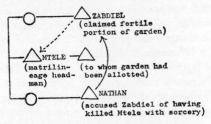

Fig. 8. The Case of 'The Fertile Patch'

relation to his children and his sisters' children]. Soon after the quarrel, Mtele became ill and subsequently died. A junior sister's son, Nathan, having just returned from working in Southern Rhodesia, came to the funeral and chased Zabdiel away, saying, 'Don't sit here crying for the one you have killed.' [Unfortunately, I have no record of who succeeded Mtele as headman.]

A third case illustrates what may happen in what I have called the second phase, when, the matrilineage having started to break up, an accusation has the function of justifying the separation. This case does not, however, represent tensions between male ortho-cousins, but between a young headman, threatened with the diminution of his following, and one of his female ortho-cousins belonging to a small group of women who lacked a male guardian in their own segment and whom he wanted to live in his section.

Case No. 6—The Diminished Following

A young married woman, Elena, had no brothers or mother's brothers. She and her mother, Cimalo, had been living in Gombe's village, to the headman's section of which they had long-standing ties of friendship, though not of kinship. Elena's mother's sister's son, Galami, persuaded them to move to a village in which he was headman of a small section. They were not, however, happy there, and came back to Gombe's village. Their leaving Galami and thus diminishing his following led to a violent quarrel between

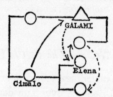

Fig. 9. The Case of 'The Diminished Following'

him and Elena, during which she alleged, by way of excuse for leaving his section, that his wife was practising sorcery against her younger sister. Elena fell pregnant soon after their return from Galami's village section, and feared that Galami had concocted, using soil on which she had urinated, a form of sorcery known as *kalamatila*, which makes childbirth difficult. When her time came, it was reported to me that she had been in labour for four days. I rushed her to the nearest mission hospital, but she died there of a ruptured uterus—probably the result, the doctor told me, of bearing down too hard, which I assume could have been caused by the fear that her classificatory brother's sorcery would prevent her from giving birth to her baby. The day after Elena's funeral, her mother, Cimalo, accused Galami of having killed her with sorcery.

The following two cases, involving the same pair of matrilineage segments, provide a further instance of the formulation of tension between segments in terms of sorcery. It is, however, rather an amorphous instance, since it reflects tension, not specifically between leaders, but generally between the two segments.

Cases Nos. 7 and 8—Redressing the Balance

In Mashawe village there live two segments of a matrilineage, the 'breast' of Angelina, which has many members, and that of Balila, which has but few. On two occasions the death of a member of the former segment has been attributed to the sorcery of a member of the latter; and, each time, the accuser (a member of Angelina's segment) has claimed that the sorcerer's motive was to reduce the disparity in numbers between the two segments.

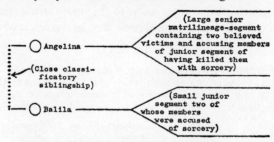

Fig. 10. The Cases of 'Redressing the Balance'

Cases, such as the above, which provide illustrations of how tensions occur between segments or between their leaders, have certain basic characteristics in common with the three introductory cases presented in Chapter 1. Firstly, misfortune is attributed to the malice of a mystical evil-doer. Secondly, the issue, either between sorcerer and victim or between accuser and sorcerer, seems to be an outcome of their competing for a strongly desired object in a situation in which there is an irreconcilable conflict in the rights, principles and claims that apply. Thirdly, there is some form of impediment—usually because of the irreconcilable nature of the conflict—to the settlement of the dispute by judicial or other rational forms of arbitration. Finally (an aspect to which I shall give due attention in Chapter 8), either the sorcerer, because of his addiction to, or choice of, illegitimate means, or the victim, because of his foolishness or recklessness, can provide material for a story with a moral.

To what extent is the function of beliefs in sorcery that Cases Nos. 4 to 8 illustrate reflected in the statistics derived from summarizing the attributes of all the cases collected? The first column of Table XVII summarizes from Table VII the percentage distribution in categories of social relationship of the links between all the sorcerers and victims involved in the 101 cases. There were 115 such links with full counting of 'multiple' cases (see above, last section of Chapter 3). The second column of this table gives a similar percentage distribution of the 112 total links between accuser and sorcerer yielded (again with full counting) by the seventy-nine cases in which accusers were identified. The first two sets of entries in the first two rows of this table show that the frequency of inter-segmental believed attacks or accusations was about twice that of intra-segmental ones. At first sight, then, the association that Cases Nos. 4 to 8 have illustrated seems to be confirmed by the statistics. If believed attacks and accusations are pointers to tensions, inter-segmental relationships seem to be more tense than intra-segmental ones. But such a conclusion may be the result of a reckless

TABLE XVII

LINKS BETWEEN (1) SORCERER AND VICTIM, (2) ACCUSER AND SOR-
CERER AND (3) ACCUSER AND VICTIM— DISTRIBUTED BY RELATION-
SHIP CATEGORY (with full counting of 'multiple' cases, i.e. cases in which
there were more than one sorcerer, victim or accuser.)

Type of Social Relationship	Percentage Distribution of Links Between			Difference (2)–(3) and Its Signifi-cance†	Ratio (2)/(3) Where Dif-ference Is Significant
	(1) Sorcerer and Victim (N = 115)	(2) Accuser and Sorcerer (N = 112)	(3) Accuser and Victim (N = 90)		
Related:					
Matrilineally:					
same segment	17·4	13·4	33·3	−19·9***	0·40
different segments	29·6	33·0	22·2	+10·8	—
segment indeter-					
minate	11·3	3·6	22·2	−18·6***	0·16
(a)	58·3	50·0	77·7	−27·7***	0·64
Not matrilineally:					
spouses	5·2	1·8	4·4	−2·6	—
co-wives, actual					
or potential	1·7	0·9	—	+0·9	—
other affines	11·3	31·2	8·9	+22·3***	3·51
others	13·9	7·1	7·8	−0·7	—
(b)	32·1	41·0	21·1	+19·9**	1·95
Unrelated (c)	8·7	8·9	1·1	+7·8*	8·05
Relationship unknown (d)	0·9	—	—	—	—
Total (a + b + c + d)	100	100	100	0	1·00

† The code for statistical significance is as follows:

Unmarked: $p > ·05$
*: $·05 > p > ·01$
**: $·01 > p > ·001$
***: $p < ·001$

interpretation of statistics. Is it possible to claim that these data show that inter-segmental tensions are twice as tense—or even more tense —than intra-segmental ones, and that accusations of sorcery are cata-lytic to lineage segmentation?

Two problems must be met if this claim is to be sustained. The first is that the high frequency of accusations in certain social relationships may be linked only indirectly with the tensions characteristic of such relationships, i.e. there may be a hidden intervening variable that explains the association. Thus, Professor Monica Wilson[1] suggested that I might test the hypothesis that, since the Cewa live in villages with their matrilineal relatives, the higher frequency among them of accusations between such relatives might simply reflect tension between people as neighbours rather than as matrilineal kinsmen. I therefore made a practice of recording both the spatial and the social relationships between the parties in each of the cases I recorded. Table XVIII

TABLE XVIII

SOCIAL AND SPATIAL RELATIONSHIPS BETWEEN (1) SORCERER AND VICTIM AND (2) ACCUSER AND SORCERER (with single counting of 'multiple' cases)

Spatial Relationship	(1) Sorcerer and Victim			(2) Accuser and Sorcerer		
	Matri-lineally Related	Not Matri-lineally Related	Total	Matri-lineally Related	Not Matri-lineally Related	Total
In same village	42	33	75	34	31	65
In different villages or at great distance	10	6	16	6	6	12
Not recorded	7	2	9	1	1	2
	59	41	100	41	38	79
Victim unknown			1			
Accuser not identified						22
			101			101

shows the distribution of these relationships. In neither sorcerer–victim nor accuser–sorcerer relationships is any association revealed between matrilineal kinship and either physical separation or physical proximity —so obviously that the application of the chi-square test is unnecessary. These data, then, do not prove the point either way. There is, however, some support for the view that accusations reflect tensions between people as relatives (in general) rather than merely as neighbours because Cewa villages, as I show in the next chapter, contain many unrelated sections, and the frequency of accusations between unrelated people is low compared with the frequency with which such people meet in the village. This argument will be developed in Chapter 7.

[1] Private communication.

The second problem, to which I alluded briefly in the last chapter, arises from the fact that the incidence of accusations of sorcery in various relationship categories is of complex determination. For convenience, I shall disregard for the moment the believed instances of sorcery (involving the relationship between alleged sorcerer and believed victim) and consider the accusations (involving the relationship between accuser and sorcerer), the latter being more important sociologically. A high frequency of accusations in a particular category is an index, not only of the degree of social tension characteristic of it, but also of the sheer frequency of interaction in it. Thus to argue that a higher frequency of accusations in one category than in another (as reflected in the table I have referred to) indicates a higher degree of tension in the former than in the latter is as naïve as contending, in a fashion not always avoided by the leader-writers of newspapers, that divorce is a more serious problem among the people of the United Kingdom than it is among South African Whites because the absolute number of divorces in any one year is greater in the former than in the latter population. Just as divorces can be compared only when considered as rates, i.e. in relation to the universe in which they occur, such as the total population or the total married population, so must accusations of sorcery be related to the universe of social interaction in which they occur.

I may approach this problem in a slightly different way by setting up a null hypothesis that no one type of relationship is characteristically more tense than another. This would mean that Ego's tense relationships would constitute a proportion, p, of all his relationships regardless of their distribution by type. Supposing that p is one-fifth and that Ego has five own siblings and twenty classificatory siblings, he might, on the null hypothesis, develop tense relationships with one own sibling and four classificatory siblings. Thus the frequency of accusations in a particular relationship category may be accounted for on the basis of the null hypothesis and cannot be taken as an index of the social tension characteristic of that category—unless the variables springing from Ego's having as many different universes of interaction as he has types of social relationships are controlled, size being only one of the possible differences between such universes.

The problem would in any case be a difficult one to resolve; and it is complicated here by the fact that, as recorded in Chapter 1, the case material did not come from a single neighbourhood. It was thus not confined to the neighbourhood for which I have full information regarding the social composition of villages. The only possible way of meeting this problem would, therefore, be to build a paradigm—empirically based if possible—which would yield a quantitative estimate of the universe of interaction a person has with each type of fellow tribesman, e.g. his siblings, ortho-cousins, lineal matrikin, agnatic relatives, affines, unrelated fellow villagers (in village sections other than his own), fellow tribesmen in other villages—and so on. With such estimates as their second terms, accusation rates or ratios would be comparable with one another, and then, but only then, could one conclude whether certain relationships have a greater expectation of accusations of sorcery than others and thus a greater underlying potential for social tension.

An added complication is the fact that Ego, whether he is taken to be accuser or sorcerer, is, as Tables X and XIV show, a person of variable age and sex; and different age–sex categories have, for obvious demographic reasons, different probabilities of interaction with other categories. Thus an old man has fewer surviving ortho-cousins than a younger one; and the chances of their being more widely dispersed, e.g. as a result of uxorilocal marriage or village fission, are greater. In general, other things being equal, one interacts more frequently with those of one's fellow men who are more numerous in type, who are in the immediate vicinity, and with whom one is linked by similar interests. Conversely, one interacts less frequently with persons who are less numerous in type, who are physically remote, and to whom one is not united by common interests.

These considerations indicate that the construction of a paradigm which would yield satisfactory second terms for comparable rates of accusation for each of the social relationship categories of Table XVII would be extremely complicated. It is an operation clearly beyond the limits set by my rudimentary statistical and demographic competence and by the localized nature of my genealogical data. I shall therefore not attempt it, but merely express the hope that this statement of the problem may prompt someone to suggest a practical solution which may guide future field workers in the collection of such data as may be used in estimating the universe of social interaction characteristic of each type of social relationship in which accusations of sorcery and witchcraft occur.

Had it been possible to construct the paradigm just sketched, it would have yielded a series of theoretical estimates each of which would have acted as a foil, a denominator or a second term, to the

M

absolute frequency of cases of accusations falling within a particular category of social relationships. Another possible solution to this problem is to take, as a foil, a figure that is derivable from the case material itself, i.e. to arrive at an accusation rate by expressing the proportion of accuser–sorcerer relationships falling in a particular category as a ratio of the proportion of accuser–victim relationships falling in that category. In effect this would be to standardize accusation frequencies by relating them to the incidence of the affiliative link between accuser and victim.

I should be explicit about the possible deficiency of this method. Being subject to social definition, the proportion of accuser–victim relationships does not provide as regular and inert a base as would an estimate of total interaction. Ceŵa social norms condemn sorcery in general, and consequently say nothing about whom one, as a sorcerer, should or should not attack. In the incidence of sorcerer–victim and accuser–sorcerer relationships, norms are therefore a constant, negative factor. In contrast to this, in the incidence of accuser–victim relationships, norms probably constitute an important influence and one that varies from one relationship to another. As I have noted (for instance pp. 145 ff.), Ceŵa norms are clear about the duties of matrilineage members towards one another, more particularly about the duties of leaders and would-be leaders towards their followers, actual or potential. A 'junior guardian' must, among other duties, undertake the investigation of misfortunes that befall his dependants. He must play the rôle that I have defined as that of accuser in those cases where sorcery is found to be the cause of the misfortune. When asked who it is who should consult a diviner, Ceŵa usually designate the own brother of the victim and probably have the 'junior guardian' in mind. Although this dogma does not represent exactly what happens, for mothers, mother's brothers and occasionally classificatory siblings may play this rôle, the fact that social norms such as this affect, in some measure at least, the distribution of accuser–victim relationships in the categories used in Table XVII may make them questionable as bases for accusation rates. On the other hand, it might be argued in favour of the use of this type of base that fluctuations in it are related to one of the factors in social tension; for, as I shall argue in Chapter 11, tense situations are often those characterized by irreconcilable conflict, ones that social norms usually leave undefined.

Table XVII compares the incidence, in categories of social relationship, of the links between sorcerer and victim, accuser and sorcerer, and accuser and victim. The first of these three distributions may be taken to reflect people's estimates of social tensions; the second, actually hostile relationships; and the third, actually affiliative relationships. There is a certain similarity between the first two distributions, brought about *inter alia* by the fact that in some instances the victim and the accuser were the same person (see end of Chapter 3). Partly because of this and partly because the second distribution reflects actual tension rather than people's estimates of tension, I shall from this point deal with only the second and third distributions.

To compare the distributions of accuser–sorcerer and accuser-victim relationships is, in effect, to examine the incidence in particular categories of social relationship of the hostile link between accuser and sorcerer and the affiliative one between accuser and victim. A comparison of the entries in the second and third columns of Table XVII will indicate whether a particular relationship-category is characterized by a predominance of accuser–sorcerer relationships or whether it shows a fairly even balance between the two. Percentages rather than actual frequencies are compared because, owing to the fact that in twelve cases the accuser was the victim himself and in one case the victim was not specified, the total for victims distinguishable from accusers is sixty-six instead of seventy-nine. With full counting of 'multiple' cases (see above, Chapter 3), there are 112 accuser–sorcerer and ninety accuser–victim relationships.

The percentage difference for each category of social relationship, together with its statistical significance, is given in the fourth column of Table XVII. A positive difference indicates a predominance in the category concerned of the accuser–sorcerer relationship. Note will be taken only of those differences that are statistically significant at or below the five-per-cent level of probability. It is only in respect of categories satisfying this criterion that the percentage ratio of accuser-sorcerer to accuser–victim relationships has been entered in the final column of the table. A ratio of more than unity, like a positive percentage difference, indicates a predominance in the category concerned of hostile links; and a ratio of less than unity, like a negative difference, indicates a predominance of affiliative links.

Adopting the interpretation of the percentage difference outlined, and observing the statistical standard set up, I may note that relationships between members of the same matrilineage segment are characterized, to an extremely significant degree, by a predominance of affiliative links; but that those between members of different segments, while predominantly hostile, are not sufficiently so to satisfy the statistical criterion. Making the doubtful assumption of the validity of the last-resource procedure I have adopted, there is in this comparison some slight support for the conclusion illustrated by Cases Nos. 4 to 8 that accusations and suspicions of sorcery are more common between segments than within them.

So much for relationships between segments of the matrilineage. What does Table XVII show about the matrilineage as a whole? It will be recalled that Cewa regard the matrilineage as the natural arena for quarrels that lead to attacks and accusations of sorcery (see Chapter 3). They usually phrase this by saying that matrilineal relatives who quarrel, being unable to avail themselves of the normal machinery of arbitration, 'leave [unspoken] words of speech with one another'. Their rarer dictum, that people who have quarrelled 'grasp [accuse] each other of sorcery', could apply to matrilineal relatives.

As to matrilineal relatives in general, Table XVII certainly shows that about half the accusers and sorcerers in the sample were in this category. There were, however, so many more accusers and victims thus related that, on balance, this category must be regarded, in terms of the conventions I have been following, as more affiliative than hostile, this statement resting on an extremely significant difference and a percentage ratio of ·64.

Among the sub-categories of matrilineal relatives, there are two that are, to an extremely significant degree, affiliative rather than hostile. These are persons belonging to the same segment (already noted) and persons whose relative segment membership is indeterminate. The latter consist mainly of mother's brothers and sisters' sons. These statistical results are not surprising for members of the same segment, in respect of whom there is a normative emphasis on mutual help, protection and vengeance. For the link between mother's brother and sister's sons, results are at variance with the impression I formed, from what people said, of the considerable degree of tension between partners in this relationship. It is possible that, in the unsystematic collection of people's opinions, I heard more of the quarrels and was told less of the quiet but faithful performance of avuncular and nepotal duties, such as those that an accuser performs for a victim.

Nevertheless, though social norms demand co-operation in these relationships, they can both be tense, especially when questions of succession or of the disposal of property are involved. I have already noted (Table VIII) a moderately significant association between matrilineal relationship of sorcerer and victim and type of quarrel, the tendency being for quarrels over social obligations and the disposal of property, especially cattle, to be characteristic of matrilineal rather than of non-matrilineal relationships. The following cases provide illustrations of the tension that such quarrels may generate in what the norms lay down to be co-operative relationships.

Case No. 9—The Independent Sister

Musiye, a woman who had borne two children, died in Bizeki village in 1949. She died of 'medicines' put in her beer by her brother, Josi, aged about forty. Musiye had long ago bought cattle with money earned by her husband

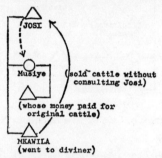

Fig. 11. The Case of 'The Independent Sister'

in Southern Rhodesia; and, when these beasts began to bear, she sold them. Josi was very angry with her and said, 'Why didn't you tell me that you wanted to sell cattle? Are there no other people in this village? No matter! Sell your cattle in the way you have already sold them!' After her death, another of her brothers, Mkawila, went to a diviner who stated that it was Josi who had killed her because of the cattle.

Case No. 10—The Ambitious Nephew

Before the Whites came, Cipanda was an important headman across the Kapoche river. Disagreeing with the policy of his chief, he retired from his headmanship and for many years lived as an unimportant village headman in another chiefdom. In his village, his junior assistant was his younger sister's son, Makanje, in whose favour he had, for reasons of personality, passed over his elder sister's son, Limbikani. After some years in what amounted to retirement, Cipanda received a reconciliatory invitation from his former chief to return to the important position he had held. However, now being old, he sent his young brother, Kasiyamadzi, in his stead, with Limbikani as his assistant. Shortly after taking up his appointment, Kasiyamadzi died; and Cipanda accused Limbikani of having killed him with sorcery. Limbikani denied this and demanded a poison ordeal. As the poison made him purge, he was considered guilty; but Cipanda, probably through a lack of interest in his former headmanship, did nothing to prevent Limbikani from succeeding to it; and Limbikani is now the incumbent, with his younger brother, Laimoni, as his assistant. My informant added, 'There is a great deal of hatred in Cipanda's family. It is only old Cipanda who holds them together. When he dies, the family will break up because his nephews will all call themselves Cipanda; some in fact already do.'

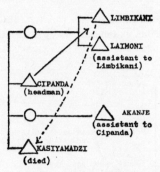

Fig. 12. The Case of 'The Ambitious Nephew'

Case No. 11—The Strong European 'Medicine'

Donaliya, who lived at Kalileshya village, went with her two children, Malia and Suŋgani (a baby boy), to her garden to hoe. She and her daughter hoed and hoed and they became hungry. They had drawn water the previous day and left it in the garden shelter. This they now used for making porridge so that they would be strong and hoe well. But, when they had eaten the porridge, the mother began to die. After a while Malia died too, and Suŋgani, who had also eaten some porridge. The people in the village saw that the sun had gone down but they had not returned; but, as they did not search for them, all three lay dead in the garden until next morning until they were found. Their bodies were carried to the village and word was sent to the territorial chief. The Chief came and took some of the porridge they had left in the garden. He gave it to a dog and the dog died. He began to search the village but could not find the 'medicines' that had killed the three people. Headman Kalileshya then went to a diviner who began to search. He found the 'medicine'; it was [potassium] cyanide;[1] and the person in whose posses-

---

[1] Informants state that this chemical, which is used in gold extraction, is sometimes stolen from mines and used for killing people. Ceŵa classify such poisoning as sorcery, since they regard European medicines and chemicals as belonging to the same general category as their own magical substances but as being stronger. Since I recount this case as it was described to me, I am unable to say whether in fact the Administration reacted as my informant said, or even if the case was reported.

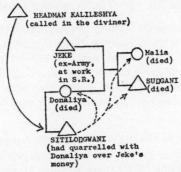

Fig. 13. The Case of 'The Strong European "Medicine" '

sion it was found, Sitiloŋgwani, the brother of Donaliya, he took to the Europeans. The Europeans did not, however, arrest him because, they said, he had not killed the deceased with an axe; and Sitiloŋgwani came back, though he has since run away to Portuguese territory. Sitiloŋgwani had quarrelled with Donaliya over some money that her husband, Jeke, had earned when he was in the Army in 1942, ten years before all this happened. (Jeke was at work in Southern Rhodesia when his wife and children died.) Sitiloŋgwani had asked Donaliya for some of Jeke's money so that he could pay his tax. She had abused him and told him to go to the War and earn some himself.

Case No. 12—The Gambler's Folly

Alisoni's fellow villagers say that he killed his younger brother, Kenala, with sorcery because, on his return from a visit to Fort Jameson, he discovered that Kenala had been gambling and had taken his [Alisoni's] tie, shirt and shoes to meet his gambling debts.

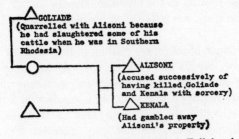

Fig. 14. The Cases of 'The Gambler's Folly' and
'The Slaughtered Beasts'

Case No. 13—The Slaughtered Beasts

Alisoni and his mother's brother, Goliade, quarrelled because, during Goliade's absence at work in Southern Rhodesia, Alisoni had taken some of Goliade's cattle and slaughtered them without his permission. When Goliade, after his return home, died, people in the village thought that he had been killed by the sorcery of Alisoni because, they said, Alisoni wanted his mother's brother's property and, anyway, was a sorcerer because he was impotent.

I shall refer again to the last two cases when discussing sorcery as a moral force (in Chapter 8). The cases of the Independent Sister (No. 9) and the Gambler's Folly (No. 12) are instances of the manner in which social control is effected—or believed to be effected—through sorcery. These cases raise the problem of distinguishing between illegitimate sorcery and legitimate mystical control by lineage elders. It may be that in them the alleged sorcerer, had he admitted the charge, might have pleaded justification for attacking his recalcitrant junior. However, the fact that the result of his attack was fatal would have made this a poor defence.

Integrating Factors

These cases have a bearing on the factors in the unity of the matrilineage, which in my emphasis on its segmentation should not be overlooked. There are a number of influences that unite the matrilineage. Segmentation cannot, of course, be stopped; but its disruptive effects can at least be postponed by astute headmanship.

The influences that delay the fragmentation of the matrilineage along its natural planes of cleavage fall into two categories. The first contains those relating to the headman; and the second, those having to do with the corporate activities of the matrilineage in Ceŵa society at large.

The importance of influences relating to the headman derives from the fact that he, like his Tale counterpart, is the keystone of the arch,[1] a fact clearly illustrated by my informant's comment on the case of the Ambitious Nephew, 'It is only old Cipanda who holds them together. When he dies, the family will break up.' This has two aspects. Firstly, positional inheritance not only increases the span of his effective dominance but also ties him more closely to his followers.

[1] Cf. p. 148.

Secondly, his social, economic and mystical power gives him effective sanctions for controlling his followers.

The headman's span of effective dominance is increased by positional inheritance because this elevates him ultimately to a point on the genealogy near which the descent lines of his followers converge—'near which', and not 'at which', because the point of convergence is a woman, the ancestress in the most ascendant generation remembered; and positional inheritance makes him her son or her brother.

To understand how positional inheritance ties the headman more closely to his followers, it should be remembered that, whereas male names pass from their holders to their sisters' sons, female ones usually go from their holders to their daughters' daughters. As Fig. 15

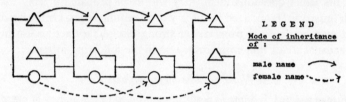

LEGEND

Mode of inheritance of :

male name

female name

Fig. 15. The Structural Implications of Sex Differences in Name Inheritance

shows, the effect of this sex difference in name inheritance (and positional inheritance follows it) is to tie the headman to all his female dependants either by a brother–sister bond or a son–mother bond (own or classificatory). In particular, it converts into a son–mother bond the avuncular bond between him and his sisters' daughters, who are perhaps the most important buds of segmentation.[1] This may have the effect of integrating all the segments of the matrilineage he leads by making him a member of each of them as they develop.

The headman has both secular and mystical sanctions for controlling his dependants. To understand the strength of the secular ones, I shall assume for the moment (this will be demonstrated below) that the matrilineage functions as a corporate group in Cewa society; and that its members therefore derive benefits from their association and enjoy the satisfaction, in terms of the Cewa normative system, of belonging to a large group.

Given this, it is obvious that the headman's task of controlling and uniting the group is greatly facilitated; for in his hands lie a powerful

[1] I am grateful to Professor J. Clyde Mitchell for suggesting that I should consider the possible structural consequences of the differing modes of inheritance of male and female names, a phenomenon which he has observed among the Yao, and which Dr Raymond Apthorpe has observed among the Nsenga (private communications).

series of sanctions. If his dependants are troublesome, he can threaten to chase them away from his village or to withhold his protection and support. Ceŵa say that long ago he could sell them into slavery. Any of these forms of expulsion would have serious consequences for them. His power to take any of these steps is restricted. Apart from the fact that it is no longer possible for him to sell his dependants into slavery, there are many social pressures opposing any step he might take towards expelling or disowning them. The pressure of public opinion is represented in an informant's dictum that a man who fails to care for (*-suŋga*, *-samala*) his dependants and leaves them to their own devices 'is not a person' (*simunthu yai*). Another informant says that if a man complains to the Chief that his dependants have run away from him, and the Chief questions them, they will in all probability reply that their 'guardian' is addicted to sorcery or to beating them. Or the headman may be deterred from taking strong disciplinary action lest his dependants attack him with sorcery, as in the following instance:

Case No. 14—The Sister without Ears

In 1949 a section headman's death was attributed to the sorcery of one of his classificatory sisters because he and she had hated each other as a result of his once having castigated her with the words, 'Thou, female dependant, thou hast no ears [art disobedient]' (*Iwe nbumba ulije matu*).

The restrictions on a headman's threatening to withhold his protection and support are well illustrated by the case of the Pretended Brother. In this case, Headman Gombe decided to disown a man he had accepted as a classificatory younger brother. The Court overruled him because he had formally accepted the man by asking him to marry the widow of another classificatory brother (pp. 277–8).

Most of the supernatural sanctions for failure to obey the headman depend on the fact that he is an elder with believed mystical powers. When the cult of the spirits was more vigorous, it was believed that the spirits overheard him as he complained (*-dandaula*) to himself about his dependants' misdeeds, and proceeded to punish the transgressors by making them or their children ill.[1] The headman was not the only person credited with mystical power over junior kin. All the elders were, and still are to some extent, believed to exercise supernatural influence of this kind. Women are said to have the power of cursing their children by expressing milk from their breasts (*kufinyila*

---

[1] The traditional Ceŵa beliefs in the mystical powers of elder relatives had many points in common with those of the Lugbara (cf. Middleton, *Lugbara Religion*, passim).

maŵele pansi) to the accompaniment of a statement such as, 'If I did not suckle this child, then no matter; but, if I did suckle him, may he die.' And even today pregnant women are warned not to quarrel with the elders lest their labour be difficult.

With the decline of the cult of the spirits, these beliefs in the mystical power of senior relatives are now often formulated in terms of sorcery. Young men who, verbally at least, echo the missionary dogma that it is nonsense to believe in the spirits, and who apparently have no fear of their intervention, nevertheless express a lively fear of the sorcery of their mothers' brothers. The mother's curse is now so rare that one of my most reliable informants, a man in his late sixties, said that he had only once observed it, and that it had then attracted such a large crowd that he could not get near enough to see properly. On that occasion, he said, the woman he observed was cursing her son, in his early twenties, who was a thief. The details of how the elders interfere with parturition are not always specified; but *kalamatila*, a kind of sorcery, is often believed to be the cause of difficult labour or death in childbirth.

Was my assumption correct that the matrilineage functions as a corporate group, and that its members derive material and psychological benefits from belonging to it? There are four parts to the answer to this question: firstly, the effect of matrilineage membership on prestige; secondly, the extent to which the matrilineage is economically corporate; thirdly, the extent to which its solidarity is enhanced by ritual; and, fourthly, taking us into the next two chapters, the extent to which it has a jural identity.

There are many instances of the prestige that is gained in Ceŵa eyes from belonging to a large group, particularly a large matrilineal kingroup. Cimbuna, which, until it broke up in 1949, was one of the largest villages in the part of the chiefdom immediately adjoining the Chief's capital, was proudly referred to by its inhabitants as 'our town', the English word being used in contradistinction to the Ceŵa term, *mudẑi* ('village'), applied to smaller neighbouring villages. In fact, so great is the felt importance of belonging to a kin-group, preferably a large one, that people who lack relatives and who have to resort to the device of fictitiously claiming kinship with one another (*kukumbana*) are objects of pity and scorn. In an enviable position are their opposites, those who are 'in the middle'. In contrast with modern slang, this Ceŵa expression means being in a fortunate position, that of having many matrikin, especially economically and socially powerful male matrikin. Ceŵa believe that the envy of sorcerers is sometimes aroused by the large size of matrilineage segments (or occasionally matrilineages) other than their own, and is satisfied by their killing off their members until some semblance of equality is reached (see, for instance, the two cases of Redressing the Balance).

Economic functions undoubtedly unite matrilineal relatives, but it is uncertain whether any of the groups that emerge from economic co-operation correspond with what I have been referring to as the matrilineage (a term standing for matrilineage remnant). When a woman's husband dies, or goes away to work for a long time, she looks to her brother for goods, such as clothes, which her husband would normally provide, and services, such as hut-building, which he would normally perform. Whether, however, the group performing these economic functions is the matrilineage as a whole or one of its segments depends on circumstances such as the depth and span of the matrilineage and on the presence or absence of competition between 'junior guardians'.

As I noted in Chapter 2, the social basis of day-to-day living is the household whose matrilineal core is a segment usually three generations in depth. This group, which is a matrilocally extended family, jointly works a common garden and lives on its produce. In contrast, the non-routine form of economic organization, the working party, is recruited from a wider field. By the promise of entertainment, and on the assumption of future reciprocity, the host matrilineage-segment induces not only members of other segments of its own matrilineage but also unrelated friends and neighbours to co-operate in tackling one of its major tasks such as weeding, starting a new garden, or building a hut or cattle byre.

It would appear that, on balance, economic co-operation, by involving groups both below and above the level of the matrilineage, does not contribute directly to its overall unity.

What of the greatest unifying influence of all, ritual? Are there any distinct ritual occasions involving a single matrilineage? And, if so, do these contribute to its solidarity? The second of these three questions has to be answered in the negative. If one makes a list of rituals affecting the daily life of the Cewa—name inheritance, mortuary rituals, female initiation, induction into the *nyau* lodge (involving as it does many aspects of male initiation)—one is struck by the fact that these are notable mainly for their effects on neighbourhood and village organization. In none of them, not even in the propitiation of the spirits, does the matrilineage emerge as an exclusive group with peculiar modes of ritual expression.

This does not mean that the third question must be answered in the negative, too. For, though the village and neighbourhood participate, the matrilineage most concerned is often of distinct ritual status. This applies especially to mortuary rituals in which the ritual friends (*adzukulu*, see above, this chapter) play their most important part. The bereaved matrilineage, weakened by its sorrow, is inactive, leaving its ritual friends to do whatever has to be done. Thus it does not lose its identity in a situation more notable for its effects on the solidarity of village and neighbourhood than on that of the matrilineage.

There are several possible explanations for the fact that, though it is often the focal point of village and neighbourhood rituals, the matrilineage lacks any rituals that are distinctly its own. One is that the traditional Ceŵa village may have been smaller than the present one, and may have consisted of a single kinship unit, in which case village rituals would have been, very largely, matrilineage rituals. Another explanation is that the decline of the cult of the spirits has affected rituals that unify at the matrilineage level of organization rather than at any other. And a third possibility is that, in an egalitarian society such as that of the Ceŵa, no kin-group, not even a chief's, has a status so inherently different from that of other similar groups that it needs ritual enforcement.

CHAPTER 5

EXTERNAL RELATIONS OF THE MATRILINEAGE

BECAUSE the matrilineage is a strictly exogamous group, marriage inevitably involves it in external relations. The matriclan (*pfuko*, plur., *mafuko*), of which it is a part, is exogamous in theory, but I have recorded several instances of marriage between members of the same matriclan—usually followed by a change in clan-name by one of the partners.

As in other societies, marriage among the Ceŵa is a clearly formalized link between two social groups; but it has neither great promise of durability nor much actual staying power. The two essential steps that put it into effect are, firstly, the passage of a token (*nsambo*)[1] from the 'junior guardian' of the bridegroom to the 'junior guardian' of the bride; and, secondly, the couple's spending the night together in a hut (*kulowana*). The token was traditionally an ivory bead; and later, a string of imported beads. It is now a money payment, sixpence being the most popular amount (see Section 4 of Table XIX). If the preferred form of marriage—with a cross-cousin or similar relative—takes place, the token is sometimes dispensed with.

As one might expect from the difference in value between this token and the bridewealth of the patrilineal Bantu, their functions are distinct. Gluckman has shown the importance of distinguishing between various types of marriage payments.[2] Some merely secure the husband's sexual, economic and other personal rights over his wife, and ensure *inter alia* that he will be able to sue in the event of her adultery. Others, such as bridewealth, go further, and transfer the woman's childbearing capacity to her husband or his kin-group. Ceŵa marriage payments and the labour service associated with traditional uxorilocal marriage are exclusively of the former type. They secure a man's rights over his wife's person and services, but do not give him rights over the

---

[1] A few informants state that there is an exchange of tokens. J. Bruwer, 'By Ons Is 'n Haantjie', refers to this payment as *cimalo* and states that it is a fowl. My informants used *cimalo* inconsistently, sometimes equating it with *nsambo* and sometimes with *nthakula*.
[2] 'Kinship and Marriage among the Lozi of Northern Rhodesia and the Zulu of Natal', pp. 199 ff.

children born of the union, who remain members of their mother's matrilineage.

This remains true even if other marriage payments have been made. An indigenous payment, known as *nthakula* or *conyamulila*, the latter implying 'of carrying [away]', is made when a man, having satisfied his wife's matrilineage that he is capable of looking after her, takes her from uxorilocal residence to a place of his own choice. Traditionally it was a goat (some say a hoe), and it is now usually five shillings. By making this payment, he gains no rights over the children, who very often return to their mother's home village. Nor is he absolved from compensating his wife's matrilineage if any of them—or his wife herself—should die.

In recent years, the Native Authorities of Fort Jameson district, presumably with the intention of 'securely binding marriage' (*kumaŋgitsa cikwati*), have encouraged a payment known to the Ceŵa by the Ŋgoni term *mcato*, and to the Ŋgoni by the Ceŵa term *cimalo*.[1] As yet, the proportion of Ceŵa making this payment, which has been fixed at thirty shillings, is very small. Even if it is made, it does not alter the nature of the rights secured by the token, but merely increases their monetary value. Its chief effect has been to increase the amounts of compensation payable in cases of adultery. Thus, if a man has 'securely bound' his marriage by handing over *mcato*, and his wife commits adultery, he may expect to be awarded damages of £3 each from his wife and her lover; and, in addition, they will have to pay a court fee of five shillings each. If he has not, the award will probably be thirty shillings each; and the court fee, half-a-crown each.

Mcato has acquired an administrative function, too. If a woman wishes to leave the Eastern Province to join her husband at his place of work, she should be in possession of a marriage certificate. This she obtains (at the cost of half-a-crown) on having her marriage registered with the Native Authority. The South Ceŵa Native Authorities, before they issue a marriage certificate, generally insist that the thirty shillings *mcato* should have been handed over by the husband's matrilineage to the wife's. This association of registration with the payment of *mcato* rests on convention rather than on legal provision.

Table XIX presents an analysis of the marriages of persons domiciled in Jeremiah village in January 1953. Section 4 of this table, to

[1] Barnes, *Marriage in a Changing Society*, p. 37, translates *cimalo* as 'legalization payment', and its function among the Ŋgoni is clearly the same as that of the *nsambo* among Kaŵaza's Ceŵa.

which I have already referred, shows that in this sample payments made in addition to the token (*nsambo*, usually sixpence) were rare.

TABLE XIX

ANALYSIS OF EXTANT AND COMPLETED MARRIAGES OF THE POPULA-
TION HAVING MARITAL EXPERIENCE, JEREMIAH VILLAGE (EXCLUDING
POTOKOSI'S SECTION), JANUARY 1953

1. *Present Marital Status*

	Male	Female	Total
Married:			
Monogamous, both present	18	18	36
Monogamous, spouse away (including two women separated)	—	8	8
Polygynous, both wives present	1	2	3
Polygynous, one wife present, one elsewhere (including two men separated)	8	8	16
Total married	27	36	63
Widowed	—	5	5
Divorced	1	3	4
Never married	32	24	56
Total population of village (excluding Potokosi's section)	60	68	128

2. *Residence of Couples Domiciled in the Village*

	Marriages		Total
	Inter-Village	Intra-Village	Married Couples
Uxorilocal	20	6	26
Virilocal	3	2	5
Not clearly either	—	3	3
Total	23	11	34

3. *Current and Completed Marriages of Persons with Marital Experience Present in the Village*

	Number
Current marriages:	
Both partners domiciled in the village	34
One partner domiciled elsewhere:	
Marriages of 'wandering' polygynists	6
Ditto, but separated	2
Monogamous, but separated	2
	44
Completed marriages:	
Ended in death	17
Ended in divorce	47
	64
Total	108

N

4. *Marriage Payments*

| | Frequency of Payment Shown for Marriages | | |
	Current	Completed	Total
Nil	2	7	9
Bead	3	14	17
3d.	1	—	1
6d.	20	29	49
1s. 0d.	4	5	9
2s. 6d.	3	1	4
5s. 0d.	1	1	2
£1	1	1	2
£1 10s.	—	1	1
£2	1	—	1
£6	—	1	1
6d. + 2s. 6d.	—	1	1
6d. + £1 10s.	2	—	2
Bead + £1 10s. + 5s.	—	1	1
No record	6	2	8
	44	64	108

5. *Outcome of Completed Marriages*

| | Informant | | |
	Male	Female	Total
Spouse died	7	10	17
Divorce	25	22	47
Total	32	32	64

6. *Reasons Advanced for Divorce*

| | Informant | | |
	Male	Female	Total
Husband 'lost' in distant labour centre	3	9	12
Husband failed to work and support wife	1	6	7
Husband otherwise at fault	3	4	7
Wife committed adultery or was morally loose	6	—	6
One of wives objected to polygyny	2	3	5
Wife otherwise at fault	6	—	6
Other reason	1	1	2
No record	4	—	4
Crude total	26	23	49
Less number of informants advancing more than one reason	1	1	2
Corrected total	25	22	47

7. *Barnes's Divorce Ratios**
   (based on figures from Section 3 above)

$$\text{Ratio A} = \frac{\text{Marriages ended in divorce}}{\text{All marriages}} \times 100$$

$$= \frac{4{,}700}{108} = 43\cdot52$$

$$\text{Ratio B} = \frac{\text{Marriages ended in divorce}}{\text{All completed marriages}} \times 100$$

$$\approx \frac{4{,}700}{64} = 73\cdot44$$

$$\text{Ratio C} = \frac{\text{Marriages ended in divorce}}{\text{All marriages other than those ended in death}} \times 100$$

$$= \frac{4{,}700}{108 - 17}$$

$$= \frac{4{,}700}{91} = 51\cdot65$$

* See J. A. Barnes, 'Measures of Divorce Frequency in Simple Societies', pp. 44–5.

Source: Hut census made in January 1953.

Section 1 of the table shows that, of the twenty-seven married men fully or partly domiciled in the village, nine were polygynists (though none had more than two wives). Of these, six alternated between Jeremiah village and the villages in which their other wives were resident; and two had deserted their other wives without having formally divorced them. The remaining one had both wives living in Jeremiah village but had built their huts at opposite ends of the village to try to keep peace between them. I gained the impression that the proportion of polygynous marriages may have been higher in Jeremiah village than elsewhere.

Sixty-one per cent of the respondents to my public-opinion survey believed that polygyny is commoner nowadays than it was long ago. It is impossible to judge whether this is a true reflection of the actual trend or merely one of the ways of harking back to the golden age. In any event, Cewa have full insight into the tensions that polygyny generates. They tell this fable which indicates that it takes the wisdom of a Solomon for a man to keep the peace between his wives, and that his only hope is to emphasize their sole common interest—that in himself:

There was once a man who had two wives who hated each other very much. He made a new garden, and divided it equally between them. Now the senior wife had a pot, and this she put on the boundary. The junior wife planted a pumpkin in her garden, and, when it grew, it bore fruit in the pot of her co-wife. It grew inside it. When the time came for harvesting pumpkins, the owner of the pumpkin said, 'I want to pick my pumpkin'; but the owner of the pot retorted, 'How can you pick it? It won't come out of my pot, and I don't want my pot broken.' And, from speaking thus, they troubled each other exceedingly. So, their husband thought of a plan for reconciling his wives. He said to them, 'I am ill and I want pumpkin. Go and get that pumpkin that is in the pot'; and the two women went and broke the pot, took the pumpkin, cooked it and gave it to their husband. And he said, 'Now may you be reconciled, senior wife and junior wife.'

Pathetic is the plight of the man who cannot keep the peace between his wives. Such a man complains:

I keep telling them to live happily together, but they won't listen. [Before I placed them in huts farther apart] I was constantly catching fowls to appease the one or the other. [Even now] I run from the one to the other, and I am just like a slave between them.

Although Cewa believe polygyny to be an important cause for people to practise sorcery against one another (cf. above, Chapter 3) this is inconsistent with the statistics summarizing the attributes of the cases collected. Table XVII shows that, with full counting, cases involving co-wives or potential co-wives (see the case of the Disappointed Widow) accounted for only 1·7 per cent of the 115 relationships between sorcerer and victim and for only ·9 per cent of the 112 between accuser and sorcerer. To these should be added those of the cases involving spouses in which informants believed polygyny to be the cause of the alleged attack or of the accusation. These cases, forming a proportion of those shown for spouses in Table XVII, amount to no more than a further 4·5 and 1·8 per cent of total cases respectively. Thus cases involving polygyny account for as little as six per cent of sorcerer–victim relationships and three per cent of accuser–sorcerer ones. And there is no significant difference between the distributions of accuser–sorcerer and accuser–victim relationships in this respect.

Cewa divorce is easy and frequent. Divorce in our sense of the term, the dissolution of an existing marriage, is formalized by handing a token to the partner not taking the initiative. If he is the husband, this is in effect the same as returning the marriage token, and is often referred to thus. Traditionally this ceremony was performed in the village by the 'guardians' concerned; and this still happens when a man whose conduct has not come up to the standards required by his wife's matrilineage is sent home by them. The Chief's court, however, is beginning to play a more prominent rôle in the granting of divorces— apparently for two reasons. Firstly, the Native Authorities have modernized a custom recorded by Coxhead in 1914,[1] whereby a divorced woman was given a string of beads to wear around her temple as a symbol of her status. Nowadays the Native Court, after making an investigation, will, if satisfied, issue a certificate, which costs the applicant a shilling, stating that she is a marriageable woman (*nbeta*). This is believed to have closed a loophole formerly resorted to by a man sued for the only kind of adultery that Ceŵa recognize, that involving a married woman. He can no longer, the Ceŵa say, use the defence that he did not know that the woman he was dallying with was married. The prudent man, they assume, will demand a woman's certificate of marriageability before he makes any advances.

Secondly, there has emerged a new ground on which a woman may seek to have her marriage dissolved—her husband's being 'lost' to the distant labour centres. Since most marriages are between members of different villages (see, for instance, Section 2 of Table XIX), his disappearance needs to be established in a wider forum than the 'meeting' (*kabuŋgwe*) of a single village.

At any rate, a good deal of the Court's time is taken up by hearings in connection with applications for certificates of marriageability. Table XXII shows that about thirty-five per cent of a sample of recorded court cases relate to these applications, which may involve the wives of both labour migrants (as the scanty records sometimes specify) and men living at home. The standard ground recorded in each case is the husband's failure to support ('clothe' and/or 'hoe for') his wife. This is, however, misleading; for, judging by what people say, many of these women applicants have probably been divorced by their husbands on grounds such as repeated adultery, barrenness, disobedience or culinary ineptitude; and many others are probably getting rid of their husbands because their matrilineages have found that they fall short of their particular ideals for sons-in-law.

A truer, though by no means absolutely true, picture of Ceŵa grounds for divorce is given by those advanced by people with experience of divorce in Jeremiah village in 1953 (see Section 6 of Table XIX). Here informants gave reasons for the dissolution of past marriages. In doing so they seldom advanced ones that placed the blame on

[1] J. C. C. Coxhead, *The Native Tribes*, 1914, pp. 29–30.

themselves; but, as the sample happens to be fairly evenly divided between the sexes, it gives a more plausible representation of what actually occurs than do the court records.

Occasionally a divorce may be granted in the absence of a socially acceptable ground. In this case the person wanting the divorce has to compensate his or her spouse. Thus a man may pay the shilling for his wife's certificate of marriageability, and add, say, five shillings 'for clothes', or, if she has a child, say, ten shillings. A woman cannot obtain a groundless divorce as easily as this. She will be required to compensate her husband for her 'unreasonable' disinclination to continue living with him by paying him £1. Adultery cases, the records of which make up about an eighth of the sample in Table XXII, do not inevitably lead to divorce. Once damages have been paid, a woman's adultery is often condoned. Repeated adultery or general moral looseness is, however, frequently cited as a reason for a husband's seeking divorce.

That the Ceŵa divorce rate has been increased by modern conditions, labour migration in particular, must be admitted. On the other hand, there are many indications that easy and frequent divorce is a longstanding Ceŵa institution.[1] These are: the absence of bridewealth, the simplicity of both marriage and divorce rituals, the tenuous position, both traditionally and currently, of the son-in-law group in the village community, and the observations of early European residents.[2]

With the Ceŵa, 'to divorce' (kusudʒula when the subject is the husband; the passive, kusudʒulidwa, when the subject is the wife) has a wider meaning than it has with us. As with us, it implies the formal dissolution of a marriage; but it has a wider application. Even a marriage that has ended because of the death of one of the spouses must be formally dissolved unless the widower or widow is to marry a member of his or her deceased spouse's matrilineage. The formal dissolution takes place about a month after the burial of the deceased spouse, at the ceremonial shaving of the heads of those who have mourned by 'keeping hair' (kusuŋga tsitsi). Traditionally a deceased man's heir either inherited the widow or went to 'fetch his bow' (kuteŋga uta), i.e. to sleep one night with her and collect the property coming to him (symbolized by the bow).

---

[1] I labour this point because it has been disputed by Bruwer, 'The Kinship Basis of Cewa Social Structure'.

[2] A. L. Hofmeyr, Het Land langs het Meer, 1910, p. 39, wrote: 'Echtscheiding vindt heel gemakkelik plaats'. Coxhead, The Native Tribes, 1914, p. 29, wrote: '. . . Divorce . . . has always been very common among the Achewa.'

The day before a shaving ceremony I attended in 1947, two of a deceased headman's widows were 'divorced' by being handed six-pence each; and the remaining two were kept on pending the return from Southern Rhodesia of the heir presumptive, one of the deceased's sisters' sons. I have no record of a man's being formally divorced after the death of his wife. This may be because I did not make specific en-quiries on this point; and all the accounts I recorded of a husband's surviving his wife were dominated by descriptions of his obligation to provide her matrilineage with a payment called 'of the spirit' (ca-mʒimu) or 'of at-the-heads' (cakumitu—a reference to the shrine in the sleeping hut at the 'head' end opposite the doorway). This payment is aimed at quietening her spirit. Actually, it is payable only if the hus-band is believed to have broken a taboo and thus caused the death of his wife (see above, Chapter 3). Judging by the regularity with which a man hands over camʒimu, whether for a deceased wife or for deceased children, he seldom succeeds in establishing his innocence. If no blame attaches to him, he may be offered a marriage with one of his wife's matrikin, usually her sister, though possibly her sister's daughter. An acquaintance of mine was offered and accepted this honour; and he did not have to get his 'junior guardian' to hand over a token for his second wife because the one handed over when he married her elder sister had united him with the matrilineage.

The fact that a widow's marriage must be formally dissolved sug-gests a right, however tenuous, of the deceased husband's matrilineage to continue the relationship sealed by the passage of the original mar-riage token. But this should not be taken to mean that by marriage a woman becomes in any sense a member of her husband's lineage as she would in a Bantu society practising lobolo, or, for that matter, among the Coorgs of South India, where the sammanda ritual has a function similar to the passage of bridewealth.[1] The right secured by the pay-ment of the Ceŵa token (nsambo) is one over a woman's person and services. It does not transfer her to her husband's kin-group.

This fact is brought out by a comparison of Ceŵa and Makhanya kinship terminology. Reader has shown that Makhanya terminology reflects a woman's assimilation to the agnatic lineage of her husband. Whereas she, the daughter-in-law, becomes for purposes of termino-logy a cognate, her male counterpart, the son-in-law, remains dis-tinctly an affine. For instance, she is 'sister' to her husband's siblings and 'child' to his parents; whereas the son-in-law is designated by

[1] Srinivas, Religion and Society among the Coorgs of South India, pp. 126 ff.

affinal terms in all contexts.[1] Ceŵa kinship terminology, on the other hand, shows no trace of assimilation of either husband to wife's matrilineage or *vice versa*. Son-in-law and daughter-in-law are both referred to by affinal terms and treated symmetrically.

The lack of assimilation in either direction points to the solidarity of the two matrilineages concerned in the marriage and to the potential weakness of conjugal links. Their actual weakness is illustrated by Section 7 of Table XIX which, for the residents of Jeremiah village in 1953, shows the percentage of all completed marriages ended in divorce (in our sense of legal dissolution before death) to be 73·4 per cent (cf. England and Wales, 1938–9: 2·6 per cent;[2] United States, 1926: 26 per cent;[3] and Union of South Africa, Europeans, 1938–44: 14 per cent).[4] It is also illustrated by the following summary of the position prevailing in Cipaŋgula village in 1949:

Of the thirty-seven persons who had married, thirteen, or thirty-eight per cent, had been divorced at least once. This group included four who had been divorced twice; and two who had been divorced three times. Taking these much-divorced persons into account, there was an average of ·57 of a divorce per person who had married.

The Ceŵa husband never secures rights to his children (unless he follows, as in a few cases coming to my notice, the almost extinct[5] Ŋgoni custom of *lobolo*). This fact is amply illustrated in the genealogies, which show that the children of divorced parents almost invariably stay with their mother or with her matrilineage (see, for instance, the children of Develiase (C.23) and Vinileŋkoni (E.25) in Fig. 3, and those of the section headman (Tenje, b.11) in No. 1 of Appendix A; the only exception in my records was D.16 in No. 4 of Appendix A); and that children whose parents live virilocally very often go to live at their mother's village of origin after they have been weaned (note the cases of one of the three children of Kuliale II (D.15 in Fig. 3) and of two of the three children of the present marriage of Tenje (b.11 in No. 1 of Appendix A). Other indications that children belong to their mother's matrilineage are: (*a*) their belonging to her matriclan (*pfuko*, sometimes *mtundu*, the latter also meaning 'tribe', 'strain' or

[1] Reader, *Makhanya Kinship Rights and Obligations*, p. 28 *et passim*.
[2] Barnes, 'Measures of Divorce Frequency in Simple Societies', Table III, citing Hajnal.
[3] *Loc. cit.*, citing Willcox.
[4] Union of South Africa, *Office of Census and Statistics*, Report on Divorces, 1913 to 1944, p. 8.
[5] Barnes, *Marriage in a Changing Society*, pp. 35–6, estimates that bridewealth is tendered in only four per cent of Fort Jameson Ŋgoni marriages.

'kind'); and (*b*) the fact that, if one of them should die, their father is assumed to have broken a taboo and thus 'cut him [the child] in the chest' (-*mdula m'cifuwa*), and has to compensate his wife's matrilineage by a payment of *camʒimu* to settle the child's spirit.

Ceŵa consider that their attitude towards divorce is essentially humane. One man, contrasting Ceŵa marriage with the traditional, but now exceptional, *lobolo* marriage of the Ŋgoni, says:

Having invested cattle in a wife, you may find that she is no good, and then all you can do is beat her, just as you would beat a slave. The Ceŵa way is better; for, if you find that your wife is useless, you do not beat her or kill her: you simply leave her.

The fact that spouses can part easily may account for the low proportion of believed attacks (5·2 per cent) and accusations (1·8 per cent) between them shown in Table XVII. Of the cases in this category, the minority that were not related to polygyny is represented by the following one, in which uncertainty of ownership created tensions that led the victim's relatives to the rather unusual belief that a man's wife, without the provocation of polygyny, had killed him with sorcery.

Case No. 15—Damages for Disputed Maiʒe

In 1952, a middle-aged man, Alufeo of Mtuŋkha village, died after only three days' illness. Four members of his matrilineage came to the conclusion that his wife, Maligalitha, had killed him by putting 'medicines' in his beer. They attributed her action to a quarrel she and her husband had had over the ownership of the progeny of a beast awarded to them as damages for the destruction of their maize crop. Alufeo had hoed a [new] garden, leaving his wife to finish it; and the crop had subsequently been eaten by someone else's cattle. Maligalitha claimed the beast awarded as damages, and the dispute with her husband came to a head when, being ill, she wanted a beast slaughtered but her husband would not agree. He then sent her home, but did not divorce her. Eventually she was awarded five of the seven surviving issue of the beast; and her husband's heirs, two.

The looseness of the Ceŵa marriage tie is probably a necessary condition for the high degree of integration of the matrilineage. Radcliffe-Brown points out that, in an extreme matrilineal society, where rights over children remain with the mother and her relatives, the close bond between brother and sister is emphasized and maintained at the expense of the bond between husband and wife.[1] Linton maintains that in

---

[1] *Structure and Function*, p. 42. See also Max Gluckman, 'Kinship and Marriage', p. 192 *et passim*.

societies organized on the conjugal basis the authentic functional family consists of a nucleus of spouses and their offspring surrounded by a fringe of comparatively unimportant blood relatives; whereas in those organized on the consanguine basis the authentic functional family consists of a nucleus of blood relatives surrounded by a fringe of comparatively unimportant spouses.[1] One might add that such spouses may not be unimportant in systems that effectively incorporate them into the lineage. These two related general propositions throw light on the relationship between the high divorce rate among the Cewa and their marked matrilineage solidarity. We should remember that the structural type Radcliffe-Brown is considering, which happens to fit the Cewa closely, is a sub-type of Linton's second category, societies organized on the consanguine basis.

Western society belongs to Linton's first category. It is a society organized on the conjugal principle. This is indicated *inter alia* by its multilineal, symmetrical kinship system which has as its focus the 'inner circle' formed by Ego's family of orientation and his family of procreation.[2] In a society of this kind, a high divorce rate is justifiably regarded as an index of social disorganization, since it threatens the group about which the whole system articulates.

Cewa society, on the other hand, belongs to Linton's second category, being organized on the consanguineal principle; and, within this general category, it belongs to the matrilineal sub-type designated in the quotation from Radcliffe-Brown. It is a society in which no device such as either bridewealth or dowry is available for reinforcing the conjugal link by assimilating one of the marriage partners to the consanguineal group of the other. Consequently, the high divorce rate among the Cewa, far from being an index of social pathology, may well be an inescapable condition for the effective consanguineal social organization on a matrilineal basis.

Position of the Father

Among the Cewa, the tendency for the conjugal link frequently to be sacrificed on the altar of the consanguineal matrilineage is reflected in the position of the father. His place in the village community is tenuous, if not temporary. As the Cewa put it, 'to be a son-in-law is to say, "I am a stranger here; this is not my home village"(*Ndinemlendo*

[1] *The Study of Man*, p. 159.
[2] Cf. Parsons, 'The Social Structure of the Family', pp. 176, 182 *et passim*.

pano; simud̯i kwathu yai)'; or, 'The work of a son-in-law is only to beget children', 'to plant seeds only' (*kubyala nbeu cabe*). Similarly, his authority vis-à-vis his wife's brother over the children he has begotten is strictly limited, as various observers have remarked.[1] The following extract from an informant's text sums up his position well:

According to Ceŵa custom, the maternal uncle is the one with authority over the child; and his authority surpasses that of the child's father. True, his father has [some] authority, but it does not compare with that of the maternal uncle. Suppose that you[2] have married at a village of unrelated people and that you have begotten children. Those children you cannot really control. If you beat your child, its maternal uncle asks you, 'Now, you, have you come here to beat children? You are a son-in-law who followed your wife [here]. Now, why do you beat children? If the child has done wrong, you should come to me, and I would compensate you for its action.' You [the son-in-law] can say nothing [to this] because he is the proprietor of the child. There is a saying of the elders, 'Here there is an aloe with its roots meeting underground,' which means that your wife's people can meet secretly with your wife and agree, 'Let us chase him away to his home village and let him stay there now.' Thus you become ashamed and go home.

The emphasis on control and punishment in this statement obscures the fact that the father is proud of 'his' children and tied to them by bonds of affection. If the view of the situation is adjusted accordingly, it can be appreciated that any man is torn by conflicting loyalties towards his children and his sisters' children. His conflict is a recurring theme in Ceŵa society, and is often cited as the reason why cross-cousin marriage is preferred. Ceŵa point out that a man looks for spouses for his children among his matrilineal dependants (particularly his sisters' children), thereby ensuring that, though his son will never succeed him, then at least his son's son (i.e. his sister's daughter's son) may do so eventually.

The case of the Fertile Patch shows how, even under indigenous conditions, a father's yielding to the temptation to favour his sons against his sisters' sons may express itself through the idiom of beliefs in sorcery; and the following case shows how this common conflict may be intensified by modern situations arising from problems of ownership of property acquired in new ways.

[1] See, for instance, Hugo, 'Die Jeugprobleem in.Ons Nyasasendingveld, Veral met Betrekking tot die Achewa', p. 42; and Eybers, *Volksgewoontes en Bygelowe in Niassaland*, p. 78.
[2] Literally 'thou'. This 'hypothetical you' is one of the rare cases where the singular forms, *iwe, u-* and *-ako*, are used even if the information is being given to someone normally addressed in the honorific plural.

Case No. 16—The Greedy Son

Headman Mceŋga acquired his cattle not from working for Europeans but by hoeing well when he was a young man and by selling his surplus maize. He bought a cow from an Ŋgoni, and by the time of his death in 1949 there were nineteen beasts descended from it. Some of these Mceŋga, during his lifetime, had given to his son, Yolami, of whom he was very fond. He had done this openly and formally, so he told me, to avoid trouble between Yolami and his own matrilineal heirs, his senior ortho-cousin, Telensi (who had been passed over in his favour), Telensi's sister's son, Ezekiel, and Anwelo, the daughter's son of Mceŋga's senior classificatory sister. Mceŋga's foresight was in vain. He left instructions that a beast named Bindura should be slaughtered at his funeral. This was done, but, though the beast had been

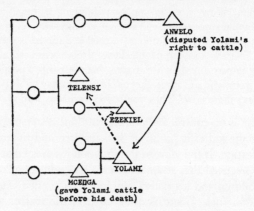

Fig. 16. The Case of 'The Greedy Son'

one of those assigned to the heirs, the son kept its hide. When, about a month after the funeral, the time came for the mourners to shave, Yolami, the son, claimed that twelve of the cattle belonged to him and only six to the heirs, whereupon the youngest heir, Anwelo, accused him of having stolen seven of those assigned to the heirs. Eventually Yolami took eleven; and the heirs, seven. Yolami said to Anwelo, 'You'll see! You've won this argument with the help of Telensi and Ezekiel. So, they'll die, both of them!' When these two men died shortly after this, Anwelo accused Yolami of having killed them with sorcery.

In this case the headman, conscious of the conflict of his loyalties to his son and to his matrikin, had anticipated the trouble between them; but the measures he took, depending as they did on oral rather than written instructions, left an element of uncertainty, from which the tension developed.

When a male member of a matrilineage happens to be living viri-locally, his wife, a daughter-in-law (*mkomwana*) of his matrilineage, is, like her male counterpart, in a tenuous position.

When I first met Headman Gombe, a polygynist living virilocally with both his wives, his second wife, Etelina, was in disgrace through having committed adultery and having quarrelled violently with her husband after a beer-drink. Gombe's sisters ostracized her almost to the point of avoiding her as they would a mother-in-law rather than joking with her as they should with a sister-in-law.

A year later, all signs of strain and disapproval had vanished. Etelina's contacts with her sisters-in-law were close and friendly. Gombe told me that, as a result of his having taken her to court, her behaviour had greatly improved, and his sisters were giving recognition to this improvement in their more friendly treatment of her.

The insecurity of the spouses of matrilineage members should not be exaggerated. Some marriages are stable, and the 'foreign' spouse achieves an important status in the village community. Notable here is the position of the son-in-law who has lived in the village for a very long time and has gained the approval and affection of the matri-lineage into which he has married. He has been so long in the village that 'his home is here; he does not remember about (or long for) his [original] home' (*paŵo n'pompano; sakumbikila ẕakwaŵo yai*). The senior among sons-in-law of this category becomes a deputy headman, and is referred to by the Ŋgoni term, *mkwekulu* (lit., 'senior affine'). He is charged with important duties, such as dispensing hospitality to travellers seeking shelter in the village, and assisting the headman in the choice of a new village site and in the distribution of land for new gardens.

Another point to be remembered is that, however insecure the social position of a particular father in Ceŵa society may be, fatherhood in general is given full recognition. Though it is a matter of small account who in particular one's father is, it is important that one should have *a* father.

There are indications of this in both speech and ritual. Ceŵa say that a father's work is to beget children, i.e. 'to place' (*kuyika*) them in their mother's womb. They are assumed to be parts of his substance, his 'seeds' (*nbeu*). The ritual of the sneeze, which Young and Banda regard as distinguishing Ceŵa from other descendants of the Maravi,[1] is a constant reminder of the importance of paternity. Suppose that a

[1] Young and Banda (editors and translators), *Our African Way of Life*, p. 10.

person's matriclan is Banda; and that the matriclan of his father is
Phili. Whenever he sneezes, he will identify himself by saying: 'A
child of Mr Phili suckled by Mrs Banda' (*Mwana waA Phili kuyam-
witsa kwaA Banda*).

The wide dispersal of this ritual suggests that it is indigenous. There
is less evidence for believing that the same applies to the custom found
among Northern Rhodesian Ceŵa today of a person's adopting as his
personal praise-name (*ciŵoŋgo*) the matriclan (*pfuko*) of his father.
Mitchell points out that this custom occurs in this area only among
tribes who have had close contacts with patrilineal peoples. It is
absent, for instance, from the Yao.[1] I have been unable to decide
whether this custom, the Tonga version of which Colson has pic-
turesquely described as a man's having 'honorary life membership' in
the clan and matrilineal group of his father,[2] is to be regarded as indigenous to the Ceŵa or the result of Ŋgoni influence. If it has come
from the Ŋgoni, it has certainly fallen on fertile Ceŵa soil.

During the Ceŵa life-cycle, there are many rituals in which the
husband-father has an important, sometimes indispensable, part to
play. Ideally it is he, rather than a ritual friend, 'hyena' (*fisi*), who
should deflower his virgin wife at the end of her puberty ceremony.[3]
And it is he who should be with her during many of the periods of
instruction associated with initiation, marriage and name inheritance
and who plays an indispensable part in the ritual ('to take the child',
kuteŋga mwana) that formally introduces the infant to the vital but
dangerous ('hot') forces involved in human reproduction (cf. above,
Chapter 3). By this ritual, the child's 'coldness', i.e. its susceptibility
to their destructive aspects, is brought to an end. Part of this ritual
consists of *coitus interruptus* with his wife; and the degree of self-
control that he exercises in this is believed to be directly related to the
child's future strength of character. To the extent that the father
'makes firm [his] heart' (*-limbika mtima*) so will the child be able to
show courage and integrity.

Perhaps most indicative of the indispensability of physiological
fatherhood among the Ceŵa is the complex of beliefs surrounding
difficult labour. When a woman has a difficult labour, it is assumed,
firstly, that her husband has been unfaithful to her during her pregnancy

---

[1] Professor J. Clyde Mitchell, private communication.
[2] 'The Plateau Tonga of Northern Rhodesia', p. 143.
[3] On this point, my investigations do not confirm Mair, 'Marriage and Family in the
Dedza District of Nyasaland', p. 107, who states that 'the girl must be deflowered by a
man other than her husband, known as the *fisi* (hyena)'.

and has thus 'cut her unborn child in the chest'. He is urged to make a full confession in order to remove the effects of his misdemeanour. If his confession fails to bring his wife's labour to an end, it is assumed, secondly, that she herself has committed adultery; and those present urge her to confess and reveal the begetter of her child. Ceŵa believe that the moment his progenitor's name is mentioned, the child comes forth.

Affinal Relationships in General

In that I have considered the rôles of husband, father and son-in-law together, I have examined the position of the father mainly in the context of his specific affinal relationships with his wife's matrilineage. Affinal relationships, both of this specific and of a more general kind, very often mediate inter-matrilineage links. This is not only because the matrilineage is exogamous and therefore affinally related to other matrilineages but also because, as I mentioned in Chapter 4, there is an equivalence of the men of a matrilineage which increases enormously the number of affinal avoidance (and joking) relationships that are observed. The whole idea of 'other people', the reference group for more general norms of conduct, tends to be based on the assumption that such people are, or will be, one's in-laws; and, of these 'other people', those of contemporary generation have the duty, as joking partners, of drawing public attention to one's misdemeanours (see above, Chapter 4).

I have noted that, among the Ceŵa, there are marked avoidance relationships between affines of proximate generations and marked joking relationships between affines of contemporary or alternate generations. Radcliffe-Brown regards both joking and avoidance as the means of organizing a stable system of behaviour in situations where affines or other categories of persons are opposed and where there is divergence of interests and therefore the possibility of conflict and hostility.[1] On the basis of this hypothesis one would not expect tensions between affines to develop to the point of their being formulated in terms of believed attacks or accusations of sorcery; for avoidance behaviour between affines of proximate generation would prevent tensions from arising; and joking behaviour between affines of contemporary or alternate generation would harmlessly discharge any that arose.

[1] *Structure and Function*, Chapters 4 and 5.

This was in fact the explanation I put forward in 1952 to account for the absence in a sample of twenty cases of either believed attacks or accusations of sorcery between affines.[1] With the extension of my sample of cases from twenty to 101, a considerable change occurred, rendering the explanation I gave in 1952 invalid (or at least unnecessary) and pointing to the dangers of generalizing from too few observations. Reference to Table XVII will show that the proportion of believed attacks between affines (other than spouses or co-wives) rose from zero to eleven per cent, while that of accusations rose from zero to thirty-one per cent. A comparison of the distributions of accuser–sorcerer and accuser–victim relationships in this category reveals an extremely significant difference, indicating that affines are much more often linked in the hostile accuser–sorcerer relationship than in the affiliative accuser–victim one.

This change in my estimates of the frequency of believed attacks and of accusations, especially the latter, in respect of which the change is much greater, calls for a re-examination of the implications of relevant theory for this problem.

The thirty-one per cent of accusations between affines recorded in Table XVII was derived from twenty-one cases. To analyse as small a sub-sample as this is statistically dangerous and cannot do more than suggest lines for future research. Table XX shows how these cases

TABLE XX

ACCUSATIONS BETWEEN AFFINES BY GENERATION AND TYPE OF SORCERER (single counting of 'multiple' cases)

Relative Generation of Accuser and Sorcerer	Classification of Sorcerer		
	'Real nfiti' (witch)	Other	Total
Same generation	—	8	8
Proximate generation	5	8	13
	5	16	21

were distributed on two variables, relative generation of accuser and sorcerer (the first mentioned in each case) and whether or not the sorcerer was classified as a 'real *nfiti*' (witch). In the eight cases of accusations between affines of the same generation, between whom joking behaviour would be appropriate, none of the sorcerers was classified as a witch; in the thirteen cases of accusations between affines of proximate generation, between whom avoidance behaviour would be appropriate, five were classified as witches.

[1] 'The Social Context of Cewa Witch Beliefs', p. 227.

The first point to dispose of, therefore, is the possibility that, among accusations between affines, there are some belonging to the more general category of cases in which a person is accused more because of his or her deviant character than because of the structural tensions involved. It will be recalled that one of the statistically significant characteristics of the witches in my sample is that their being accused is seldom preceded by a quarrel (cf. end of Chapter 3). The following case appears to be one belonging to the general category in which character rather than structure determined the direction of the charge and where the affinal relationship concerned was probably irrelevant.

Case No. 17—A Notorious Witch

Dailesi died during her third pregnancy. Although before her **death** she had quarrelled with her elder sister, Manjose, 'they always blame Maŋgose

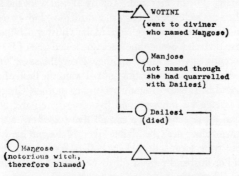

Fig. 17. The Case of 'A Notorious Witch'

[Dailesi's husband's mother] in that family because she is a notorious **witch**'. And so it was on this occasion. Dailesi's brother, Wotini, went to the diviner, and Maŋgose was the one named.

The same seems to be true of the following case. I give a close translation of the informant's statement in order to convey how suspicions become aroused and how rumours develop on the basis of them. It also shows, incidentally, the measures that may be taken to escape the attentions of someone regarded as an addicted witch.

Case No. 18—The Inedible Children

Lowase, the daughter of Cisese, gave birth to a boy baby, but he died. In the course of time she gave birth to a girl baby, but she died. Soon after this she herself began to suffer from sores on her breasts, without knowing that the one who had brought these sores to her was Baileti (her mother's sister's husband's mother). At night Baileti used to come and suck her breasts so that the sores on them would get better quickly. But this aroused people's suspicions, and they said, 'Come, let us go and divine.' Those who went to the

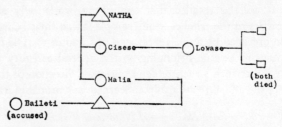

Fig. 18. The Case of 'The Inedible Children

diviner were Loŵase's mother, Cisese, and her mother's brother and sister, Natha and Malia. The diviner said: 'Tell me if you want me to name the one who killed Loŵase's children.' They therefore gave him two shillings and he began to explain: 'Baileti, the mother of Malia's husband, is the one who wants to kill Loŵase [herself]. Some time back she killed one of Loŵase's children, and more recently she has killed another. Now she says, "The flesh of the children wasn't tasty, but nauseating; now I want the flesh of their mother."'

On hearing this, Loŵase, together with her mother, Cisese, said, '[From] here at this village we must go and live elsewhere'; and Natha said, 'No, don't. I'll find a place where we can all live together.' So, with them, he started his own village near the Mzime river. Malia and her husband came to live there and were soon followed by Baileti. As soon as she arrived there, Loŵase and her husband moved off to Nyasaland to live in her husband's home village. There they had a child called Natha [after his mother's brother] and he is alive to this day because they stayed in Nyasaland until after Baileti died, when they returned to the Mzime.

But that person Baileti was a bad person. She was in the habit of changing into a night bird. On one occasion a person with the necessary 'medicines' caught this bird and it changed back into Baileti, who said, 'It's me, please.' Now [that she's dead] the people in the village are no longer troubled.

Another of the accusations between affines, this time between two of the same generation, may reasonably be regarded as belonging to a wider category, that including cases in which strong motives were involved. In this respect it resembles the case of Revenge through First Aid, in which the same motive, sexual jealousy, led to an accusation between unrelated persons. In the following case a dispute between a man and his sister-in-law, arising from their different interpretations of the freedom of the joking relationship, led to this man's being held responsible for her death by her husband. Since accuser and accused had married into the same matrilineage, they were classificatory brothers rather than what Ceŵa usually conceive of as affines.

Case No. 19—The Virtuous Sister-in-Law

Maliseni tried on several occasions to seduce his wife's sister, Violeti, but she consistently rejected his advances. Violeti's husband, Bvalani, knew about

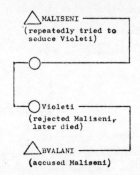

Fig. 19. The Case of 'The Virtuous Sister-in-Law'

his attempts; and, when Violeti died, he accused Maliseni of having killed her with sorcery in revenge for being rejected.

Having disposed of some of the cases which, while involving accusations between affines, may better be regarded as belonging to other more general categories, I am left with those in which the affinal relationship *per se* seems to have been crucial in the tensions being expressed in the idiom of sorcery.

Perhaps the best way of approaching these remaining cases is to consider further the rôle played by affines in Ceŵa society. I have already remarked that one's affines are often conceived of as the reference group for proper conduct, and that, in particular, those of contemporary or alternate generation have the duty, as joking partners, to draw attention to a person's misdemeanours. When such misdemeanours are serious enough to be regarded as sorcery, and when the miscreant's matrikin may, through doubt or reticence, be unwilling to accuse one of their own number of it, the duty of formulating the accusation may fall on an affine. The affine is thus an outsider who forces the matrilineage in which he has interests to recognize the sorcery in its midst.[1] This seems to have happened in the following case.

Case No. 20—The Jealousy of the Barren

In 1949 Kambia died as a result of vengeance magic given her in some snuff by the husband, Fuŋgulani, of her younger classificatory sister, Gelesi. Fuŋgulani had told Gelesi's elder sister, Loliwe, of his intention to take this step because, he said, he had been to a diviner in Southern Rhodesia who had informed him that his and Gelesi's three children who had died in Southern

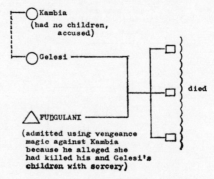

Fig. 20. The Case of 'The Jealousy of the Barren'

Rhodesia had been killed by the sorcery of Kambia. The diviner had explained that Kambia, who was barren, was jealous of her younger [classificatory] sister's fecundity. In spite of Fuŋgulani's admission that he had killed Kambia, Kambia's relatives did not take any action against him because, they said, Kambia had deserved to die. [This may have been the reason why, if the attack constituted murder by poisoning, there was no prosecution by the Administration.]

In the next two cases it again fell to an affine to try to expose sorcery in the matrilineage to which she was linked.

Case No. 21—The Repossessed Garden

Thamaŋga, a village elder, gave his wife's sister, Cabe, a garden. Later he took it back, and in her anger she said, 'Thou, we'll see the manner in which

---

[1] This explanation occurred to me as a result of two seminars in the Department of Social Anthropology and Sociology in the University of Manchester, to which the main contributors were Professor Max Gluckman and Dr E. L. Peters; and my view of the moral implications of the outsider's rôle was clarified in subsequent discussions with them.

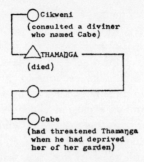

Fig. 21. The Case of 'The Repossessed Garden'

thou shalt stay in thy garden' (*Iwe, tione m'mene udʒakhalila m'munda mwako*). When Thamaŋga died, his sister, Cikweni, went to a diviner who told her that he had been killed by the sorcery of Cabe.

Although Cabe's use of the second person singular (instead of the honorific plural) and her castigation of Thamaŋga were appropriate to their joking relationship, she expressed herself ominously.

Case No. 22—The Carpenter's Tools

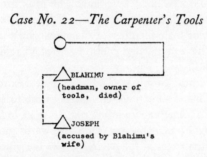

Fig. 22. The Case of 'The Carpenter's Tools'

When Headman Blahimu died after drinking *kacaso* with his junior classificatory brother, Joseph, Blahimu's wife, who had seen Joseph inviting her husband to drink with him, accused Joseph of having killed him by putting 'medicines' in his drink. People believed that Joseph wanted full ownership of Blahimu's carpenter's tools, which at the time he had on loan.

Relationships between Village Sections

So much for the external relations of the matrilineage brought about by marriage. I shall now turn to those connected with neighbourhood. The origins of neighbourship lie in the circumstances that bring village sections together, thus linking them in co-operation and dispute.

The headman of a Ceŵa village is the headman of its founding section, the one to which the other sections have become attached. The bonds that tie these subsidiary sections to the founding one are of various kinds. Kinship sometimes plays a part. If lineage segmentation has taken place without an explosion violent enough to break up the village, the derivative segments may, for a while at least, occupy distinct sections. This, the reader will remember, was what happened in Cimbuna village up till 1939. In this case, actual matrilineal kinship existed between the section of Headman Cimbuna and that of Headman Mceleka, his senior relative (see above, Chapter 4).

Some sections may be bound together not by actual, but by putative, matrilineal kinship. Potokosi came from Portuguese territory and claimed to be Jeremiah's mother's brother (Chapter 4). Although he and Jeremiah were unable to explain the actual link between them, they assumed that this link existed, i.e. that their two sections belonged to the same matrilineage. I remember how, whenever Potokosi joined Jeremiah and me on Jeremiah's verandah, he took great pains not to come into contact with the sleeping mats of Jeremiah's wives, whom, as a putative senior male member of their husband's matrilineage, he had to avoid. This exaggerated caution served to reinforce a link of questionable validity.

Putative matrilineal kinship pushed to its logical extreme is common matriclanship. This is sometimes advanced as the reason why a subsidiary section has joined the founding one. In 1946, in Mceleka village, the people of Tenje's matrilineage (who afterwards moved to Matope village) gave as their reason for having joined the village the fact that they belonged to the same matriclan as Headman Mceleka.

Of other types of kinship bonds uniting village sections, the most notable is the patrilateral link between the founding matrilineage and the matrilineage fragments developing from the virilocal marriages of its male members, typically those of the headman and his predecessors (see above, Chapter 4). The children of these virilocal marriages belong to their mothers' matrilineages, which are usually domiciled elsewhere. In the early stages of a marriage of this kind, the children often move to their mother's village of origin where they are cared for by her mother or sisters. As the marriage becomes stable, so do they tend more and more to remain living in their father's village. The headman's eldest son (in the typical case) is a 'junior guardian' in charge of the local matrilineage fragment. He keeps constantly in touch with their 'senior guardian' in their mother's village. As time goes on, the headman's son becomes an independent 'headman' of the local matrilineage fragment and thus of the section that develops around it.

Even kinship ties that Ceŵa regard as unimportant may form links between village sections when people wish for other reasons to reside in a village. One instance is Ŋguzi's section which joined Mceleka village because Ŋguzi was the half-sister (father's daughter) of Tomu, one of the elders of Mceleka's matrilineage. Another is Mwaiŋga's section, which has been included with Jeremiah's in Fig. 3. Mwaiŋga (C.1) is Jeremiah's father's brother's daughter and the widow of his mother's mother's brother's son, Dauti (C.2).

According to some informants, the traditional Ceŵa village was a small kinship unit. Its present large size and complex composition may be in some part the result of the insecurity of the recent past and the administrative policy of the present. There is, however, some reason for believing that its large size, and presumably its social complexity, is of more remote origin. In 1831, before the Ŋgoni invasion, Gamitto remarked on the large size of two Ceŵa chiefs' villages, that of Fumo (territorial chief) Mugurura, which had 'over a thousand huts', and that of Mambo (paramount chief) Mucanda, which was 'extremely large both in huts and in the number of its inhabitants'.[1] Perhaps more useful for our purposes is the fact that he describes as 'small' a Maravi village which consisted of twenty huts and contained sixty to eighty inhabitants.[2] Today, in Kaŵaza's part of the Reserve, such a village would also be regarded as small. It would be between a third and two-thirds of the size of the average 'administrative' village[3]—depending on whether the comparison is in terms of huts or of inhabitants. Gamitto also records that there was a continual state of civil war among the Maravi arising from succession disputes and petty quarrels between territorial chiefs.[4] This may have led to the association in the same village of unrelated matrilineages even before the turmoil of the Ŋgoni invasion.

However remote its origin, the tendency for matrilineages to cluster for reasons of external relations is a feature of the modern Ceŵa village. For ease of control, the Administration has from time to time laid down various minima for village size.[5] So it is that there now exist links

---

[1] *O Muata Caʒembe*, pp. 111 and 113.   [2] *Ibid.*, p. 30.
[3] Cf. above, Chapter 4.   [4] *O Muata Caʒembe*, pp. 52–4.
[5] For instance, the present ten-taxpayer rule. For further details, see Chapter 4.

based on expediency, whether on account of the need for security long ago or because of the requirements of the Administration more recently. As an instance there is the link between the two largest sections of Jeremiah village, Jeremiah's and Cimseleti's (see above, Chapter 4).

The links I have thus far mentioned are summarized in Fig. 23 (A to E). One type of link, (F), remains to be discussed. Many Ceŵa

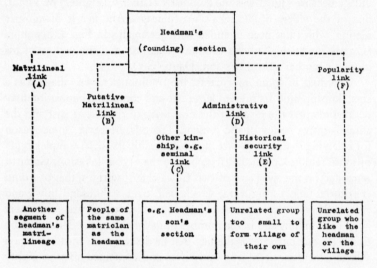

Fig. 23. Types of Links between Ceŵa Village Sections

villages are well in excess of the minimum size laid down by the ten-taxpayer rule; and the importance of belonging to a large social group has already been mentioned. The list of links between village sections would therefore be incomplete without some reference to the fact that some of them come together and remain united as a result of sheer sociability and a feeling of congeniality towards fellow villagers.

That this sociability is subject to individual variation and is stimulated or extinguished by a particular headman's personality or by the attractions of a particular village is shown by the fact that Ceŵa opinions are divided on whether it is preferable to live in a large or a small village. My public-opinion survey in 1947 showed that sixty-four per cent of informants[1] preferred living in small villages; and twenty-six per cent, in large ones; ten per cent showed no preference.

[1] The effective sample for this item was 156—for the reasons given in Chapter 2.

Those who favoured living in small villages maintained that they had the following advantages (in descending order of frequency of mention):

(a) Quarrels, noise, arson and adultery are rare.
(b) The inhabitants reach agreement quickly, especially since they are likely to be kinsmen.
(c) There is less mutual killing (*kuphana*) and less sorcery (*ufiti*).

Those who favoured living in large villages claimed these advantages for them:

(a) Their richer social life; and
(b) Their providing a better basis for co-operation in ritual and subsistence activities.

Noting these advantages leads me to the next section. Before proceeding to it, I should note that the second reason cited for living in small villages, the rapidity in reaching agreement between kinsmen, conflicts with a prevalent opinion that kinsmen are more prone to practise sorcery against one another because their quarrels are not subject to the legal arbitration that is applied to quarrels between unrelated persons (see Chapter 3). Perhaps such discrepancies arise from people's feeling that 'the grass on the other side of the fence is greener'. The majority, living in large villages, long for smaller ones, forgetting some of their drawbacks.

Co-operation and Dispute in the Village

Between the matrilineages forming the cores of the sections of a village, and between those of adjacent or historically associated villages, there exist patterns of co-operation and reciprocity. From time to time these require adjustment and revision by judicial institutions at the level of the village and, taking us into the next chapter, of the Chief's court.

The most formal co-operation has to do with ritual. When a matrilineage is weakened by being in a ritually dangerous state resulting from a crisis of life, especially bereavement, members of other matrilineages come to its assistance as 'ritual friends' (*adzukulu*, see Chapter 4). This co-operation may have been traditionally on the basis of paired matriclans as it is among some other tribes.[1] Nowadays, however, the distinction between matriclans is less important in ritual contexts than that between the weakened matrilineage, on the one hand, and non-members of it, on the other.

[1] See, for instance, Colson, 'Clans and the Joking-Relationship among the Plateau Tonga of Northern Rhodesia'.

Less formal co-operation between one matrilineage and another or, even more specifically, between segments or individual members of different matrilineages, occurs in working parties organized for various purposes such as weeding a garden, building a hut or starting a new patch of cultivation. Participants in these are usually drawn from the same neighbourhood (see Chapter 2). The host matrilineage segment recruits helpers from neighbours not only in its own village but also in adjacent ones, especially those of long association, such as the derivatives of Cimbuna village.

My references to Cewa attitudes regarding the desirability of large or small villages point to some of the disputes that occur between neighbours. When people live cheek-by-jowl in huts that lack clearly defined courtyards, and when over-population brings their gardens uncomfortably close to one another, it is not surprising that friction should sometimes arise between them. An important modern influence in these conditions generating friction is land shortage, the background to which was presented in Chapter 2.

As I mentioned in the last chapter, the duties of a 'guardian', whether senior or junior, include settling quarrels among his dependants, and supporting them when they are in conflict with the members of other matrilineages. There is adequate judicial machinery for resolving conflict, especially if the opponents belong to different matrilineages. If they belong to different matrilineages within the same village, e.g. to different village sections, their respective 'junior guardians' refer their quarrel to their 'senior guardians', who are usually their respective section headmen. These headmen then take the matter up with the village headman (if, that is, he is not one of them, as he may be). One of the most onerous duties of the village headman is to receive petty complaints and to resolve differences. Cewa recognize this when they say, 'The headman is the rubbish heap' (*Nfumu ndi kudzala*). One village headman I knew well told me that, if people came to his hut during the night to have a quarrel settled, he always pretended to be sound asleep; and his wife's standing instructions were, when they wakened her, to get up and put them off until morning. Often, he said, people had forgotten about their quarrel by morning, and he heard no more about it.

If a quarrel is serious enough to persist, and if the village headman considers its settlement to be within his competence, he calls a meeting (*kabuŋgwe*) at which to discuss it. Cewa say that long ago practically all cases were settled at this level. It would not be accurate to describe this as a village headman's court; for many villagers, especially elders, participate, and the headman's main function is to formulate the collective opinion of the participants. The most active participants are men, though the women, sitting in a segregated group, may join in if they feel strongly on a particular point.

The village 'meeting', like any other part of the Ceŵa judicial machine, is a forum in which rancour is removed by patient examination and persuasion in terms of a code of morals and law assumed to be accepted by those participating.

This emphasis on compromise and, incidentally, the part that women may play during a case, are well illustrated by a village meeting that I attended in 1952.

The meeting had been called to settle what was primarily a quarrel between Daniel and his wife, Elizabeth. They had become estranged because Elizabeth had had a difficult labour followed by the death of her baby. It had been established (in Ceŵa opinion) that Daniel's adultery while his wife had been pregnant had been the cause of this misfortune, and he had been made to compensate his wife's matrilineage by paying cam*z*imu (see above, this chapter). Soon after this, Daniel built a new hut midway between the two sections to which he and Elizabeth belonged, and tried to induce his wife to live in it. She refused, and this led to an impasse from which divorce seemed to be the only escape. It was at this stage that Elizabeth, on retiring one night, found that her sleeping mat and the sack on which her smallest child slept had been removed from her hut. She reported this to her brother, the section headman, who told her to sleep in another hut, and promised that he would investigate the matter in the morning.

Meanwhile, early the following morning, Tabetha, an elderly widow living in an adjoining section of the village, discovered the mat and sack on the verandah of her married daughter's hut. Suspecting sorcery, she started complaining (*kudandaula*) loudly so that all could hear of the threat to her daughter's safety. In this way, Elizabeth heard of the whereabouts of her property and collected it. She then sought out her husband, and abused him for having taken her property, whereupon he assaulted her and destroyed her winnowing basket and enamel basin with a hoe.

The enquiry into these events could not be held that day because the headman of Daniel's section could not be found. Early the following morning, practically all the adult men and women of the village assembled, and interested elders from neighbouring villages joined them. Taxed with having placed Elizabeth's property on Tabetha's .daughter's verandah, Daniel pleaded an alibi. He and two friends, he said, had gone to drink beer at a nearby village; and, since the beer was good, had stayed there all night. Unfortunately for him, his two friends could only confirm that the beer was good—so good that it had rendered them incapable of knowing whether Daniel had been with them throughout the night or not.

Seeing his case collapse, Daniel said that he would admit the charge against him, but 'with a sore head' (*mutu uŵaŵa*), i.e. under protest. The immediate and unanimous rejoinder of the meeting was, '[To say] "I admit it with a sore head" is no admission at all' (*Nadzomela mutu uŵaŵa nikudzo-mela liti*). It was only during an adjournment, when it was easier for Daniel to climb down, that a small group of elders induced him to make an un-qualified admission and to agree to offer his wife a 'pardon fowl' (*ŋkhuku yopepeza*).

Throughout the discussion of this case, old Tabetha clung tenaciously to two 'exhibits', the sleeping mat and the sack, and called out from time to time in this vein: 'And what about these? Only sorcerers spread mats on people's verandahs without permission. For a long time we have been wondering about the deaths that have occurred in this village; now we are learning who the sorcerers are. To spread mats is to kill by sorcery'—and so on.

If the village meeting is unable to arrive at a satisfactory solution the case is taken to the Chief's court. Informants assured me that there was an increasing tendency to take to the Chief what formerly would have been settled in the village at a meeting such as the one just described. I shall return to this point presently.

If the contestants belong to different villages, the case may be tried by what amounts to a neighbourhood meeting. All the important local village and section headmen are present. No one in particular presides, though the two headmen of the village sections most directly con-cerned play the most conspicuous rôles. Again, however, the tendency seems to be to take a case of this degree of complexity direct to the Chief's court, to which we now turn.

CHAPTER 6

THE POSITION OF THE CHIEF

AT the village or neighbourhood 'meeting', the contestants' 'senior guardians' (or their deputies) are present as a matter of course; for these are the section or village headmen. It is when a case goes to the Chief's court that the principle that litigants should be supported by their 'guardians' is occasionally forgotten, and the Chief or his court assessors may have to remind people of its importance. In those few instances in which a person tries to approach the Court independently, the ridicule that is showered upon him is a forcible reminder that it is considered proper that judicial contests should mobilize the matrilineages of the contestants. This is shown by the following incident which also reiterates the principle operative at lower levels of the judicial system, that a miscreant should freely acknowledge his wrong.

In 1952, Chief Kaŵaza Maniŋu turned a man out of his court because he had admitted the charge against him, not because he freely acknowledged being in the wrong, but 'because the Chief says so'. As the man left, the Chief remarked to me and to his assessors that the difficulty had arisen because the man had been accompanied by his father and not by his mother's brother.

Another aspect of this mobilization of matrilineages for judicial contests is the fact that the matrilineage, through its headman, is held responsible for the court-debts of its members.

Some years previous to 1947, Chief Kaŵaza Soŋgani's court found that Headman Gombe's younger brother had committed adultery, and ordered him to pay damages. Since he had neither cattle nor money, the Court ordered Gombe to pay the damages on his behalf. Gombe refused, saying that the Court should rather imprison his younger brother, whereupon the Court seized his bicycle as security against the payment, which he eventually made.

The Chief's court is becoming more and more involved in the minutiae of village life. In part this may be the result of overcrowding and the predominance of links other than kinship between neighbouring village sections. Driven more by circumstances than by inclination

to live with their neighbours, members of one section may not necessarily respect the opinion of the headman of another who happens also
to be headman of the village as a whole. Another factor is the political
ambitions of chiefs. Village headmen are sometimes charged with con-
tempt of a chief's court because they have tried to settle cases that a
chief considers beyond their competence. On the other hand, I once
heard the late Chief Kaŵaza Soŋgani tell the contestants in a case, both
of whom were from the same village, one with an Nseŋga-speaking
headman, to 'go home and speak Nseŋga', by which he meant go
home and settle the case out of court, since it was one that needed a less
formal approach.

Modern Bases of Authority

The modern form of Northern Rhodesian Indirect Rule was cast in
Ordinances passed in 1929 and 1936;[1] but the general policy of dele-
gating administrative and judicial functions to native chiefs dates back
to the early days of administration by the British South Africa Company.[2] As I have mentioned in Chapter 2, Chief Kaŵaza Soŋgani
started his career as a Divisional Messenger of the B.S.A. Company's
Administration. Later, after he had succeeded to the chieftainship, and
as Northern Rhodesian chiefs' authority was made legally effective,
he was gradually taken into the extensive hierarchy of Indirect Rule.

Thus today his successor, A Kaŵaza Maniŋu, has a legally established position which enables him to participate in the legislative,
executive and judicial processes of local government. He is a member
of the Ceŵa Native Authority Council, which comprises Paramount
Chief Undi, the twelve Fort Jameson Ceŵa territorial chiefs, and
'Departmental Councillors' (akin to Ministers) for Administration,
Education, Public Works, Agriculture, Health and Water, and
Forestry. This body has the power to promulgate orders and rules on
a wide range of specified subjects, including, for instance, the control of
liquor brewing and consumption; the prevention of soil erosion, deforestation and the pollution of water supplies; and the suppression of
prostitution.[3] It has set up a Native Treasury, the 1953 estimates of
which (summarized in Table XXI) give some idea of the scope of its
administrative functions.

[1] Northern Rhodesia, *Laws*, Native Authorities Ordinance, No. 32 of 1929; Native
Authority Ordinance, No. 9 of 1936; and Native Courts Ordinance, No. 10 of 1936.
[2] For details, see Barnes, *Politics in a Changing Society*, pp. 111 ff.
[3] For details, see Native Authority Ordinance, Sections 8 and 17, and Government
Notices sanctioning new categories of orders made under Section 8(x).

TABLE XXI

SUMMARY OF THE ESTIMATES OF THE CEŴA NATIVE TREASURY, 1953

Estimated Revenue	£	*Estimated Expenditure*	£
Share of Native Tax	7,800	Administration:	
Court Revenue	1,500	Personal Emoluments	4,059
Licence Fees (e.g. arms, dog,		Other Expenditure	2,169
beer, store)	1,860	Education	3,827
Local Fees and Dues:		Public Works	1,173
Local Levy	1,500	Water Development	1,462
Others	1,959	Agriculture	1,008
Grant from Provincial Native		Postal Services	114
Treasury Fund*	1,625	Health	1,618
		Miscellaneous	441
		Forests	102
	£16,244		£15,973

* This fund, from which expenditure on various purposes, e.g. welfare, may be made on the authority of the Provincial Commissioner, is derived from a share of the Native Tax (twenty per cent in Fort Jameson district).

Source: Northern Rhodesia, *Eastern Province*, Chewa Native Treasury Estimates, 1953, Fort Jameson, on file at Fort Jameson.

As to Chief Kaŵaza's judicial function, he constitutes, with three paid assessors, the Kaŵaza Native Court, which has the power to impose a sentence of up to a £20 fine, six months' imprisonment, ten strokes with a cane, or a combination of these punishments; and to try civil cases involving not more than £100 except in cases concerning inheritance and marriage in which the limit is higher. In keeping with A Kaŵaza Soŋgani's having been Paramount Chief of the Southern Ceŵa (see Chapter 2) the powers of this court are greater than those of other Ceŵa territorial chiefs except Chief Mkanda Mateyo, who, having been Paramount Chief of the Northern Ceŵa, has been granted equal recognition. Appeals lie from the Kaŵaza Native Court to the Ceŵa Appeal Court, which comprises Paramount Chief Undi, two paid assessors, the 'Departmental Councillors' and unpaid tribal elders; and from this court, to the subordinate courts (of District Commissioner and Provincial Commissioner) and the High Court of Northern Rhodesia. The decisions of the native courts are subject to revision by the subordinate courts.

The jurisdiction of a native court such as A Kaŵaza's is wide and flexible, even though, in addition to the limits that have been mentioned, there is the usual restriction to a geographical area as well as the specific exclusion from its competence of three types of cases, viz.

(*a*) those in which a person is charged with an offence leading to some-one's death or an offence punishable with death or imprisonment for life; (*b*) those relating to witchcraft (including sorcery); and (*c*) those involving non-natives.[1]

More positively, the Ordinance specifies that native courts shall administer (*a*) 'the native law and custom prevailing in the area of the jurisdiction of the court, so far as it is not repugnant to justice and morality' or inconsistent with the provisions of other laws in force in Northern Rhodesia; (*b*) rules and orders made under the Native Authority Ordinance; and (*c*) the provisions of Ordinances and laws which the court has been authorized to administer.[2] Since the Ad-ministration often makes suggestions to Native Authority Councils regarding orders they should consider making, there is a good deal of uniformity in the legislation administered by native courts throughout Fort Jameson district, whether Ceŵa, Ŋgoni or Kunda.

To the Ceŵa the distinction between civil and criminal law is not as crucial as it is to us. A native court, finding someone guilty of assault or theft, will order him—in the same hearing—both to pay a fine and to compensate the person whom he has wronged; provision has been made for this in the Native Courts Ordinance.[3] Similarly, wrongs such as adultery and damage to property are righted by the payment, not only of compensation, but also of a court fee; this fee is, however, more akin to an order for costs than to a fine. For this reason, the distinction between civil and criminal cases has been disregarded in Table XXII.

Traditional Bases of Authority

It would be a mistake to confine the search for Kaŵaza's authority to the modern legislative provisions under which he and his associates have been taken into the administrative and judicial machine. As the descendant of a woman chief, Manyika, to whom Undi five or six generations ago assigned the Milanzi area on the north-eastern side of the Kapoche, Kaŵaza's authority rests on tradition as well as formal recognition by the present-day Administration.

Ceŵa use the term 'chief' (*nfumu*) for a village section 'chief', a village 'chief' (both of whom I call headmen), a 'chief of country' (whom I call a territorial chief) and the paramount chief. When he passed through Undi's country in 1831, Gamitto recorded that it was

---

[1] Native Courts Ordinance, Section 11.
[2] *Ibid.*, Section 12.
[3] Native Courts Ordinance, Section 14(1).

divided into provinces governed by chiefs whom he designated as 'Mambos',[1] and that these were subdivided into districts governed by 'Fumos'.[2] Elsewhere, in reference to Undi's people (whom he called Maraves), he makes a distinction between the village headman 'Muéne-muzi' (now written *mwini mudʒi*) and the territorial chief, 'Muéne-zico' (*mwini dʒiko*),[3] who presumably had the status of Fumo.

This hierarchy of 'chiefs' contains three basic categories: the paramount chief, the territorial chief and the village headman. It is true that territorial chieftainships are not all of the same order of devolution from the paramountcy, but this is a matter of historical accident and does not necessarily determine their present relative status. Thus, among Southern Ceŵa chiefs, Kaŵaza and Mwaŋgala, whose chieftainships devolved from Undi direct, do not on this account enjoy a status superior to that of Kathumba and Ziŋgalume, who obtained theirs through Cimwala and Mwaŋgala respectively. All four are territorial chiefs; and such differences as exist between them are the result of other factors, such as present size of territory and population and (in Kaŵaza's case) the fact that a recent incumbent was a man whose ability and industry were early recognized by the Administration. In some cases, however, priority of devolution does determine status. Thus Cimwala and Citikwele, having received their chieftainships from Undi direct, play an important part in his installation.

It should be added that village headmen are not all of the same status. Certain of them rank as the 'lieutenants' (*ambili*, sing., *mbili*) of the territorial chief. They are distinguished from their peers by having the right (known as *thambwe*) to organize female initiation ceremonies and the *nyau* mimes.[4] The council of *ambili* helped the chief in the administration of his country, and, in particular, were charged with calming him when he was angry.

As a territorial chief, A Kaŵaza belongs to the category most often mentioned in traditional accounts of relationships between matrilineages and between villages. '[He] of the country' (*adʒiko*, the territorial chief), as the dispenser of land, was someone to whom and to whose successors headmen and villagers were under a perpetual obligation. This they acknowledged by paying him tribute (*mitulo*).

---

[1] I noted in Chapter 4 that *Mambo* is a term of address reserved for important chiefs and certain types of diviners.
[2] *O Muata Caʒembe*, 1854, pp. 53–4.
[3] *Ibid.*, p. 83.
[4] Again there are many similarities between Ceŵa and Yao in these respects. Cf. Mitchell, *The Yao Village*, Chapter 4.

P

Tribute consisted of food for the tribal granaries from which visitors and the destitute were fed, and people—men for war, and men and women as slaves for the chief's service or for trading to the Arabs for cloth and guns. People found guilty of sorcery—or rather those of them who were not killed by the poison ordeal itself or executed following it—were an important source of these slaves. Gamitto mentions another source, captives made during the incessant civil war arising from succession disputes and petty quarrels between 'Fumos'.[1] In addition the chief had a claim on ivory, the skins of certain animals and the feathers of certain birds obtained from his territory. The special relationship between 'lieutenants' (*ambili*) and the territorial chief was expressed by their having to pass on to him the lion's share of the 'fees' (mainly fowls, hoes and reed mats) paid in connection with girls' initiation and boys' entry into the *nyau* society.

The position of the territorial chief is entrenched in traditional rituals, especially those relating to the land. If accidents occurred in the human reproductive cycle, e.g. the pregnancy of an incompletely initiated girl, the death of a pregnant woman or the birth of a stillborn child, these were taken to be threats to the chief, his people and his land. If a girl became pregnant before the end of her first puberty ceremony, the 'little maidenhood' (*cinamwali caciɲono*), which might extend over four or five months, her condition, known as *cimbwili-mbwinda*, was said to have blinded the chief (*-doola m'maso*, 'make holes in [his] eyes'). A special ceremony had to be performed, and the chief had to be suitably compensated. Similarly, the corpse of a woman dying in childbirth was regarded as a threat to the fecundity of other women and to the fertility of the land. It therefore had to be cut open to relieve the dangerous tension (*nphamvu* = 'strength') that it harboured; and it could not be buried, but was either thrown into a deep pool or tied in the branches of a tree. To repair the mystical damage done to the chief, the woman's matrilineage had to send him her sister or some other girl to be his slave, or, if they were fortunate, make him a gift of a large goat.

The ceremony that reflects most clearly the traditional authority of the territorial chief is the installation of a village headman. This is important because it is still regularly performed and because in it are expressed the principles that the village headman is subordinate to the chief and that he has a definite mandate for good government from the people of his village and neighbourhood. This ceremony is an instance

[1] *O Muata Caʒembe*, pp. 52–4.

(a)

(b)

PLATE V. INSTALLATION OF HEADMAN OF
KAYANZA VILLAGE, 1948

(a) Chief Kaŵaza Soŋgani instructs his son to perform ritual shown below,
i.e. to raise the cloth suddenly and shout, 'Mr Kayanza here! Mr Kayanza
has returned!' (b) a ritual friend (with bald head) sits on the mat next to
neophyte headman's chair.

of the handing on of a name, and has certain features common to ceremonies of its kind. Those of special significance for present purposes are brought out in the following abridged description:

The ritual starts at a mourning ceremony held in connection with the death of the previous headman. The ceremony may be the shaving that occurs about a month after the funeral when beer, known as *moŵa wabona*, is brewed; or, especially if there is doubt about the succession, at a feast held roughly a year later (called *caka*, 'year'). At whichever it happens to be, when the beer is a day off maturing (*cale*), a libation of it and an offering of maize-flour are made to the spirit of the deceased headman; and a final decision is taken about who is to succeed him. The following morning, when the beer has matured (*wakupya*), the neophyte headman is led by a ritual friend to the chief's capital where the crucial part of the installation takes place. The chief presents the neophyte with a piece of cloth which is placed over his head. He then instructs someone present, e.g. his son or one of his councillors, to remove the cloth suddenly as he shouts, 'Mr So-and-so here! Mr So-and-so has returned!', using the deceased headman's name, which the neophyte has now formally inherited. The neophyte is now led back to his village, placed on a mat and instructed by his villagers and neighbours on how to be a successful and acceptable headman. Anyone, male or female, old or young, may instruct him—and perhaps his wife—provided he or she hands over a small gift while doing so.

The point that is relevant at present is the fact that the crucial part of the installation is performed at the chief's capital and at the chief's behest. Every time a village headman is installed, the people of his village and its neighbourhood are reminded that the territorial chief has the right to veto their choice by failing to present the piece of cloth and have the name called.

The Work of the Chief's Court

The Chief's court, with its both traditional and modern foundations, is a place towards which local interest and sentiment are directed. During my stay in the Reserve, A Kaŵaza's court used to sit twice a week; and on court days large crowds gathered at Kagolo. These included, not only litigants and their supporting 'guardians' and headmen, but also those who came to see how the affairs of state were conducted. 'Why are you at court today?' I once asked of a young man whom I knew well. His reply would have delighted Durkheim: 'I attend court to gain wisdom. Wisdom does not come from one person [me] but from your fellow men. If you see someone else doing wrong, you know what not to do.' The headman who had accompanied me to court intervened: 'What about those who do wrong knowingly and even admit it?' The young man could not reply. He was gaining wisdom outside as well as inside the court.

The crowd usually assembled long before the court would be likely to open. There was an animated exchange of news between those from different parts of the chiefdom or from neighbouring chiefdoms. One could always find a group of people tightly packed round the *nsolo* board—a stout plank with four long lines of holes cut in it on which a game resembling draughts is played with pebbles. The elder Kaŵaza was an expert player. Seated at the *nsolo* board in such close contact with his subjects that one had to distinguish him by his white beard and his unusual flowing white robes, he gave a curiously blended impression of autocrat and democrat, one that is not far wrong of either the Ceŵa chief of tradition or his modern counterpart, the president of a native court. Sometimes it would be time for court to begin before the game had finished; and some of the most incisive comments on evidence and the most astute judgments I heard Chief Kaŵaza Soŋgani make were irregularly punctuated by the grunts and jargon peculiar to the *nsolo* player.

What types of disputes are taken to the Chief's court? Table XXII

TABLE XXII

ANALYSIS OF 333 CASES COMING BEFORE THE KAŴAZA NATIVE COURT, ENTERED IN CASE RECORD BOOKS COVERING THE PERIODS, 5.4.47 TO 5.6.47; 24.6.48 TO 15.9.48; AND 22.12.48 TO 29.1.49

	%	%
1. *Offences under Legislation Administered by the Native Authority*		
Agriculture, e.g. failing to make contour ridges	6·0	
Hygiene, e.g. failing to keep village sites cleared	6·0	
Education: failure, once having entered a child for a school course, to send it to school	7·5	
Control, e.g. failure to carry out a lawful instruction of the Native Authority; contempt of court	2·7	
	—	22·2
2. *Disputes between Matrilineages*		
Applications for divorce and the issue of a certificate of marriageability	35·4	
Adultery	13·2	
Damage to crops	10·2	
Assault, verbal abuse and slander	9·3	
Sundry damages, including theft and infection with venereal disease	9·7	
	—	77·8
		100·0

is an analysis of 333 cases entered in three case record books which I borrowed from Chief Kaŵaza's court clerk in 1949. The records were made during the periods, April to June 1947, June to September 1948 and December 1948 to January 1949, and thus cover different seasons of the year. The cases fall into two main categories. The first includes those involving offences under Native Authority rules and orders and under laws administered by the native courts. The second consists of disputes between the members of different matrilineages. In the first category typical fines were: 2s. 6d. for not keeping a child at school once he had been entered for a course; 10s. for failing to keep a village site clear of weeds and grass; 10s. for failing to make contour ridges in a garden; and £1 for dancing *nyau* (this was before the ban on *nyau* was lifted). In the second category typical awards of damages and costs (court fees) were: 10s. damages and 3s. court fee for assault; 8s. damages and 1s. court fee for the destruction of crops by cattle; 7s. damages and 2s. court fee for killing someone's pig; and 30s. each damages and 2s. 6d. each court fee for adultery (wife and lover).

There were a few minor seasonal variations revealed by these records. Obviously there were more actions for damages to crops in the April-to-June period when crops awaited ripening than in the two others covered, while women tended to put their divorces in order more in the slack season (June to September in this case) than in the other, busier seasons.

The general atmosphere of the Court and the nature of Ceŵa judicial processes are brought out in the following cases:

The Fixing of Compensation: Lawrence gave Robert a beast to look after on the understanding that he would give him a present in return for caring for it. Robert now refuses to return the beast unless Lawrence pays him 25s. Lawrence affirms that this is too much because Robert has had milk from it which he has sold to the ghee factory, and asks the Court to order the return of his beast. The Court finds that 25s. is too much, and orders the return of the beast provided Lawrence pays Robert 10s., which sum he hands over in court. In addition Lawrence pays a court fee of 2s. 6d.

Division of Property on Divorce: A divorced couple place 2s. 6d. each before the Court as a deposit against court fees. The ex-husband asks for an order permitting him to take ground-nut seed from their joint store. The ex-wife objects that, though he is entitled to a share of their maize, he is not entitled to any ground-nuts because she bought them with money she made from making pots. The Court persuades her to agree to his taking a small quantity of ground-nuts for seed. No fees are charged.

A Claim for Damages Postponed: A man with a swollen eye complains that he was assaulted during a quarrel arising from the sale of some ground-nuts for which he was paid short. The Court orders him to come back in a week, by which time it will be possible to assess the extent of the damage to his eye. It would be fruitless, says the presiding assessor, to pass judgment until this is known.

Egenesi's Pig: A girl, Egenesi, complains that her pig has been killed by some boys. Asked who they are, she says, 'Many boys.' An assessor jokingly calls out, 'Many boys!', but there is no response from the boys waiting outside. The court messenger goes out and brings in nine boys, six of them aged about five or six and three of them about ten or eleven. One of the smaller ones acts as spokesman and gives a long description of how they decided to eat the pig, how their first attempts to catch it failed, but how they eventually caught it, killed it and ate it. Egenesi and the spokesman agree about the size of the pig. Members of the Court obviously enjoy the story, and everyone in court thinks it highly amusing. There is a general straightening of faces, however, and the presiding assessor says that the boys should be heavily punished because they are also in the habit of stealing fowls. A shilling is collected from each of the nine boys' 'guardians'; 7s. is handed to Egenesi's grandmother and 2s. is taken as a court fee.[1]

A Difficult Divorce Case: Malina applies to the Court for a divorce because, she says, her husband 'does not hoe and does not come to her house', i.e. does not support her or live with her. The presiding assessor reminds her that she came once before, complaining that her husband had a venereal disease and that she did not want to sleep with him, and that the Court then ordered her to do so because her husband had stated that, if he infected her, he would stand the consequences. Malina replies that her present application has nothing to do with the previous case. She claims that her husband took her to his village and left her there pregnant when he went to work in Southern Rhodesia. After her child was born, her husband's relatives sent her home.

The Court asks her husband whether what she says is true. He says it is and adds that he did not bring her back to his home village again because she refused to go with him, saying that his relatives had chased her away. The Court then investigates the reasons for their having chased her away, and discovers that it was because they were afraid of being held responsible if she or her child had died while they were with them. The presiding assessor suggests that the husband is being unfair to Malina because he has recently contracted a bridewealth marriage with an Ŋgoni woman and has not the same degree of control over Malina as he has over his Ŋgoni wife. This

---

[1] At the time of this case a shilling represented about two days' wages in local unskilled employment.

hypothesis is not developed further, and the Court tries to patch up the marriage by suggesting that the husband should build Malina a hut in her home village and let her live there. Asked if she would agree to such a plan, Malina replies that she will have nothing to do with him in any case. The Court rules that she has no reasonable ground for divorce and must therefore pay her husband £1 compensation and a court fee of 1s. The husband agrees to divorce her on this condition.

The presiding assessor advises Malina not to get married again for six months and tells her that he is tired of having her come to Court. This, he says, is the fifth time. He urges her if she is pregnant to say so now so that there will not be another case later on. She says she is not pregnant. He asks her whether her husband has left a hoe in her house, by which he means any property. She laughs and says her husband does not know how to use a hoe.

The couple and their 'guardians' leave the Court. The presiding assessor reminds his colleagues that they forgot to ask whether this was a marriage in which *mcato* (see above, Chapter 5) was handed over. If so, he says, the husband is entitled to its return. The assessors and others present decide that, if the husband had paid *mcato*, he would have applied for its return.

Estranged Newlyweds: Olipa complains that her husband Sindikani, has infected her with a venereal disease. Before their marriage they had had a liaison as a result of which she became pregnant. When her relatives said that Sindikani had made her pregnant, he denied this, but, because his own brother told him that he could not deny it since he had slept with her, he agreed to admit responsibility and to marry her. They were married. Three days later Sindikani went away to work. When he came home for short holidays from work, he did not go to his wife at all.

Questioned by the Court, Sindikani admits that he does not live with his wife, and adds that he has no intention of going back to her. He affirms that he is not diseased and therefore could not have infected Olipa. He states that his reason for not going back to her is that, on the very night of their marriage, two young men banged on the door of her hut, wanting to come in. When he asked who was there, one of them gave his name as D. C. Paŋgaẁanthu. His wife later admitted to him that D. C. Paŋgaẁanthu had come to the village in order to meet her.

The Court makes an interim order that the couple should go to the hospital to be tested for venereal disease. The presiding assessor adds that, if Sindikani is proved free of disease, Olipa will have a very serious charge to answer, since she will have accused him falsely when she has actually been infected by someone else.

Even this cursory examination of the functioning of a Ceẁa native court leaves the impression that well-developed judicial machinery exists for handling most of the clashes that arise between persons belonging to different matrilineages. Furthermore, this machinery works because under Indirect Rule the people are operating institutions that they regard as their own. Although they may complain that, by traditional standards, adulterers, sorcerers and thieves are too lightly dealt with, there is no doubt that by and large the people are willing participants in this institution of social control. Their position in this respect contrasts sharply with that of urban Africans in South Africa, who are subjected to a host of laws and regulations that are alien to the normative order that they implicitly or explicitly cherish, and to whom punishment brings little or no disgrace. The Cewa, on the other hand, are so enmeshed in the principles underlying their judicial institutions that to get involved in a case (*kuteŋga mlandu*) is a matter of serious social consequence.

When the Judicial Machine Fails

The Chief's court and, lower down, the village or neighbourhood 'meeting' constitute a system that is usually effective in removing uncertainties and tensions from human relationships. There are, however, occasions on which this machine breaks down—because it is incompetently handled, because ill-fortune intervenes, because malefactors escape its meshes, or because the disputes it seeks to adjust cannot, by their very nature, be resolved. In such instances the persisting tensions may be expressed through the medium of beliefs in sorcery.

Incompetent handling of the judicial machine is illustrated in the following case.

Case No. 23—The Chief Who Judged His Own Case

Thomu of Bizeki village died in 1946 as a result, so people believed, of someone's preparing a 'medicine-line' (*mkhwekhwe*) for him. Thomu's sister's son, Joinala, had committed adultery with one of the wives of a territorial chief. The chief concerned had judged the case himself and had ordered Thomu on behalf of his nephew to pay him three head of cattle. Thomu had appealed to the Paramount Chief's court which had ordered the return of all the cattle on the ground that the award had been excessive. After Thomu's death, his widow and her matrikin consulted a diviner who told them that Thomu had been killed by the sorcery of the territorial chief whose decision had been reversed.

An instance of where ill-fortune intervened and nullified the work of the Court was the case of the Cow's Four Limbs, in which a beast awarded as damages for adultery died before those to whom it was awarded could enjoy the benefits of owning it.

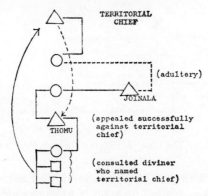

Fig. 24. The Case of 'The Chief Who Judged His Own Case'

The judicial machine can operate only when malefactors are brought within its range. The following case shows how, in Ceŵa belief at least, a wronged person may be driven to sorcery if he cannot follow the proper course of suing the person who has wronged him. To convey the reasoning that the informant (who happened to be the mother's sister's husband of the victim) imputes to the sorcerer, I have made as literal a translation as possible of the text from which it is taken.

Case No. 24—Revenge through First Aid

In Kamutu village, a little boy, Solomon, was in the cattle byre watching the milking of the cows. While there, he began bleeding from the nose. Ciŋkhuni, when he saw this, took his 'medicines' and gave them to the child's maternal grandmother, Maluŵa, telling her that they were for a bleeding nose. Maluŵa began preparing soft porridge in which to administer the 'medicines' to Solomon. The child's mother, Johana, refused, saying, 'Don't give those "medicines" to the child,' but Maluŵa persisted [and the child died].

He who took 'medicines' for killing that child was Ciŋkhuni. He killed the child because its maternal uncle, Dokotala, committed adultery with the wife of Ciŋkhuni when Ciŋkhuni was [at work] in Southern Rhodesia. When Dokotala committed adultery, they caught him, but he escaped and the following day ran away to Southern Rhodesia. When Ciŋkhuni heard that his wife had committed adultery at home, he started on his journey home. When he arrived there, he found that Dokotala had already run away to Southern Rhodesia. Because of this Ciŋkhuni was sorely troubled. He kept

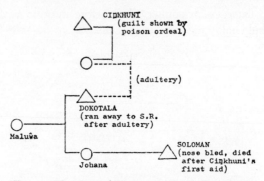

Fig. 25. The Case of 'Revenge through First Aid'

asking himself 'What shall I do?' He asked himself in his own heart; and thereupon he began to search for a way in which he could kill the children of Dokotala's sister, Johana. When he saw that child bleeding from the nose, he said [to himself], 'The time has come.' But, as I have explained, the child's mother tried to prevent the administration of the 'medicines' while its grandmother insisted that they should give them to stop the bleeding from the nose. She [the grandmother] gave him those 'medicines'. This was when the sun was at four o'clock. It's true that his nose stopped bleeding; but when they asked him [how he felt], he said his head was sore. After a short while, at six o'clock, the child died. A great sorrow! Ciŋkhuni, the person who had provided the 'medicines', began to ask, 'In whose family is there a death?' Not realizing his deceit, Johana answered, 'In mine.' The next day they buried Solomon, and, after a week, Johana, her sister and brother moved away from the village to one where they had formerly lived; and, in time, other members of her family did likewise. Their dispersal caused Ciŋkhuni to be sorely troubled, and [in an attempt to clear himself] he said he wanted to drink ordeal poison. The people secretly agreed to an ordeal. When he drank the poison, he did not vomit, which indicated that he was a sorcerer; whereupon he was greatly ashamed.

There are two main types of cases in which the judicial machine fails because the conflicts it seeks to resolve cannot be contained or adjusted by its decisions. In the first type, the parties are driven by strong motives, such as political or sexual rivalry, which are not likely to be amenable to, or satisfied by, judicial rulings. In the second type of case, the parties belong to the same matrilineage and cannot therefore avail themselves of the higher levels of the judicial machine.

An instance of how a judicial ruling failed to contain political rivalry will be found in the case of a Sister's Treachery, in which the

Chief had laid down that the sections of two unrelated men, Headman Gombe and A Cenje, should live together in the same village and that the former should be its headman. Their competition was not resolved by this decision, and it is not surprising that Gombe came to believe that Cenje was practising sorcery against him. Incidentally, in both this case and that of Revenge through First Aid, which I have just presented, it is interesting to note that, as the story is narrated, the sorcerer, unrelated to the victim, in practice effected his nefarious purpose by utilizing the trust placed in him by one of the victim's matrilineal relatives.

Another instance of how an unresolved conflict may be expressed through beliefs in sorcery is to be found in another of the cases concerning Headman Gombe (the Pretended Brother). Exasperated by the anti-social conduct of Kazingachile, Headman Gombe tried to get the Court's sanction for his disowning him as a member of his matrilineage, but, when he failed, he accused Kazingachile of sorcery.

One reason why, in Cewa eyes, strong motivation may prevent the judicial machine from containing and adjusting conflicts is that its decisions may not be sufficiently satisfying to someone who has been seriously wronged. People may believe that such a person's righteous indignation may be too strong to be satisfied with mere material compensation for the wrong he has suffered and that, to appease his anger, he may be driven to illegitimate action in the form of sorcery. Although they seem to have a sympathetic understanding of what drives him to sorcery, they do not condone the extremity of the measures he takes. Like the audience of a dramatic tragedy, they feel for him but cannot excuse him.

Case No. 25—The Broken Friendship

Two young men, Thawani and Batizani, were unrelated friends living in the same village. Batizani went to work in the district and returned home one night to find his friend Thawani committing adultery with his wife. He refused to take any legal action against Thawani; but, soon after this, went to Nyasaland. He returned from Nyasaland on a Thursday. On the Friday Thawani became unwell, and by the Saturday he was dangerously ill. People began to ask Batizani, 'Seeing that you came back on Thursday and your friend became dangerously ill on Saturday, what are we to think here in the village?' After they had spoken thus, on the Sunday Thawani died. Their own village headman being away, they called in the headman of a neighbouring village to question Batizani. Everyone, especially Thawani's brother, Waitisoni, believed that Batizani had brought 'medicines' with him from Nyasaland, where 'medicines' are reputed to be powerful, and had killed his former friend with them. The fact that he had refused to take any legal action against him was taken as a sign of his intention to kill Thawani with sorcery.

Note how the informant emphasizes that the sorcerer would not take any legal action against his victim, as a sensible man would have done, to appease the rancour in his heart awakened by not only the trespass on his rights but also the breach of the friendship.

In three of the cases just mentioned, the Broken Friendship, a Sister's Treachery, and Revenge through First Aid, the sorcerer and his victim were not kin to one another and strong motives were assumed to be operating. In the next chapter I shall consider further this link between strong motivation and deviation from the central Ceŵa dogma that victims of sorcerers are victims of their matrikin.

Meanwhile it should be remembered that such cases are exceptional, that the judicial machine usually succeeds in adjusting relationships between disputants who are of different matrilineages. In fact, the more crucial weaknesses of the judicial system are revealed by the cases that never reach the Chief's court, those between members of the same matrilineage. The 'guardians', both senior and junior, are responsible for settling such cases, but they are probably too closely involved in the issues before them to be impartial. Since personal qualifications are important in succession to headmanship, a 'guardian' may have his own ambitions at the back of his mind when he tries to settle an issue involving a potential supporter. At any rate, Ceŵa are fully aware of the fact that it is within the matrilineage that the judicial machine most often breaks down—in the Ceŵa sense of failing to effect a settlement satisfactory to the contestants. Hence it is here that they believe sorcery to operate. It is matrikin, they say, who tend to practise sorcery against one another because, when they quarrel, they are likely 'to leave [unspoken] words of speech with one another' (*kusiana mau oyaŋkhula*). These words have to remain unspoken largely because the opportunities for speaking them formally are limited, with the result, according to Ceŵa neo-Freudian reasoning, that they find an outlet in sorcery. On the basis of this belief, disputes between members of the same matrilineage tend to breed accusations of sorcery when misfortune befalls one of the disputants.

CHAPTER 7

BELIEVED ATTACKS AND ACCUSATIONS
BETWEEN UNRELATED PERSONS

REFERENCE to Table XVII shows that believed attacks and accusations between unrelated persons amount in both instances to only nine per cent of the sample. These figures are low in relation to those of opposed categories such as persons matrilineally related (fifty-eight and fifty per cent respectively) or persons related in any way (ninety and ninety-one per cent). Comparisons of this kind revive the question, discussed in Chapter 4, of the wisdom of attaching importance to absolute figures (even though, as here, expressed as percentages) without relating these to the universe of interaction of the types of persons involved.

For unrelated persons, however, I can offer a safer estimate—even though still a crude one—of the universe of interaction than for any other category of social relationship. This is because Ceŵa villages almost invariably comprise a number of unrelated sections, and there is therefore a large proportion of anyone's neighbours and economic co-operators who are not his kinsmen. As I pointed out in Chapter 4, it was not possible on the basis of my statistics to falsify the tentative hypothesis that, since Ceŵa matrikin live together, the higher frequency of accusations of sorcery between them may reflect tensions between people as neighbours rather than as *matrilineal* kinsmen. It does seem possible, however to falsify the alternative hypothesis that accusations reflect tensions between people as neighbours rather than as kinsmen in general. In other words, accusations between unrelated persons are low both absolutely and relatively to the large universe of interaction characteristic of them as a result of the social composition of Ceŵa villages. The same is true of believed attacks.

My main task in this chapter will be, not so much to explain the low incidence of believed attacks and accusations between unrelated persons, as to define the exceptional conditions under which this general rule does not apply. The explanation for the generally low incidence in this category of social relationships is not far to seek. Since unrelated persons can avail themselves of the arbitration of the Chief's court, many of their disputes can be settled before they reach explosive proportions. The exceptional cases, those constituting nine per cent of sorcerer–victim and of accuser–sorcerer coincidences, require more careful examination.

I have already presented some instances in which the sorcerer was believed to have taken the unusual course of attacking someone unrelated to him. All these cases were characterized by a belief that strong motives were operating. In the case of the Broken Windscreen, there was competition for goods in short supply; in the cases of the Cow's Four Limbs, the Chief Who Judged His Own Case, Revenge through First Aid, and the Broken Friendship, sexual jealousy was involved; and in the case of a Sister's Treachery, rivalry for village headmanship.

These cases suggest that the relatively few instances in which sorcery is believed to operate between unrelated persons are ones in which there was a tense relationship between the persons involved as sorcerer and victim.[1] Is this hypothesis supported by the statistics that summarize the attributes of all the cases collected? I shall first approach the question in the typically Ceŵa idiom of belief: When a sorcerer attacks an unrelated victim, is his attack usually preceded by a quarrel?

TABLE XXIII

To Test Association between Social Relationship (in Three Categories) of Sorcerer and Victim and whether or not a Quarrel was Believed to Precede the Sorcerer's Attack

Sorcerer and Victim Were	Quarrel Preceded Attack	No Quarrel Preceded Attack	Total
Related matrilineally	41	18	59
Related non-matrilineally	22	9	31
Unrelated	9	1	10
	72	28	100
Victim not specified			1
$\chi^2 = 1 \cdot 808$; $\cdot 50 > p > \cdot 30$			101

Table XXIII shows how the 101 cases were distributed in respect of these two variables. There is no significant association between them. Though as many as nine of the ten believed attacks on unrelated victims were preceded by quarrels, there was also a high proportion of quarrels preceding attacks on kinsmen, whether matrilineal or non-matrilineal.

[1] This applies also to accuser and sorcerer. See pp. 217–8.

BELIEVED ATTACKS BETWEEN UNRELATED PERSONS 217

Admittedly the proportions were lower for related than for unrelated, but the numbers involved are too small to eliminate the possibility that the results obtained could have resulted from chance.

It may be more fruitful to ask: In those believed attacks preceded by quarrels, did sorcerers and unrelated victims show a tendency to quarrel over issues different from those in which sorcerers and related victims were involved? Table VIII showed a moderately significant association between the *kind of quarrel* preceding the believed attack and whether sorcerer and victim were matrilineally related or not. The first part of Table XXIV represents a rearrangement of the same data,

TABLE XXIV

QUARRELS PRECEDING (1) BELIEVED ATTACKS AND (2) ACCUSATIONS
OF SORCERY

Attack or Accusation Believed to be Linked with	(1) Sorcerer and Victim			(2) Accuser and Sorcerer			
	Related	Un-related	Total	Related	Un-related	Relation-ship Unknown	Total
Quarrels over social obligations, cattle and other property	31	1	32	29	0	10	39
other issues, including sexual jealousy and politics	32	8	40	23	9	8	40
No Quarrel	27	1	28	18	0	4	22
	90	10	100	70	9	22	101
Victim not identified			1				
			101				
Significance of association	$\chi^2 = 7\cdot411$; $\cdot05 > p > \cdot02$			$\chi^2 = 15\cdot626$; $\cdot01 > p > \cdot001$			

and shows a moderately significant tendency for sorcerers and their unrelated victims to have quarrelled over issues such as sexual jealousy and political rivalry rather than over the typical bones of contention between sorcerers and their related victims, such as social obligations, cattle and other property, or, in fact, to have quarrelled at all. However, this finding must be taken with reserve because, owing to the small frequencies in some of its cells, the table does not satisfy the conditions sometimes specified for the applicability of the chi-square test.[1]

If we depart from the usual Ceŵa idiom and study the relationship, not between sorcerer and victim, but between accuser and sorcerer, a similar conclusion emerges. The second part of Table XXIV shows a clear separation of the categories of related and unrelated accusers and

[1] See, for instance, Siegel, *Nonparametric Statistics*, pp. 46 and 178, citing Cochran.

sorcerers in regard to both whether a quarrel preceded the accusation and the nature of the issue (if any) over which they quarrelled. Although the association shown in this part of the table is of a higher degree of significance than that in the previous one, it has to be taken with the same reserve owing to the possibility that, on account of low cell-frequencies, the chi-square test has been inappropriately applied.

A return to Table XVII will show that, in terms of the interpretations adopted when the table was introduced, links between unrelated persons are hostile rather than affiliative; for, though they make up less than ten per cent (with full counting of 'multiple' cases) of either sorcerer–victim or accuser–sorcerer links, they make up only one per cent of accuser–victim coincidences. Statistically, this predominance of hostile accuser–sorcerer links over affiliative accuser–victim links is moderately significant for the relationship category (unrelated persons) being examined. In other words, the proportion, in this category, of accuser–sorcerer links so exceeds that of accuser–victim ones that the percentage difference is moderately significant; and the percentage ratio is 8·05.

I noted (end of Chapter 3) that, of the ten cases in which first sorcerer and first victim mentioned were unrelated, only one was not preceded by a quarrel and that the remaining nine were preceded by quarrels about love (five cases), politics (two cases) or unspecified issues (two cases). Some of these cases have already been presented.

Unrelated accusers and sorcerers showed a similar trend—partly because, where they were unrelated, so usually were sorcerer and victim, and we are examining almost exactly the same set of cases, though from a different angle. In all nine cases in which the first accuser and first sorcerer recorded were unrelated, either a severe quarrel or intense rivalry had preceded the accusation. In four of these cases, the sorcerer's motive was assumed to be sexual jealousy, his wife or betrothed having been seduced by a close relative of the victim; and the accuser, recognizing this strong motivation, and aware of the guilt of the victim's relative, had little or no difficulty in inferring who the sorcerer was. In the fifth case, there had been a serious quarrel at work on a tobacco farm between the victim and the African foreman (*kapitao*), and the latter was blamed for her death. The remaining four cases arose out of political rivalry: in two, the accuser and sorcerer were village-section leaders competing for overall headmanship of the village; in the third, they were supporters of rival candidates for an important chieftainship; and, in the last, the victim's wife accused a territorial chief of having killed her husband, who, before his death, had succeeded in an appeal to the Paramount Chief against a decision of the territorial chief (The Chief Who Judged His Own Case).

Some of these cases have already been presented in other contexts. The following two are added by way of illustrating the two main types of issues that led to believed attacks and accusations of sorcery between unrelated persons:

Case No. 26—Revenge Taken Rather Far

Zechariah betrothed a girl and then went to work in Southern Rhodesia. After he had been there three years, the girl said, 'How's this? When he left me, I was but a child. Now I am a grown woman. Now I'll form a liaison with a man.' This she proceeded to do, with Abelo. Zechariah received a letter from his sister in which she reported the infidelity of his betrothed; and he wrote back to her, 'How is it that my betrothed has taken on with Abelo? Did he not know that I had betrothed her? She will see [i.e. experience] something!' And he signed his letter with the drawing of a lion. After a month, lions came and took one of Abelo's beasts. Next day they caught another; and, the following day, yet another. But when the lions came to catch Abelo himself, they failed to get him, and went back again to Southern Rhodesia where they were received by their master [Zechariah]. Zechariah now procured 'medicines' which he sent through the air, and with them he killed Abelo's mother, three of his sisters, two of his mother's sisters, two of his younger brothers, his mother's mother and his mother's brother. The accuser, Abelo, did not need to make enquiries; to him it was obvious who the sorcerer was.

Case No. 27—Supporters of Rival Candidates

Katete and Kasinda were rivals for a chieftainship, that of Kabambo (see His Uncle's Bed). One day a messenger reported to one of Katete's friends, Filipo, that one of his rival's supporters, Cimteŋgo, on hearing of the Paramount Chief's intention to support Katete's candidature, had said that he disagreed: that Katete might have a right to succeed, but only after the death of Kasinda. He had added the threat, 'If Katete doesn't die, there'll be a war' (*Ngati A Katete sadʒafa mpaka ŋkhondo idʒacitika*). Subsequently Filipo was informed by some of Katete's relatives that they overheard Cimteŋgo saying, 'The moon is old. If Katete is alive by the next moon, he will be lucky.' Filipo claims that Cimteŋgo has been attempting to kill Katete with sorcery.

It may be worth noting that, in the case of Revenge Taken Rather Far, Zechariah's action, in that it was in some measure justified, might

Q

have been classified as vengeance magic rather than sorcery; for the definition of sorcery that I have adopted includes the idea that it is illegitimate. Against this it may be argued, however, that Zechariah could have sued Abelo in the Chief's court instead of adopting the extreme measures he chose; and that, in any case, he took his revenge rather far.

This case is a good illustration of Mayer's contention[1] that 'People who have both possibilities may still prefer to accuse each other of witchcraft rather than pick a legal quarrel' because 'they do not want to be reconciled. What they want is an excuse for rupture.' This excuse is imputed to Zechariah, who, it is assumed, found the killing of his rival or of his rival's cattle and relatives the only satisfying way of avenging as serious a wrong as that of being cuckolded. This idea should not, however, make one forget that the people concerned actually believe that sorcery is being perpetrated.

My survey of believed attacks and accusations of sorcery between unrelated persons, though it rests on poor foundations because of the small numbers involved, points to the same conclusion as that reached in the last chapter. It would appear that the judicial machine is adequate for adjusting most relationships between members of different matri-lineages (including the category I have been considering in this chapter, unrelated persons), but that in a few instances it fails because of parti-cularly strong motivation or some similar impediment to its normal operation, and the unresolved or unresolvable conflicts are then ex-pressed in the idiom of sorcery.

[1] *Witches*, p. 13, commenting on my paper, 'The Social Context of Cewa Witch Beliefs'.

CHAPTER 8

SORCERY AS A MORAL FORCE

AN hypothesis often expressed or implied by those social anthropologists and psychologists who have written on witchcraft and sorcery is that beliefs in these phenomena serve to reinforce social norms by dramatizing them.[1] These beliefs, it is argued, buttress a society's values by providing—in the person of the sorcerer or witch—a symbol of all that is defined as anti-social and evil, and thus a rallying point for the forces of morality and good. The fear of being accused of mystical evil-doing is, according to this view, a sanction for moral conduct. A few writers[2] suggest that it is not only the sorcerer or witch who plays a morally relevant rôle but also his victim. This is because his misfortune is sometimes retrospectively attributed to his own misconduct or to that of a close associate. Thus the fear not only of being accused but also of being attacked by sorcery or witchcraft may be an important factor in social control.

Whichever character one examines, mystical evil-doer or victim, sorcery and witchcraft emerge as conservative social forces; and their conservative character is brought into sharp relief when they operate under conditions of social change, a subject that will be considered in the next chapter. As Malinowski put it, when writing of sorcery:

> In whatever way it works, it is a way of emphasizing the *status quo*, a method of expressing the traditional inequalities and of counter-acting the formation of any new ones. Since conservatism is the most important trend in a primitive society, sorcery on the whole is a beneficent agency of enormous value for early culture.[3]

The normative function of Cewa beliefs in sorcery has been illustrated in many of the cases already presented in other contexts. For instance, in the case of the Virtuous Sister-in-Law, Maliseni, who had persisted in trying to commit adultery with his married sister-in-law

[1] See, for instance, Hunter (now Wilson), *Reaction to Conquest*, p. 317; Kluckhohn, *Navaho Witchcraft*, pp. 63–4; Starkey, *The Devil in Massachusetts, passim*; and Nadel, 'Witchcraft in Four African Societies', p. 28.

[2] For instance, Malinowski, *Crime and Custom*, pp. 86 and 93–4; Fortune, *Sorcerers of Dobu*, pp. 175 ff.; and Whiting, *Paiute Sorcery*, pp. 84–5 *et passim*.

[3] *Crime and Custom*, p. 317.

though she had always refused his advances, after her death was accused of having killed her with sorcery. Even when the blame attaches to the victims of the attack or to their close relatives or friends, the moral is the same. In the case of the Cow's Four Limbs, it was the close relatives of the wrongdoer who died as a result, so people believed, of the cuckolded husband's mother's sorcery; and much the same applies to the case of a Revenge Taken Rather Far. All these cases have the implication that adultery and similar wrongs may well lead to more serious consequences than being sued in the Chief's court.

In this chapter I shall examine the extent to which the case material supports the hypothesis that beliefs in sorcery buttress social norms. My procedure will be to present an outline of Ceŵa norms and then to consider whether the ideal behaviour they prescribe is sanctioned by beliefs that underlie the real or imagined events reported. For obvious reasons of scientific procedure, the two sets of data to be compared must be independent of each other; and the outline of norms will therefore be based on all available evidence *except* cases involving beliefs in sorcery.

An Outline of Ceŵa Norms

The following account of Ceŵa norms is based on: (*a*) people's expressed conceptions of socially desirable conduct and characteristics; (*b*) their actual sanctioning of everyday behaviour; (*c*) their definitions of abnormal behaviour; (*d*) their accounts of misfortunes, with their tendency retrospectively to attribute moral weaknesses or transgressions to the victims concerned; (*e*) the norms of conduct as well as the norms of misconduct[1] upon which Ceŵa judges seem to be basing their assumptions; and (*f*) the moral implications of folk-lore and ritual.

I collected a considerable amount of material on conduct that Ceŵa commend and personality traits that they admire by asking informants to speak or write about 'a good person' (*munthu wabwino*). Sometimes I asked them to describe more specifically their conception of a good man, a good woman, a good headman or chief (*nfumu*), or a good teacher. Realizing that these descriptions would be idealized, I tried to supplement them by observing everyday behaviour and by recording people's evaluations of the actual conduct of others. One method of obtaining such evaluations was to ask a few semi-literate people living in different villages to keep diaries for me. What they wrote threw much light on their conceptions of conduct worthy of praise or blame;

[1] Cf. Gluckman, *The Judicial Process*, Chapter 3.

for they often showed that their enjoyment of the company of the good
or their shocked amazement at the conduct of the bad was of sufficient
interest to warrant the arduous task of recording it.

The statements about ideal character show that the Cewa have a keen
appreciation of the intrinsic and instrumental value of harmonious
human relationships. The good man is the meek one who pleases all,
gives offence to none, and is wise, generous and sociable. The good
woman and the good child, in accordance with their inferior status,
have two important qualities in common, obedience and a willingness
to be of service in their respective spheres of housekeeping and errand-
running. Both pay respect to elders—for reasons that will be mentioned
presently.

Esteemed people are depicted as being conscientious in fulfilling
their obligations, whether these be defined by kinship bonds or by
wider social links. Good men help their dependants, and take pains to
entertain visiting friends or even passing strangers; and their wives,
children and sisters' children support them in these duties.

'To converse congenially' (kuceza) is valued for its own sake; and
Cewa obviously enjoy the company of others. At the same time they
are fully aware of the rewards for being sociable and pleasing to others.
Sometimes these expected rewards are cited in support of a recommended norm. A child is enjoined to be willing to run errands in order
that he may be clothed or helped in some other way by those who wish
to send him. A woman is told that her best way of achieving the
security of a stable marriage is for her to cook well and be both faithful
and sexually responsive to her husband; and she is warned that, if she
offends the elders when she is pregnant, she cannot expect to bear her
child without trouble.

There is considerable agreement between theory and practice in the
sense that conduct conspicuous enough to bring praise or blame in
everyday life usually exemplifies or violates the norms just described.
The good man of verbal description is meek; and the bad man of everyday rebuke and gossip is aggressive and short-tempered. Similarly, the
bad woman is headstrong, impudent, lazy, domestically incompetent
or promiscuous; and the bad child is disobedient. The sociable, hospitable person, constantly recommended in theory, enjoys in practice
great popularity and is therefore in an enviable position. His opposite,
the recluse who avoids the company of others or spends too much time
in the company of his wife instead of that of his male friends, is the
subject of disapproval and derision.

The conventions of polite social intercourse are adjusted to the smooth running of the wheels of interaction. I realized this through having to learn and practise them. I had to seek permission to join company (a formal request never refused); and I had to sit down as soon as possible and on as low a seat as I could find lest people should think I was expecting the honour of being given a chair. I had to be properly settled before expecting a greeting, had to acknowledge all greetings individually, and had to repeat, for each one who asked me, my answers to questions about my health and whence I had come and whither I was going. I had to ask such questions of others and to assist those who spoke to me by punctuating their remarks with interjections that showed my interest in what they told me, such as '*Kodi?*' (Really?), '*Inde*' (Yes), '*A-a!*' (Now you don't say!), '*Basi!*' (Enough said!) and '*Cabwino*' (Good). I had to seek permission before leaving, and felt ashamed on being told by my language teacher that both the way I had clapped my hands on approaching the group and the intonation of my farewell had been effeminate.

The intensely social orientation of the Ceŵa is reflected in the sanctions they apply to transgressors. Underlying all those sanctions that they deliberately mete out (as opposed to those that one may infer to be operating indirectly through mystical belief) is a marked sense of shame (*manyaẓi*). People are deterred from immoral conduct, not so much by the punishment that a court imposes, nor by the damages it may award, but rather by the associated derision of other people and the consequent feeling of shame. Shame is said to make grown men weep and to drive impetuous transgressors to suicide. If a person who has been insane 'feels shame again' at his nakedness, this is taken to be a sign of his recovery.

When someone is warned that his conduct will lead to the personal disaster of feeling ashamed, the 'reference group', those among whom he should not lose face, may be designated as 'other people', or, more specifically, as his age-mates, the people of another village, his affines— present or future—or his joking partners (see Chapters 4 and 5), who may, in jest, speak many a true word.

An implicit reference *point* (rather than group) is the headman. 'A headman is born!' is the joyful cry attending the birth of every boy; and rightly so, since (cf. Chapter 4) the merits of a man's personality often take him further than would his genealogical position alone. As one might expect, the ideal headman, to whose position most men secretly aspire, is the epitome of approved conduct. He is a meek person, serenely self-controlled, who is generous to his dependants and hospitable to strangers. He has the knack of readjusting disturbed human relationships and of persuading people of the wisdom of his decisions rather than forcing them to accept these. Some of the norms defining the ideal headman's rôle probably spring from an appreciation of its great difficulty. He is a person who should refrain from gambling; who should drink only in moderation, if at all; who should remain at a beer-drink only a short time lest violence occur and he be called upon to give evidence before the chief and have to admit that he was drunk; and who should not leave his village or section except for work in his garden or for duty at the chief's capital.

Many of the norms prescribing the teacher's rôle are of a similarly preventive character and point to the difficulties brought about by Western differentiation and the new distribution of power. The teacher should not take advantage of his comparative wealth and prestige by seducing other men's wives or his senior pupils; nor should he punish children without due permission; nor should he show disrespect towards the village headman.

The high degree of social orientation, which I have remarked on, is found in the Ceŵa definition of insanity, a condition attributed, incidentally, either to sorcery or to seizure by an angered ghost (ciwanda)—angered because the sufferer or one of his associates has failed to perform a ritual such as purification after a bereavement. In descriptions of 'mad people' (ŵanthu ŵamisala) given by my informants and by witnesses at Lunacy Inquiries,[1] socially disrupting symptoms are emphasized—rather than, as in our society, the patient's loss of self-identification and orientation. The actions of mad people that are noted are that they burn down huts, destroy crops and livestock, assault people, talk to themselves, undress in company without shame and wander into and stay in the bush where they behave like wild animals. The last symptom, incidentally, is related to an interesting though rather obscure negative value. Just as the night is a 'lonely time' to the Irish,[2] so is the bush a 'lonely place', a 'wilderness' (cipululu), to the Ceŵa. It is the antithesis of normal living, and the attitude towards it represents the obverse of the emphasis on sociability.

As I have remarked, violent and aggressive behaviour is strongly disapproved. There are constant reminders of this in everyday life. I

[1] I made notes on those concerning Ceŵa from a file entitled 'Lunacy Inquiry from 1939 to 1944' kept at Fort Jameson.
[2] Arensberg, The Irish Countryman, p. 187.

have often seen adults separate children who have started fighting 'lest their quarrel be the cause of enmity between their parents'. Verbal abuse (*kutukwana*) is regarded in almost as serious a light as actual physical violence (*ndeu*). Anyone who loses his temper (*-pya mtima*, lit., 'burns [in his] heart') is the subject of strong condemnation. If a case is being heard at a village meeting (*kabuŋgwe*) or before a chief, and one of the litigants loses his temper, the action goes against him, no matter how strong his position in other respects. This is in keeping with the principle already noted (Chapter 5) that the function of Ceŵa judicial institutions is the removal of hatred from human hearts by patient examination and persuasion in terms of a commonly accepted code. To lose one's temper during a trial is to defy this principle.

By Ceŵa standards, it is difficult to comply with this principle; for to do so involves experiencing the shame of admitting that one has done wrong. Perhaps this is why Ceŵa emphasize the desirability of freely acknowledging when one is in the wrong, and why courts take great pains to induce the loser of an action to say 'I admit [it]' (*Nabvomela*), 'I was at fault' (*Nalakwa*) or 'I have been foolish' (*Napusa*). As I shall mention when I deal with the moral implications of ritual, Ceŵa believe that confessing (*kuulula*) a wrong is an effective means of staving off its normal mystical consequences.

What are the lessons of Ceŵa misfortunes? What moral weaknesses, if any, are attributed retrospectively to the victims or their close associates? As I made clear in Chapter 1, the case material I collected during the course of field work was not confined to misfortunes attributed to sorcery, from which the numbered series of cases in this book have been taken, but included misfortunes in general. Those of them that were not attributed to sorcery, but to natural causes, to other people's actions and omissions and to the intervention of lineage spirits, provided instances of the retrospective dramatization of norms. In other words, their victims, like the victims of sorcery, were sometimes believed to deserve what befell them because they or their close associates had disregarded social norms.

This makes it possible for someone whose sorcery is blamed for a misfortune to shift the blame on to some other mystical agency. He would, however, be limited by the fact that such a course is notorious. Many Ceŵa believe (cf. Chapter 3) that sorcerers are in the habit of killing people who are being punished by a spirit or who have been cursed, thus throwing their guilt on to someone who in a fit of temper may have said more than he intended.

It will be recalled that, in Table I, the 194 cases of misfortune recorded during the course of my field work were classified *inter alia* according to whether or not they had moral implications in regard to the previous actions of the victim or of someone associated with him. In eighty-three cases, the victim of the misfortune had, in terms of Ceŵa social norms, been at fault; and, in a further thirty-four, someone closely associated with him, such as a kinsman or friend, had been at fault. Of these 117 cases with moral implications, seventy-one were ones involving beliefs in sorcery; and forty-six did not involve such beliefs. The types of misdemeanours of which victims or their associates had been guilty are shown in Table XXV. My present concern is

TABLE XXV
Types of Misdemeanour Attributed to the Victim or His Associate in the 117 Cases in Table I that had Moral Implications

Type of Misdemeanour	Cases Involving Beliefs in Sorcery	Cases not Involving Beliefs in Sorcery	Total
Failure to discharge traditional obligations	16	7	23
Sexual promiscuity	1	16	17
Being a sorcerer	17	—	17
Being conspicuously fortunate	12	—	12
Being quarrelsome, aggressive, etc.	9	1	10
Failure to perform ritual, breach of taboo, etc.	—	10	10
Dishonesty, theft, etc.	4	6	10
Adultery, sexual jealousy, etc.	7	—	7
Being mean or avaricious	5	—	5
Others (drunkenness, lack of virility, being unsociable)	—	6	6
	71	46	117

$$\chi^2 = 78 \cdot 811; p < \cdot 001$$

with the second column, which summarizes the transgressions of the forty-six victims or victims' associates in those cases in which their misfortunes were not attributed to sorcery. The following—in descending order of frequency—are the more important of the traits or actions attributed to the victims (or their associates) where the misfortune was not connected with sorcery: sexual promiscuity; failure to perform a ritual or to observe a taboo; failure to discharge a traditional obligation; and dishonesty, theft and similar misdemeanours. Examples of case summaries from these categories are:

Sexual Promiscuity (of the victim's husband): Leonora, a young woman who had had one child, began to suffer from swellings in the groin. These became worse, and she died. People said that her death was the result of a venereal disease, known as 'the disease of Songea [a place in Tanganyika Territory]' (*nthenda yaSoŋgea*), which she had contracted ('taken', *-teŋga*) from her husband who had been infected with it by prostitutes in Southern Rhodesia. Her relatives sued her husband in Chief Mlolo's court and were awarded damages of £6, the court fee being 5s.

Failure to Observe a Taboo (by victim's wife): Mkanjo went to work in a mine in Southern Rhodesia, taking his wife with him. One day, as he was operating a pneumatic drill, a loose piece of rock came away and killed him. His wife argued that his death was the result of the hatred of the African foreman (*kapitao*) who, she said, must have deliberately marked the position of the hole on a loose piece of rock. Mkanjo's relatives refused to believe this, saying that his wife must have committed adultery and thus broken the strict sexual taboo imposed on the wives of all those engaged in dangerous or delicate operations, such as mining, iron smelting and *kacaso* distilling.

Failure to Perform a Ritual (by victim and later her relatives): Otina, a young married woman without children yet, was preparing food when a rooster approached, and began to eat it. She tried to chase it away, but it turned on her and pecked her on the eyebrow. Her relatives considered this such an unusual occurrence that they consulted a diviner, who found that the spirit of Otina's mother's mother was angry because Otina 'is eating alone without preparing anything for us'. Otina's relatives were Christians, and told the diviner that they could not make beer to appease a spirit. Otina died three weeks after the rooster's attack.

Failure to Discharge Traditional Obligations (by victim's lover): Sitelia, an unmarried girl, became pregnant and died in childbirth. This, people said, resulted from the fact that the baby's father was not present to make a traditional confession of his adulteries committed while Sitelia was pregnant (cf. Chapter 5) because there was no prospect of his marrying her, since, although he was her cross-cousin, his relatives were Roman Catholics and could not allow him to marry a cross-cousin.

Theft (by victim): Mcele, a middle-aged man, stole a coat. Its owner procured property-protective magic (*cambo*) which followed up (*-londola*) the thief, killing him and two of his relatives.

It is interesting to note the frequency with which modern influences occur in these examples, which were taken at random from my records. Labour migration, prostitution, greater differentiation of work, loyalty to Christian principles—all these are features of modern life which directly or indirectly increase the difficulty of conforming to traditional norms, and probably multiply the cases in which punishment is believed to befall those who defy them. The relevance of modern social changes to beliefs in sorcery will be taken up in the next chapter.

My records of court cases (see Chapters 5 and 6) are not full enough to exemplify for the Cewa Gluckman's insight that native judges use reasonable norms of conduct as a means of attacking evidence.[1] They show, however, that Cewa judges have clearly formulated norms of conduct at the backs of their minds when they try to settle disputes. For instance, in the 'Fixing of Compensation' and the 'Division of Property on Divorce', the Chief's court had no hesitation in upholding the norm of generosity by tempering the avarice of the man who, having looked after another's cow and enjoyed the proceeds of the sale of its milk, wanted a relatively large money payment before he returned it to its owner, and in persuading the divorced wife to give her ex-husband some of the ground-nut seed that she had acquired by her own efforts. Similarly, the importance of being ready to admit a wrong is upheld by the unanimous rejoinder of the village meeting to Daniel that '[To say] "I admit it with a sore head" is no admission at all' (see end of Chapter 5), and by an analogous response on the part of Chief Kawaza Manipu to the man who admitted his wrong 'because the Chief says so' (Chapter 6). The much-admired shrewdness basic to wise leadership is illustrated by the Court's familiarity with what Gluckman calls the 'norms of misconduct'[2] when the judges indicate to Olipa in the case of the 'Estranged Newlyweds' that they suspect her of covering up her infidelity by accusing her husband of having infected her with venereal disease.

Reference to Table XXII shows that much of the Kawaza Native Court's time is devoted to cases involving conduct likely to disturb normal social relationships, including adultery, assault, slander, theft and damage to crops. Furthermore, the Court departs from its usual leniency when dealing with more serious invasions of rights and more violent breaches of the peace. For instance, in January 1947, I was present when Chief Kawaza Sopgani imprisoned a man for six months because he stole clothes, and a boy for two months because he was in possession of a knife when the court messenger (*kapasu*) tried to arrest him for breach of a service contract with a White farmer.

The Cewa have their share of Africa's rich heritage of oral folk-lore. This includes ideophones, idioms, proverbs, maxims, riddles, fables

[1] *The Judicial Process*, p. 82.
[2] *Ibid.*, p. 129.

and songs. These folk-lore elements vary in the extent to which they have explicit moral references. Proverbs and maxims are the most directly didactic; fables and songs the most densely obscured in symbolism.

Many proverbs and maxims refer to social life by extolling the virtue of good neighbourliness or by warning of the consequences of anti-social conduct. Thus, 'If your companion's beard catches alight [and] you extinguish [the fire] for him, tomorrow he'll extinguish [one in] yours'; and 'Good requites companionate good; evil requites companionate evil'. Certain idiomatic expressions facilitate the development of social skills, such as the shrewd recognition of the deception of others. For instance, 'sharpness of tongue' (*kutwa kwalilime*) means the ability to tell lies that resemble truthful statements and is something that a wise leader or judge must be on the look-out for. The primary function of riddles appears to be providing entertainment and training in general mental alertness. Among those I collected, few had any moral implications.

Songs and fables deal with a wide variety of subjects, both traditional and topical, and their function would seem to be the provision of entertainment and vicarious social experience rather than the pointing of morals. The words of songs vary in intelligibility. Those accompanying mundane tasks such as pounding maize are usually straightforward, though not necessarily didactic, commentaries on current affairs. Those pertaining to traditional dances, such as the secret *nyau*, the *cimbumbuli* and *cigwiti* of the older people and the *ciŵele* and *citelele* of the younger ones, have a more obscure symbolism. The main moralizing function of songs of all kinds would appear to be to acquaint people with the realities of human behaviour rather than to lay down appropriate forms of conduct.

Fables are more articulate in painting a shrewd picture of human deceit, chicanery and cunning. Most of them have animal characters who tend to play constant rôles. Hare (*Kalulu*) is usually the hero, and personifies the slyness that helps the weak to overcome the strong and villainous. Tortoise (*Fulu*) resembles him in many ways, though he achieves his ends through the boldness of simplicity rather than the deceptiveness of cunning. Lion (*Mkaŋgo*, *Cilombo*) represents the powerful, pompous authority against which these two are often successfully pitted; Hyena (*Fisi*), the greed and lack of principle that moralists even as liberal as Hare and Tortoise find abhorrent; and Baboon (*Mkhwele*), the stupidity of the dupe whom cleverer characters find useful as a cat's paw or scapegoat. Thus, it is Hare who bribes and tricks his way out of Lion's clutches; Tortoise who alone succeeds in catching the wily Hare with bird-lime on his shell-back; Hyena who puts an end to the generosity of the hospitable (human) headman by eating all his pigs instead of the single one he was invited to take; and Baboon who dies when Hare succeeds in putting the blame on to him for killing Lion's children.[1]

The general impression given by these animal tales, which Cewa share with many other Africans, is one of 'business ethics' in a bush setting. The unprincipled principles they extol contrast sharply with both the asserted norms of Cewa precept and the operative norms of sanctioned conduct. The line between types of actions that are held up for emulation and those that are models for detestation[2] is so thin that one can only assume that the tales perform a function similar to that of cartoon films and detective novels in our society; they provide adventure to compensate for the dullness of respectability; negative example to satisfy the smugness of those who observe the norms; standardized day-dreams to reassure the small and weak; and vicarious experience to sharpen the wits of those who would improve their understanding of social behaviour. In this last respect, they resemble the legends of the Andamanese[3] in being a means of giving exercise to interest in human character.

The most outstanding human character in fable is Pimbilimani [of] Original Plan (*Pimbilimani Nzelu Zayekha*). He shows much of Hare's resourcefulness and cunning when he pits himself against the unprincipled malevolence of his mother and maternal uncle. In addition, he illustrates the advantage of the human privilege of having a following; for he effects his plans, not only by organizing his human agemates, but also by commanding a band of animal helpers. The plot of the Pimbilimani story, though not the mental processes of its characters, has a Hamlet-like quality which I have been unable to penetrate for present purposes, but which makes it worth reproducing for some reader who may be more successful. It is included with a few other illustrations of Cewa stories in Appendix B.

In at least two respects, the folk-lore to which I have referred accords with the other sources of normative conceptions I have examined. It emphasizes frankness and ingenuousness in social life.

[1] The stories in which these incidents occur are given in Appendix B.
[2] Cf. Smith, *African Symbolism*, p. 13.
[3] A. R. Brown, *The Andaman Islanders*, p. 395.

Its characters never justify their motives with complicated rationaliza-
tions. Their morality seems to be practical and down-to-earth. Harmonious social relationships are highly valued, that men should not
only desire them but also develop the shrewdness needed for bringing
them about. Ceŵa folk-lore gives a realistic picture of human motives
(especially when they are projected into animals) and shows that their
being hidden is not conducive to bearable social life.

When we move to the field of ritual, we expect the emphasis to shift
from the appeal of intrinsic rationality to that of symbolic appropriateness.[1] This shift in fact occurs to the extent that, in their ritual,
Ceŵa express certain values, such as fertility and virility, that have not
yet cropped up in my exploration of the more direct indicators of
norms. At the same time, even in the field of ritual itself, Ceŵa show
the uncomplicated, ingenuous and yet shrewd appraisal of social life
that I have noted in other contexts. This may partly explain the great
difficulty I had in getting informants to conceive of the possibility
that elements of their ritual might have meanings going beyond their
everyday connotations. In any event, I have to record my failure to
penetrate Ceŵa ritual symbolism. I tried, but the combined effect of
deficient training on my part and a lack of articulateness on the part of
my informants prevented me from making much headway. For
instance, I failed to discover any referent symbolically associated with
the removal of hair, which plays an important part in mortuary rituals.
I was repeatedly told that it was simply hair that was being shaved off
and thrown away! One of the few objects to which informants gave a
symbolic meaning without much hesitation or without much coaxing
from me was the string of white beads placed round the neck of the
recipient of the name in the ritual of nominal reincarnation (*kuponya
nyumba*, see below, this chapter). This, they said, stood for a 'pure
heart' (*mtima woyela*), which was their expression for the meek and
generous disposition that they hoped the recipient would assume with the
name. Other objects whose symbolism was clear included the 'activating
agents' (*viẑimba*, sing., *ciẑimba*) used in magical concoctions, especially
the 'medicines' with which diviners doctor themselves (see Chapter 3).

The fact that the Ceŵa have a rational approach to human society
and the norms controlling it does not mean that supernatural sanctions
have no appeal to them. On the contrary, they show the utmost respect
for the complex of mystical beliefs centring on ritual purity and impurity. As shown incidentally in one of the cases of misfortune given

[1] Cf. Parsons, *The Structure of Social Action*, pp. 210-11.

in this chapter, ritual purity, which is achieved mainly by a taboo on sexual intercourse, especially illicit sexual intercourse, is considered necessary for performing difficult or dangerous operations such as mining, smelting or distilling. It is also necessary at all the crises in the life cycle—birth, puberty, marriage and succession to headmanship or chieftainship. The most protracted period during which ritual purity is required of parents, more particularly by their abstention from illicit sexual intercourse, is the ten or eleven months from conception to 'when the child first smiles'. As I have noted in Chapters 3 and 5, difficult labour is attributed to the ritual impurity of either husband or wife, the commonest assumed cause of such impurity being infidelity of either of them during the period of pregnancy; and the child is not removed from his state of susceptibility ('being cold', *kuẓiẓila*) until the ritual of 'taking the child' (*kuteŋga mwana*) formally introduces him to the 'hot' forces abounding in the village. A feature of this ritual that is relevant here is the belief, already mentioned, that to the extent that the father succeeds in bracing himself (*kulimbika mtima*, 'making firm [his] heart') to forgo the pleasure of full intercourse, so will the child show firmness of character.

Another aspect of the *mdulo* complex of beliefs that is relevant here is the notion that the breach of a taboo will not affect the one who breaks it, but that some innocent person connected with him will suffer. This supernatural sanction is backed by secular authority in that, usually, persons who break *mdulo* taboos at inauspicious times are successfully sued in the Chief's court for the damages believed to result from their misdemeanour or even negligence.

The ultimate effect of this coincidence of ritual prescription and secular sanction is the preservation of social relationships conducive to effective human reproduction. Through the obscurer channels of symbolism and mystical belief the values of the fertility of the soil and the fecundity of animals and men are supported. A link between such values and the *mdulo* complex is to be found in the belief that a woman who has died in childbirth should be cut open to release the harmful tension (*nphamvu*, 'strength'), and her corpse either thrown into a deep pool or tied in the branches of a tree lest its 'heat' should destroy the fertility of the soil (see above, Chapter 6).

Matching these ritual prescriptions, there is intense preoccupation with ideas of virility. The standards that men set up when they complain that they are losing their sexual powers are stringent, to say the least. In this connection, a subtle conception of the place of women in

Ceŵa society is shown in the belief that, if a woman should have an orgasm before her sexual partner, the latter, unless he makes a quick confession of his inadequacy and is appropriately treated, will develop a wasting disease that invariably proves fatal. Of the six miscellaneous cases shown in the last line of Table XXV, two were of this kind.

Before turning to the details of the ritual of cardinal importance in sustaining the Ceŵa moral code (that of nominal reincarnation), I shall dispose of the normative aspects of rituals associated with death, puberty and marriage.[1]

In brief, mortuary rituals comprise the magical protection of corpse and grave-site from the attacks of sorcerers, followed by burial, grave-watching for two or three nights and a series of mourning ceremonies. The first of these ceremonies, which occurs on the day following the burial, consists of the tying of mourning bands (milaʒa, sing., mlaʒa) on the heads of those persons, such as wives or sisters of the deceased, chosen to be chief mourners. At this time their heads are shaved for the first time to allow the growth of a fresh crop of hair which will be kept as a sign of mourning. About a month later there is a ceremony, attended by dancing and beer-drinking, at which beer that is a day off maturity (cale) is offered to the deceased's spirit, and, the following day, the mourning bands are removed and the mourners' heads finally shaved. At the ceremony following the death of an important person, the nyau mimes were traditionally produced; but during the long period when, in Northern Rhodesia, these were banned directly or indirectly by the Administration, a young people's dance, ciwele, took their place. About a year later, if the deceased was an important person, an anniversary feast (called caka, 'year') is held— again to the accompaniment of dancing and beer-drinking. The theme of the last two ceremonies, especially where dancing, beer and libations are concerned, is the forgetting (kuiwala) of the deceased and the settling (kukaʒikika) of his ghost at the graveyard—away from the village where it might interfere with the welfare of the living. This theme, though expressed in supernatural terms, has an important secular aspect. It facilitates the readjustment of the members of the group to the loss of one of their number, and accords well with the emphasis I have noted elsewhere on the maintenance—in this case in spite of the accident of death—of harmonious human relationships.

The outstanding feature of the puberty and marriage rituals (which

---

[1] Fuller descriptions of all three types of rituals, as well as of nominal reincarnation, will be found in my paper, 'Notes on Some Ceŵa Rituals' (in preparation).

usually coalesce in the case of the girl's ceremony) is their emphasis on formal instruction. The Ceŵa do not leave the important process of education for the fullest phases of living to ill-defined emotional nuances of their ceremonials. In their matter-of-fact way, they ensure that the neophyte knows verbally at least how to meet every situation he is likely to encounter in his new, full adult status. To us, who have become partially immunized by the constant stream of spoken and written words with which we are bombarded, Ceŵa attention to verbal detail appears obsessional. A girl is not simply told that she must see to the comfort of her husband. She is told that she must first go to the bush and gather firewood; then bring it back; then make a fire; then go to the water-hole to draw water—and so on—leading eventually to but one small detail of her wifely duty, providing warm water for the washing of her husband's legs. Every other duty that may be in store for her is similarly presented in great detail. Ceŵa assign a much greater value to words than we do. We believe in the power of words only if by some association they have become charged with interest or, at the worst levels of education and propaganda, fear. To the Ceŵa, words have a high face value, and 'to give words' (*kupatsa mau*) means to deliver a charge of unfailing, intrinsic worth.

This is not to say that the occasions on which words are given are not charged with emotion. Words are delivered on occasions the importance of which warrants their being given special attention. But the fact that all words likely to be of use at some time in the future are included, that nothing is left to vague hints and obscure symbols alone, points to the down-to-earth conception of human relationships that I described earlier.

A notable feature of the puberty ceremonies, especially those activities of the *nyau* society that may be equated with boys' initiation, is the inclusion of both positive and negative objects and actions for evaluation, i.e. the setting up of values and behaviour patterns both for emulation and detestation, with as thin a line between the two as is the case with folk-lore characters and themes.

The most conspicuous negative values associated with *nyau* are to be found in the suspension, during its production, of normal rules of respectful and decent behaviour. Even in its present form, which represents a degeneration resulting from years of being banned, orgiastic features are prominent. The characters in the dance, their faces masked and their voices made falsetto, drop all respect-forms in speech, use abusive and obscene language, dance naked if there are no Whites

R

present, and assault people freely, especially those who are entering the society, i.e. in effect, those who are undergoing tribal initiation. Informants say that long ago their behaviour was even more violent, that they could take property and assault any person and rape any woman who got in their way; and that people used to hide in their houses to avoid such incidents. Apart from the fact that the dancers were generally supposed to be the spirits—only initiated members of the society knew that they were not—and could not be identified, no legal action would have been taken against them even if it had been possible to identify them. In a society remarkable for its tight controls in everyday life on aggression and violence, the period of *nyau*-production was—and in some measure still is—one during which such controls were dramatically lifted.

These negative values, i.e. objects and activities held up for detestation, are prominent in the induction of new members into the *nyau* society. If someone defecates near the place in the bush where neophytes are taught and dances are practised (the *liunde* or *dambwe*), the boys are made to pick up and pretend to eat the faeces, and are told to examine them carefully because 'they must be familiar with things that, in the village, are looked upon as filthy'. Similarly, they are made to wash in urine and carry out other humiliating actions, such as dancing *cimwaŋgalala*, an erotic display by means of which a well-brought-up Ceŵa wife arouses her husband's ardour.

In both the boy's (*nyau*) and the girl's (*cinamwali*) puberty ceremonies, the instructions given are typical of those of rites of passage. The neophyte is enjoined 'to give up childishness' (*kuleka cibwana*) and to take on a character befitting an adult man or woman. The girl in particular is warned that she should always help the elders and avoid quarrelling with them when she is pregnant lest she should lack someone to help her when her time comes to bear her child. And, as I have noted, she is instructed in the details of how to satisfy her husband's every need. She is warned that she should not look at her husband's face, since it is the one she has seen before, but should rather watch his belly because it is wont to change with hunger; that, when he performs 'the work of the house', i.e. when he has sexual intercourse with her, she should be responsive lest he complain that he sleep with a dead person who has not been properly instructed; and that she should be hospitable to his guests that he may enjoy their hospitality when he visits them. Like the *nyau* entrant, she is put through many tests of humiliation, patience and endurance.

PLATE VI. *NYAU* AND *CIWELE*

(a) Two *akasinja* dancers perform near the drumming team; (b) *Malia*, a male masked dancer, caricatures Ceŵa womanhood; (c) *Makanja*, the dancer on stilts; (d) *Nswala*, model of an antelope, danced after dark by a man inside it—here parked in the bush; (e, f) *Ciwele* drums and dance.

One of my informants remarked that, whereas the girl has one initiation, the boy has two. This is not altogether correct; for the girl's ceremony has two distinct phases, one at her first menstruation ('little maidenhood', *cinamwali caciŋono*) and one at her first pregnancy ('big maidenhood', *cinamwali cacikulu* or *cisamba*). What he was referring to was the fact that the boy, in addition to entering into *nyau*, plays an active part in his wife's initiation. With her he goes through certain rites of attachment, such as eating together (in a society in which men and women usually eat separately), the mutual shaving and the mixing of pubic and axillary hair, and the ritual *coitus* that brings to an end her dangerous 'cold' condition. It is only if the girl is unmarried that someone else, such as one of her cross-cousins, is invited to play the rôle of 'hyena' (*fisi*) and perform this vital service for her by deflowering her ('eating [her] maidenhood', *kudya cinamwali*). Corresponding with the instructions his wife receives, the boy is told how he should be a good husband, especially how he should avoid being unfaithful to her when she is pregnant and thus injuring her unborn child by 'cutting it in the chest'.

The taking of names[1] is a ritual in which the central figure, a neophyte about to take over the earthly name of a departed spirit, may be of almost any age. Very often he or she is a child to whom the name is transferred because its former proprietor has complained—by making some member of the matrilineage ill—that he or she is being forgotten. On the other hand, the person concerned may be a man advanced in years who, on succeeding to a headmanship, is receiving the name of his predecessor. If the name is an important one, such as that of a headman, the weight of responsibility of its associated office is symbolized by the recipient's manifest unwillingness to receive it and by his having to be captured by force or by stealth and put through the ceremony.

This ritual resembles the rituals of puberty and marriage in providing much scope for verbal instruction. The notable respect in which it differs from them is that the instruction is more general in its reference. The specific duties of the married adult give rise to a wealth of detailed precepts, whereas the task of being a worthy successor to a person of cherished memory may be conceived of in but a few general maxims. The normative importance of nominal reincarnation lies, not

[1] Because of its subtle play on the word 'nominal', I find Stefaniszyn's translation of *kuponya dzina* ('to throw [the] name') highly appropriate (cf. 'African Reincarnation Re-Examined'). My investigations confirm his finding that there is no belief that the receiver of the name is possessed by the deceased's spirit, i.e. according to belief, reincarnation is purely nominal.

so much in the volume of words that pass, as in the fact, especially true
of succession to headmanship, that the new status is one of honour
and importance which on no account should be betrayed by unworthy
conduct. Another difference between the ritual I am describing and
those of puberty and marriage is that the latter involve individual
sponsors (*aphuŋgu*, sing., *phuŋgu*) and specialist instructors (*anyam-
kuŋgwi*, sing., *nyamkuŋgwi*) who are entrusted with the detailed supervision of neophytes, whereas the former involves a wide circle of
people of diverse status, any of whom may instruct (-*laŋga*) the
recipient of the name, provided he (or she) accompanies his advice
with a small gift. Typically these advisers remind the neophyte of his
new genealogical position by telling him what his relationship now is
to each of them; and then urge him to be of good heart like his predecessor, or, if his predecessor's conduct was not exemplary, simply
'to give up childishness', to be meek, generous and polite, and to avoid
violence, abuse and unkindness.

The ritual of nominal reincarnation is important because of its
spirit of rebirth and rededication and because the neophyte is expected
to aspire either to the standard actually set by his predecessor or to the
one people wish he had set. It is a recurring public reminder of the
Ceŵa conception of desirable traits and proper conduct.

From the clues that I have presented—precept and example in
everyday life, the retrospective explanation of misfortunes, and the
analysis of court judgments, folk-lore and ritual—it is possible to
construct a picture of Ceŵa norms. Its broad base is a clear conception
of the value of orderly social life. This conception is brought into
sharper relief by the relatively dispassionate contemplation of its opposite, which is not far removed from the Hobbesian state of nature, in
which the bush rather than the village is the frame of reference, and
people's conduct would approximate to the destructiveness of the
madman or the 'mutual killing' (*kuphana*) that Ceŵa sometimes
ascribe to the pre-European era of their recent history.

Orderly social life is promoted, and the state of nature—of wild
animals in the bush—is avoided, not only by teaching people in
suitably susceptible states the basic principles of good living, but also
by giving them, through both initiation and folk-lore, a familiarity
with aberrant conduct and a clear understanding of the mechanism of
the social order and therefore a keener perception of how it may be
operated for the common good. It is this intellectual aspect of their
morality that appears to make the Ceŵa sensitive to shame; for the

advantages of proper conduct are so clear to them that only a fool could be immoral.

On a more mystical, less rational level, the values of fertility and fecundity are preserved in beliefs relating to the effects, both on the power of the soil and on the human reproductive process, of the careless handling of natural forces. The consequences of these beliefs are, however, in conformity with the more rational conceptions of the social good; for they encourage conduct which, while insupportable by scientific standards, involves serious consideration of the effects of one's actions on other people's welfare.

Sorcerers Often Personify Evil

To what extent do the beliefs represented in the case material serve to buttress the norms I have outlined? Firstly, do Ceŵa sorcerers serve as symbols for distinguishing and stigmatizing socially disapproved conduct and characteristics? Secondly, do their victims exemplify Ceŵa conceptions of unwise, if not anti-social, tendencies?

TABLE XXVI

CHARACTERISTICS OF THE FIRST SORCERERS NAMED IN THE 101
CASES IN TABLE I IN WHICH THE MISFORTUNE WAS ATTRIBUTED
TO SORCERERS ATTACKING NON-SORCERERS

Characteristics	Number of Cases
Socially disapproved:	
Already a known sorcerer	17
Jealous or greedy	9
Quarrelsome or threatening	7
Involved in sinister activities, e.g. incest, hunting magic	5
Impotent or sterile	4
Other socially disapproved characteristics	7
	—
	49
Not socially disapproved	52
	—
	101

Table XXVI shows that forty-nine, or slightly under half, of the 101 sorcerers in the sample were believed to have had anti-social traits before being involved in the real or believed episode recorded. Of these forty-nine, seventeen, or about a third, were described as already or habitually sorcerers; and all but two of the seventeen were, or would have been, classified as 'real nfiti' (witches) rather than 'killers-for-malice'. With only two exceptions, my records do not reveal what more specific traits may have been hidden in this sub-category—traits which might originally have created the reputation of being a sorcerer. One man (Katuule, see below, Chapter 10) acquired such a reputation because he was in the habit of entertaining others with conjuring tricks; and another, Alisoni of the Gambler's Folly and the Slaughtered Beasts, because he was impotent.

A further third of the forty-nine cases (nine plus seven) were ones in which the sorcerer was described as jealous, greedy, quarrelsome or threatening; and the remainder were ones in which he or she was involved in activities of a sinister nature associated with sorcery, or was impotent or sterile, or was considered a bad character for some reason other than those already cited.

Those falling into the first sub-category, i.e. alleged sorcerers who, when they were accused, already had the reputation of being sorcerers, provide an instance of how the normative function of beliefs in sorcery may interact with their function of expressing unresolved tensions. The case of the Notorious Witch illustrates this. Although before her death the victim had quarrelled with her elder sister, it was her husband's mother, Maŋgose, who was accused of having killed her 'because they always blame Maŋgose in that family because she is a notorious witch'. In other words, the tension between sisters was not expressed in the accusation because it could be deflected on to someone defined by social norms as an appropriate scapegoat. I did not personally know the alleged witch in this case, but I did know Alisoni of the Gambler's Folly and the Slaughtered Beasts, just referred to. I noted that he was said to be impotent, was highly strung, volatile, and, in general, temperamentally unsuited to playing the rôle of the Ceŵa ideal man, who, as I tried to show in the last section, is defined as meek, controlled and unaggressive. This unfortunate misfit figured in the two cases mentioned as well as in three others not included in the sample because my records on them were not full enough.

An example of how an accusation of sorcery may result from a person's being involved in practices of a sinister nature is the following:

Case No. 28—His Niece's Head

In 1950, an adolescent girl, Adelaida, on going to fetch water, disappeared. When the people of her village missed her, they searched, but could not find her. Then someone discovered her head on the hut-verandah of her mother's brother, Kamaŋgani, and, near it, the footprint of a small leopard. Kamaŋgani had the reputation of using *nfumba* magic for enticing other people's crops from their gardens into his. The people accused him of sending a leopard-familiar to kill his sister's daughter so that he might have her skull to put in his grain-store to increase his maize at other people's expense. He denied the accusation and invited them to search his hut for the familiar. While they were doing so, the leopard escaped through a window. His guilt, in the eyes of the people of the village, was confirmed when he ran away. He went mad; and the last time they saw him—in 1951—he was wandering around naked. He has not been seen since, and probably died in the bush.

It is easy to slip into the Ceŵa way of thought and assume the guilt of this man and thus overlook the tragedy that may befall someone who firmly believes in sorcery including the possibility of his being a sorcerer himself.

The characters of accused sorcerers vary from those of unmitigated scoundrels like Kaziŋgachile, the Pretended Brother, to tragic figures like Eledia, the first wife of the Backsliding Christian, whom, people believe, the course of events drives into socially disapproved behaviour.

Victims May Get Their Deserts

The case of the Backsliding Christian provides a convenient link with the second way in which beliefs in sorcery may vindicate social norms, i.e. by attributing socially disapproved behaviour to the victim. Headman Gombe and his first wife, Eledia, had married while still young, and had both become Christians. Many years later, by which time Gombe was employed as an evangelist by one of the missions, he made a girl, Etelina, pregnant and married her, with the result that he was discharged from the mission. Eledia, a conforming Christian, did not adjust herself—as Ceŵa norms would demand—to her husband's polygyny, and the tension that developed between the co-wives culminated in her being accused of trying to kill Etelina and Gombe with sorcery. Although, as I have noted, Eledia was in a rather tragic way to blame for not having adjusted herself to her husband's polygyny, so, too, was one of the victims of her believed sorcery, Gombe, in that, from one viewpoint at least, he had been unwise to destroy her happiness and his career with the mission; and he got, or narrowly escaped, his due. (For details, see Chapter 10.)

I may now refer to the first column of Table XXV in order to check whether the characteristics of victims in cases involving beliefs in sorcery provide confirmation—of a negative kind—of my account of

Ceŵa norms based on other lines of evidence. This column shows the distribution, according to the misdemeanour attributed to the victim or his associate, of seventy-one cases having moral implications and involving beliefs in sorcery (including seventeen cases in which sorcerers were victims of people's physical or magical vengeance, of their own sorcery or of the sorcery of others—see first summary of Table I). In descending order of frequency of mention, the following are the moral defects of which the victims or their close relatives or friends were believed to be guilty: being a sorcerer; failure to discharge traditional obligations; being conspicuously fortunate; being quarrelsome, aggressive, etc.; being involved in adultery or similar misdemeanours; being mean or avaricious; being dishonest; and (only one case) being sexually promiscuous.

A comparison of this distribution with that shown in the second column of the table, for cases not involving beliefs in sorcery, reveals that, with the exception of two categories of misdemeanour, viz. failure to discharge traditional obligations and dishonesty, there is virtually no overlapping, the general association of types of misdemeanour with types of sanction being statistically of extreme significance though, as in an earlier table (Table XXIV), there is some doubt, because of low cell-frequencies, about the applicability of the chi-square test. Thus, when misfortunes are attributed—in part at least—to the sexual promiscuity of the victim or his associate (usually his sexual partner or someone ritually 'cold'), they are almost exclusively regarded as the consequence of contracting a venereal disease or of breaking an *mdulo* taboo, i.e. this general category of misdemeanour is almost entirely sanctioned by beliefs not necessarily involving sorcery. Conversely, cases of sexual jealousy, involving adultery and analogous situations, are sanctioned (in this sample) entirely by beliefs in sorcery. The difference would appear to be that, while both types of misdemeanours are likely to arouse strong feelings on the part of those wronged, the type sanctioned by beliefs in sorcery, i.e. misdemeanours relating to adultery, etc., involve more fundamental conflicts of rights, given the background of marital insecurity in a society with a high divorce rate.

Two cases that I have already considered in other contexts provide straightforward examples of how the misfortune of a victim of sorcery may be attributed to a wrong he has committed. In the case of the Gambler's Folly, Kenala gambled away his elder brother's property, and, so people believed, was subsequently the victim of his brother's sorcery; and, in the case of the Broken Friendship, Thawani was believed to have been killed by the sorcery of Batizani whose friendship he had betrayed by committing adultery with his wife. Other cases of a similar kind are the following:

Case No. 29—Youthful Impudence Punished by Death

Absolom was a boy of about fifteen years. One day, the cattle he was herding strayed into the garden of his mother's sister, Bwanji, and started eating the crops there. When Bwanji's husband, Mkawila, returned to the village, he started abusing Absolom. Absolom struck him. Mkawila then said,

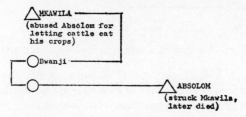

Fig. 26. The Case of 'Youthful Impudence Punished by Death'

'It is not right that I should be beaten by a child; the child [doing so] should die.' After only two weeks Absolom suffered from a headache and died the same afternoon. The people said to Mkawila, 'See, you, his [classificatory] father, said the child should die. See, he's died now.' They reported the matter to the Chief who, however, refused to take any action because, he said, he dealt only with cases in which people had seen 'medicines' being poured [i.e. with cases he might refer to the Administration as suspected murder by poisoning].

Case No. 30—The Unfair Polygynist

Lilani was killed by the sorcery of his new wife. He had angered her by spending a longer time with his first wife than with her.

Case No. 31—Death from the Disease of the Dogs

In May 1950, a puppy belonging to Alibeti went mad, and he caught it and tied it up. It escaped, and he caught it again; but this time it bit him on the finger. He went to the dispensary at Kaŋkhomba village, but, as there was no medicine there for this complaint, they advised him to go to the St Francis Mission Hospital, which, however, he neglected to do. In August he began to be ill. He vomited and could not drink water, just as a dog cannot when it has the disease of the dogs. His father and mother tried various remedies,

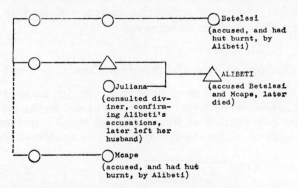

Fig. 27. The Case of 'Death from the Disease of the Dogs'

but to no avail. Alibeti complained to his father, saying, 'I am being killed by your kind [*mtundu*, which may be translated here as "matrikin"], Father,' without naming any of them specifically. His father listened sympathetically to this allegation because he was very fond of his son, something that had already incurred the anger of his matrikin. Alibeti then went mad and burnt down the huts of two of his father's matrikin, of Mcape, his father's mother's mother's sister's daughter, and of Betelesi, his father's mother's sister's daughter's daughter, accusing them of practising sorcery against him. He died, and Betelesi stayed away from his funeral. His mother, Juliana, then consulted a diviner who confirmed her son's accusations; and, for this reason, she subsequently left her husband.

In this last case, not the victim, but an associate, his father, was the one who had been unwise. He had not resolved the conflict of loyalties a man feels towards his children and his matrikin; and, as a result, he lost, not only his beloved son, but also his wife 'who had been with him for many years and borne him many children'.

Sometimes cases related to structural opposition illustrate the principle that a person who is conspicuously fortunate may be believed to be the victim of sorcery. The man who wins a succession dispute, especially if his victory is attributable to personal rather than genealogical qualifications, is, in Cewa eyes, conspicuously fortunate and in danger of the sorcery of his opponents. This was, temporarily at least, the position of Katete in the case of the Supporters of Rival Candidates, which was linked with that of His Uncle's Bed. Although Katete's genealogical qualifications were weaker than those of his rival, Kasinda, his personal ones were strong, and it was at the time when people thought that he had secured the Paramount Chief's support that his friend, Filipo, believed him to be the victim of the (unsuccessful) sorcery of Cimteŋgo, one of Kasinda's supporters.

The following case illustrates further this type of situation:

Case No. 32—A Disappointed Candidate's Revenge

Thilani was the rightful heir to a junior headmanship, but was passed over in favour of Ziloni, who, though junior to him both genealogically and in years, was popular and looked upon as a more suitable candidate. Thilani

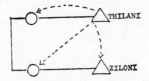

Fig. 28. The Case of 'A Disappointed Candidate's Revenge'

quite openly—'as if he were mad'—threatened Ziloni, saying, 'I [shall] kill you this year' (*Nikupha caka cino*). He carried out his threat, so say those who heard him make it, by putting 'medicines' into Ziloni's beer. Subsequently he was believed to have killed with sorcery his own mother and her sister, the mother of Ziloni, both of whom had sided with Ziloni against him.

'Being conspicuously fortunate' can sometimes be the result of being carried along by the tide of social change, and will be examined further in the next chapter.

Conclusion

In general, my case material confirms the view that beliefs in sorcery provide a medium for the dramatization of social norms. Although about half of the sorcerers in the sample were believed to have had no anti-social traits before becoming involved in the cases recorded, they were nevertheless now sorcerers, serving as symbols of social evil. The moral stigmata of those who had already shown them before being accused or suspected of sorcery covered a representative range of anti-social conduct, and portrayed, if negatively, a series of cherished Ceŵa norms, such as meekness, self-control and generosity.

As to victims of sorcery, two-thirds of the 118 cases involving beliefs in sorcery—including those of vengeance on sorcerers—were ones in which anti-social or socially inadequate behaviour was attributed either to the victim or to someone closely associated with him. Although their misdemeanours were different from those of victims of misfortunes ascribed to causes other than sorcery, they were nevertheless, again, violations of widely accepted Cewa norms, including those violated by the sorcerers in the sample.

CHAPTER 9

SORCERY AND SOCIAL CHANGE

I N the cases presented in the last chapter, there was confirmation of the widely held view that sorcery—and the same would hold for witch-craft—is a conservative force. This view implies that beliefs in sorcery afford the means, not merely of preserving the general shape and the periodic rhythms of a society in a relatively unchanging environment, but also of increasing its resistance to outside influences. Wilson (*née* Hunter) indirectly supports this implication when she writes of the brake that such beliefs place on the adaptation of the Pondo to modern conditions:

... These very forces which make for stability hamper initiative [i.e. in changing to the European mode of living]. Traits which make a man un-popular are often socially valuable [i.e. in the modern situation].[1]

As an instance she records the Pondo belief that modern fertilizer is a medicine the use of which causes neighbouring fields to rot.

Similarly, Brown and Hutt, discussing witchcraft in relation to problems of administration and development, say that

... it tends to accentuate the conservatism of the Hehe. No man must be too much in advance of his neighbours, or there is a danger that a jealous warlock will kill him by witchcraft. Thus a man must not wear clothes which differ too markedly from those of his neighbours, nor must he seek methods of gaining wealth or social superiority which involve too great a departure from traditional tribal life.[2]

Kluckhohn maintains that witch beliefs among the Navaho have the function *inter alia* of preventing the undue accumulation of wealth and tempering too rapid a rise in social position.[3]

It would appear from these statements that rapid social changes are likely to cause an increased preoccupation with beliefs in sorcery and witchcraft. *A priori*, this would seem to be true whether we approach

[1] *Reaction to Conquest*, p. 317.
[2] *Anthropology in Action*, p. 182.
[3] *Navaho Witchcraft*, p. 63.

the problem either in terms of changes in the values defining ideal conduct or in terms of the dynamics of social relationships. This is because one of the effects of social change is to bring new values and norms into conflict with indigenous ones; and another is the creation of new relationships and the fundamental modification of old ones.

Economic Advances Strain Relationships

In my attempt to check these views empirically against Ceŵa material, a good starting-point is the well-known tendency for returning labour migrants to arrange to enter their home villages under cover of darkness (see above, Chapter 3). I remember one evening being disturbed by funereal wailing in the village where I was camped. When I asked about the death I assumed must have just occurred, I was told that it had actually taken place some months before and that people were wailing because one of the deceased's kinsmen had just returned from Southern Rhodesia and had learned for the first time of the loss he had suffered during his absence. The explanation given for this practice of returning after dark is that, if the matrikin of the returning migrant see the goods he brings back with him, they will expect to be given a share of them, and, if they are disappointed, will practise sorcery against him.

The migrant's problem can be approached in terms either of values or of relationships. During his absence he has acquired typically modern aspirations to a higher standard of living and the tendency to devote his earnings towards this end rather than invest them in the social relationships that dominate life in the Reserve. His new attitudes conflict with those of his conservative elders and others who have not moved far out of the egalitarian economy of the Reserve. Reconciling the two sets of attitudes is a difficult task; and concealing the rewards of his labours is one of the ways of evading it.

As to relationships, the migrant, usually a younger man, is the dependant of his 'senior guardian', and is one of the leaders, or 'junior guardians', of the matrilineage segment to which he belongs. These two relationships involve him in obligations to assist both the matrilineage in general, through the headman, and his more immediate dependants in his own segment.

Some returning migrants make a conscientious attempt to share their gains. Thus an easy compliance with custom and little disturbance are reflected in this account a young man gave me of his return from a

journey to work in Southern Rhodesia, which he and his father and
two friends had undertaken some ten years previously, when he was
about twelve years old. After about six months' work, he relates,

Our homeward journey began in May 1937. I had altogether two pounds,
ten shillings. . . . On leaving work, we went to buy at the store. I bought
shorts, a shirt, a belt, a sweater, a hat and tennis shoes. . . . We began our
journey home [on foot]. . . . We took four weeks and arrived home in the
fifth week. Everyone rejoiced exceedingly, especially my mother, who danced
very much. I perceived that my elder [classificatory] brother, Patisoni, . . .
rejoiced, and so did my elder [own] brother, Kadze. Seeing that I had ten
shillings [of my money left], I took half a crown to give to my mother, but
she refused it; I gave Kadze two shillings, and he bought a pair of shorts and
a shirt. And with the half crown my mother had refused I bought shorts,
and with two shillings I bought hoes, one for my mother and one for me.
I gave a shilling to another [classificatory] mother, the mother of Patisoni.
And half a crown I kept that I might give it to my other [classificatory]
mothers. . . . The tennis shoes I had bought I gave to another elder brother.

Another informant, partly because of greater sensitivity and possibly because he undertook his journey at a more independent age,
when he was about sixteen, finds the problem more difficult. Fresh
from a journey to Southern Rhodesia lasting nearly two years, he
reports on what happened after he had travelled from the Southern
Rhodesian high veld down to the Zambezi ferry by lorry.

When we had crossed the Zambezi, the boy from a village near home with
whom I was travelling and I got on our bicycles (which we had bought for
twelve pounds each in Salisbury) and took four days to reach home. Each
night we slept in villages, buying food with our money; we got it at reasonable prices.
We entered our home villages at seven or eight o'clock in the evening
because this is one of our customs. There are certain people who have bad
hearts, as if sorcerers, who, if they see you coming with a big bag with many
blankets and nice pillows, say: 'That person has come back with many
things.' If you don't give them a shirt or some money or something, they
start seeking 'medicines' with which to kill you. We do this only in our home
villages. On the road there's nothing to fear.
When I was in Southern Rhodesia, I earned good money, and on returning I had thirteen pounds, a bicycle and other things, such as shorts, [long]
trousers, six shirts and a jacket. When I came back I was in great trouble and
confusion, not knowing how to take my money and divide it among my
relatives. Some I gave ten shillings; another, a pound; and another, two
pounds. In July 1950, I had sent home five pounds to my mother so that my

relatives could buy a beast. On my return they rejoiced, saying, 'You've done well because you have bought a "bank".'

The sort of situation that this young man probably feared is illustrated by the following case:

Case No. 33—A Maternal Uncle's Schemes Foiled

A young man called Sitifana returned from work in Southern Rhodesia with much property. Among his matrikin, there were many who were poor and who wanted the property to be divided among them. One of them, his

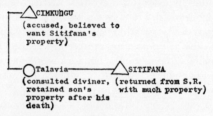

Fig. 29. The Case of 'A Maternal Uncle's Schemes Foiled'

mother's brother, Cimkuŋgu, killed him with 'medicines'. Sitifana's mother, Talavia, went to a diviner who confirmed her suspicions against her brother, Cimkuŋgu. Talavia now retains her late son's property, arguing that Cimkuŋgu is not entitled to it, having killed him.

Such a situation need not necessarily involve labour migration. Those who prosper locally are subject to the same fears.

Case No. 34—A Sawyer's End

Solomon died of epilepsy in 1950. People say that this illness dated from when he drank a small gourdful of beer given him by his classificatory mother, Idesi. He remembered afterwards that it had given him a queer

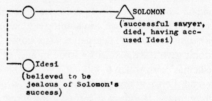

Fig. 30. The Case of 'A Sawyer's End'

sensation, and he attributed his subsequent illness to it. He believed that Idesi was practising sorcery against him because he owned a saw and made good money by sawing planks for sale. Idesi, who was poor, 'did not feel good on seeing him well-off', and, so he reasoned, wanted to kill him.

The cases I have been considering are ones in which the tension may be attributed very largely if not entirely to modern social conditions. Relationships between matrilineage members are in part expressed by the devolution and control of property among them.[1] One of the headman's rights and responsibilities is to make decisions regarding how property should be disposed of. Property is an important means of expressing his status of leadership and his relationships with his following. Under the traditional system, the property whose distribution symbolized his power consisted of small-stock and grain and various items passing through his hands and ultimately reaching territorial and paramount chief, as well as occasional parcels of guns, cloth and slaves that might come his way. In modern times, although tribute has been largely displaced by tax, the value of other forms of property that the headman disposes of has increased considerably, but so has the tendency for his dependants to question his right to dispose of it. This is because it is usually his dependants who go away on labour journeys and earn money. They often send some of it home, as the sixteen-year-old boy did, and it is sometimes invested in cattle. When the labour migrants return, they tend to question the implicit assumption that the property which they have helped to acquire belongs to the matrilineage as a whole and that its disposal is in the hands of the matrilineage authorities. Quarrels sometimes arise in this situation and may lead to accusations and suspicions of sorcery, as in the following case:

Case No. 35—A Refusal to Divide

In Malume village, a young man, Cimkhwakhwa, went away to work, and, on his return, handed £1 of his earnings to his mother's brother, Kakalulu, who added it to other money at his disposal and bought a beast.

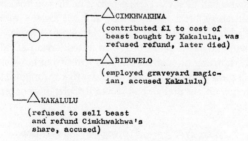

Fig. 31. The Case of 'A Refusal to Divide'

[1] I am grateful to Professor Max Gluckman for drawing my attention to this point.

s

Cimkhwakhwa subsequently wanted the beast sold and the proceeds divided and his share separated. Kakalulu refused to carry out his wish, and there was bad feeling between them. Cimkhwakhwa died, and his younger brother, Biduwelo, employed a graveyard magician to keep a vigil at his grave. The graveyard magician reported that he had seen Kakalulu approaching the grave, and had beaten him. When Kakalulu died soon after this, his death was attributed to the retaliatory action of the graveyard magician.

Two cases of this kind have to do with quarrels that resulted when a woman elder of the matrilineage tried to interfere in the disposal of cattle bought with the earnings of junior members, including her son.

Case No. 36—Not Merely Chicken-Pox

Robert lives uxorilocally in a village adjoining that in which his mother's putative sister's son, Bvalani, similarly lives uxorilocally. At present Bvalani is away at work in Southern Rhodesia. Bvalani's mother, Kuliale, and another of her sons, Cipatsilo, live in a village a considerable distance away from those where Robert and Bvalani are married. Robert went to a diviner about two of

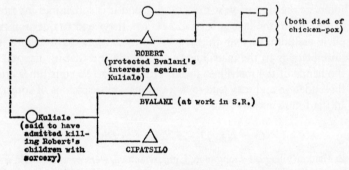

Fig. 32. The Case of 'Not Merely Chicken-Pox'

his children who had died of chicken-pox. The diviner told him it was his distant classificatory brother, Cipatsilo, and the latter's mother, Kuliale, who had killed his children with sorcery. He went to Kuliale's village and questioned her, and she is said to have admitted having killed the children because Robert, acting on instructions in a letter from her son Bvalani, had refused to sell some of Bvalani's cattle in order that she might buy clothes for herself. Summing up, the diviner had said to Robert, 'It's not merely chicken-pox: it's cattle.'

Case No. 37—A Mother's Intervention

Two classificatory brothers, Enea and Soliade, went to Southern Rhodesia together, and, from money they earned there, bought a beast. Enea returned

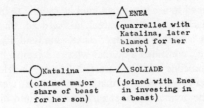

Fig. 33. The Case of 'A Mother's Intervention'

before Soliade, and a quarrel arose between him and Katalina, Soliade's mother, who claimed that Soliade had the major share in the beast. According to village gossip, Enea killed Katalina with sorcery.

The cases thus far reviewed appear to have arisen from the uncertainty connected with ownership of, or partial rights to, two new elements in Ceŵa culture, money and cattle, and this uncertainty has led to a jockeying for position which is conducive to tensions that are difficult to resolve by means other than accusations of sorcery.

The people involved in disputes over money earned by labour migrants need not necessarily belong to the same matrilineage, as in the following case, in which the alleged sorcerer and his believed victim were cross-cousins.

Case No. 38—Money from Johannesburg

Jemusi and his mother's brother's son, Cimutu, went together to work in Johannesburg. Cimutu returned home first, bringing £25 that he had been given by Jemusi to invest for him at home. Cimutu, however, without telling anyone at home, spent this money himself. Jemusi meanwhile stayed at work in Johannesburg for eighteen years. His kinsmen begged him to come home

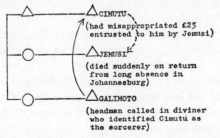

Fig. 34. The Case of 'Money from Johannesburg'

because they longed to see him again, and he came. On his arrival he complained of a headache, and within a week he was dead. The village headman, Galimoto, Jemusi's mother's younger sister's son (and, like Jemusi, a cross-cousin of Cimutu), consulted a diviner who said Jemusi had been killed by the sorcery of someone who had wasted £25 of his. Headman Galimoto invited the diviner to his village so that he could make a clearer identification. At the village, the diviner threw some 'medicines' into his bowl, which he had filled with water, and saw the image of Cimutu, with a 'medicine-horn' in his hand, on the surface of the water. He called Cimutu and, pointing to the image, said, 'Who's this?' Cimutu admitted that it was himself. The diviner said, 'Do you still deny that you killed Jemusi?' Cimutu went to his hut, crying with shame. Headman Galimoto said that the case should be taken before the Chief; but, before any action could be taken, Cimutu ran away in the middle of the night and went to Cape Town, where he was subsequently killed in a street accident.

New Bones of Contention

The most conspicuous expression of modern conflicts of values in accusations and believed instances of sorcery is to be found in the objects of competition in quarrels and rivalries that preceded them. Such objects of competition and other issues of quarrels were referred to incidentally when I considered, in this respect, differences between those sorcerers and victims matrilineally related and those not so related (see end of Chapter 3); differences between related and unrelated sorcerers and victims (see above, Chapter 7); and differences between related and unrelated accusers and sorcerers (Chapter 7). Of the categories into which the issues of quarrels fall, some, such as headmanship and the failure to discharge obligations towards kinsmen, include issues that could have arisen under the indigenous social system. Others, such as land, cattle and other forms of property, are clearly modern. Others, again, such as adultery, sexual jealousy and divorce, may, according to circumstances, be attributed to indigenous or to modern value-conflicts, or to both.

An examination of Table XXIII and the first part of Table XXIV shows that, of the 101 cases, there were seventy-two preceded by quarrels. Since two issues were involved in seven of these, there were altogether seventy-nine issues. These have been classified in Table XXVII. It appears that just over half of the issues could have arisen

TABLE XXVII

Indigenous or Modern Influences reflected in the Issues of Quarrels preceding Accusations of Sorcery or Instances of Believed Attack by Sorcerers

Accusation or Instance Preceded by Quarrel over	Cases f	%
Issue that could have arisen under indigenous conditions, e.g. involving headmanship, obligations between kinsmen, sexual jealousy	44	55·7
Issue apparently brought about by modern influences, e.g. involving cattle, other property, land rights	19	24·0
Issue that could have arisen under indigenous conditions but which seems to have been aggravated by modern influences, e.g. conflict of Ceŵa and Christian values, adultery related to labour migration	9	11·4
Unspecified issues	7	8·9
	79	100·0

under indigenous conditions; that about a quarter were brought about by modern conditions; and that just under an eighth were ones in which indigenous stresses might have been aggravated by modern conditions.

How Deep Do Changes Go?

One of the propositions established by studies in the introduction of Western medicine to non-Western societies is that techniques diffuse more readily than their underlying scientific rationale.[1] It might be added that, even within Western society itself, there is often relatively limited understanding of the scientific basis of medical practice and that attitudes towards medical practitioners frequently resemble those that non-Western patients hold towards their priests and medicine-men.

A clear example of the acceptance of a technique without an appreciation of its rational basis is to be found in the Ceŵa enthusiasm for injections. People will willingly submit to a course of injections—or to a single one—whether or not their condition has been diagnosed as one amenable to such treatment. For instance, as I have noted in Chapter 3, Ceŵa sometimes seek treatment for venereal disease in the belief, not that they have such a disease, but that the injections, or even a single injection, will have a generally prophylactic effect. This is because they

[1] For a convenient summary of the literature on this point, see Caudill, 'Applied Anthropology and Medicine'.

regard the syringe as containing powerful *maŋkhwala* (magical sub-stances), and they recognize its use as a far more effective method of getting these into the bodily system than their own of rubbing them into incisions made in the skin (*kútemela* [*maŋkhwala*]) or washing with them (*kusamba*) or administering them orally (*kumwetsa*).

Even educated Ceŵa tend to place European medicines in the same category as Ceŵa *maŋkhwala* and thus to attribute to the former the supernatural properties of the latter. A slightly educated man came to me, complaining of a stiff neck, which, he said, must have been the result of sorcery. I offered him some embrocation, but expressed my doubt that European medicine could help an African complaint such as his appeared to be. He dismissed my objection by saying (cf. Chapter 3):

> God created many trees. There is no reason why the Europeans should not have acquired some of the good trees which can be effective against the bad ones.

My public-opinion poll (see above, Chapter 2) included ques-tions about modern medical services, such as one about the relative merits of outlying mission hospitals and the Government African Hospital in Fort Jameson. I noted a tendency on the part of most of the persons I interviewed myself, who included a number of better-educated ones, to explain their choice of hospital in terms, not of medical skill, but of 'strong medicines' (*maŋkhwala yanphamvu*). An-other interesting outcome of questions about medical services was that what little opposition people expressed towards going into hospital was often explained by their fear that Africans employed at the hospitals would use the 'strong medicines', over which they had con-trol, for killing some of their patients. Again this revealed a tendency to identify European medicines with Ceŵa *maŋkhwala*. Thus the translation of *maŋkhwala* as 'medicines' is more satisfactory to the Ceŵa than it is to me; for to them European medicines are substances with not only chemical and biological properties but also magical properties.

Religious principles of explanation seem to have been taken over more readily than scientific ones. As I mentioned in Chapter 2, al-though the rate of formal, lasting conversion is low, the influence among the Ceŵa of Christianity is extensive. It crops up in wide-spread observance of the Sabbath, avoidance of cross-cousin marriage, abstinence from beer (or more secretive drinking of it, in which case it is referred to as *tobwa*, a non-alcoholic drink, instead of *moŵa*), and prayers and readings from the scriptures at funerals. Muluŋgu, the aspect of the Ceŵa Supreme Being now identified with the Christian God, is referred to as being in control of the course of events; but it is difficult to determine the extent of influence attributed to him before the advent of the missions.

Though the Christian rationale co-exists with explanations of events in terms of sorcerers, spirits and taboos (such as those of the *mdulo* complex), its influence is nevertheless considerable. This is probably because it has been grafted on to a well-developed branch of Ceŵa explanatory principles, that invoking the Supreme Being. The impact of Christianity has, however, sometimes resulted in strain. In the case of the Backsliding Christian there was conflict between Christian values, firmly embraced by Headman Gombe's first wife, Eledia, and the Ceŵa assumption that polygyny is fitting to the status of headman. In a chronologically earlier case involving the same couple (the Disappointed Widow), there was again a conflict between Christian teachings about polygyny (then accepted by them both) and the Ceŵa custom of nepotal widow-inheritance.

Cataclysmic Searches for Adjustment

The stresses and strains of modern life periodically build up to breaking point and express themselves in a blended modern idiom when anti-sorcery movements sweep across the country. Brief descriptions of some of those affecting the Ceŵa have been given earlier (Chapter 3). Both the Mcape and Bwanali-Mpulumutsi movements focused attention on the evil propensities of sorcerers, and thus portrayed, negatively, some cherished Ceŵa norms. The Bwanali-Mpulumutsi movement, with its emphasis on the confession of past misdeeds as an essential part of the cure of repenting sorcerers, was particularly effective in this respect. This is brought out in the following extract from a report by an informant who made the arduous journey from near Chief Kaŵaza's capital in Northern Rhodesia to Mpulumutsi's headquarters in Portuguese territory:

After we had been treated and given 'medicines' to take away with us, we retired. Some people woke up with headaches, and went and complained of them to Mpulumutsi. He said to them, 'You've been eating your fellow men.' One confessed, 'Yes, I've eaten two of my children.' Another said, 'I've eaten my mother-in-law and her husband.' A third admitted to having brought a human head with him and to having used flesh from it as a 'relish' to eat with his maize-flour porridge on the very journey to Mpulumutsi! He had thrown it away just before arriving. Mpulumutsi warned these people that they should give up their evil practices. After that he gave them 'medicines' to drink.

Those who, having been treated with Mpulumutsi's 'medicines', fail to confess their sorcery, or resume it after having confessed, are sure to die. Many die on their way home to their villages. [In reply to a question] No, I didn't see any dead people, but on the way to Mpulumutsi's I saw a number of trees from which bark had been stripped in order to make coffins for those who had died by the way.[1]

Barber, reviewing certain 'messianic' movements that have occurred among American Indian tribes, asserts that the function of a messiah is to proclaim a stable order to replace the state of insecurity resulting from deprivation and the disorganization of the 'controlling normative structure' of a society in a culture-contact situation.[2] This general proposition seems to fit the two movements I am considering. Western influences have affected both the social structure and the normative system of Cewa society. The rural masculinity rate has dropped, and those who have been drawn, even temporarily, into the vortex of modern industry have been exposed to new conflicts of values which have made them more prone to doctrines of salvation and reform.

In contrast, however, to the assumption frequently made about the conservative nature of beliefs in sorcery, an assumption generally vindicated by the material I have presented in this chapter, the more specific doctrines of the anti-sorcery movements have not always supported indigenous norms against intrusive ones, but have rather achieved a relatively consistent blending of the old and the new. As Worsley has pointed out, 'millenarian' movements, far from being nativistic flights from reality, as Linton claimed they were, are rather 'desperate searchings for more and more effective ways of understanding and modifying' a confused environment.[3] Since both the movements closely affecting the Cewa were well integrated with modern as well as indigenous aspects of life,[4] their function has been to rearrange and synthesize the old and the new rather than, as I have shown to be the case with other aspects of Cewa beliefs in sorcery, to conserve indigenous norms threatened by modern ones.

[1] Recorded in Marwick, 'Another Modern Anti-Witchcraft Movement in East Central Africa', pp. 104–5.
[2] Barber, 'Acculturation and Messianic Movements'.
[3] 'Millenarian Movements in Melanesia', pp. 24–5.
[4] Cf. Richards, 'A Modern Movement of Witch-Finders', pp. 450–1; and Marwick, 'Another Modern Anti-Witchcraft Movement in East Central Africa', passim.

CHAPTER 10

BIOGRAPHICAL: THE LIFE AND DEATH
OF HEADMAN GOMBE

In case the material presented in earlier chapters may have the appearance of being impersonal, in that it represents the summarized attributes of all the cases I collected and retained for analysis, or unconnected, in that it draws illustrations from individuals randomly distributed among them, I shall in this chapter present a consecutive account of events in the life of a Ceŵa headman whom I got to know intimately. This will not be a complete biography, nor will it contain an analysis of the subject's personality which normally serves as a unifying theme in an attempt to portray someone's life history. It will do nothing more than present in a connected sequence a series of episodes that illustrate some of the tensions that arise in the course of Ceŵa life and show how some of these are resolved *inter alia* by reference to beliefs in sorcery.

The cases of believed sorcery presented in this chapter are not in chronological order, since some of them, such as the case of a Poison Ordeal Long Ago, have been included to provide historical background for more recent ones. The following summary, which links approximate dates, main events and cases of believed sorcery, may give perspective to the series.

Approximate Time Scale	*Main Events*	*Sequence of Cases of Believed Sorcery*
1890		
		A Poison Ordeal Long Ago
	Gwilani's adultery	
	Birth of Gombe	
	Destruction of village by Mlumpham'madzi	
1900	Move to Gombe's father's village in Mpezeni's country	

Move to Mlolo's country

1910

Gombe works for wages in
    Moçambique

Works in Tete and brings
    back salt which helps his
1920   relatives during a drought
Marries Eledia
Starts mission training
Death of Gwilani

The Disappointed Widow
Works as evangelist in various
    villages
Short trip to Southern
    Rhodesia

1930   Village moves to Mzime
Death of Gombe's parents
Becomes village headman
Starts work in Southern
    Rhodesia
Joined by Eledia   A Jealous Husband's
Younger brother in charge of   Revenge
    new village
Return to service with mission

1940   Second marriage (to Etelina)   The Backsliding Christian
Discharged from mission   The Vanishing Hyena
Pitani's section joins village   The Coveted Cattle
Loss of Macenga's section   Three Possible Causes
Loss of Jolobe's section   The Live Hare
Death of Blahimu   A Sister's Treachery
Death of baby in Cipapa's   The Pretended Brother
    section

                                    Children Shouldn't Tell
                                    Tales

1950   Work in Fort Jameson   The Game That Ran Away
        Death of Gombe
        Gombe's younger brother
            chases Etelina away

Early Life

Gombe was born a few years before the turn of the century in a
village in what is now Portuguese territory lying to the south of the
Northern Rhodesian border. His birth came at the close of a disturbed
period, the sixty-odd years during which the Ceŵa and their neighbours were either enslaved or repeatedly raided by the Ŋgoni (see
above, Chapter 2). Even before and after this period, conditions among
the Ceŵa seem to have been unstable. Just before the Ŋgoni con-
quests and raids started, Gamitto remarked on the continuous succession wars among their forbears, the Maravi (see Chapter 5); and one
of Gombe's earliest memories of the time at the end of it was the
flight of his two elder sisters, his parents and his matrilineal relatives
into the bush to escape the wrath of a matriclansman, Mlumpha-
m'madzi, who claimed a relationship with Gombe's matrilineage and
wanted its members to join his own following in a village near Domwe
mountain not far from the present Nyasaland–Moçambique border.
When they refused, he destroyed their village. The privations resulting
from this incident prompted Gombe's father to leave his affines' village and to move north with his wife and children to his home
village in the country of the Ŋgoni chief, Mpezeni, in what is now
Northern Rhodesia. A few years after this, the power of the Ŋgoni
having been broken (see Chapter 2), Gombe's father's village section
left Mpezeni's country and for many years lived in a village in the
country of the Ceŵa chief, Mlolo.

Gombe was able to relate, having heard it from his elders, an even
earlier incident. About the time of his conception, his mother's
brother, Gwilani, had committed adultery. His mistress had become pregnant but had died in childbirth, her baby surviving. Her
matrilineage authorities insisted on the baby's being cared for by
Gwilani's matrilineage; and he was given to Gombe's mother. 'He
sucked one side; and I, the other,' explained Gombe. The child's
relatives even demanded that Gombe should be abandoned and the
orphaned baby given all Gombe's mother's milk, but his mother
would not agree to this. The two boys spent their childhood together

and the orphan was returned to his matrikin at about the age of six or seven.

Since his father had moved to virilocal residence, Gombe's paternal grandparents and his paternal classificatory fathers played a more important part in his upbringing than is usual with a Ceŵa child. And, when the time came for Gombe to take a wife, his father found a bride for him among his own matrilineal dependants.

During the second decade of this century, Gombe had his first experience of working for wages during two trips of a few months each into Moçambique, one of them as far afield as Tete on the Zambezi. With some salt that he brought back with him from Tete he was able to buy grain for his relatives whose crops had failed. It was on his return from these journeys that he married Eledia, a member of his father's matrilineage, and they both became Christians. During the early 1920's he went to one of the missions to train as an evangelist.

Contact with Gombe's matrikin was not broken for long by his father's having taken him away from their village to the south. By the time his father's people had moved west from Mpezeni's country to Mlolo's, they had been joined by some of Gombe's mother's relatives, including his mother's brother, Gwilani, and his wife, Namkuŋgwi, and their daughter, Zana. It was in relation to this family that, some years later, Gombe had to face a conflict between his duty as a uterine nephew (as prescribed by Ceŵa norms) and his adherence, which his wife shared, to the principles of Christianity.

Case No. 39—The Disappointed Widow

Soon after Gombe's marriage to Eledia, his mother's brother, Gwilani, died. According to Ceŵa custom Gombe should have married his uncle's widow, Namkuŋgwi. Freshly converted to Christianity, and fully supported by his wife, Gombe refused to contract what would have been a polygynous marriage; and Namkuŋgwi began to hate the young couple. A few years later, by which time Gombe and Eledia had two children, her hatred was intensified by a quarrel between Namkuŋgwi's daughter, Zana, and Eledia over damage to winnowing baskets and pots that each other's goats had caused. The day after this quarrel Eledia found some sinister objects, including a dead lizard, on the threshold of her hut, and that day her baby started to be ill, and it died the next day. Some time after this, the issue of Gombe's inheriting his uncle's widow was again raised, and, once more, Gombe refused. Namkuŋgwi threatened him and Eledia felt very insecure. 'I wasn't happy until the day she died,' she explained to me many years later. One of the causes of her insecurity was that, when Gombe was being trained as an evangelist, they both lived at the mission and had to leave their remaining child in the village. One day they received word that their child was ill, and hurried back to the village to find that it was suffering from a sore chest. 'Its

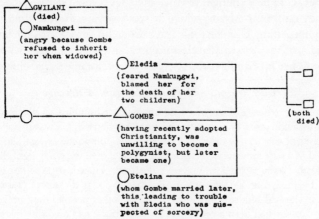

Fig. 35. The Cases of 'The Disappointed Widow' and
'The Backsliding Christian'

illness was an amazing thing' (*cinthu codabwitsa*), said Eledia, 'because the child was well and playing with its fellows until the early afternoon. Then it began crying "*Mayo, Mayo* [a cry of distress which may be related to *mai*, 'mother']" and went on like this until it died next day just after midday.' Although a sore chest is a symptom of *mdulo* (see Chapter 3), Gombe and Eledia were convinced that this child, like their other one, had been killed by Namkuŋgwi's sorcery, though they took no action against her.

These incidents made Gombe and Eledia take precautions about their subsequent children. Their third child was a girl, Evelina; and their fourth, a boy, Andalasoni. When Andalasoni was born, the people in the village told Eledia that she should leave Evelina with them, but she refused, saying, 'No, I'll look after her myself [at the mission] because the children get finished [i.e. die off] in the village.' Similarly, when, between 1926 and 1933, they lived in a succession of villages in which Gombe worked as an evangelist, they kept both these children, and their next one, a boy, Edisoni, with them.

Work in Southern Rhodesia

The salary that Gombe received from the mission was small, and, to make ends meet, he found it necessary on two occasions during his period of service as an evangelist to take unpaid leave and work in

Southern Rhodesia. The first trip, taken in 1928, was a short one; the second, between 1933 and 1938, was for over three years. During the second trip Gombe was joined by Eledia who, in the company of her brother, Gombe's younger brother and a few other relatives, made the journey on foot to Mazoe, where he was working. A year after Eledia had joined him, Gombe took leave from his employer and he and Eledia paid a visit to his classificatory sister, Khumbiza, who was living at her husband's place of employment, a mine near Selukwe.

Case No. 40—A Jealous Husband's Revenge

One day when Eledia was accompanying Khumbiza to fetch water, Khumbiza collapsed on the path and lost consciousness. She did not come round until she had been carried back to the compound, when she complained of a sore arm and chest. She vomited and died the same night. Before her death Eledia begged Khumbiza's husband, Tilauzi, to take her to the mine hospital, but he refused, saying that she was a 'knave' (*mambala*) because she had hidden money given her by other people, the implication being that she had been a prostitute. Only after she had died did Tilauzi go to the hospital. The authorities were angry with him for not having brought her for treatment. There would have been an enquiry, but there was an accident at the mine and the doctor was too busy attending to the injured. Gombe and Eledia were convinced that Tilauzi had killed his wife with sorcery.

Khumbiza left a small child, and Gombe and Eledia took it back with them to Mazoe where Gombe resumed work. Being semi-literate, he was made a time-keeper and his fellow workers were jealous of him and caused him much trouble. Khumbiza's child died and Gombe and Eledia linked its death, though not very clearly, with the jealousy of Gombe's fellow workers.

Apart from the incidents that have been related, Gombe and Eledia enjoyed their time at Mazoe. They had many letters from those they had left at home, and the news was good. Eventually Eledia's maternal uncle came to tell them that her mother was seriously ill. Gombe left work and they set out for home immediately. By the time they arrived, Eledia's mother was well again, but they decided to stay on in the Reserve, where Gombe rejoined the service of the mission.

Village Headmanship and Polygyny

Shortly after Gombe's first trip to Southern Rhodesia in 1928, the village in which his and his wife's relatives were living in Mlolo's country had to move farther west, into Kaŵaza's. The villagers were

displaced by White tobacco farmers who secured their title to the land
in terms of the North Charterland Concession (cf. Chapter 2), which
made it possible for them, on payment of a small amount of compensation, to dispossess native inhabitants. The village, along with others in
the same part of Mlolo's country, moved to the Mzime valley in
the west of Kaŵaza's chiefdom. Gombe's father moved with his
matrilineage, though by now his own children and grandchildren
formed a group within it large enough to warrant its living in its own
section. Gombe, as the senior male member of this matrilineage
fragment, became its nominal headman, though his absence in Southern
Rhodesia and, on his return, in the service of the mission, made it
necessary for him to leave his dependants in the care of his father and,
later, his younger brother.

A year or two before Gombe's departure on his second trip to
Southern Rhodesia, his mother and father died, their deaths being
within a short time of each other. At about the same time, a quarrel
involving an accusation of sorcery caused bitter feeling between the
headman of the village and the members of a number of its sections,
all unrelated to the headman and not closely linked with each other.
These formed a new, separate settlement, and Gombe as headman of
one of them was put in charge of the new village as a whole.

Gombe's thus becoming a village headman was one of the reasons
for his leaving employment with the mission five or six years later.
The other reason, related to the first, was a conflict between the
Christian rule of monogamy, which Eledia strongly supported both as
a Christian and as his first wife, and the social demands of headmanship. A headman needs women to make beer and to cook food for
guests; and, as his sisters are often not as amenable to his control as an
extra wife would be, he often finds it convenient to become a polygynist. In any event, after resuming service with the mission on his
return from Southern Rhodesia, Gombe made a woman called Etelina
pregnant. She was a marriageable woman (*nbeta*) because her husband
had some years previously become a 'lost one' (*mcona*) in Southern
Rhodesia and she had obtained a divorce. Gombe married her and was
discharged from the mission. This was a devastating blow to Eledia
and caused a permanent estrangement between them. It would probably have led to their being divorced if they had not been relatives.
And in one sense Gombe's second marriage was bitter fruit of the
sacrifice of his first one; for Etelina's pregnancy ended in a miscarriage,
and she never succeeded in bearing him any children. However, she

proved an asset as a domestic help, and her skill as a potter brought her in enough money for her own clothes, which were always a striking contrast to the shabby clothes of the neglected, resentful, embittered Eledia.

Gombe took his (not unexpected) discharge from the service of the mission more philosophically, and found compensations in the prestige of village headmanship. As he remarked to me about ten years later, 'Even if they [the missionaries] turn us out, it's no matter because God hasn't done so'; and he proceeded to inveigh against the immorality of African church elders 'who despise us for our polygyny and yet are adulterous themselves' as well as that of a White missionary who, he claimed, had had to be sent away because he made an African school-girl pregnant twice and gave her an abortifacient on each occasion. 'They are not fit people to judge us,' he added. He certainly seemed to be a conforming Christian in all respects other than his polygyny and a lively belief in sorcery, which latter he shared with most Ceŵa Christians of my acquaintance.

Case No. 41—The Backsliding Christian (see Fig. 35)

Eledia could find no solution to the problem that faced her. Traditionally she should have rejoiced, or at least outwardly remained calm, at her husband's taking a second wife and thus relieving her of some of the heavy chores that befall a headman's lady. But a deep attachment to Christianity, as well as about twenty years of happy marriage in, because of Gombe's employment away from home, a much closer association with her husband than most Ceŵa women have, made it difficult for her to adjust to the new situation. Furthermore, she was supported in her feud against her husband and his second wife, not only by his sisters, but also by her matrilineal relatives represented locally by those who had married some of the sisters. The support she won from these allies made it possible for her to control her three children in accordance with her wishes and in some instances against the wishes of her husband, who, wanting to emulate his own father, was annoyed at being denied authority over them, as, for instance, when Eledia and her mother's brother found a wife for her son, Andalasoni, without even consulting Gombe. The tension between Gombe and Eledia mounted. In 1947, Gombe and his second wife, Etelina, discovered a horn hidden among their possessions in Etelina's hut, and, though Eledia denied any knowledge of it, they believed she was practising sorcery against them. Soon after this, Gombe killed a goat, and, knowing that Eledia did not eat goat's flesh, gave her some for the children, promising her a chicken for herself the following day. She abused him and he struck her. Her matrilineal relatives took him before the Court, but he managed to win the case by producing the horn and reporting her alleged sorcery to the court officials, who reprimanded her.

Trouble with Other Sections

These domestic issues were not Gombe's only worries. Since he had been made village headman largely by chance, the headmen of the other sections in his village were jealous of his position and plotted against him. Their number had by now been increased through a link with the past that had unpleasant associations. Pitani, the sister's son of Mlumpham'madzi, who had terrorized Gombe's home village when he was a child, came from Portuguese territory with a large following and attached himself to Gombe's village. He then did his best to take over the village headmanship, his claim to it being that he was a senior matrilineal relative of Gombe's. Gombe, in turn, claimed that Pitani was no more closely related than through being a putative clansman as a result of Pitani's ancestors having been the captives of Gombe's. The Chief accepted Gombe's contention and left him in charge of the village; though Gombe still lacked a feeling of permanent security because, happening to be a favourite of the Paramount Chief, he felt that the Territorial Chief might be prejudiced against him. Furthermore the Chief's ruling did not prevent Pitani from intriguing against Gombe whenever he had an opportunity.

Such an opportunity arose once when Gombe committed a well-intentioned but carelessly conceived act of neighbourliness which normally would have been appropriate to a headman's rôle. He once spent the afternoon visiting a friend in a neighbouring village. On his way back he sat on the verandah of a hut belonging to a member of Cipapa's section in his own village. Its occupant proudly told him that his wife, one of Cipapa's sisters, had just had a baby; and he went into the hut to see it. He asked the parents what its sex was, when it was born and whether it sucked well. He noticed that the child's mother did not answer his last question and that the child was snuffling. Having said a prayer for the baby and having given its father threepence (at the time the equivalent of about half a day's wage of an unskilled labourer in local employment) as a present for it, he went home. That night the baby died. Its mother's brother, Cipapa, and certain of his elders, wanted to take action against Gombe, saying, 'How is it that he went into a birth-hut (cikuta) and killed our child [by mdulo, since the child was 'cold'; and he, they assumed, 'hot']?' (see Chapter 3).

T

They were, however, dissuaded from taking this course by Cenji, a highly respected 'senior affine' (*mkwekulu*) of their matrilineage; but Pitani, who had nothing whatever to do with the incident since it had not occurred in his section, made it the excuse for slandering Gombe as village headman and trying, though unsuccessfully, to raise opposition against him.

Other disputes with section headmen were of more serious consequence, one of them leading to Gombe's being himself accused of sorcery. Basic to Gombe's difficulties in this connection was the fact that the other sections of his village had been made subordinate to him mainly because they had quarrelled with the headman of their former village and had nowhere else to go. The former headman had quarrelled with Cenji, the influential senior affine of Cipapa's section, and he had disliked the headmen of the other two sections, Jolobe and Maceŋga, because the former had the reputation of being a sorcerer and the latter consistently failed to provide labour from among his dependants for clearing the village site of weeds when the Administration periodically ordered the headman to have this done.

Jolobe's section lived for some years in Gombe's village, but the tension between the two headmen mounted. It culminated in Gombe's believing that Jolobe was the victim of a magical trap he had set for sorcerers, and, after Jolobe's death, in Gombe's being accused by Jolobe's relatives of having killed him with sorcery.

Case No. 42—The Vanishing Hyena

A child of one of Gombe's sisters died. Gombe sought the help of his friend, Headman Blahimu, who possessed graveyard magic, and together they magically 'closed' the child's corpse, the hut in which it lay, the gravesite and the graveyard against attack by sorcerers. Only then did they permit the people to start funereal wailing. Their suspicions of Jolobe were immediately aroused by the fact that, having ascertained the cause of the wailing and knowing well that there was a bereavement in the village in which he lived, he callously went off to a neighbouring village and drank beer while the funeral took place, and, on his return, had the effrontery to ask for a share of funeral porridge. Gombe and Blahimu kept him under careful observation and discovered that every day for the week following the burial he came back early from his garden and sat on a termite heap, staring in the direction of the graveyard. For this reason they kept a vigil at the graveside for four nights (an unusually long period, especially since the deceased was only a child), and, after that, they 'closed' the grave by setting a magical snare for any sorcerers who subsequently might try to exhume the corpse. An inspection of the graveyard soon after this showed that a hyena had approached the grave but that its spoor vanished at the point where the magical snare had been set. Almost immediately Jolobe began to be ill, and within a week he was dead. Before his death he abused his friend, Ŋombe, from another village, saying that he had misled him into believing that the graveyard had not been magically 'closed' and it would be safe for them to go there [to eat the corpse understood]; and he asked that those who had doctored the grave should come and remove the effects of their magic. Gombe was called to him, but, when asked to neutralize his magic, replied, 'I've slept badly [i.e. have had sexual intercourse] and cannot in my present ['hot'] state go and dig the neutralizing "medicines".' Soon after this, one of Blahimu's relatives died in his village, and similar precautions were taken; and again Gombe and Blahimu found evidence of a hyena's approaching the grave. Similarly, Ŋombe became ill and sent for Blahimu and Gombe, asking them to remove the effects of their magic, but they made the same excuse and he died. Jolobe's section accused Gombe of having killed their headman with sorcery and went to live in the new settlement area to the north of the Great East Road.

The tension between Gombe and the leader of the second section, Maceŋga, did not lead to an accusation of sorcery, possibly because Maceŋga was a lay preacher and would not have cared to admit a belief in it; but it was nevertheless serious. It came to a head when some children belonging to Maceŋga's section fouled the village water-hole by diving in it after fish. Gombe made the mistake of having their 'guardians' fined by the Chief's court instead of asking Maceŋga to reprimand them. This incident gave Maceŋga legitimate cause for complaint and he used it in a successful application to the Chief for permission to form an independent village.

It is difficult to judge whether there were any grounds for Gombe's suspicion that Cenji, the senior affine of Cipapa's section, was trying to seize his headmanship. Cenji had few matrilineal relatives who might have formed a following for him, and only one of them, the husband of one of Gombe's uterine nieces, was living in the village. At any rate Gombe feared him, perhaps because he was influential in Cipapa's section and because he was a successful diviner. The following is based on Gombe's account of the incident:

Case No. 43—A Sister's Treachery

Gombe's elder sister, Tapita, became ill, and, as a brother should, he procured 'medicines' for her from a herbalist in a neighbouring village. After they had been administered, Cenji came secretly to Tapita and said,

'You, Tapita, you're ill and I know why. It is because your brother, Gombe, is trying to kill you. I know this because I dream [i.e. am a diviner]. Now, is it good that you should die?' Tapita loyally replied, 'But if it is in fact he who wants to kill me, no matter, let him kill me.' Cenji said, 'No, it's not good that you should die. Rather let us kill him and you stay alive.' 'But who will care for all us children [Gombe's dependants] if we kill him?' she objected. 'You're all big enough to look after yourselves,' he replied. Finally, Tapita agreed and asked, 'How can we kill him?' He said, 'No, I'll kill him, but you give me a token (*nsambo*) that I may kill him well.' Tapita gave him six shillings and told him to get on with it.

Meanwhile, the 'medicines' Gombe had procured from the herbalist proved ineffective and Tapita's illness grew worse. On the point of death, she sent for Gombe and said, 'My brother, I'm dying and I want to confess';

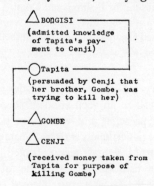

Fig. 36. The Case of 'A Sister's Treachery'

and she proceeded to tell him all that had happened. Gombe listened, and, when she had finished, said, 'Really?' and she said, 'Yes.' Gombe came back to his house and wept and prayed to God, saying, 'If it's I who wanted to kill Tapita, God, chastise me; but if it isn't, let Tapita live.' And Tapita recovered. When she was well again, Gombe asked her, 'Those words you spoke, Tapita, shall we not go and ask Cenji about them?' Tapita said, 'No, don't.' Gombe said, 'No, I don't agree with you and Cenji. I'll question you both together.'

In fear Tapita took more money to give to Cenji and said, 'Hurry up and kill Gombe. He wants to question us.' Gombe did not know what steps Cenji may then have taken, but he felt no ill effects. In the course of time he took Cenji to the Chief's court and made sure that Tapita and her husband, Boŋgisi, were present. In response to the Chief's demand, Cenji, with shaking hands, surrendered eight shillings, saying that Tapita had given him this amount, asking him to kill Gombe. Boŋgisi admitted knowledge of the transaction and its purpose, and, when the Chief asked him why he had not reported it to Gombe, he had no words in reply. The Chief held the eight shillings and said, 'O.K.! (*Cabwino!*) If Gombe dies this year, we'll know it's you, Cenji, who will have killed him'; and he sent them all back to the village.

When I recorded this case, I felt that it might have been coloured by Gombe's suspicious, almost paranoid, nature; and, since I knew Tapita well, I tried to get her account of it. I found her evasive and reticent about the incident, and I wondered whether I had been justified in suspecting Gombe's version of being greatly distorted. After much prodding, she gave me an account of it that left me with the impression that she was trying to put me off with a plausible story. It was to the effect that she had been delirious when she was ill and had spoken a good deal of nonsense. She confirmed that her brother had procured 'medicines' from the herbalist he told me about, and gave me a detailed account of how her illness had seriously interfered with the hoeing of her husband's and her garden. She then linked the incident with the death of Jolobe by pointing out that she recovered from her illness at the time that Jolobe died, and added that Jolobe's relatives accused Gombe of having killed Jolobe with sorcery in order to make her well. She concluded by saying that it was her belief that it was Jolobe's mother who had tried to kill her. They had quarrelled because Jolobe's mother had accused her of using *nfumba* sorcery to drive the grass and weeds from her [Tapita's] garden into hers. During her illness, she said, she had seen fire going from the hut of Jolobe's mother to her grain store, and she therefore believed that Jalobe's mother had attacked her with sorcery (this being possible, she said, because they happened to belong to the same matriclan) by placing 'medicines' in her grain store.

Although Cenji was someone whose confidence I also enjoyed, the dangers of hunting with the hounds and running with the hares made me fear I might destroy my good relationships with the members of the village if I pursued the question further.

This case, though it has some obscurities, illustrates three important points. Firstly, the headman of a village has to move carefully lest his actions—even those that are consistent with his rôle as a brother or a matrilineage elder, or as a keeper of the peace among unrelated people —provide his adversaries with an excuse for leaving him and diminishing his following. Secondly, the fact that Cenji is believed to have worked through his would-be victim's sister seems to be an acknowledgment of a corollary to the Cewa dogma that sorcerers attack their own matrikin, i.e. if they wish to attack unrelated people, they may consider it more effective to work through their victims' matrikin. Thirdly, Gombe's prayer suggests that he feared the possibility that he might be a sorcerer—the same kind of fear that drove Kamaŋgani mad in the case of His Niece's Head.

Eccentrics in the Village

Of the various people whom Headman Gombe had at one time or another to control, at least three were believed to have inherently evil propensities that would make 'sorcerer', my generic term for the Ceŵa mythical evil-doer, rather strained as a designation for them. In Ceŵa terms, they were 'real *nfiti*' (witches) rather than 'killers-for-malice'. One was Byalani, a matrilineal descendant of the wife of Gombe's mother's mother's brother, Kamudzi. Another was Katuule, a member of Gombe's section, a classificatory mother's brother of his first wife, Eledia, and the second husband of his eldest sister, Luŵa. And a third was an old woman, Mwatsiliza, belonging to a minor section of the village which joined it after the ones thus far mentioned.

Gombe's control of Byalani was negative in that he would not allow him to settle in the village. He appeared, however, to be on friendly terms with him. It was Gombe's sister, Tapita, who explained why it was considered wiser to forgo the advantage of having Byalani and his immediate family added to Gombe's total following and rather have them stay in the neighbouring village from which Gombe's had been derived.

Case No. 44—A Poison Ordeal Long Ago

When Headman Kanyumba died in the 1890's, what Ceŵa consider to be a proper investigation into the cause of his death was carried out. His uterine nephew and heir, Gwilani, arranged for ordeal-poison to be administered to all the adults of the village including himself. One woman, the wife of another of the deceased headman's nephews, Zigwile, picked up her child and ran away to a nearby hill and could not be found while the ordeal was being held. During the ordeal only one person failed to demonstrate her innocence by vomiting. This was Mtuŋgamadzi, one of Headman Kanyumba's widows. Byalani is her daughter's son, and is believed to have inherited her evil propensities. She was chased away from the village, and he, too, is prevented from living in its modern successor. Zigwile's wife, who ran away, taking her child, was adjudged guilty, too, especially since, on their return to the village the same evening, her child let the cat out of the bag by saying, 'When you were looking everywhere for us, you were actually treading on us because we had changed into rocks.' Zigwile's wife, too, was chased away; though many years later Zigwile was foolish enough to remarry her. He died soon after this.

Gombe's and Tapita's suspicions of Byalani were confirmed by the death of Musani, the husband of their younger sister, Mwasamala, though they had no clear evidence of his guilt, and they attributed to him a motive that was not in keeping with the idea of his being a witch rather than a killer-for-malice or, in this case, a killer-for-greed.

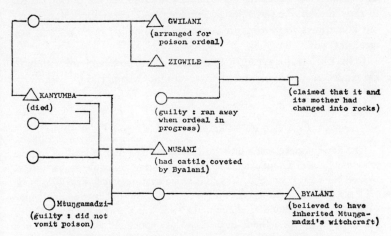

Fig. 37. The Cases of 'A Poison Ordeal Long Ago' and
'The Coveted Cattle'

Case No. 45—The Coveted Cattle (see Fig. 37)

Musani became ill, and, because he had no matrilineal relatives to act on his behalf, his wife's people (members of Gombe's matrilineage) went to consult a diviner. The diviner said that it was the spirit of his mother's brother who was making him ill. 'But,' objected Tapita, 'when he died, blood came out of his mouth, ears and nose. Spirits don't kill people like that: they just strike them dead without leaving any signs. Musani's life was obviously cut short by someone's putting something in his beer. The one who did it was the one who expected to inherit his cattle, Byalani.' It is conceivable that, in the absence of a matrilineal heir, Byalani, who was Musani's father's daughter's son, might have secured the cattle. [I have no record of whether he in fact did.]

The case of Katuule was a clearer illustration of the conception of 'real *ufiti*' (witchcraft), an addiction rather than an act committed in a fit of passing malice. Katuule had always been eccentric. As a member of Gombe's father's matrilineage, he had been known to the members of Gombe's section from an early age. During his boyhood he had had several attacks of insanity, and on one occasion he had had to be tied up with strands of bark, and left with a pile of wood preventing him from falling into the fire, while his relatives sought 'medicines' with which to treat him. He took a delight in performing conjuring tricks (*matseŋga*), and on two occasions these tricks were confused with the anti-social tricks of a witch, and he had to submit to the poison ordeal to clear himself. He was a jovial, amiable person, very fond of hunting, but sometimes forgetting to come back from his hunting trips for weeks on end.

In his old age, his eccentric background began to catch up with him. He tended to be blamed for illnesses among his matrikin.

Case No. 46—Children Shouldn't Tell Tales

One day I noticed that a little girl, Neli, the daughter of Evelina and the granddaughter of Gombe and Eledia, was wearing an amulet at her throat. I asked her what it was and she said it was a charm (*cithumwa*). 'Who made it?' I asked. 'Cenji,' she replied. 'What's it for?' 'Someone tried to injure me.' 'Who was it?' 'Katuule.' I thought that this was too delicate a subject to pursue further with a child; and, when the opportunity arose, I consulted Cenji himself, the maker of the charm and a well-known diviner. He confirmed what Neli had told me. It started, he said, when Neli discovered

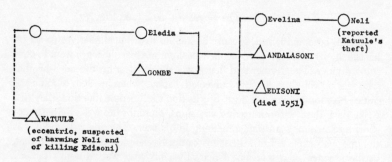

Fig. 38. The Cases of 'Children Shouldn't Tell Tales' and 'The Game that Ran Away'

Katuule stealing sweet stem from the garden of her grandmother, Eledia. She reported this to Eledia, and Katuule was very angry, and had been trying to kill her with sorcery. She had been seriously ill, and, when consulted by her matrilineage elders, he had divined the cause as explained and provided her with the protective charm. It was of a kind, he added, that would turn the sorcerer's 'medicines' back upon himself; and he saw signs of this happening to Katuule whose health was declining.

When another member of Eledia's matrilineage, her younger son, Edisoni, became seriously ill, Katuule was again suspected.

Case No. 47—The Game that Ran Away (see Fig. 38)

Edisoni attended school in a neighbouring village. When he had completed his course there, he went to school in Fort Jameson. Very soon he began to suffer from chest trouble, and they took him to the hospital in Fort Jameson, but to no avail. They therefore brought him back to the village where he became very ill indeed. Some said that he was suffering from *kudʒidyela* ('eating of himself'), a condition believed to result if a youth has his first nocturnal emission and fails to report this and be treated with strengthening 'medicines'. But most people said it was a 'disease coming from people', i.e. the result of someone's sorcery. His mother, Eledia, consulted a diviner, who gave Edisoni some 'medicines' which, if he washed himself with them, would alert him to his attackers. The first time he used these, he saw someone approaching his hut from the shrubs at the edge of the village; and he asked to be moved to another hut. From the second hut he heard people talking, and one of the things they said was, 'That game of ours has run away; it isn't here any longer.' The next morning he was very much worse, and asked that his father, Gombe, be fetched from Fort Jameson, where he was working. However, he died before his father could get to him, and all Gombe could do was build a brick covering over his son's grave. Although Edisoni had not identified the person he had seen approaching or any of the people he had heard talking, Eledia felt convinced that it was Katuule who had killed him.

She even blamed Katuule for the death of her elder son, Andalasoni, which occurred when he was working on a farm near Lusaka. She believed that Katuule had somehow succeeded in sending him 'medicines' that killed him.

Katuule and his wife, Luŵa, seemed to be well aware of the hostility felt towards them, and, when I last saw them, were living in a rudely constructed hut in their maize garden. When I remarked on this to their fellow villagers, they laughed and passed it off by saying that Katuule had always been fond of the bush. When I asked if this was a reference to his being a hunter, they said that he had seldom killed anything bigger than birds. More confidentially, people told me that he was living away from the village because he realized that people knew he was a sorcerer. One informant added that he had even converted his wife to sorcery, and that, as she had taken to it late in life, it had not suited her body and she had developed leprosy. Had I not noticed that her skin had become lighter and her fingers deformed? [I had not.]

It was this informant, a close friend of Gombe's younger brother, who gave me the explanation of Gombe's death (see below, this chapter) that was linked with this couple and which was supported by a minority of people in the village.

The two cases in which old Mwatsiliza was accused of sorcery may be regarded as preludes to the case of the Diminished Following, having occurred four or five years previous to it.

Mwatsiliza belonged to a small matrilineage fragment that attached itself to Gombe's village. Mwatsiliza was herself a cross-cousin of Jolobe, and, since Gombe and Jolobe belonged to the same matriclan, Gombe called her his cross-cousin (*msuŵani*) although their relationship could not be traced genealogically. Mwatsiliza's section consisted of her own segment and that of her sister, Cimalo. The headman of her segment was her son, Galami, though in 1947, when the first case occurred, he was too young to have an undisputed right to its leadership, and his mother and her sister, Cimalo, tended to be more directly dependent on the village headman, Gombe.

Case No. 48—Three Possible Causes

Mwatsiliza's daughter, Telezia, became ill, and Mwatsiliza went to a diviner who said her illness had been caused by the spirit of Mwatsiliza's mother, Nakhoza. Telezia then died, and, after her death, Mwatsiliza and her sister, Cimalo, went to another diviner who accused Mwatsiliza of having herself killed Telezia with sorcery. This led to a quarrel, and Mwatsiliza's son, Galami, went to yet another diviner, who asserted that Telezia's death had been caused by her husband's committing adultery when she was pregnant, and thus killing her by *mdulo*.

Case No. 49—The Live Hare

After Telezia's death, her baby, Yaliwe, died suddenly while being carried on Mwatsiliza's back. Everyone, including Molisi, Mwatsiliza's younger son, said that Mwatsiliza was the sorcerer who had killed the child. Mwatsiliza's sister, Cimalo, was suspected, too; and both submitted to the poison ordeal. Cimalo was unaffected, but Mwatsiliza is said not only to have defecated but also to have passed a live hare, which hopped away. Her guilt for the deaths of both Yaliwe and Telezia was now considered to be conclusively proved.

It is interesting that, in the first of this pair of cases, three explanations for the misfortune were given. The first and the last were in line with the interests of the person who consulted the diviner, assuming that Galami, as potential headman, wanted to retain his mother's support. In the case of the Live Hare, Molisi's accusation of his mother may possibly have sprung from his competition with Galami for headmanship, since his accusation, if proved, as it was proved by the ordeal, would discredit Galami's judgement.

Some five years later, Galami, who was living at his wife's village,

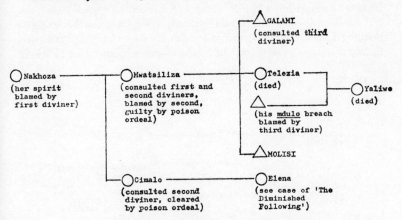

Fig. 39. The Cases of 'Three Possible Causes' and
'The Live Hare'

tried to build up a following there by inducing Mwatsiliza, Cimalo and their children to join him; but, as I related in the case of the Diminished Following, his attempt to hold them failed, ending in two accusations of sorcery.

One of the eccentric persons with whom Gombe had to deal was an unmitigated scoundrel rather than one conforming with the stereotype of the addicted 'real *nfiti*'.

Case No. 50—The Pretended Brother

In 1949, Kaziŋgachile came from Nyasaland and claimed membership of Gombe's matrilineage. Although he was unknown to any of the local members of it (he claimed closest affiliation with Gombe's classificatory brother, Taulo, who was at work in Lusaka), he was accepted as a member, and in the course of time was sent to marry the widow (*kulowa cokolo*) of another of Gombe's classificatory brothers in a village a few miles away.

After a while, Kaziŋgachile showed seriously anti-social characteristics. Firstly, he cut bark from a tree in the burial ground (something only a sorcerer would do). Secondly, he was caught in the act of collecting soil soaked in his wife's urine; and, though he protested that he was trying to regain her lost affection by making a love potion with it, people suspected him further of sorcery. There was a story, too, of how, while hoeing with his wife in their garden, he had suddenly disappeared, his footprints coming mysteriously to an end in the middle of the garden.

Gombe decided to disown him, and informed the Chief's court accordingly. This did not, however, absolve him (or his matrilineage) from responsibility for Kaziŋgachile's further misdeeds; for, when Kaziŋgachile stole one of Taulo's cattle and sold it in a neighbouring village, and Gombe, acting on behalf of Taulo, sued the buyer for its return, the Court refused to grant this, finding that the fact that Gombe had chosen Kaziŋgachile to inherit a widow

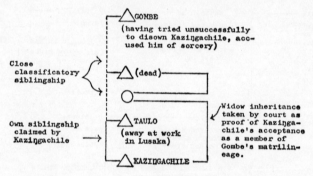

Fig. 40. The Case of 'The Pretended Brother'

on behalf of his matrilineage was sufficient proof of his being a relative; and that from this it followed that, although Gombe had later disowned him, he was in fact still responsible for his actions.

Recalling his sinister actions, Gombe accused Kaziŋgachile of sorcery, and he returned to Nyasaland.

Death and Explanations

On my way to the Ceŵa Reserve in 1952, I learned of Gombe's death from an official of the Administration. He told me that Gombe had been killed in a motor accident in Fort Jameson. It had been established that both he and the driver of the car in which he had been travelling had been drunk. As the car swerved from side to side, Gombe had tried to jump out and had been crushed between the car and the bank at the side of the road. The driver had been convicted of manslaughter and sentenced to eighteen months' imprisonment.

In the village, seventy-five miles away, two constructions were placed on this tragedy. A minority of informants put the blame on Gombe's eldest sister, Luŵa, who, they said, had been taught sorcery by her husband, Katuule. The motive that they attributed to her was that, being poor, she often used to beg for things from her brother who usually denied her them, since he favoured one of his younger sisters, the wife of Musani (the victim in the case of the Coveted Cattle), who had been recently widowed.

The other version had to do with the alleged infidelity of Gombe's second wife, Etelina. Gombe himself once told me that he had had occasion to reprimand Etelina for 'wandering about' (*kuyenda-yenda*), which implied that she was promiscuous; and when his friend, Headman Blahimu, died in 1947, he became very depressed because he believed that it was his [Gombe's] anti-adultery magic (*likaŋkho*) that had killed him. His suspicions had been aroused as early as 1941, when he had had a violent quarrel with Etelina, and she had run away. For two weeks he had searched for her without success because she had run away to Blahimu, who had sheltered her in his kitchen. He then decided to employ anti-adultery magic. Without her knowing it, he administered it to her and to himself and then had intercourse with her. Then, at a Christmas beer party, Blahimu paid them a visit and committed adultery with her, becoming very ill as a result. In fear of his life, he told one of Gombe's friends, though not Gombe himself, that it was Gombe's *likaŋkho* that had caused his illness. On this occasion he recovered.

In 1947, Gombe again became suspicious, and once more administered *likaŋkho*, which this time he obtained from Nseŋga country. Blahimu came soon after this for some beer being sold at Gombe's village and again committed adultery with Etelina. This time he became very ill and sent for Gombe, asking him if he could help him (not specifying what he meant by this). Gombe tried to give him an antidote, but he was unable to take it and died.

An informant who was a member of Blahimu's section gave me a different account of his death (see the case of the Carpenter's Tools), attributing it to the sorcery of a junior classificatory brother who wanted to inherit Blahimu's carpenter's tools and who killed him by putting 'medicines' into his *kacaso*.

The explanation of Gombe's death given by the majority of his friends and relatives was that Etelina, whom he had taken with him when he went to work in Fort Jameson, formed liaisons with various men there, including the man who was driving the car in which he met his death. Some said that this man left the door only partly shut and deliberately pushed him out. Others thought that he met his death through more mystical causes: that Etelina's lover used sorcery to make the accident happen. In any event, one of the first things Gombe's younger brother did on becoming acting headman was to chase Etelina away to her home neighbourhood, accusing her of 'spoiling' (*kuonoŋga*) the village.

Headman Gombe's life is not typical in all respects. For one thing, both his family of orientation and later his family of procreation most of the time lived virilocally. For another, he became a Christian during a period when conversion was relatively rare. In spite of these divergences from my estimate of the average Ceŵa headman, his story nevertheless serves to illustrate in a unified way both the origins of social tensions in Ceŵa life and the various possible ways in which these may be resolved. It presents some of the conflicts that impinge on an individual Ceŵa living in modern times of change, and some of the disjunctions he encounters when he becomes enmeshed in the social machinery of section, village and chiefdom. It shows, too, that the tensions springing from value conflicts or structural oppositions may be redressed—or articulated and sharpened until they are resolved more drastically—by a variety of belief systems, including sorcery. In the next chapter I shall consider *inter alia* the conditions under which sorcery rather than, say, the intervention of lineage spirits or the breach of *mdulo* taboos, tends to be invoked as an explanatory principle.

CHAPTER 11

RECURRING THEMES IN ALL CONTEXTS

IN this chapter I shall try to summarize the features common to the contexts in which Ceŵa attribute their misfortunes to sorcery. I shall also examine those contexts in which sorcery is not usually invoked, since these, as negative instances, will throw light both on the ingredients of social tension and on the factors that lead to the expression of tension in terms of sorcery rather than of some alternative explanatory principle.

As I pointed out in the first chapter, I adopted my order of presentation in the interests of intelligibility and not in an attempt to induce generalizations from specific instances. Since I am following the hypothetico-deductive method, I shall present my summary of the contexts of Ceŵa sorcery as data that may be checked against hypotheses to which writers on witchcraft and sorcery have at least implicitly subscribed.

A Moral Theory of Causation

The first point to note is that the material presented in preceding chapters provides ample confirmation of Evans-Pritchard's pioneering insight that beliefs in mystical evil-doers explain the course of events by relating the occurrence of misfortune to disturbances in the moral relationships between persons.[1] In its general form this proposition applies equally to sorcerers and witches, since, as Evans-Pritchard puts it, 'Both alike are enemies of men';[2] and the fact that their practices are deemed anti-social and illegitimate makes them appropriate agents to whom to attribute human misfortunes. It is true that the Ceŵa conceive of other agents affecting the course of events, and sometimes attribute their adversities to these; but the largest category in my sample of serious misfortunes, and one comprising a slight majority of all cases, was that in which they were attributed to sorcery.

[1] *Witchcraft among the Aʒande*, passim.
[2] *Ibid.*, p. 387.

As Gluckman in reviewing Evans-Pritchard's Azande book has remarked, 'Witchcraft as a theory of causation embraces a theory of morals.'[1] This particular aspect of Evans-Pritchard's insight, to which Malinowski's statement of the conservative function of sorcery (cited in Chapter 8) was a precursor, is also confirmed by my material from the Ceŵa. I have shown in Chapter 8 that retrospective explanations of misfortunes may have moral overtones and that this applies to those in which sorcery is invoked. Many features of the cases presented in the course of the book, as well as the attributes of the majority of the 101 cases summarized in the tables, illustrate the widely held view that beliefs in witchcraft and sorcery have the function of reinforcing social norms by dramatizing them. The moral overtones of such cases do not comprise a single context of sorcery so much as an aspect of all contexts.

Table XXVI shows that about half the sorcerers first mentioned in the 101 cases were believed to have had anti-social traits even before they were suspected or accused of sorcery. This moral aspect of all contexts of sorcery sometimes had reference to the believed victim when his misfortune was attributed to his own or his associates' foolishness or failings. Thus about sixty per cent of believed victims or their close associates had been considered guilty of a misdemeanour directly related to the attack made on them (Table XXV).

The conservative nature of beliefs in sorcery is thrown into prominence when, as a result of social change, the moral implications of the indigenous philosophy of causation conflict with those of an intrusive one. That there is such a conflict between norms springing from the basic clannishness of Ceŵa society and those derived from the greater differentiation of urban-industrial civilization is suggested by three of my findings. Firstly, as Table XXVII shows, modern objects of competition, such as cattle, money and other property, crop up clearly in about a quarter of the cases, and may have been involved in about a further tenth of them. Secondly, the norms defining new relationships, such as those between unrelated fellow employees, produce conflicts that are sometimes expressed in suspicions or accusations of sorcery. Thirdly, indigenous conflicts of norms, such as those laying down a man's relationships with his children and his sister's children, may be exacerbated by his owning modern kinds of property.

In contrast to the cases presented, the anti-sorcery movements represent a reaction to the newly created or recently increased value

[1] *Custom and Conflict*, p. 86.

conflicts just mentioned. They tend to be, in Worsley's terms, desperate searchings for more effective ways of understanding and modifying a confused environment (see above, Chapter 9).

Formulating and Redressing Tense Relationships

The second important proposition to be checked against the material is the one that beliefs in sorcery provide a means by which tense relationships may be formulated, and sometimes redressed, as a result of their clearer, more incisive, or even more explosive, expression.[1] This proposition may be tested against phenomena of two distinct orders. The relationship between sorcerer and victim provides a pointer to the estimates the people themselves make of the incidence of tensions in their society, whereas the relationship between accuser and sorcerer provides a more objective, external assessment of this incidence. It should be noted at once that the first order of data, though it generalizes specific instances of people's beliefs, does not yield a picture of the society's tension points that corresponds with the one they paint in their general statements. For instance, it will be recalled that, while both male and female informants express the view that most sorcerers are women, the sex-ratio of those involved in the cases collected shows males to comprise a much larger proportion than would be expected from such a general statement. Similarly there is a difference between people's general estimates of the frequency with which polygyny leads to sorcery and the proportion of specific instances, real or believed, in which polygyny is involved. I shall return to this point in a later section.

Although it is important to maintain the distinction between the imaginary sorcerer–victim link and the real accuser–sorcerer link, it should be noted that their respective distributions in categories of social relationship do not yield fundamentally different pictures of structural tensions in Cewa society. This is partly, though not wholly, because victim and accuser are, in just over a sixth of the seventy-nine cases where the accuser was identified, the same person. The two distributions of hostile coincidences both show, somewhat in line with generally expressed belief, that matrilineal relatives are involved to a considerable degree as sorcerers and victims and as accusers and

[1] There is no single source that I can offer for this hypothesis. It represents my development of a suggestion made to me in conversation by Professor J. Clyde Mitchell about fifteen years ago. Aspects of it are at least implied in the writings of those authors cited in Appendix C.

U

sorcerers, and that unrelated persons are involved to a correspondingly lesser extent in these hostile links.

The use of this method of detecting the tension points in a social structure leads to methodological difficulties that I have been unable to solve in this study. In particular, it raises the question whether and how it is possible to standardize either type of frequency distribution in such a way that the incidence of believed attacks or of accusations in a given category may be compared with that in another. When the tables show, for instance, that the cases include very few accusations associated with polygyny, does this statement have any meaning until it has been related to the polygyny rate of the population of whose misfortunes the cases are a sample?

Thus far I have considered only the first part of the proposition being examined in this section, i.e. the question whether tense relationships are formulated in terms of sorcery. The second part is to the effect that, if tense relationships are thus formulated, the clearer expression of these relationships has the effect of resolving or adjusting them. If it does have this effect, the proposition may be regarded as an instance of a wider principle that beliefs in sorcery have a social function in that they contribute to maintaining the pattern of the social system while facilitating its adjustment to changing internal and external conditions.

Though, as I shall try to show presently, the comparative sociology of sorcery and witchcraft throws much light on this problem, it needs to be examined, too, in terms of the general sociology of tension and conflict. If accusations and believed attacks are to be regarded as signs of conflict and stress, and thus as social mechanisms for amplifying tensions so that they may be perceived and disposed of, it is convenient to regard them as particular instances of what some sociologists call 'conflict', and others, 'tension'. Following Gluckman's usage, I reserve 'conflict' for oppositions of principle and motive that are covert, underlying and usually inherent in social structure. For their overt manifestations I use 'dispute', 'rivalry', 'quarrel', 'combat', etc.[1] What have general sociologists written of the social functions of tension and conflict, and are their conclusions applicable to the particular instance being considered? The most notable contributor here is Simmel, who, unlike the generation of sociologists who followed

---

[1] This is Gluckman's usage in *Custom and Conflict*, but as the book consists of broadcast lectures, he does not define all his terms explicitly. In a personal discussion, Professor Gluckman stressed that many sociologists and anthropologists are trying to make the single word 'conflict' serve too many purposes.

him, sees conflict, not simply as a pathological phenomenon, but also more subtly as sometimes an essential ingredient in the balance and virility of a social group.[1] Similarly, von Wiese regards even open combat as sometimes a healing, rather than a contaminating or destructive social process.[2] In the field of comparative sociology, Gluckman, who, however, acknowledges the inspiration of colleagues of his generation, such as Evans-Pritchard and Fortes, has consistently applied this dynamic approach to problems of both social cohesion and social change;[3] and in general sociology Coser[4] and Bernard[5] have recently revived interest in the functions of tension and conflict.

If the underlying conflicts and tensions that lead to accusations and suspicions of sorcery and witchcraft are to be regarded as instances of general forms of social interaction that sociologists examine, then these more specific forms should have corresponding social functions. Some anthropologists have developed this specific instance of the sociology of conflict; and, to exemplify their approach, I shall examine contributions by Wilson, Nadel, Gluckman, Mitchell and Turner to the proposition that accusations of mystical evil-doing contribute to the maintenance of the pattern of a social structure or to its development through time. Wilson[6] shows how differences in the witch beliefs of the Pondo and the Nyakyusa are directly related to differences in social structure. Nadel[7] presents a similar study but one based on data from four varied societies from the same cultural group. Gluckman[8] takes the case of the daughter-in-law or sister-in-law among the patrilineal, virilocal Zulu in order to show how accusations of witchcraft facilitate 'the working out through time of two contradictory social processes within the group' of agnates forming the core of the homestead. Although there are strong animosities among these men, they seldom accuse one another of witchcraft, but rather accuse their women-affines. In doing so, they reveal, not to themselves but to the outside observer, that the rôles of these women have conflicts built into them; for, though it is through the children born to these women that the lineage maintains and gathers strength, yet it is by this very

[1] *Conflict*, p. 13 *et passim*. See also Coser's useful summary of Simmel's central thesis, *Social Conflict*, p. 31.

[2] Becker, *Systematic Sociology*, p. 272.

[3] *Custom and Conflict*, p. 1 *et passim*; Malinowski's *Sociological Theories*, p 10; and 'Some Processes of Social Change', p. 254.

[4] *Social Conflict*.

[5] 'The Sociological Study of Tension.'

[6] 'Witch Beliefs and the Social Structure.'

[7] 'Witchcraft in Four African Societies.'

[8] *Custom and Conflict*, Chapter 4, especially pp. 98–9.

process that husbands develop their own independent interests, in favour of their sons, and thus hasten the segmentation of the lineage.

In a similar manner, Mitchell[1] shows the part played by accusations in Yao society, not merely depicting a model of the society stopped for examination at the moment of analysis, but also setting it in motion to show the rôle of accusations in a developing sequence, at the same time providing a matrilineal parallel to Gluckman's Zulu study. Turner[2] takes this approach further. He contends that a social system, like an organic one, moves dynamically through space and time, and, in so doing, exhibits growth and decay. As changes occur, tensions develop; and, when these become critical, the system goes through a cataclysmic change which Turner, for want of a better term, calls a 'social drama'. A social drama affords the sociologist a brief glimpse of the society's inner workings in that it reveals 'a limited area of transparency on the otherwise opaque surface of regular, uneventful social life'. In that it is a moment at which persons or groups try to manipulate the social structure to their own advantage, it may be either an index or a vehicle of change. Many of the social dramas that Turner presents include accusations of witchcraft. Both Gluckman[3] and Turner[4] make the important point that certain deep-lying conflicts in a social structure are not susceptible of the rational adjustment provided by the judicial process and can be expressed only in mystical beliefs, including those in witchcraft and sorcery, which ascribe the surface disturbances to the wickedness of individuals. The inherent disharmonies in the social system are thus cloaked under an insistence that there is harmony in the values of a society. This theory of harmony is stated in ritual. The view of these two writers agrees with Nadel's contention that witch beliefs enable a society to continue functioning though it is fraught with conflicts and contradictions which it is helpless to resolve.[5]

The idea that accusations and suspicions of sorcery represent explosions by which the social system is periodically revised and readjusted receives support from Cewa data. As I tried to illustrate in Chapter 4, accusations of sorcery play a part in the development of the matrilineage. In the first phase of this development, during which the group remains united, accusations between segment leaders represent their attempts to achieve overall control. In the second phase, once

[1] *The Yao Village*, Chapter 6.
[2] *Schism and Continuity*, pp. 93 and 161–2.
[3] Most explicitly in *Politics, Law and Ritual in Tribal Society*, Chapter 6.
[4] *Schism and Continuity*, pp. xxi and 122 ff.
[5] 'Witchcraft in Four African Societies', p. 29.

division has started, and these attempts have been abandoned, accusations have the function of accelerating and justifying the incipient separation. The first phase is represented by the succession dispute between Katete and Kasinda in the case of His Uncle's Bed; and the second, by the case of the Diminished Following, in which accusations against Galami and his wife made by Cimalo and her daughter, Elena, provided an irrefutable excuse for their leaving Galami's village-section.

In a less obvious and spectacular way, accusations of sorcery bring to the surface, and thus to the possibility of adjustment, conflicts that have eluded settlement by the machinery of conciliation such as joking and avoidance relationships and the arbitration of the Chief's court. Finally, the idea that beliefs in sorcery have the function of formulating and adjusting social tensions is supported, though not conclusively proved, by the fact that, in about three-quarters of the cases, the believed attack or the accusation was linked in people's minds with a preceding tense relationship between sorcerer and victim or between accuser and sorcerer (see Table XXIV). The remaining quarter raises a problem which will be discussed towards the end of the next section.

The Genesis of Tensions

If I am to characterize the cases in which a tense relationship preceded the believed attack, I must again digress for a moment from the comparative sociology of sorcery and witchcraft to the general sociology of tension and conflict. What does the latter branch of knowledge say of the genesis of tense relationships? The writings of the German systematic sociologists contain many useful hints. Von Wiese, sometimes regarded as the writer who took the formalism of this school to its logical if sterile conclusion, has a good deal to say about the conditions that cause competition to develop through suspicious opposition ('contravention') to actual violence or the threat of it ('conflict').[1] He attributes the more dissociative forms of interaction to competition that has got out of hand. Normally, according to von Wiese, when two or more persons compete, they are involved in a non-violent form of interaction in which they bid for the favour of a third party (which may be conceived of in the plural, as in commercial competition for a market), and in so doing they observe whatever rules that may apply in the situation in which they interact, and they maintain a relationship with each other. When this

[1] Becker, *Systematic Sociology*, Chapters 18–20.

process gets out of hand, it develops into social tension (contravention) in which the contending parties suspect each other of violating the rules prescribing their interaction and in which the relationship between them is strained to the point of rupture. Subjectively this is an insecure and uncomfortable phase of interaction.

How does competition get out of hand and develop into tension? At first sight two factors seem to be involved, firstly, the strength of motivation towards the scarce status, power, person or resource[1] for which the parties compete; and, secondly, the degree to which the situation is one that is flexible, and thus subject to manipulation and jockeying for position, or is one in respect of which there are underlying, built-in conflicts of claims, duties or loyalties.

The first of these two factors is obvious and needs little elaboration. To say that the competitors are strongly motivated towards a highly valued goal is to imply that they are driven by imperative biological needs or by secondary needs that cultural conditioning has implanted. A sociological analysis is concerned not so much with the origins of such needs as with their variations in magnitude and their response to social stimuli.

The second factor needs further study. Whether competition will occur at all and whether it will develop into tense rivalry will depend on whether the situation in which it occurs is relatively circumscribed or relatively self-regulative. In the former type of situation, competition may be virtually eliminated by a rigid social structure which separates persons who might otherwise compete with one another; in the latter, people are free at least to compete and may develop tense relationships if each starts manipulating to his own advantage the norms defining their interaction.[2] An important rider to the operation

---

[1] I owe some of these phrases to Coser's definition of 'conflict' which, in some respects, resembles von Wiese's definition of 'competition'. See *Social Conflict*, p. 8.

[2] The following are a few of the many examples which may be cited in support of this principle. Evans-Pritchard (*Witchcraft among the Azande*, pp. 104–5) reports that Zande commoners refrain from accusing nobles of witchcraft because *inter alia* 'their contact with these people is limited to situations in which their behaviour is determined by notions of status'. Gluckman ('Kinship and Marriage among the Lozi of Northern Rhodesia and the Zulu of Natal', p. 180) contrasts the attitudes of Lozi and Zulu to sororal polygyny and ascribes the potentially greater tension it would cause among the Lozi to the fact that among them the relative status and inheritance rights of wives are not fixed, whereas among the Zulu they are. Von Wiese (Becker, *Systematic Sociology*, pp. 260 and 254) maintains that 'doubt and contravention go hand in hand' and that 'a highly accessible secular structure will manifest much more competition than an isolated, sacred structure for in the former there are few traditional bonds whereas in the latter tradition so fortifies institutional barriers that freedom may be virtually non-exixtent'. Barnes (*Politics in a Changing Society*, p. 33), discussing Ŋgoni succession, states that 'the contradiction between superordination by age and by status of mother among half brothers brought up in the same vicinity led to conflict. . . .'

of the second factor is that circumscription of behaviour will be likely to succeed in eliminating competition and preventing tension only if the set of relationships that mediates it is legitimate, in the sense of conforming with the primary values of the society.

The two factors leading to the development of tension from competition need to be taken together if they are to be illustrated from the case material. This is because they frequently balance each other. The same degree of tension may conceivably develop from a strong dose of uncertainty or conflict associated with a weak dose of motivation as from the opposite type of combination or from medium doses of each factor.

The case material shows that goals competed for by those who ultimately suspect or accuse each other of sorcery often have to do with such fields of aspiration as leadership of a following, ownership of property, or success in love or in tribal politics. The material also shows that competition can only occur because of uncertainty or because there is no established procedure or precedence, and that it will probably be intense because of conflicting norms defining the competitors' rights and rôles. Thus there may be conflict between the claims of genealogical position and those of personal qualification, or conflict between a headman's traditional right to dispose of his matrilineage's property and the newly made claims of those of his followers who have gone to the labour centres. These new claims arise from the increasing capacity of young adults to earn money and the increasing number of objects on which they can spend their income. Above all, new ranges of goods offer them the choice of raising their own standard of living, instead of ploughing back their income into established relationships. The fact that cattle frequently crop up in quarrels culminating in accusations of sorcery is related to their being—on any appreciable scale—a new element in Ceŵa culture and one about which there are consequently no clear precedents.

In addition to strong motivation and weak circumscription of competitive behaviour, there is a third ingredient in social tension which should not escape notice because, like the postman in Chesterton's story, it is a familiar constant and therefore tends to be invisible. This is the fact that there is a personal relationship between the parties involved in a believed attack of sorcery, whether or not it is followed by an accusation. With a few exceptions, all the writers whose works I have examined on this point state or imply that the relationship between mystical evil-doer and victim or, more rarely, between accuser and

mystical evil-doer, is a personal one, one in which the parties expose in
their interaction, not merely single rôles or single facets of their social
personalities, but complex rôles, or all facets. In other words, their
relationships are nearly always of the kind that Gluckman calls 'multi-
plex' [1] and that some other sociologists call 'total', as opposed to
'segmental'.[2] Certainly in all the real or imagined episodes I have
recorded, the *dramatis personae* have been enmeshed in such personal
relationships.

The most notable of the exceptions referred to in the last paragraph
is Kluckhohn, who reported a tendency among the Navaho for distant
and totally unrelated witches to be blamed for people's misfortunes.[3]
This general statement of the position among the Navaho is not, however, consistent with some of the cases presented in the same study.[4]
Furthermore, after writing *Navaho Witchcraft*, Kluckhohn found that
more recent data did not entirely confirm his earlier conclusions in this
respect, and that gossip about local witches was commoner than his
first impressions had led him to believe.[5] Other exceptions are writers
on Oceania, where, though the issue is clouded by definitions that
diverge from those used elsewhere, there is some evidence that sorcery
is believed to operate between communities as well as between persons
in the same community.[6]

There may, however, be a good reason for the apparent inconsistency in Kluckhohn's material.[7] It is conceivable that both statements he recorded were correct. It might be argued that, in some cases,
it is not possible to link a given misfortune with a previous quarrel or
even a moral lapse on the part of the victim. Since, however, the
general belief in witchcraft or sorcery is nurtured and maintained by
those instances where there is a clear-cut link between social tension
and mystical evil-doing, there may be a tendency for witchcraft or
sorcery to be invoked even when no such link is discoverable. This
flywheel effect of beliefs in specific attacks by evil-doers may cause
people to attribute a misfortune, not to 'just one of those things', but
to 'just one of those witches (or sorcerers)'. As Evans-Pritchard re-

---

[1] *The Judicial Process*, p. 19.
[2] For instance, Coser, *Social Conflict, passim.*
[3] *Navaho Witchcraft*, p. 55.
[4] *Ibid.*, Part III.
[5] This information was contained in a commentary that the late Professor Kluckhohn
was kind enough to send me on my paper on 'The Social Context of Ceŵa Witch Beliefs'.
[6] I review some of the relevant literature in 'Witchcraft as a Social Strain-Gauge'.
[7] In *Closed Systems and Open Minds*, Gluckman and Devons have made a detailed
criticism of this aspect of Kluckhohn's work.

corded, if the trouble is slight, Azande merely dismiss it as 'witch-craft' much as we might say 'bad luck'.[1]

This brings to mind the thirty per cent of cases in which no quarrel preceded the believed attack or accusation. In these instances the blame for a misfortune was laid at the door of someone who was not necessarily in a tense relationship with the victim or the accuser. Such persons were usually eccentric, and, as Table IX shows, about two-thirds of them were classified as witches ('real *nfiti*'). They seemed to provide a reserve of people who could be accused when the misfortune to be explained could not clearly be attributed to a tense social relationship. It is significant that they tended to be regarded as witches rather than as 'killers-for-malice'. Had Kluckhohn's data been susceptible of classification on Evans-Pritchard's criterion, he might possibly have found that the distant believed attackers were witches, while the ones involved in closer relationships were sorcerers.

Although, in this thirty per cent of my cases, the trouble was seldom slight, there seemed to be no clear-cut link between it and social tensions. People had to look around for someone to blame; and, in directing their accusation or gossip, they were probably influenced more by the personal deviance of those they blamed than by structural conflicts.

Alternatives to Sorcery

The fact that no more than fifty-five per cent of serious misfortunes were attributed to sorcery raises the question why it is that certain misfortunes are not necessarily explained in this manner. There would appear to be alternatives to sorcery as a means of expressing and resolving tensions.[2] What are the conditions under which sorcery rather than one of these alternatives is the preferred mode—though 'preferred' must be read in terms, not of conscious personal choice, but of unanticipated social functioning?

I can attempt an answer to this question by examining a series of contexts ranging from near the negative pole, where sorcery is typically not the mode of explanation, nor an accusation of it the mode of expression, to near the positive pole, where it, rather than one of its alternatives, is the preferred mode.

It is difficult to find a relationship category that qualifies in an absolute sense as the negative instance. The nearest approach to it is

---

[1] *Witchcraft among the Azande*, Chapter 4.
[2] This is in line with the insight of E. J. and J. D. Krige, who consider that witchcraft must be regarded as only one of a number of mechanisms for resolving tensions (*The Realm of a Rain Queen*, p. 264).

the relationship between spouses. Here, because there is a high loading of the motivational factor, especially in cases involving polygyny, and a close personal relationship, one might expect, as the Ceŵa do themselves, a high incidence of tension formulated in terms of sorcery. Yet this relationship, together with the closely linked one involving co-wives, accounts for only seven per cent of believed attacks and only three per cent of accusations (cf. Table XVII). While these are percentages derived direct from absolute frequencies, and therefore suspect in the absence of a universe of interaction that could be used for standardizing them, their small size is nevertheless in strong contrast to the Ceŵa doctrine that one informant expressed in the double statement, 'Polygyny and cattle finish people'; and I would probably not be far wrong if I assumed that, if they were available, their standardized forms would be small.

As I suggested in Chapter 5, the most probable explanation for the rarity of believed attacks or accusations of sorcery between spouses is the weakness of conjugal ties, a weakness associated with the solidarity of the Ceŵa matrilineage. If tension develops between spouses, they can easily part, and usually do part, before it grows into the intense hatred that is characteristically expressed in terms of sorcery. Although Ceŵa marriage is a personal, or total, relationship, it has nevertheless a strong element of contract in it; and there is no idea of romantic love to cause the partners to regard divorce as a personal disaster. It is a relationship which may, in the interests of matrilineage solidarity, be easily contracted out of; and it does not require sorcery as a catalytic agent in the process of separation.

Furthermore, among the Ceŵa in contrast to the Zulu,[1] it is not a man's wives who are the main foci of structural conflicts but rather his sisters and, more commonly, those 'buds of segmentation', his uterine nieces.

The exceptions to this near-negative instance, the cases in which spouses were believed to have attacked each other with sorcery or to have accused each other of such attacks, fall into two categories. The cases involving spouses and yielding five per cent of sorcerer–victim and two per cent of accuser–sorcerer relationships amounted to seven. Of these, four were ones in which polygyny or adultery was involved, i.e. strong motivation and intense rivalry seemed to arouse hostility to which mere divorce was an inadequate outlet. In two of the remaining cases, where believed attack and accusation coincided, in that the

---

[1] I am grateful to Professor Max Gluckman for pointing out this contrast to me.

victim was also the accuser, special circumstances made divorce an impossible or an unsuitable means of ending tension. In the case of the Backsliding Christian, Gombe and Eledia, though estranged, did not obtain a divorce because they were related to each other and Eledia was a member of a locally domiciled matrilineage remnant. In the case of Damages for Disputed Maize, divorce would not have been a solution to the rancour between Alufeo and Maligalitha because it would not have settled their dispute, which was over the ownership of a beast bought from the proceeds of a surplus maize crop, to the production of which both of them had contributed. The remaining case was that of the Pretended Brother, the one in which Gombe, having concluded that Kaziŋgachile was a scoundrel, accused him of trying to kill his [Kaziŋgachile's] wife with sorcery.

Another way in which tensions between spouses may be resolved is through the medium of the *mdulo* complex of beliefs. The death of a child can often be attributed to the breach of a taboo by someone closely related to him, such as one of his parents (and occasionally by someone more remotely connected, such as the possibly unrelated headman of his village). As I remarked in Chapter 5, judging by the regularity with which a man hands over compensation (*camʒimu*, 'of the spirit'), whether for a deceased wife or for a deceased child, he seldom succeeds in establishing his innocence to the charge of having thus killed a member of his family of procreation. Yet no lasting blame attaches to him; his payment easily clears him.

Further from the negative pole, but still on the negative half of the scale, is the category comprising links between unrelated people. As I pointed out in Chapter 7, the frequency with which unrelated people are believed to attack each other with sorcery, or accuse each other of it, is low, not only in an absolute sense, but also relative to the fact that many of a given person's village neighbours (those in sections other than his own) are usually not his kinsmen. The low rates of believed attack or of accusation in this relationship category point to the effectiveness of the means of resolving tensions between unrelated persons, more particularly, the judicial process. They may suggest, too, that unrelated persons are less often the loci of the kinds of structural conflicts that Gluckman and Turner (see above, this chapter) consider can be redressed only by ritual (as against rational arbitration).

One of the episodes in Gombe's life history illustrates another fact that should be taken into account when examining the conditions under which sorcery is or is not invoked in the formulation of tension, i.e. the likelihood of sustaining so serious a charge. Since the persons concerned in this episode may have been unrelated, it is appropriate to consider it here. When Gombe made the mistake of entering a birth-hut and of exposing himself to the charge of having killed by *mdulo* the baby he visited (see above, Chapter 10), Pitani, who coveted his headmanship, took the opportunity of trying to discredit his rival. The situation in which these two competed was one which might well have been conducive to an accusation of sorcery, since motivation was strong and Pitani's claim to the headmanship a matter of dispute, and since the Chief had made a ruling with which Pitani was dissatisfied. Yet Pitani did not accuse Gombe of sorcery, but tried to persuade people that Gombe had been guilty of a relatively minor tort. Apart from the fact, which should not be overlooked, that he may not have *believed* Gombe to be a sorcerer, he was probably aware of his difficulty, as a somewhat unpopular newcomer, in sustaining a charge of sorcery.

Relationships between members of the same matrilineage fall at the positive end of the scale, the incidence of believed attacks and accusations between them being high. Here Ceŵa insight is a good guide. As I mentioned in Chapter 3, informants point out that the matrilineage is the natural arena for quarrels about succession to office and the ownership and disposal of property. In other words, there are present the strong motives often found as ingredients in tensions expressed in terms of sorcery. Furthermore, these motives are given relatively free play as a result of conflict between the principles governing competitive interaction. Thus competition can at least take place and is likely to develop into intense rivalry. The third ingredient, the invisible constant, is also present; for all the relationships are highly personal and, what is equally important, they cannot, like conjugal links, be quietly dismantled.

Where Ceŵa insight is probably clearest is in the explanation of why the resulting tension is likely to be expressed through the medium of sorcery. Informants state that, because matrilineal relatives cannot sue one another in the Chief's court, they often 'leave words of speech with one another', and that their smouldering hatred flares up from time to time in the form of attacks of sorcery.

In this, the near-positive instance, there is a clear illustration of the hypothesis that one of the conditions for the resolution of tension in terms of sorcery is that alternative ways of expressing it are not available.

Wider Applications

The formulae to which the Ceŵa material conforms will not necessarily apply under conditions prevailing in other societies with different modes of life and social organization. There are, in fact, societies, both non-literate and 'modern', which lack beliefs in witchcraft and sorcery or, while having them, show far less preoccupation with them than, say, the Azande or the Ceŵa. No easy explanations for their absence or unimportance can be put forward. Only careful, detailed comparison and analysis, going well beyond the task I have set myself in this book, may reveal whether in such societies a freedom from the fear of witchcraft or sorcery is to be attributed to the absence of strongly motivated but slightly regulated competition in personal relationships or, more probably, to the presence of alternative forms of expression, such as singing contests, slanging matches, feuds, war, actual homicide (as opposed to the mystical form of it in sorcery and witchcraft), art forms, sport—and so on. Furthermore, if safe comparisons are to be made, the societies concerned should, by the process of diffusion, have had equal opportunities of accepting these institutions, the task of sociological analysis in this respect being to explain why witchcraft or sorcery took on in some societies and not in others to which they became known.

What are the reasons for the virtual absence in modern society of beliefs in sorcery and witchcraft (as they are defined in this book)? The existence of what I have referred to as the invisible constant, the fact that, in sorcery and witchcraft, the accuser, accused evil-doer and believed victim are joined by intimate bonds, may indicate the direction in which an analysis should proceed if it is to answer this question. The point in history when beliefs in witchcraft and sorcery began to decline seems to have been when small-scale, intimate communities began to be displaced by large, impersonal, urban complexes. Their decline does not seem to have been associated with the growth of religion, which, on the contrary, during some periods, such as the Reformation in Europe and the late seventeenth century in New England, seems rather to have encouraged them by multiplying uncertainties of conscience among Protestants and by confusing witches with heretics in those parts of Christendom where loyalty to an authoritarian Church with narrowly defined goals was demanded. Nor may their decline be attributed entirely to the rise of rationalism. A more probable cause is the emergence of a large-scale society in which many relationships are impersonal and segmental. In such a society, disturbances in those relationships that remain personal and total may be isolated, compartmentalized and expressed in forms that do not necessarily require a belief in mystical personal influence, a belief which is basic to the formulation of social tensions in terms of sorcery and witchcraft.

APPENDIX A

ADDITIONAL GENEALOGIES

1. *Tenje's Section, Matope Village*

THIS genealogy illustrates the typical social composition of a Ceŵa village-section.

2. *Matope's Section, Matope Village* (abridged)

This genealogy represents a variation from the typical pattern, caused by an abnormally high proportion of virilocal marriages.

3. *Hut Plan of Matope Village*

Note that Tenje's section (Huts Nos. 39–47) is segregated from the other sections of the village because, at the time when it was studied, it had only recently joined the village.

4. *Cimseleti's Section, Jeremiah Village* (see end folder)

This genealogy illustrates the typical social composition of a Ceŵa village-section. Note that it includes the small section of Maiwase (B.13), the second wife of Cuzu (B.12). Maiwase's section appears to be developing into an independent one; it is already spatially segregated.

The legend and hut plan of Fig. 3 apply to this genealogy.

5. *Potokosi's Section, Jeremiah Village* (see end folder)

This genealogy deviates from the typical pattern in having an abnormally high proportion of virilocal marriages; and it is complicated by (*a*) the inter-twining of long-associated matrilineages and (*b*) the fact that the section has recently come from Portuguese territory, where many of its members have been left.

The legend and hut plan of Fig. 3 apply to this genealogy.

297

APPENDIX A, Nos. 1, 2 and 3

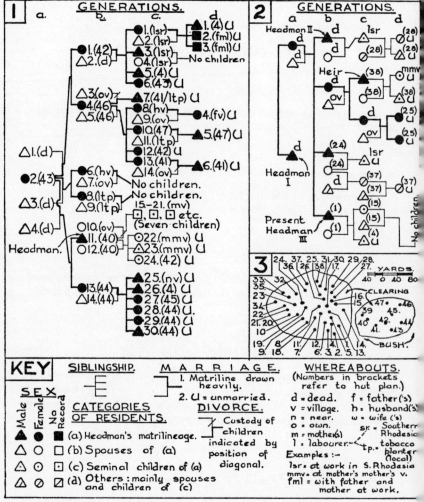

Genealogies of two of the sections and hut plan of Matope Village, Fort Jameson
District, Northern Rhodesia

(Diagram reproduced by kind permission of the Editor of the *South African
Journal of Science*)

(1) Tenje's, illustrating the typical social composition of a Cewa village section.
(2) Matope's (abridged), illustrating a variation from the typical pattern caused by
an abnormally high proportion of virilocal marriages.
(3) Hut plan: Tenje's section (Huts Nos. 39–47) is segregated from the other
sections because it joined the village only recently.

SOME EXAMPLES OF CEŴA STORIES

1. *Hare and Lion's Children*[1]

LION had four children. One day he met Hare and asked him, 'Would you like to work as the nurse of my children?' Hare said: 'Yes, Great Chief, I should like to very much.' So, Lion then left all his children with Hare and went to hunt game. While he was away, Hare played with the children on the sand, saying, 'You and you wrestle with each other, and the one that falls is game.' One fell down, and was eaten. This went on until three children had been eaten and only one remained. Then Hare said, 'All right, you who remain and I shall wrestle and we'll see who is knocked over.' They actually wrestled and Hare was knocked over, but he said to the lion cub, 'If you eat me, with whom will you remain?' And they wrestled again, and the lion cub was knocked down, and Hare ate him.

Now Hare said, 'But what am I to say to Lion?' He made a plan and took thorns and scratched himself all over his body and began to weep. Lion returned and on arrival asked, 'Why are you crying, Hare?' Hare replied 'Sorry, Great Chief, but Baboon seized all the children and ate them.' And Lion said, 'Now what are we to do?' Hare replied: 'I have already thought of a plan. I shall tie you in a bundle of sweet potatoes, and then we'll go and trade with the baboons.' They actually did as they had planned, and Hare carried the bundle to the baboons, asking them, 'Who wants to buy sweet potatoes?' He called them all to come close, but one of the baboon children who was there kept saying, 'There is a big eye in the bundle.' Hare therefore said, 'Come on, let us go and trade in the house.' And they all entered the house. Then Hare closed the door. Lion sprang out of the bundle and caught all the baboons, and that was the end of them.

2. *Hare, Tortoise and Their Fellow Animals*[2]

It happened like this. All the animals could not drink water because all the streams had run dry. They came to an agreement that they would dig for water; and they sent Antelope to go and beg a water-charm[3] from Rock

---

[1] My translation of the original told by Vinancio Nthukwa.
[2] My translation of the original told by Kosmos Banda.
[3] *Ciẓimba ca madẓi. Ciẓimba* usually means an activating agent added to otherwise inert

Rabbit (Hyrax), who lived on a hill; for Rock Rabbit appears to live without drinking water, and we do not know where he drinks it. Rock Rabbit told Antelope to go and dig beside the *caŋgaluce* tree to be found in the *dambo*. Antelope ran fast, but, as he descended the hill, he fell down and forgot what Rock Rabbit had said.

When Antelope came to his fellow animals, he named another tree; and, when they dug, they found no water. Then they sent another animal to Rock Rabbit, but he did exactly the same as Antelope. This happened again and again, until nearly all the animals had been sent and had returned without the charm. There remained only Hare and Tortoise. But Hare refused to go and beg the charm from Rock Rabbit, and his fellow animals chased him away, saying, 'If you come and beg water here, you'll die of thirst.' And, having spoken thus, they sent Tortoise to beg for the water-charm. When he arrived, Rock Rabbit said: 'But I've already said that you must dig beneath the *caŋgaluce* tree in the *dambo*.' And Tortoise listened carefully, not wishing to forget what he had been told; and, on his return, he did not fall down. Thus Tortoise returned safely, and they succeeded in digging a water-hole.

At the water-hole they placed a guard who might keep Hare away if he came to drink water there. But Hare always came with honey in order to bribe the one on guard to let him drink water. And all the animals failed to guard the water-hole properly because they liked honey. But there came the time for Tortoise to guard the water-hole. He didn't care for honey, and he asked the others to smear bird-lime on his back so that, when Hare came, he would think that his shell was something to sit on. When Hare arrived, he saw what he thought to be a small stone, and he sat on it, dangling his legs in the water. And, because he knew nothing about Tortoise's plan, he thought that there was no one guarding the water-hole; but in fact he was sitting on Tortoise's back. And he began to boast, saying that they were now afraid of him because they had failed to place a guard at the water-hole. When Hare wanted to depart, he found that he was stuck, and he tried in many ways to get away, but in vain.

Eventually the others found him there, properly stuck. And when all the animals had assembled, Elephant said, 'You are going to die today.' And he asked him, 'Where do you want to be killed?' And Hare replied: 'I want you to kill me in a bush, because, if you try to kill me on a stone, I'll certainly remain alive, and, if you try to kill me in a bush, I'll certainly die because dirt will get into my eyes.' And all the animals shouted together: 'Kill him by throwing him into a bush so that he'll really die.' But in fact the bush was very soft and he was not killed when he landed there. He ran away as fast as he could, and was saved.

After a few days, the rains came again, and the water-supply was restored.

---

root concoctions to make them potent. But for its un-African flavour, 'spell' might have been a better translation than 'charm'.

3. *Hyena and the Hospitable Headman*[1]

Long ago there was an hospitable [human] headman who used to receive all who came to his village. If they needed food, he gave it to them. Now there was a certain person who went to the village of the hospitable headman, and his name was Lion. Lion came to the village and approached the headman, saying, 'I need a sleeping place because time has overtaken me so that I am unable to pass on to my home village.' And the headman gave him a place to sleep in, and he asked his guest: 'Have you food with you that you may eat today?' And his guest replied, 'No, I have no food because I thought that I would reach home today.' So, the hospitable headman said: 'Lion, go into the cattle byre and eat one large ox.' And Lion in fact went there and caught one beast, as the headman had told him, and, having eaten it, went to the hut the headman had given him for the night.

Next day, at daybreak, Lion went to take leave of the headman and to thank him for the hospitality he had enjoyed in his village. And the headman said, 'Go to the byre and eat one other beast before you leave for home.' And Lion caught one other beast, and, having eaten it, went on his way.

Now, when Leopard heard about this from Lion, he, too, made a journey to the village of the hospitable headman, arriving there in the afternoon. He approached the headman and said: 'I would like a place to sleep in because time has overtaken me, and I cannot get home today.' The headman said: 'Go and sleep in that hut'; and he asked him, 'Have you food with you that you may eat today?' And Leopard replied, 'No, I have no food because I thought that I would reach the place to which I am going before the end of the day; so, please help me.' And the headman told Leopard: 'Go to the goat-pen and catch one big goat.' And Leopard went and caught one and ate it.

Next morning, at daybreak, Leopard went to the headman to take his leave and thank him for the hospitality he had enjoyed. But the headman said, 'Go again to the goat-pen and take another little goat and eat it before going home.' And Leopard went and caught one, as his host had told him, and then went home.

When he arrived home, he told Hyena the story of the hospitable headman who received people well, giving them food according to their kind. When Hyena heard this, he made a journey to the village of the hospitable headman, and, having arrived, said to him: 'I would like somewhere to sleep because the place to which I am going is so far that I shall be unable to reach it today.' And the headman said, 'All right, sleep in that hut over there'; and he asked him, 'Have you food with you that you may eat today?' And Hyena replied: 'No, I have no food because I thought that I would reach the place to which I am going before the end of the day; so, please help me.' And the headman told Hyena, 'Go to the pig-pen and eat one large pig'; and Hyena went and caught a large pig and ate it. When he had finished, he went to sleep in the hut the headman had assigned to him.

[1] My translation of the original told by Thandford Phili.

In the middle of the night, Hyena awoke and went to the pig-pen and caught all the pigs and took them to the bush. But the people heard the noise and came out of their houses; and, when they saw it was Hyena, they killed him.

So, Hyena died because of his thieving ways; and the headman gave up helping people who came to sleep at his village because of the case of Hyena. Hyena brought misfortune to all the people who sought the headman's hospitality. And that is why, even to this day, people hate Hyena for his thieving ways and for his having ended the friendship between people and the hospitable headman.

4. *Pimbilimani of Original Plan*[1]

A certain person had a male child whose name was Pimbilimani of Original Plan. And one day Pimbilimani's mother went to the stream to get water. When she had drawn water, she was unable to raise the jar on to her head, and Lion came along. She said, 'Please, Lion, help me put this on my head.' Lion replied: 'And if I put it on your head, what will you give me?' And that woman said, 'But I'll give you my child to eat; he's at the village.' Lion agreed, and helped her with the jar.

Next morning Lion came, and the woman said, 'But wait a little, and while I prepare the traps on the verandah of the house, you hide yourself near at hand; and, when the trap falls, I'll tell him to go and see the trap that has fallen; when he comes, then you can catch him.' The trap fell, and the woman said 'Pimbilimani, go and see the trap that has fallen,' but the child said, 'But my trap falls twice'; and the trap fell again, and he said, 'That trap of mine falls three times'—and thus he did not go.

And the woman said to Lion, 'All right, now I'll tie you in a bundle of grass, and I'll tell Pimbilimani to go and lift the bundle of grass, and at that time you can catch him'; and the woman actually tied up a bundle of grass with Lion inside it. She told Pimbilimani: 'Go and carry the bundle of grass on the path.' Pimbilimani told his companions, 'My companions, come along, let's go and carry the bundle of grass on the path.' His companions assented, and Pimbilimani said, 'But first you must shoot at this bundle of the adults.' They made small bows and began to shoot at the bundle. Very soon Lion ran away. And Pimbilimani took the grass to his mother.

Lion went again to the mother of the child and said, 'I've been unable to eat your child; now, therefore, I am going to eat you, his mother.' But the boy's mother said, 'But I'll buy him a white cloth and, when he is in the boys' hut, you'll know which he is and you'll be able to catch him.' And the boy's mother bought her son a white cloth; but, when he went to the boys' hut, he tore up the whole of that cloth and divided it among his companions. When Lion came, he asked: 'Which is Pimbilimani in here—the one with a white

---

[1] My translation of the original by Natalia Banda.

cloth?' But Pimbilimani replied, 'Look, we've all got white cloths; so, whom are you going to catch?' Therefore Lion did nothing.

From that time, Pimbilimani realized that his mother wanted to feed him to Lion. So, he killed his mother and made a belt from the skin of her belly.

At the village of his maternal uncle, they heard that Pimbilimani was very famous. And his uncle called him to his village. On his journey there, Pimbilimani took these animals: a mouse, a wood-borer, a spider, a rat and a water-rat. And he began his journey. After walking a long way, he found there was a big hill shutting off the whole path; and he took the mouse and it made a tunnel through it. And they all went on. Secondly, they came to a big lake which was impossible to cross; so, they took a spider-web so that it could be their bridge, and on it they actually made a bridge and they all crossed the lake. They went on many miles, and they encountered an enormous tree shutting off the whole path; but Pimbilimani simply took the wood-borer and told it to make a hole through the tree; and it actually made a hole, and they all went on well. Fourthly, they came to a big bush; now he sent the water-rat, saying, 'Now make our path that we may go in it'; and the water-rat actually made a path through the bush. Eventually they came to the village of his maternal uncle. All these things that he had encountered on the road had been caused by the sorcery of his maternal uncle.

His uncle killed a beast, and they cooked food. When they were cooking, Pimbilimani sent the rat, saying, 'Go and look at the food.' The rat actually went, and returned, saying, 'They've put "medicines" in your food; so, you must eat our food.' And so it happened that Pimbilimani did as the rat had said.

Next morning, at daybreak, his uncle took his bow and shot a pigeon which was in a nearby tree. He actually killed the pigeon, but the arrow remained in the tree. And he told Pimbilimani to climb up there so that he could retrieve the arrow. And Pimbilimani said, 'But you must look after this belt of mine.' And his uncle tied the belt round his belly. Now, when Pimbilimani had climbed up, his uncle uttered a magical address, saying to him, 'You, if you saw this tree being planted, let the tree not go up; but, if you did not see the tree being planted, let the tree go right up!' And the tree actually went up very high. And he, too, right up there, Pimbilimani, said, 'But I, too, if you recognize that belt of mine that you tied round your belly, it doesn't matter. But if you don't know where I got that belt, belt of mine, contract on the belly!' And the belt gripped very hard on his uncle's belly, so that that person told the tree to come down. And in this way they failed to overcome each other.

ACKNOWLEDGEMENTS TO OTHER WRITERS ON SORCERY AND WITCHCRAFT

MY approach to the sociology of sorcery has been influenced mainly by the material on African societies, especially the writing of the following:

Evans-Pritchard, whose pioneering study of witchcraft, oracles and magic as components of a people's philosophies of causation and morality (*Witchcraft among the Azande*, 1937) has become the model and source of definitions and lines for further development for all subsequent research workers.

Monica Wilson (*née* Hunter), who relates witchcraft to jealousy and hatred, reports on the social categories to which accused witches belong and explores the moral implications of witchcraft in a changing society (*Reaction to Conquest*, 1936), links differences in beliefs with differences in social structure ('Witch Beliefs and the Social Structure', 1951), presents classified lists of cases, and refers to accusations as well as believed attacks (*Good Company*, 1951, and [with three collaborators] *Social Structure*, 1952).

J. D. Krige, who, attributing witchcraft and sorcery to interpersonal tensions, shows the importance of institutional controls on the expression of such tensions in terms of witchcraft and sorcery (*The Realm of a Rain Queen* [with E. J. Krige], 1943, and 'The Social Function of Witchcraft', 1947).

Schapera, who distinguishes between the prevalence of beliefs in sorcery and people's preoccupation with them, which may be no more marked than ours with fears of traffic accidents, and, on finding a large proportion of his sample of believed attacks between persons in close personal association, suggests that an important difference between modern and Tswana society is that separation may be resorted to as a means of avoiding tensions in the former but not in the latter ('Oral Sorcery among the Natives of Bechuanaland', 1934, and 'Sorcery and Witchcraft in Bechuanaland', 1952).

Gluckman, who has appreciated the wide applicability of Evans-Pritchard's concepts (*Economy of the Central Barotse Plain*, 1941, 'The Logic of African Science and Witchcraft', 1944) and has shown the part played by conflicts built into social processes in the genesis of accusations of witchcraft (*Custom and Conflict*, 1955).

Nadel, who, though he handles too many variables for clarity, shows the link between key social relationships in a society and the form taken by its witch-beliefs ('Witchcraft in Four African Societies', 1952, and *Nupe Religion*, 1954) and accounts for the shortcomings in Malinowski's contribution to this branch of sociology ('Malinowski on Magic and Religion', 1957).

Mayer, who provides a concise but penetrating summary of the sociology of witchcraft (*Witches*, 1954).

Mitchell ('A Note on the African Conception of Causality', 1951, and *The Yao Village*, 1956) and Turner (*Schism and Continuity*, 1957), who analyse the part played by accusations of witchcraft in the developmental sequences of community life.

Among writers on other areas and periods, I have found the following stimulating:

Malinowski, who analyses the emotional and social aspects of magic and witchcraft (which he does not distinguish from sorcery) (*Magic, Science and Religion and Other Essays*, 1948 [main essay first published in 1925]) and recognizes the conservative function of beliefs in sorcery (*Crime and Custom*, 1926).

Kluckhohn, who, in spite of an unsuccessful psychological analysis, offers some useful sociological hints (*Navaho Witchcraft*, 1944).

B. B. Whiting, who examines sorcery as a form of social control (*Paiute Sorcery*, 1950).

M. A. Murray, who, though straining to support a doubtful hypothesis, has insight into the moral aspects of witchcraft (*The Witch-Cult in Western Europe*, 1921, 'Witchcraft', 1929, and *The God of the Witches*, 1933).

Ewen, who, more soberly, documents the links between witchcraft, religion, satanism and politics in British history (*Witch Hunting and Witch Trials*, 1929, and *Witchcraft and Demonianism*, 1933).

Davies, who carries Ewen's work further, especially regarding politics (*Four Centuries of Witch-Belief*, 1947).

Starkey (*The Devil in Massachusetts*, 1950), who, through imaginative use of sources such as Burr (*Narratives of the Witchcraft Cases, 1648–1706*, 1914), builds up a plausible picture of the rôle of accusers in the special moral climate of late seventeenth-century New England.

SELECT ANNOTATED BIBLIOGRAPHY
OF THE CEŴA

Notes:

1. This bibliography contains a few references to other 'Nyanja-speaking peoples' where similarities to the Ceŵa are close.

2. The following works are listed in both this and the General Bibliography: Barnes, 1951 and 1954; and Marwick, 1952a.

3. If an item is not in English, the language in which it is written is indicated in square brackets at the beginning of the note referring to it.

4. Square brackets in the title show what part of it has been omitted in the abbreviated form (if any) used in footnote references.

5. The places of publication of lesser-known journals referred to are as follows:

Die Basuin	Bloemfontein
Die Huisgenoot	Cape Town
Die Koningsbode	Cape Town
Op die Horison	Cape Town
Theoria	Pietermaritzburg

ANON.

n.d. *Cinyanja Spreekwoorde.* No publisher or place of publication. Probably Mkhoma, Nyasaland: Dutch Reformed Church Mission Press.

[Afrikaans] A selection of proverbs in Nyanja.

n.d. *Mdulo.* No publisher or place of publication. Probably as for previous item at a date early in the twentieth century.

[Archaic Afrikaans] Symptoms and believed causes of *mdulo*, a disease attributed to ritual contamination; occasions on which steps to avoid it are taken.

Anuário da Província de Moçambique

1952–3. Lourenço Marques: A. W. Bayly and Co., Ltd.

[Portuguese] Contains population figures for the Tete district.

ATKINS, Guy

1950a. 'The Nyanja-Speaking Population of Nyasaland and Northern Rhodesia (a Statistical Estimate)', *African Studies*, 9, 35–9.

Refers to 1948–9, includes Nseŋga-speaking Fort Jameson Ŋgoni, and makes estimates of Ceŵa under non-Ceŵa chiefs.

1950b. '[Suggestions for an] Amended Spelling and Word Division of Nyanja', *Africa*, 20, 200–18.

The basis of the orthography used in this study.

1952. (ed.) *Uŋkhoswe waaNyanja* by Bennett E. MALEKEBU, q.v.

AXELSON, Eric

1940. *South-East Africa, 1488–1530*, London: Longmans, Green and Co.
Deals with Portuguese settlement at Sofala and on the Zambezi in the early sixteenth century, and refers to early Arab penetration.

BANDA, Hastings

1946. (ed. with T. Cullen YOUNG, q.v.) *Our African Way of Life.*

BARNES, J[ohn] A[rundel]

1951. *Marriage in a Changing Society*, Rhodes-Livingstone Papers, No. 20, Cape Town: Oxford University Press for Rhodes-Livingstone Institute.
Fort Jameson Ŋgoni marriage, including influences on Ceŵa and *vice versa.*

1954. *Politics in a Changing Society*, Cape Town: Oxford University Press for Rhodes-Livingstone Institute.
Detailed history of Ŋgoni invasion, early administration and land in Fort Jameson district.

BARRETTO, Manoel

1667. *Report upon the State and Conquest of the Rivers of Cuama*, trans. in Vol. 3, 463–95 and 502–8, of *Records of South-Eastern Africa*, collected by George M'Call THEAL, q.v.
Early references to the Maravi.

BEADLE, B. A.

1873. (trans.) 'Journey of the Pombeiros P. J. Baptista and Amaro José [across Africa from Angola to Tette on the Zambeze]', q.v.

BOCARRO, Antonio

1876. 'Extracts from the Decade Written by Antonio Bocarro', in Vol. 3, pp. 254 ff., of *Records of South-Eastern Africa*, collected by George M'Call THEAL, q.v.
Written in seventeenth century. Contains journal of Gaspar Bocarro who went from Tete to Kilwa in 1616.

BRITISH SOUTH AFRICA COMPANY

1889–1892 ⎫
1892–1894 ⎬ *Report on the Company's Proceedings and the Conditions of the*
1896–1897 ⎭ *Territories within the Sphere of Its Operations.*

1897–1898 ⎫
1898–1900 ⎬ *Report on the Administration of Rhodesia.*
1900–1902 ⎭

Early administration, cattle, labour migration.

BRUWER, J[ohannes P. van S.]

1937–8. 'Die Rasse onder Wie Ons Kerk Arbei', *Die Basuin*, 8, 2, 14–15; 8, 4, 17–19; 8, 5, 18–20; 9, 1, 14–16; 9, 3, 5–6; 9, 4, 15–16; 9, 5, p. 6.
[Afrikaans] Some items of traditional history.

1939. 'Huweliksgewoontes onder die Acewa', *Die Basuin*, 10: 1, p. 13; 2, 12–14; 3, 9–11; 4, p. 10.
[Afrikaans] Ceŵa marriage customs.

1943. 'By Ons Is 'n Haantjie', *Die Huisgenoot*, 14 May.
[Afrikaans] Entertaining account of Ceŵa marriage.

1943–4. 'Godsbegrippe, Aanbidding en Geloof in Bonatuurlike Magte onder die Acewa van Noord-Rhodesië', *Op die Horison*, 5, 146–9; 6, 5–11.
[Afrikaans] Northern Rhodesian Ceŵa cult of spirits, supreme being, magic, sorcery and divination.

1948. 'Kinship Terminology [among the Ceŵa of the Eastern Province of Northern Rhodesia]', *African Studies*, 7, 185–7.

1949. *Die Gesin onder die Moederregtelike Acewa*, unpublished M.A. thesis, University of Pretoria.
[Afrikaans] Northern Rhodesian Ceŵa: traditional history, everyday life, village composition; development and structure of the family and its part in tribal life; recreation; the three-generation system. Rich in linguistic idiom and ethnographic detail. Being centred on the elementary family, misses the importance of consanguineal organization.

1950. 'Note on Maravi Origin and Migration', *African Studies*, 9, 32–4.
Suggests origins of names 'Cewa' and 'Malawi'.

1951. 'Korswelverhoudings en die Belangrikheid Daarvan by Begrafnisge-bruike', *Op die Horison*, 13, 24–33.
[Afrikaans] Joking relationships. Identifies funeral friends with grand-children.

1952a. 'The Kinship Basis of Ceŵa Social Structure', Correspondence in the *South African Journal of Science*, 49, 17–20.

1952b. 'Remnants of a Rain Cult among the Acewa', *African Studies*, 11, 179–82.
Traditional rain-cult described to the author at the time of the 1948 drought.

BURTON, [Sir] R[ichard] F[rancis]

1873. (trans. and annotator) 'Lacerda's Journey to Cazembe in 1798', q.v.

BYATT, H. A.

1900. 'Chewa-Land', *British Central Africa Gazette*, 30 June.
Early administrator's impressions.

CENTRAL AFRICAN STATISTICAL OFFICE

1952. *Report on the 1950 Demographic Sample Survey of the African Population of Northern Rhodesia.*
Estimates population, crude death-rates and infant mortality rates.

1954. *Monthly Digest of Statistics for the Federation of Rhodesia and Nyasaland,* 1, 3.

CLARK, J. Desmond

1950. 'A Note on the Pre-Bantu Inhabitants of Northern Rhodesia', *The Northern Rhodesia Journal,* 11, 42–52.

CODRINGTON, R.

1896. 'Central Angoniland (Extracts from a Report)', *British Central Africa Gazette,* 15 September.
Some Nyasaland Ceŵa who resisted Ŋgoni.

1898. 'The Central Angoniland District [of the British Central Africa Protectorate]', *Geographical Journal,* 11, 509–22.
Ceŵa defences against Ŋgoni; clothing; early administration.

COXHEAD, J. C. C.

1914. (ed.) *The Native Tribes [of North-Eastern Rhodesia],* Royal Anthropological Institute Occasional Papers, No. 5.
Political organization, land tenure, marriage, divorce, early administration.

1922. *Northern Rhodesia: A Handbook,* Livingstone: Government Printer.

CUNNISON, Ian

1960. trans. of GAMITTO, q.v.

DEARE, George Russell ('A Durban Man')

1929. 'Eighteen Months with the Last of the Slave Raiders' and other titles, *Week-End [Natal] Advertiser* (Durban), six consecutive articles, 6 April to 11 May.
Independence of Cimwala and Undi in 1897.

DE LACERDA E ALMEIDA, Francisco José Maria

1873. 'Lacerda's Journey to Cazembe in 1798', q.v.

DOS SANTOS JÚNIOR, J. R.

1944. *Algumas Tribos do Distrito de Tete,* Pôrto: República Portuguesa, Ministério das Colonias.
[Portuguese] Physical anthropology of tribes of the Tete district of Moçambique. Contains climatic data and population statistics.

DOS SANTOS, João

1609. *Ethiopia Oriental,* trans. in *Records of South-Eastern Africa,* collected by George M'Call THEAL, q.v. (Vol. 7, pp. 290 ff.)
[Portuguese] Early references to tribes on north bank of Zambezi.

DULY, A. W. R.

1948. 'The Lower Shire District: [Notes on Land Tenure and Individual Rights]', *Nyasaland Journal*, 1, 2, 11–44.
Includes a reference to Undi as the great chief of the Maravi.

DU PLESSIS, J.

1905. *A Thousand Miles in the Heart of Africa*, Edinburgh: Oliphant, Anderson and Ferrier.
Records a visit to Central Nyasaland at the beginning of the twentieth century.

EAST AFRICAN STATISTICAL DEPARTMENT

1954. *Unpublished Official Source*, Letter dated 1 March.
The Nyanja-speaking population of Tanganyika Territory.

EYBERS, Jessie H.

1942. *Volksgewoontes en Bygelowe in Niassaland*, Stellenbosch: the Author and C. S. V.-Boekhandel.
[Afrikaans] Systematic though sometimes expurgated ethnography of the Nyasaland Cewa.

FOÀ, Édouard

1901. *Du Cap au Lac Nyassa*, Paris: Plon-Nourrit et Cie, 2nd ed.
[French] Undi's capital at the turn of the century. Ŋgoni raids.

FRASER, R. H.

1945. 'Land Settlement in the Eastern Province of Northern Rhodesia', *Human Problems in British Central Africa*, 3, 45–9.

GAMITTO, A[ntonio] C[andido] P[edroso]

1854. *O Muata Cazembe*, Lisboa: Imprensa Nacional. Trans. as *King Kazembe* by Ian CUNNISON, Lisboa: Junta de Investigações do Ultramar: Centro de Estudos Políticos e Sociais, Estudos de Ciências Políticas e Sociais, Nos. 42 and 43, 1960.
[Portuguese] Includes detailed, objective, systematic and highly competent series of observations on Maravi and Cewa life in 1831–2, covering *inter alia* tribal dispositions; chieftainship, headmanship and matrilineal succession; material culture, including iron-working; diet; dress; trade; judicial procedures; religion, including rain-making; funeral friendship; sorcery; and the poison ordeal.

GARBUTT, H. W.

1911a. 'Native Customs in Nyasa (Manganja) Yao (Achawa)', *Proceedings of the Rhodesia Science Association*, 11, 87–96.
Maŋanja nepotal inheritance of widows; witchcraft.

1911b. 'Witchcraft in Nyasa (Manganja) Yao (Achawa)', *Journal of the Royal Anthropological Institute*, 41, 301–5.

GENTHE, Hugo

1897. 'A Trip to Mpezeni's', *British Central Africa Gazette*, 1 August.
Effects of an Ŋgoni attack on a Cewa village.

HAMILTON, R. A.

1954. 'The Route of Gaspar Bocarro from Tete to Kilwa in 1616', *Nyasaland Journal*, 7, 2, 7–14.
Critical examination of G. Bocarro's route journal.

1955. 'Oral Tradition: Central Africa' in *History and Archaeology in Africa*, ed. by R. A. HAMILTON, London: School of Oriental and African Studies.
Reconciles the conflict between myths of local creation and of the immigration of the Maravi by suggesting that the latter apply, not to the whole people, but chiefly to invaders who encountered long-established lineage-organized peoples.

HETHERWICK, Alexander

1929. *Dictionary of the Nyanja Language*, London: Lutterworth Press for United Society for Christian Literature.
Revision of David Clement SCOTT's *Encyclopaedic Dictionary* (q.v.). Retains some of its ethnographic notes.

HODGSON, A. G. O.

1933. 'Notes on the Achewa and Angoni [of the Dowa District of the Nyasaland Protectorate]', *Journal of the Royal Anthropological Institute*, 63, 123–66.
Notes on: Cewa origin; conquest by Ŋgoni; *mdulo* (disorder resulting from ritual contamination); initiation; marriage and domestic relations; clans; *nyau* (mimes produced by men's secret society); rain-making; funerary rituals; and beliefs in spirits.

HOFMEYR, A. L.

1910. *Het Land langs het Meer*, Stellenbosch: De Christen Studenten Vereniging van Zuid Afrika.
[Dutch] Divorce; supreme being; spirits; witchcraft.

HUGO, G. F.

1940. 'Die Jeugprobleem in Ons Nyasasendingveld Veral met Betrekking tot die Achewa', *Op die Horison*, 2, 38–43.
[Afrikaans] Nyasaland Cewa: traditional initiation; maternal uncle's authority; effects on youth of Christianization.

JOHNSTON, Sir Harry H[amilton]

1894. *Report by Commissioner Johnston of the First Three Years' Administration of the Eastern Portion of British Central Africa*, London: H.M. Stationery Office, C. 7504, Africa No. 6.
An administrator's impressions of the Nyanja-speaking peoples, including Cewa.

1897. *British Central Africa*, London: Methuen and Co.
Tribal dispositions at the turn of the century. Nyanja beliefs relating to ritual contamination (*mdulo*); sorcerers' fire, necrophagy, familiars; the poison ordeal; methods of addressing harmful medicines.

1873. 'Journey of the Pombeiros P. J. Baptista and Amaro José [across Africa from Angola to Tette on the Zambeze]', trans. by B. A. BEADLE in *The Lands of Cazembe*, q.v.
Simple route journal of two bondsmen sent from Angola to Cazembe in 1806 and who travelled from Cazembe to Tete in 1810, returning to Angola in 1810–11. Refers to Mkanda (Mocanda) as 'Caronga'.

'W. D. L.'
1950. ' "Machemba"—Primitive Citadels', *Nyasaland Journal*, 3, 34–7.
Cewa fortifications in Central Nyasaland.

1873. 'Lacerda's Journey to Cazembe in 1798', trans. and annotated by Sir Richard Francis BURTON in *The Lands of Cazembe*, q.v.
Translation, with extensive footnotes and map, of the diary of F. J. M. DE LACERDA E ALMEIDA on his journey through Maravi country.

1873. *The Lands of Cazembe*, London: John Murray for the Royal Geographical Society.

LAWSON, Audrey
1949. 'An Outline of the Relationship System of the Nyanja and Yao Tribes in South Nyasaland', *African Studies*, 7, 180–98.
Kinship in Nyanja homestead organization.

LIVINGSTONE, David and Charles
1866. [*Narrative of an Expedition to*] *the Zambesi and Its Tributaries*, New York: Harper and Brothers.
References to Undi's 'empire'; *Pondoro* (lion diviner); witchcraft and the poison ordeal.

'W. H. M.'
1896. 'The Achewa', *British Central Africa Gazette*, 15 December.
Clothing; wooden hoes; and fortified villages.

MACDONALD, J.
1893. 'East Central African Customs', *Journal of the Anthropological Institute*, 22, 99–122.
Importance of having a following; slavery; detection of witches. Which tribes referred to not always clear.

MAIR, Lucy P.

1951. 'Marriage and Family in the Dedza District of Nyasaland', *Journal of the Royal Anthropological Institute*, 81, 103–19.

Domestic organization in area of Ŋgoni, Ceŵa and Ntumba admixture.

MAKUMBI, Archibald J.

1955. *Maliro ndi Myambo ya Acewa*, Cape Town: Longmans, Green and Co.

[Nyanja] Ceŵa customs relating to funerals of various types, with incidental references to *nyau* (mimes produced at certain funerals by a men's secret society).

MALEKEBU, Bennett E.

1952. *Uŋkhoswe waaNyanja*, Annotated African Texts: I: Maŋanja, ed. by Guy ATKINS, Cape Town: Oxford University Press for School of Oriental and African Studies.

[Nyanja with English translation and notes] Excellent account of guardianship of female dependants (*nbumba*) among the South Nyanja who, in this respect at least, closely resemble the Ceŵa. Editor's notes include some references to burial friendship.

MARWICK, M[axwell] G[ay]

1950. 'Another Anti-Witchcraft Movement in East Central Africa', *Africa*, 20, 100–12.

The Bwanali-Mpulumutsi movement of 1947.

1952a. 'The Social Context of Ceŵa Witch Beliefs', *Africa*, 22, 120–35 and 215–33.

Ceŵa social organization and beliefs in witchcraft [referred to as sorcery in this study], followed by an analysis of twenty cases of misfortune attributed to witchcraft [sorcery].

1952b. 'The Kinship Basis of Ceŵa Social Structure', *South African Journal of Science*, 48, 258–62.

Ceŵa consanguineal organization described and illustrated by genealogies.

1956. 'An Experiment in Public Opinion Polling [among Preliterate People]', *Africa*, 26, 149–59.

Discussion of technical problems involved.

1961. 'The Role of the Social Anthropologist in Assessing Development Programmes' in *Social Research and Community Development*, ed. by Raymond APTHORPE, Conference Proceedings of the Rhodes-Livingstone Institute, No. 15, Lusaka: Rhodes-Livingstone Institute.

Presents, with qualifications, results of the public opinion poll referred to in the last entry.

1963a. 'History and Tradition [in East Central Africa through the Eyes of the Northern Rhodesian Ceŵa]' *Journal of African History*, 4, 375–90.

1963b. 'A Note on Ordeal Poison in East Central Africa', *Man*, 63, 45-6.

(in preparation) 'Cattle Ownership and Labour Migration [Two Aspects of Recent Ceŵa Adjustment]'.

1968. 'Notes on Some Ceŵa Rituals', *African Studies*, 27, 3-14.

MICHAELIS, H. A.

n.d. *A New Dictionary of the Portuguese and English Languages* (in two parts), New York: Frederick Ungar Publishing Company.

Useful for checking Portuguese origin of certain Ceŵa words.

MOGGRIDGE, L. T.

1902. 'The Nyasaland Tribes: Their Customs and Their Ordeal Poison', *Journal of the Royal Anthropological Institute*, 32, 467-72.

MONTEIRO, José Manoel Corrêa

1854. *O Muata Cazembe* by A. C. P. GAMITTO, q.v., who was second-in-command and chronicler of the expedition led by MONTEIRO.

MURRAY, A[ndrew] C[harles]

1897. *Nyasaland en Mijne Ondervindingen Aldaar*, Amsterdam: Dusseau.

[Dutch] Nyasaland Ceŵa dress, language and religion at the turn of the century.

1931. *Ons Nyasa-Akker*, Stellenbosch: Pro-Ecclesia Drukkery.

[Afrikaans] History of Dutch Reformed Church Mission in Nyasaland. Includes Nyasaland Ceŵa indigenous religion, creation myths and poison ordeal.

MURRAY, S. S.

1932. *A Handbook of Nyasaland*, London: Crown Agents for the Colonies.

Includes ethnographic sections dealing with Ceŵa and Cipeta.

NORTH-EASTERN RHODESIA

1903. *Official Handbook*, Fort Jameson: Administration Press.

Early activities of white settlers. Indirect rule.

NORTHERN RHODESIA

1951. *Census, 1951*, Lusaka: Government Printer.

1929. *Report on Native Affairs for the Year 1929*, Livingstone: Government Printer.

1937. *Department of Native Affairs*, Annual Report on African Affairs, Livingstone: Government Printer.

1947. *Department of Native Affairs*, Annual Report on African Affairs, Lusaka: Government Printer.

1951. *Department of Native Affairs*, African Affairs: Annual Report, Lusaka: Government Printer.

NORTHERN RHODESIA—*contd.*

1952. *Department of Native Affairs*, African Affairs: Annual Report, Lusaka: Government Printer.

1953. *Department of Native Affairs*, African Affairs: Annual Report, Lusaka: Government Printer.

1929. *Laws*, Native Authorities Ordinance, No. 32 of 1929.

1936. *Laws*, Native Authority Ordinance, No. 9 of 1936.

1936. *Laws*, Native Courts Ordinance, No. 10 of 1936.

1948. *Laws*, Witchcraft Ordinance, No. 5 of 1914 as amended by No. 47 of 1948.

1943. *Report of the Ecological Survey* by C. G. TRAPNELL, q.v.

1947. *African Representative Council*, Debates.

(Various) *Unpublished Official Sources*. See appended list.

NTHARA (alt. NTARA), Samuel Yosia (alt. Josia)

1945. *Mbiri ya Acewa,* Zomba: Nyasaland Education Department.
    [Nyanja] A popular vernacular tribal history.

1949a. *Headman's Enterprise*, trans. and ed. with a preface by [T.] Cullen YOUNG, London: Lutterworth Press.
    Fictitious presentation of changes brought about by the advent of Christianity.

1949b. *Nchowa*, London: Longmans, Green and Co.
    [Nyanja] Fictitious biography of a Nyasaland Cewa woman.

NYASALAND PROTECTORATE

1946. *Report on the Census of 1945*, Zomba: Government Printer.

1951. *Unpublished Official Source*, Letter from the Chief Secretary, Nyasaland Government, dated 20 February 1955, concerning African population statistics.

POOLE, E. H. Lane

1929–30. 'The Date of the Crossing of the Zambezi by the Ngoni', *Journal of the African Society*, 29, 290–2.
    Fixed at November 1835. Good summary of repercussions.

1932. *Human Geography of Fort Jameson District*, unpublished MS., deposited at the Rhodes-Livingstone Institute, Lusaka.
    Detailed study of topography, climate, cultivation and seasonal activities in Fort Jameson district.

1949. *Native Tribes [of the Eastern Province of Northern Rhodesia]*, Lusaka: Government Printer, 3rd ed.
    Includes a fairly comprehensive history of the Maravi and their descendants in Northern Rhodesia, of the Ŋgoni invasions, and of the advent of Europeans to what is now the Eastern Province of Northern Rhodesia.

PRETORIUS, J. L.

1949. 'The Terms of Relationship [of the Ceŵa]', *Nyasaland Journal*, 2, 44–52.
Detailed on terminology and associated behaviour patterns among
Nyasaland Ceŵa. Identifies gravediggers with grandchildren.

PRICE, Thomas

1952. 'More about the Maravi', *African Studies*, 11, 75–9.
Disputes existence of modern tribe designated by variant of the name
Maravi.

RANGELEY, W. H. J.

1949. ' "Nyau" in Kotakota District', *Nyasaland Journal*, 2, 35–49, and 3,
19–33.
The most detailed study of *nyau* (mimes produced by men's secret society)
on record.

1951. 'Some Old Ceŵa Fortresses in the Kotakota District', *Nyasaland
Journal*, 4, 54–7.

1952. 'Two Nyasaland Rain Shrines', *Nyasaland Journal*, 5, 31–50.

1953. 'Mbona—the Rain Maker', *Nyasaland Journal*, 6, 8–27.

1954. 'Bocarro's Journey', *Nyasaland Journal*, 7, 15–23.

RATTRAY, R. Sutherland

1907. *Some Folk-Lore Stories and Songs in Chinyanja*, London: Society for
Promoting Christian Knowledge.
[Nyanja with annotated English translation] Ŋgoni customs, for the most
part borrowed from Cipeta and Ceŵa, including birth, girl's initiation,
marriage, death, poison ordeal, graveyard vigil, divining, change of
village site, rain-making, hunting, stories, songs and dances.

READ, Margaret [Helen]

1942. 'Migrant Labour [in Africa and Its Effect on Tribal Life]', *International
Labour Review*, 45, 605–31.
Effects of labour migration on Ŋgoni and Ceŵa compared.

1956. *The Ngoni of Nyasaland*, London: Oxford University Press for International African Institute.
Includes some references to Ceŵa.

RITA-FERREIRA, António

1958. *Agrupmento e Caracterização Étnica dos Indígenas de Moçambique*,
Lisboa: Ministério do Ultramar, Junta de Investigações do Ultramar.
[Portuguese with English summaries] Ethnic grouping of African popula-
tion of Moçambique. Shows Zimba to be a division of Ceŵa.

SCOTT, David Clement

1892. *A Cyclopaedic Dictionary of the Mang'anja Language*, Edinburgh: Foreign Mission Committee of the Church of Scotland.
Includes ethnographic notes.

SMITH, M. M.

1949. *Nkhani ya Idesi*, London: Longmans, Green and Co.
[Nyanja] Fictitious biography of a Nyanja woman.

STANNUS, H. S.

1910. 'Notes on Some Tribes [in British East Africa]', *Journal of the Royal Anthropological Institute*, 40, 285–335.
Sound, thorough study of many aspects of Nyanja life, including sorcery, steps taken against sorcerers; enumeration; barter equivalents of slaves; trade goods and local products; and funeral friendships.

STEENKAMP, D. J.

1945. 'Die Voedsel van die Acewa', *Op die Horison*, 7, 8–16, 59–69, and 107–115.
[Afrikaans] Nyasaland Ceŵa diet.

STEFANISZYN, B.

1954. 'African Reincarnation Re-Examined', *African Studies*, 13, 131–46.
Nominal reincarnation among Ceŵa and neighbouring peoples.

STEGMANN, J. J.

1933. 'Die Godsbegrip van die Acawa' [*sic*], *Die Koningsbode*, 44, 255–6 and 368–70.
[Afrikaans] Nyasaland Ceŵa indigenous religion.

STEGMANN, (?) (her late husband's initials, J. J., given)

1951. 'Kan en Behoort die Heidense Inisiasie deur 'n Christelike Vervang te Word?', *Op die Horison*, 13, 2–12.
[Afrikaans] Indigenous Nyasaland Ceŵa girl's initiation and new form of initiation introduced by Dutch Reformed Church Mission.

STEYTLER, John George

n.d. *Ethnographic Report on the Achewa Tribe of Nyasaland*, unpublished MS. prepared as a class assignment at Yale University.
Thorough, comprehensive ethnography of the Nyasaland Ceŵa. Rich in linguistic detail. The original source of references to the Ceŵa in the Yale Cross-Cultural Index (now Human Relations Area Files).

1939. *Educational Adaptations with Reference to African Village Schools*, London: Sheldon Press.
Careful examination of Nyasaland Ceŵa culture as providing foundations for Western education.

STIGAND, C. H.

1907. 'Notes on the Natives of Nyasaland, North-Eastern Rhodesia and Portuguese Zambesia', *Journal of the Royal Anthropological Institute*, 37, 119–32.
Miscellany of notes in varying detail on Ŋgoni, Yao, Cewa and Cipeta. At some points not clear which are referred to.

1909. 'Notes on the Tribes in the Neighbourhood of Fort Manning, Nyasaland', *Journal of the Royal Anthropological Institute*, 39, 35–43.
Cewa defences and Mwase's resistance to the Ŋgoni.

TEW (now DOUGLAS), Mary

1950. *Peoples of the Lake Nyasa Region*, Ethnographic Survey of Africa, ed. by [C.] Daryll FORDE, East Central Africa, Part I, London: Oxford University Press for International African Institute.
A synthesis of literature on the tribes of the region in which the Cewa live. Useful for tribal interrelationships, history and basic culture.

THEAL, George M'Call

1896. *The Portuguese in South Africa*, London: T. S. Unwin.
Early Portuguese settlement in south-eastern Africa.

1898–1903. *Records of South-Eastern Africa*, London: Wm. Clowes and Sons, Ltd, for the Government of the Cape Colony.
Contains translations of many early Portuguese records.

THOMSON, H[ugh] H.

n.d. *The Mbang'ombe Chieftainship*, unpublished notes.

THOMSON, T[homas] D.

n.d. *Preliminary Notes on the Constitution of Mwase's Chewa*, unpublished MS.
Describes the exceptionally well-organized Cewa kingdom of Mwase Kasuŋgu.

TRAPNELL C[olin] G.

1943. [*The Soils, Vegetation and Agriculture of*] *North-Eastern Rhodesia*, Report of the Ecological Survey, Lusaka: Government Printer.

UNITED KINGDOM

1900. *Statutory Rules and Orders*, The North-Eastern Rhodesia Order in Council.

1911. *Statutory Rules and Orders*, The Northern Rhodesia Order in Council.

1928. *Statutory Rules and Orders*, The Northern Rhodesia (Crown Lands and Native Reserves) Order in Council.

1936. *Statutory Rules and Orders*, The Northern Rhodesia (Native Reserves) Amendment Order in Council.

1947. *Statutory Rules and Orders*, The Northern Rhodesia (Native Trust Land) Order in Council.

VAN DER WALT, L. B.

1932a. 'Bygeloof in Verband met Tuinmaak', *Die Basuin*, 3, 3, p. 17.
[Afrikaans] 'Superstitions' relating to gardening.

1932b. 'Bygeloof in Verband met Siektes', *Die Basuin*, 3, 4, p. 6.
[Afrikaans] 'Superstitions' relating to illnesses.

VAN HEERDEN, J.

1951. 'Die Aanbidding en Gebede van die Heiden', *Op die Horison*, 13, 4,
11–17.
[Afrikaans] Nyasaland Ceŵa indigenous religion, including some prayers
to the spirits.

WERNER, Alice

1906. *The Natives of British Central Africa*, London: Archibald Constable and
Co., Ltd.
An entertaining, though not always reliable, introduction to Nyasaland
tribes at the turn of the century. References, where distinct, are most often
to Nyanja, Maŋanja and Yao.

WINTERBOTTOM, J. M.

1950. 'Outline Histories [of Two Northern Rhodesian Tribes]', *Human
Problems in British Central Africa*, 9, 14–25.
Includes a synthesis of Maravi traditions. Contains a mistaken reference
to the use by Lacerda of the name Cheva; and mistakenly gives the
Mkanda matriclan as Phili.

YOUNG, [T.] Cullen

1946. (trans. and ed. with Hastings BANDA) *Our African Way of Life*, London: Lutterworth Press for United Society for Christian Literature.
Nyasaland Ceŵa and Maŋanja life by three African authors, with a
translator's preface containing brief notes on Ceŵa origin and distribution; matrilineal organization; marriage; magic; and initiation.

1949. (trans.) *Headman's Enterprise*, by S. Y. NTHARA, q.v.

1950. 'Kinship among the Ceŵa of Rhodesia and Nyasaland', *African Studies*,
9, 29–31.
Traditional history. Regards Ceŵa as 'mother tribe' from which Nyanja
and others derived.

NORTHERN RHODESIA, *Unpublished Official Sources*

Eastern Province (formerly *East Luangwa District* and *East Luangwa Province*)
District Note Books (2 vols.), kept at Fort Jameson.

Annual Reports, Fort Jameson Division, 1912–13, 1914–15 and 1915–16, on
file at Fort Jameson.

Annual Reports, Fort Jameson Sub-District, 1917–18 and 1921–2, on file at Fort Jameson.

Annual Reports, Fort Jameson District, 1938, 1946 and 1951, on file at Fort Jameson.

Sundry Documents:

Recommendation from District Commissioner, Fort Jameson, to Provincial Commissioner, Eastern Province, dated 4 July 1934, recording Chief Kaŵaza's service as 'Paramount Chief of the Southern Chewa . . .', on file at Fort Jameson.

Certificate in possession of Chief Mkanda Mateyo, signed on 3 June 1935 by H.E. the then Governor of Northern Rhodesia, Sir Hubert Young, recording his service as 'Paramount Chief of the Northern Chewa . . .'

File entitled 'Lunacy Inquiry, from 1939 to 1944', Fort Jameson.

Annual Report of the Medical Department, 1951, on file at Fort Jameson.

Annual Report: Department of Agriculture, 1951, on file at Fort Jameson.

Chadiza Tour Report, No. 2 of 1952, on file at Fort Jameson.

Chewa Native Treasury Estimates, 1953, on file at Fort Jameson.

Provincial Team, Eastern Province Agricultural Economic Review, Report by a Sub-Committee (consulted early in 1953), on file at Fort Jameson.

Memorandum, dated 8 January 1953, recording areas of Ceŵa Reserve chiefdoms, on file at Chadiza.

Department of Forestry, Check List of Trees and Shrubs, loaned by the Provincial Forestry Officer, Fort Jameson.

Miscellaneous Interviews and Letters

Verbal communication from Native Courts Adviser, Lusaka, November 1952.

Discussion, early in 1953, with Provincial Medical Officer of the Eastern Province in Fort Jameson.

Verbal communication from Agricultural Supervisor, Katete, early in 1953.

Letter in March or April 1953 from District Commissioner, Fort Jameson, informing me of installation of A Obster Cibvuŋga as Paramount Chief Undi.

Letter, dated 29 September 1954, from Conservator of Forests, Ndola, regarding tentative identification of the Northern Rhodesian variety of *mwabvi* tree.

Letter, dated 4 April 1955, from Provincial Veterinary Officer, Fort Jameson, regarding cattle and small-stock statistics.

GENERAL BIBLIOGRAPHY

(See *Notes* at the beginning of the Select Annotated Bibliography
of the Cewa on p. 307)

ARENSBERG, Conrad M., *The Irish Countryman*, New York: The Macmillan Company, 1937.

BARBER, Bernard, 'Acculturation and Messianic Movements', *American Sociological Review*, 6, 1941, 663–9.

BARNES, J[ohn] A[rundel], 'Measures of Divorce Frequency in Simple Societies', *Journal of the Royal Anthropological Institute*, 79, 1949, 37–62.

Marriage in a Changing Society, Rhodes-Livingstone Papers, No. 20, Cape Town: Oxford University Press for Rhodes-Livingstone Institute, 1951.

Politics in a Changing Society, Cape Town: Oxford University Press for Rhodes-Livingstone Institute, 1954.

BECKER, Howard, *Systematic Sociology* [: *on the Basis of the* Beziehungslehre *and* Gebildelehre *of Leopold von Wiese*], New York: John Wiley and Sons, 1932.

BERNARD, Jessie, 'The Sociological Study of Tension' in *The Nature of Conflict*, Paris: UNESCO for International Sociological Association, 1957.

BROWN, A[lfred] R[eginald] [Radcliffe-], *The Andaman Islanders* (see RADCLIFFE-BROWN, A. R.).

BROWN, G. Gordon, and A. McD. Bruce HUTT, *Anthropology in Action*, London: Oxford University Press for International Institute of African Languages and Cultures, 1935.

BURR, George Lincoln (ed.), *Narratives of the Witchcraft Cases 1648–1706*, New York: C. Scribner's Sons, 1914.

CAUDILL, William, 'Applied 'Anthropology and Medicine' in *Anthropology, Today*, ed. by A. L. KROEBER, Chicago: Chicago University Press, 1953.

COLSON, Elizabeth, 'The Plateau Tonga of Northern Rhodesia' in *Seven Tribes of British Central Africa*, ed. by Elizabeth COLSON and Max GLUCKMAN, London: Oxford University Press for Rhodes-Livingstone Institute, 1951.

'Clans and the Joking-Relationship among the Plateau Tonga of Northern Rhodesia', *Kroeber Anthropological Society Papers*, 8 and 9 (the Walter B. Cline Memorial Volume), 1953, 45–60.

COSER, Lewis A., [*The Functions of*] *Social Conflict*, Glencoe, Ill.: The Free Press, 1956.

CUNNISON, I[an], *Kinship and Local Organization on the Luapula*, Communications from the Rhodes-Livingstone Institute, No. 5, Livingstone, 1950.

DAVIES, R. Trevor, *Four Centuries of Witch-Belief*, London: Methuen and Co., Ltd, 1947.

EVANS-PRITCHARD, E[dward] E[van], *Witchcraft* [*, Oracles and Magic*] *among the Azande*, Oxford: The Clarendon Press, 1937.

EWEN, C. L'Estrange, *Witch Hunting and Witch Trials*, London: Kegan Paul, Trench, Trubner and Co., Ltd, 1929.

Witchcraft and Demonianism, London: Heath Cranton Ltd, 1933.

322

FISHER, R[onald] A., *The Design of Experiments*, Edinburgh: Oliver and Boyd, 1935.

FORTES, Meyer, *The Dynamics of Clanship [among the Tallensi]*, London: Oxford University Press for International African Institute, 1945.

FORTUNE, R. F., *Sorcerers of Dobu*, London: George Routledge and Sons, Ltd, 1932.

GLUCKMAN, Max, *Economy of the Central Barotse Plain*, Rhodes-Livingstone Papers, No. 7, Livingstone: Rhodes-Livingstone Institute, 1941.

'Some Processes of Social Change [Illustrated from Zululand]', *African Studies*, 1, 1942, 243–60.

'The Logic of African Science and Witchcraft', *Human Problems in British Central Africa*, 1, 1944, 61–71.

Malinowski's Sociological Theories, Rhodes-Livingstone Papers, No. 16, Cape Town: Oxford University Press for Rhodes-Livingstone Institute, 1949.

'Kinship and Marriage [among the Lozi of Northern Rhodesia and the Zulu of Natal]' in *African Systems of Kinship and Marriage*, ed. by A. R. RADCLIFFE-BROWN and [C.] Daryll FORDE, London: Oxford University Press for International African Institute, 1950.

Custom and Conflict [in Africa], Oxford: Basil Blackwell, 1955.

The Judicial Process [among the Barotse of Northern Rhodesia], Manchester: Manchester University Press for Rhodes-Livingstone Institute, 1955.

Politics, Law and Ritual in Tribal Society, Oxford: Blackwell, 1965.

(ed.) *Essays on the Ritual of Social Relations*, Manchester: Manchester University Press, 1962.

(ed.) *Closed Systems and Open Minds*, Edinburgh: Oliver and Boyd, 1964.

HAGOOD, Margaret Jarman, *Statistics for Sociologists*, New York: Henry Holt and Company, 1941.

HOGBIN, H[erbert] Ian, *Law and Order in Polynesia*, New York: Harcourt Brace and Company, 1934.

HOLE, Christina, *Witchcraft in England*, London: B. T. Batsford Ltd, 1945.

HOMANS, George C[aspar], 'Anxiety and Ritual', *American Anthropologist*, 43, 1941, 164–72.

The Human Group, London: Routledge and Kegan Paul, Ltd, 1951.

HUNTER, Monica, *Reaction to Conquest* (see WILSON (née HUNTER), Monica).

KLUCKHORN, Clyde, *Navaho Witchcraft*, Papers of the Peabody Museum of American Archaeology and Ethnology, Harvard University, 22, 1944, No. 2.

KRIGE, E[ileen] Jensen, and J[acob] D[aniel] KRIGE, *The Realm of a Rain Queen*, London: Oxford University Press for International Institute of African Languages and Cultures, 1943.

KRIGE, J[acob] D[aniel], 'The Social Function of Witchcraft', *Theoria*, 1, 1947, 8–21.

LINTON, Ralph, *The Study of Man*, New York: D. Appleton-Century Company, 1936.

MALINOWSKI, Bronislaw, *Crime and Custom [in Savage Society]*, London: Kegan Paul, Trench, Trubner and Co., Ltd, 1926.

A Scientific Theory of Culture and Other Essays (with a preface by Huntington CAIRNS), Chapel Hill: University of North Carolina Press, 1944.

MALINOWSKI, Bronislaw—*contd.*
Magic, Science and Religion and Other Essays, ed. by Robert REDFIELD, Glencoe, Ill.: The Free Press, 1948.
MARWICK, M[axwell] G[ay], 'The Social Context of Cewa Witch Beliefs', *Africa*, 22, 1952, 120–35 and 215–33.
'Witchcraft as a Social Strain-gauge', *The Australian Journal of Science*, 26, 1964, 263–8.
MAYER, P[hilip], *Witches*, Inaugural Lecture, Grahamstown: Rhodes University, 1954.
MIDDLETON, John, *Lugbara Religion*, London: Oxford University Press for International African Institute, 1960.
MITCHELL, J[ames] Clyde, 'The Yao of Southern Nyasaland' in *Seven Tribes of British Central Africa*, ed. by Elizabeth COLSON and Max GLUCKMAN: Oxford University Press for Rhodes-Livingstone Institute, 1951.
'A Note on the African Conception of Causality', *Nyasaland Journal*, 4, 1951.
The Yao Village, Manchester: Manchester University Press for Rhodes-Livingstone Institute, 1956.
MURRAY, Margaret A., *The Witch-Cult in Western Europe*, Oxford: The Clarendon Press, 1921.
'Witchcraft' in *Encyclopedia Britannica*, London, 14th ed., 1929.
The God of the Witches, London: Sampson, Low, Marston and Co., Ltd, 1933.
NADEL, S. F., 'Witchcraft in Four African Societies: [an Essay in Comparison]', *American Anthropologist*, 54, 1952, 18–29.
Nupe Religion, London: Routledge and Kegan Paul, 1954.
'Malinowski on Magic and Religion' in *Man and Culture*, ed. by Raymond [W.] FIRTH, London: Kegan Paul, 1957.
PARSONS, Talcott, *The Structure of Social Action*, New York: McGraw-Hill Book Company, Inc., 1937.
'The Social Structure of the Family', in *The Family* ed. by Ruth Nanda ANSHEN, New York: Harper and Brothers, 1949.
RADCLIFFE-BROWN, A[lfred] R[eginald] (BROWN, A. R.), *The Andaman Islanders*, Cambridge: The University Press, 1922.
Structure and Function [in Primitive Society], London: Cohen and West, 1952.
READER, D[esmond] H., *Makhanya Kinship Rights and Obligations*, Communications from the School of African Studies, University of Cape Town, New Series, No. 28, Cape Town, 1954.
RICHARDS, Audrey I., 'A Modern Movement of Witchfinders', *Africa*, 8, 1935, 448–61.
Land, Labour and Diet [in Northern Rhodesia], London: Oxford University Press for International Institute of African Languages and Cultures, 1939.
Bemba Marriage and Present Economic Conditions, Rhodes-Livingstone Papers, No. 4, Livingstone: Rhodes-Livingstone Institute, 1940.
SCHAPERA, I[saac], 'Oral Sorcery among the Natives of Bechuanaland' in *Essays Presented to C. G. Seligman* ed. by E. E. Evans-Pritchard *et al.*, London: Kegan Paul, Trench, Trubner and Co., Ltd, 1934.
'Sorcery and Witchcraft in Bechuanaland', *African Affairs*, 51, 1952, 41–52.
SIEGEL, Sidney, *Nonparametric Statistics*, New York: McGraw-Hill Book Company, Inc., 1956.

SIMMEL, Georg, *Conflict*, trans. by Kurt H. WOLFF, Glencoe, Ill.: The Free Press, 1955.

SMITH, Edwin W., *African Symbolism*, Henry Myers Lecture, London: Royal Anthropological Institute, 1952.

SRINIVAS, M. N., *Religion and Society among the Coorgs of South India*, Oxford: The Clarendon Press, 1952.

STARKEY, Marion L., *The Devil in Massachusetts*, New York: Alfred Knopf, 1950.

STEFANISZYN, B., 'Funeral Friendship in Central Africa', *Africa*, 20, 1950, 290–306.

TAFT, D[onald] R[eed], *Criminology, a Cultural Interpretation*, New York: The Macmillan Company, 1950.

TEW (now DOUGLAS), Mary, 'A Further Note on Funeral Friendship', *Africa*, 21, 1951, 122–4.

TURNER, V[ictor] W., *Schism and Continuity [in an African Society]*, Manchester: Manchester University Press, 1957.

UNION OF SOUTH AFRICA, *Office of Census and Statistics*, Report on Divorces, 1913 to 1944.

UNITED NATIONS, *Statistical Handbook*, New York, 1951.

WHITING, Beatrice Blyth, *Paiute Sorcery*, Viking Fund Publications in Anthropology, No. 15, New York: Viking Fund, 1950.

WILSON, Monica (*née* HUNTER), *Reaction to Conquest*, London: Oxford University Press for International Institute of African Languages and Cultures, 1936.

Good Company, London: Oxford University Press for International African Institute, 1951.

'Witch Beliefs and the Social Structure', *American Journal of Sociology*, 56, 1951, 307–13.

with Selma KAPLAN, Theresa MAKI and Edith M. WALTON, *Social Structure*, Keiskammahoek Rural Survey, Vol. 3, Pietermaritzburg: Shuter and Shooter, 1952.

WISDOM, John Oulton, *Foundations of Inference in Natural Science*, London: Methuen and Co., Ltd, 1952.

WORSLEY, P[eter] M., 'Millenarian Movements in Melanesia', *Human Problems in British Central Africa*, 21, 1957, 18–31.

INDEX AND GLOSSARY

Dutch Reformed Church Mission: 64
duties of 'guardians': 145, 156, 174 f.,
196, 208 f., 214, 269
dʒiko (plur., *maiko*), country, territory
of a chief: 29, 203

East African Statistical Department:
21n., 311
'eating of himself' (*kudʒidyela*), disease
believed to follow unreported first
nocturnal emission: 275
eating together, ritual of: 136, 237
economic factors in matrilineage solidarity: 166
eni (sing., *mwini*), proprietors, owners,
guardians: 10n., 137n.
Erythrophloeum sp.: 88
etiquette: 13, 130, 224
Europeans (Whites): 30, 41, 53, 56 ff.;
Ceŵa attitude towards, 51 ff., 57 ff.,
93
Evans-Pritchard, E. E.: 68n., 80 f.,
281 f., 285, 288n., 290 f., 305, 322
evil disposition of sorcerer: 11, 221 f.,
239 ff.
Ewen, C. L'E.: 306, 322
exogamy of matrilineage: 125
Eybers, J. H.: 181n., 311

fables: 230 f., 299 ff.
failure to resolve conflict leads to sorcery: 8, 11, 95, 147, 179, 195, 210 ff.,
220, 292 ff.
familiars of sorcerers: 5, 7 f., 77 ff., 80,
219, 240, 269
family (*banja*): 44
Fanakalo, 'Kitchen Kaffir': 5
father–child relationship: 67, 180 ff.
father's rôle in reproduction: 180 f.,
183
father's rôle in ritual: 184 f., 233
fecundity valued: 233
fellow-workers, competition between:
3, 97
female lieutenants of headman: 139 ff.
fertility of soil valued: 233
field work methods: 12 ff.
fire of sorcerers: 78
Fisher, R. A.: 4n., 323
fisi, 'hyena', ritual friend in particular
context: 138, 237
flexibility of relationships and tension:
253, 288 f.

Foà, E.: 55n., 311
folk-lore, moral implications of: 229 ff.
a following highly valued: 139, 149 ff.,
231, 261, 269, 302 f.
foreign diviners, prestige of: 89
foreign 'medicines', prestige of: 84, 214,
256
formal instruction in initiation and
name-inheritance: 234 ff.
formality between proximate generations: 135
formulation of questions about misfortunes: 13 f.
Fortes, M.: 139n., 140n., 144, 148, 285,
323
Fortune, R. F.: 221n., 323
fortunes of matrilineage segments: 140
fowl (*ŋkhuku*): as diviner's fee, 91, 106;
as gift of appeasement, 43, 60, 174
Fraser, R. H.: 57n., 311
friendly familiarity of alternate generations: 134 f.
funeral friend—see ritual friend
funerals—see mortuary rituals

Gamitto, A. C. P.: 21n., 46n., 54, 87n.,
126n., 137, 138, 144, 193, 202 f.,
261, 311
Garbutt, H. W.: 311
gender, common, of sorcerer and
witch: 9n.
genealogical position, succession to:
136, 146, 162 f., 238
genealogies: additional, 297 ff.; conventions used in, 10, facing 116, 149
general beliefs checked against specific
instances: 98 ff.
genesis of tensions: 287 ff.
Genthe, H.: 53n., 54n., 312
girls' initiation (*cinamwali*): 59 f., 67,
203 f., 234 ff.
Gluckman, M.: 52n., 82n., 169, 179,
190n., 222n., 229, 251n., 282, 284 ff.,
288n., 290, 292n., 293, 305, 323
God: 15, 63 f., 73, 257, 270
Gombe, Headman: 164, 183, 199,
212 f., 241, 259 ff., 293 f.
grandchildship (*cidʒukulu*): 134 f.,
136 ff.
grave-watching: 77 f., 85 ff., 252, 268
graveyard magic: 77 f., 85 ff., 252, 268
Great East Road (*Mteŋgamahule*): 48
grounds for divorce: 175 f.

z